Becker Professional Education, a global leader in professional education, has been developing study materials for the ACCA for more than 20 years. Thousands of students studying for the ACCA Qualification have succeeded in their professional examinations studying with its Platinum and Gold ALP training centers in Central and Eastern Europe and Central Asia.

Nearly half a million professionals have advanced their careers through Becker Professional Education's courses. Throughout its 60-year history, Becker has earned a strong track record of student success through world-class teaching, curriculum and learning tools.

Becker Professional Education has been awarded ACCA Approved Content Provider Status for its ACCA materials, as well as materials for the Diploma in International Financial Reporting (DipIFR).

We provide a single solution for individuals and companies in need of global accounting certifications and continuing professional education.

D1825924

Becker Professional Education's ACCA Study Materials

All of Becker's materials are authored by experienced ACCA lecturers and are used in the delivery of classroom courses.

Study Text: Gives complete coverage of the syllabus with a focus on learning outcomes. It is designed to be used both as a reference text and as part of integrated study. It also includes the ACCA Syllabus and Study Guide, exam advice and commentaries and a Study Question Bank containing practice questions relating to each topic covered.

Revision Question Bank: Exam style and standard questions together with comprehensive answers to support and prepare students for their exams. The Revision Question Bank also includes past examination questions (updated where relevant), model answers and alternative solutions and tutorial notes.

Revision Essentials Handbook*: A condensed, easy-to-use aid to revision containing essential technical content and exam guidance.

*Revision Essentials Handbook are substantially derived from content reviewed by ACCA's examining team.

Becker Professional Education
is an ACCA approved content provider

BECKER

PROFESSIONAL EDUCATION®

ACCA

P3 BUSINESS ANALYSIS

REVISION QUESTION BANK

For Examinations from September 2017 to June 2018

BECKER
PROFESSIONAL EDUCATION®

This training material has been prepared and published by Becker Professional Development International Limited: www.becker.com/acca

ISBN: 9781785664014

Acknowledgement

Past ACCA examination questions are the copyright of the Association of Chartered Certified Accountants and have been reproduced by kind permission.

ACCA

P3 BUSINESS ANALYSIS

REVISION QUESTION BANK

For Examinations from September 2017 to June 2018

BECKER
PROFESSIONAL EDUCATION®

This training material has been prepared and published by Becker Professional Development International Limited: www.becker.com/acca

ISBN: 9781785664014

Acknowledgement

Past ACCA examination questions are the copyright of the Association of Chartered Certified Accountants and have been reproduced by kind permission.

CONTENTS

Question   *Page*   *Answer*   *Marks*   *Date worked*

> The current exam format is a 50 mark case study question and a choice of two from three 25 mark questions. Questions of different mark allocations are provided for additional syllabus coverage.

CASE STUDIES

		Page	Answer	Marks
1	National Museum *(ACCA D08)*	1	1001	50
2	EA Group *(ACCA D12)*	5	1008	50
3	Midshire Health *(ACCA J13)*	8	1012	50
4	MachineShop *(ACCA D13)*	12	1017	50
5	ReInk *(ACCA J14)*	15	1023	50

ENVIRONMENTAL ANALYSIS

6	IL *(ACCA D09)*	18	1028	25
7	CoolFreeze *(ACCA Pilot J11)*	19	1030	25
8	Nesta *(ACCA J13)*	22	1033	25

COMPETITION AND CUSTOMERS

9	Helen Bradshaw *(ACCA J05)*	23	1036	20
10	Housham Garden *(ACCA D13)*	24	1039	25

STRATEGIC CAPABILITY

11	AutoFone *(ACCA J08)*	25	1042	35
12	Moor Farm *(ACCA D12)*	29	1047	25
13	DRB Electronic Services *(ACCA Pilot J11)*	30	1049	25

ORGANISATIONAL INFLUENCES

14	i- compute *(ACCA D11)*	32	1051	25

COMPETITIVE ADVANTAGE STRATEGIES

15	Ramon Silva *(ACCA D05)*	33	1054	20

CORPORATE LEVEL STRATEGY

16	Excalibur Sportswear *(ACCA D01)*	34	1056	20
17	Ambion *(ACCA J10)*	35	1058	25

STRATEGY DEVELOPMENT

18	Environment Management Society *(ACCA PilotJ11)*	37	1060	25
19	Graffoff *(ACCA D12)*	38	1062	25

ORGANISING AND ENABLING SUCCESS

20	Sensational Sounds	40	1065	25

Question		Page	Answer	Marks	Date worked
MANAGING STRATEGIC CHANGE					
21	Pharmacy Systems International *(ACCA J08)*	40	1067	25	
BUSINESS AND PROCESS CHANGE					
22	Country Car Club *(ACCA J08)*	42	1071	25	
23	Flexipipe *(ACCA J12)*	44	1075	25	
24	Chemical Transport *(ACCA J13)*	45	1078	25	
25	Bridge *(ACCAJ14)*	46	1081	25	
E-BUSINESS					
26	Viva Espana	48	1083	25	
27	The Management Press *(ACCA D10)*	49	1086	25	
28	Cronin Auto Retail *(ACCA J11)*	50	1088	25	
29	BA Times *(ACCA D13)*	51	1091	25	
PROJECT MANAGEMENT					
30	ASW *(ACCA D08)*	53	1095	16	
31	Mahem *(ACCA J12)*	55	1098	25	
32	Institute of Independent Analysts *(ACCA J14) adapted*	57	1100	40	
PROJECT CONTROL AND LEADERSHIP					
33	8-Hats Promotions *(ACCA J11)*	58	1104	25	
34	Homedeliver *(ACCA D11)*	60	1107	25	
PRICING					
35	ITTrain *(ACCA J14)*	62	1110	25	
FINANCE AND STRATEGY					
36	Green Socket	63	1113	25	
37	Gift designs Co *(ACCA D06)*	64	1116	20	
RATIO ANALYSIS					
38	OneEnergy *(ACCA J09)*	65	1117	25	
STRATEGY IMPLICATIONS OF MANAGEMENT ACCOUNTING					
39	Despard	67	1119	10	
40	World Engines *(ACCA D12)*	68	1120	25	
41	ATD *(ACCA D13)*	69	1123	25	
PEOPLE					
42	Rick Hein *(ACCA J09)*	71	1126	25	
43	Academic Recycling Company *(ACCA J13)*	73	1129	25	

Question		Page	Answer	Marks	Date worked
RECENT EXAMS					
December 2014					
1	Roam Group	74	1132	50	
2	Stella Electronics	78	1137	25	
3	TKP	80	1139	25	
4	Noble Pets	81	1142	25	
June 2015					
1	2Tel	2	15	50	
2	Yvern	6	19	25	
3	OfRoad	8	20	25	
4	TMZ	10	22	25	
September/December 2015 [1]					
1	QTSBA	2	15	50	
2	Institute of Certified Operations Managers	6	18	25	
3	Mantis & Gear	8	19	25	
4	Cooper University	10	21	25	
March/June 2016					
1	QTP	2	15	50	
2	Shop Reviewers Online	6	18	25	
3	The Holiday Company	8	19	25	
4	Westoria Public Health Authority	10	21	25	
	Marking scheme		23		
September/December 2016					
1	Skod Light Bulb Industry	2	13	50	
2	Webfilms	6	16	25	
3	Retail World	8	17	25	
4	Maratec	10	19	25	
	Marking scheme		21		

Tutorial note: *The model answers to past ACCA exam questions are considerably longer and more detailed than would be expected from any candidate in the examination. They should be used as a guide to the form, style and technical standard (but not length) of answers that candidates should aim to achieve. However, these answers may not include all valid points mentioned by a candidate – credit will be given to candidates mentioning such points.*

---

[1] Since the introduction of four exam sessions a year ACCA now publishes sample questions from the September and December and March and June examinations.

Question 1 NATIONAL MUSEUM

Introduction

The National Museum (NM) was established in 1861 to house collections of art, textiles and metalware for the nation. It remains in its original building which is itself of architectural importance. Unfortunately, the passage of time has meant that the condition of the building has deteriorated and so it requires continual repair and maintenance. Alterations have also been made to ensure that the building complies with the disability access and health and safety laws of the country. However, these alterations have been criticised as being unsympathetic and out of character with the rest of the building. The building is in a previously affluent area of the capital city. However, what were once large middle-class family houses have now become multi-occupied apartments and the socio-economic structure of the area has radically changed. The area also suffers from an increasing crime rate. A visitor to the museum was recently assaulted whilst waiting for a bus to take her home. The assault was reported in both local and national newspapers.

Thirty years ago, the government identified museums that held significant Heritage Collections. These are collections that are deemed to be very significant to the country. Three Heritage Collections were identified at the NM, a figure that has risen to seven in the intervening years as the museum has acquired new items.

Funding and structure

The NM is currently 90% funded by direct grants from government. The rest of its income comes from a nominal admission charge and from private sponsorship of exhibitions. The direct funding from the government is based on a number of factors, but the number of Heritage Collections held by the museum is a significant funding influence. The Board of Trustees of the NM divide the museum's income between departments roughly on the basis of the previous year's budget plus an inflation percentage. The division of money between departments is heavily influenced by the Heritage Collections. Departments with Heritage Collections tend to be allocated a larger budget. The budgets for 20Y2 and 20Y3 are shown in Figure 1.

Figure 1: Section budgets; 20Y2 and 20Y3

Collection Sections	Number of Heritage Collections	Budget ($000s) 20Y2	Budget ($000s) 20Y3
Architecture	2	120.00	125.00
Art	2	135.00	140.00
Metalwork	1	37.50	39.00
Glass		23.00	24.00
Textiles	1	45.00	47.50
Ceramics		35.00	36.00
Furniture		30.00	31.50
Print and Books		35.00	36.50
Photography		15.00	15.50
Fashion		10.00	10.50
Jewellery	1	50.00	52.50
Sculpture		25.00	26.00
Administration		60.50	63.00
Total		621.00	647.00

The head of each collection section is an important position and enjoys many privileges, including a large office, a special section heads' dining room and a dedicated personal assistant (PA). The heads of sections which have "Heritage Collections" also hold the title of professor from the National University.

The departmental structure of the NM (see Figure 2) is largely built around the 12 main sections of the collection. These sections are grouped into three departments, each of which has a Director. The Board of Directors is made up of the three directors of these departments, together with the Director of Administration and the Director General. The museum is a charity run by a Board of Trustees. There are currently eight trustees, two of whom have been recently appointed by the government. The other six trustees are people well-known and respected in academic fields relevant to the museum's collections.

Figure 2: Current Organisational Structure

Board of Trustees

Board of Directors	Director General		
Director of Art and Architecture	Director of Industrial Art	Director of Media and Contemporary Art	Director of Administration
Head of Architecture	Head of Metalwork	Head of Print and Book	Finance
Head of Art	Head of Glass	Head of Photography	Purchasing
	Head of Textiles	Head of Fashion	Marketing
	Head of Ceramics	Head of Jewellery	Property Services
	Head of Furniture	Head of Sculpture	Visitor Services

Government change

One year ago, a new national government was elected. The newly appointed Minister for Culture implemented the government's election manifesto commitment to make museums more self-funding. The minister has declared that in five years' time the museum must cover 60% of its own costs and only 40% will be directly funded by government. This change in funding will gradually be phased in over the next five years. The 40% government grant will be linked to the museum achieving specified targets for disability access, social inclusion and electronic commerce and access. The government is committed to increasing museum attendance by lower socio-economic classes and younger people so that they are more aware of their heritage. Furthermore, it also wishes to give increasing access to museum exhibits to disabled people who cannot physically visit the museum site. The government have asked all museums to produce a strategy document showing how they intend to meet these financial, accessibility and technological objectives. The government's opposition has, since the election, also agreed that the reliance of museums on government funding should be reduced.

Traditionally, the NM has provided administrative support for sections and departments, grouped together beneath a Director of Administration. The role of the Director General has been a part-time post. However, the funding changes introduced by the government and the need to produce a strategy document, has spurred the Board of Trustees to appoint a full-time Director General from the private sector. The trustees felt they needed private industry expertise to develop and implement a strategy to achieve the government's objectives. The new Director General was previously the CEO of a major chain of supermarkets.

Director General's proposal

The new Director General has produced a strategic planning document showing how the NM intends to meet the government's objectives. Proposals in this document include:

(1)   Allocating budgets (from 20Y4) to sections based on visitor popularity. The most visited collections will receive the most money. The idea is to stimulate sections to come up with innovative ideas that will attract more visitors to the museum. Visitor numbers have been declining (see Figure 3) since 20X8.

Figure 3: Visitor numbers 20X8–20Y1 (000s)

	20Y1	20Y0	20X9	20X8
Age 17 or less	10	12	15	15
Age 18–22	5	8	12	10
Age 23–30	10	15	20	20
Age 31–45	20	20	18	25
Age 46–59	35	35	30	30
Age 60 or more	40	35	35	30
Total	120	125	130	130

(2)   Increasing entrance charges to increase income, but to make entry free to pensioners, students, children and people receiving government benefit payments.

(3)   Removing the head of sections' dining room and turning this into a restaurant for visitors. An increase in income from catering is also proposed in the document.

(4)   Removing the head of sections' personal assistants and introducing a support staff pool to reduce administrative costs.

(5)   Increasing the display of exhibits. Only 10% of the museum's collection is open to the public. The rest is held in storage.

(6)   Increasing commercial income from selling posters, postcards and other souvenirs.

The Director General has also suggested a major re-structuring of the organisation as shown in Figure 4.

Figure 4: Proposed Organisational Structure

Reaction to the proposals

Employees have reacted furiously to the Director General's suggestions. The idea of linking budgets to visitor numbers has been greeted with dismay by the Director of Art and Architecture. "This is a dreadful idea and confuses popularity with historical significance. As previous governments have realised, what is important is the value of the collection. Heritage Collections recognise this significance by putting the nation's interests before those of an undiscerning public. As far as I am concerned, if they want to see fashion, they can look in the high street shops. Unlike fashion, great art and architecture remains." The Director of Art and Architecture and the two professors who hold the Head of Architecture and Head of Art posts have also lobbied individual members of the Board of Trustees with their concerns about the Director General's proposals.

The Director of Industrial Arts and the Director of Media and Contemporary Art have contacted powerful figures in both television and the press and as a result a number of articles and letters critical of the Director General's proposals have appeared. A recent television programme called "Strife at the NM" also featured interviews with various heads of collections criticising the proposed changes. They were particularly critical of the lack of consultation; "these proposals have been produced with no input from museum staff. They have been handed down from on high by an ex-grocer", said one anonymous contributor.

Eventually, the criticism of staff and their lack of cooperation prompted the Director General to ask the Board of Trustees to publicly back him. However, only the two trustees appointed by the government were prepared to do so. Consequently, the Director General resigned. This has prompted an angry response from the government which has now threatened to cut the museum's funding dramatically next year and to change the composition of the Board of Trustees so that the majority of trustees are appointed directly by the government. The Minister of Culture has asked the museum to develop and recommend a new strategy within one month.

Required:

(a)   **Analyse the macro-environment of the National Museum using a PESTEL analysis.**

(20 marks)

(b)   The failure of the Director General's strategy has been explained by one of the trustees as "a failure to understand our organisational culture; the way we do things around here".

Assess the underlying organisational cultural issues that would explain the failure of the Director General's strategy at the National Museum.

Note: requirement (b) includes 2 professional marks.   (20 marks)

(c)   Johnson, Scholes and Whittington identify three strategy lenses; design, experience and ideas.

Examine the different insights each of these lenses gives to understanding the process of strategy development at the National Museum.

Note: requirement (c) includes 2 professional marks.   (10 marks)

(50 marks)

Question 2 EA GROUP

Introduction

The EA Group has a portfolio of companies that currently specialise in alternative energy supply and associated products and services. It grew out of Power of the Sun (POTS) Co, one of the pioneers of solar heating, which still remains an autonomous company in the Group. The profits generated by POTS funded the initial development of the Group, which now comprises 12 companies. Only four of these companies are considered in this scenario.

Power of the Sun (POTS) Co

POTS Co was one of the first companies to realise the potential of solar powered energy solutions and it pioneered the use of the technology, particularly in government and city council (public sector) buildings. From 2000 to 2010 its net profit regularly exceeded 15%. Recent results for the company are shown in Figure 1. The approximate size of the overall market is also given (sector turnover).

All figures in $m	2016	2015	2014	2013
Sector turnover	357·00	357·00	356·00	355·00
POTS sales revenue	107·10	100·00	96·10	88·80
Gross profit	22·50	21·00	22·10	22·20
Net profit	7·50	7·00	8·70	9·80

Figure 1: Selected data for POTS Co

Although POTS was the main source of the profits which drove the expansion of the EA Group, many employees within POTS feel that it is now relatively neglected. Consumer surveys suggest that the brand is not as well recognised as it was and respondents who did recognise it saw it as a tired and traditional brand. Many of its most gifted managers have been promoted into the EA Group headquarters or other companies within the Group. It was expected that their expertise, gained with POTS, would help improve the performance of acquired companies. However, despite this loss of valuable resources, POTS still has recognised expertise and many valuable contacts and contracts in the public sector which the EA Group has been able to exploit. These contracts, particularly with city councils, have allowed the company to retain a significant presence in the solar powered energy market at a time when competitors have withdrawn from, or scaled down, their operations.

Neach Glass

The EA Group acquired Neach Glass in 2008. Neach Glass was founded by Kevin Neach to provide high quality glass products. These were used in the original solar panels developed by POTS and a close relationship was built up between Kevin Neach and the managing director of POTS, Ken Nyg. Ken later became chief executive officer (CEO) of the EA Group. The glass panels continue to be used in POTS products. In 2008, Kevin Neach informed Ken Nyg that Neach Glass was on the brink of going into administration. As a result, the EA Group acquired the company to help secure the supply of a vital component in the POTS product. Since that time, financial and management resources have been invested in Neach Glass in an attempt to improve market share and profitability. Some of POTS's best managers have been transferred to the company. Data for Neach Glass is shown in Figure 2. Again, the estimated size of the total market is shown as sector turnover.

All figures in $m	2016	2015	2014	2013
Sector turnover	88·20	89·00	89·50	90·00
Neach turnover	7·94	7·12	7·16	6·30
Gross profit	1·45	1·28	1·22	1·07
Net profit	0·72	0·57	0·57	0·45

Figure 2: Selected data for Neach Glass

ENCOS

In 2012, Ken Nyg recognised that other alternative energy sources other than solar power were becoming increasingly important. Council managers were increasingly requesting a combination of power sources with control systems that could be used to switch the power source to reflect the most economic combination of sources. As a result of this, the EA Group acquired ENergy COntrol Systems (ENCOS), a company with innovative control systems for monitoring power use and matching it to the most suitable and cheapest source of supply. ENCOS was acknowledged as a technical leader, but had little marketing expertise and few contracts in the public sector. ENCOS's control systems have sophisticated mathematical algorithms which are now used in many private sector applications. It has an excellent record in profitable delivery, with each contract carefully estimated and a detailed analysis of gross profit reported per contract. Financial data for ENCOS is shown in Figure 3. The market sector turnover is again given.

All figures in $m	2016	2015	2014	2013
Sector turnover	81·00	76·00	71·50	70·00
ENCOS turnover	21·00	17·00	14·30	13·30
Gross profit	5·00	4·00	2·75	2·55
Net profit	3·35	3·00	1·85	1·65

Figure 3: Selected data for ENCOS

Steeltown Information Technology

Steeltown City Council is the second largest city council in the country. Two years ago, responding to government initiatives to outsource non-core activities, it decided to outsource its information technology department to the private sector. The department developed and implemented bespoke in-house systems to support the departments of the council (housing, education, social services etc). Trade unions in the council mounted a vigorous campaign against the plan and employees were overwhelmingly against it. Many of the employees had worked for the council for many years and had experienced a stable work environment. However, this opposition hardened the council's resolve and they forced through the plan, citing the union's restricted working practices as a major problem. The council invited private sector companies to tender for the work and resources of the department.

The EA Group were keen to broaden their technological services to the public sector and saw this as an opportunity to acquire an organisation that could spearhead its growth. As Ken Nyg said "we must avoid being too narrow in focus. We started out in solar energy, before broadening out into other energy sources and services. We now wish to broaden again into information technology services in general and the acquisition of the Steeltown City Council's information technology department is a perfect vehicle for this. We see clear technology synergies with ENCOS who are technical leaders in control software design and development."

Steeltown Information Technology, as the company is now called, has entered into a 10-year exclusive contract with Steeltown City Council to supply information technology services. The contract price is based on current costs, plus inflation, plus a 5% gross profit margin. The contract will be renegotiated after five years, when it is expected that savings made by the company can be passed on to the council.

The IT director and his deputy, who both vigorously opposed privatisation, have not been transferred to the new company. They both took voluntary redundancy from the council. Other managers are philosophical, glad that the uncertainty of the last two years was behind them. One manager commented that although "he was against outsourcing in principle, now the sale has been agreed, let's get on with it". Very few new systems have been developed in the last two years whilst the future of the department was being discussed. There is now a backlog of applications to develop for a number of council departments. Users in these departments usually find it very difficult to specify system requirements in advance and there have been very few successfully implemented IT solutions.

Although the Steeltown City Council contract is on a cost plus basis, managers who have always been budget and service-driven will be expected to profitably deliver solutions to other potential customers in the public sector.

As part of preparing for strategic change at Steeltown Information Technology, the EA Group wishes to benchmark its performance. They have been provided with the information given in Figure 4.

	2016	2015	2014	2013
User satisfaction [1]	48%	46%	45%	44%
Faults reported [2]	200	250	375	425
User satisfaction (nationwide) [3]	45%	44%	44%	43%

[1]   Measured by internally constructed and analysed user surveys at Steeltown City Council
[2]   Measured by reported faults in software at Steeltown City Council
[3]   Reported by city councils throughout the country

Figure 4: Data for Steeltown City Council information technology department

As another part of their preparation for strategic change at Steeltown Information Technology, the EA Group also wish to understand the contextual factors that will affect such change. They want to explore these factors before they firm up their proposed strategy for the newly acquired company.

Required:

(a)   **Analyse the performance of each of the four companies described in the scenario and assess each company's potential future contribution to the EA Group portfolio of businesses.**   (24 marks)

   Professional marks will be awarded in part (a) for the clarity and structure of the answer.   (4 marks)

(b)   Time, scope, capability and readiness for change are four contextual factors that affect strategic change.

   Evaluate the potential influence of these four factors at Steeltown Information Technology on any strategic change proposed by the EA Group.   (12 marks)

(c)   **Discuss the principles, together with the advantages and the disadvantages, of benchmarking in the context of Steeltown Information Technology.**   (10 marks)

(50 marks)

Question 3 MIDSHIRE HEALTH

Introduction

In 2016 Terry Nagov was appointed as Chief Executive Officer (CEO) of MidShire Health, a public authority with responsibility for health services in Midshire, a region with a population of five million people in the country of Etopia. Like all health services in Etopia, MidShire Health is funded out of general taxation and is delivered free of charge. Terry Nagov was previously the CEO of a large private company making mobility appliances for disabled people. He had successfully held a number of similar executive positions in companies producing consumer products and goods for the consumer market. He was appointed to bring successful private sector practices and procedures to MidShire Health.   Etopia had experienced a prolonged economic recession and such appointments were encouraged by the government of Etopia who were faced with funding increased health care costs. They perceived that private sector expertise could bring some order and greater control to the functioning of public sector services. One of the government ministers publicly commented on the apparent "anarchy of the health service" and its tendency to consume a disproportionate amount of the money collected through general taxation. The government was keen on establishing efficiencies in the public sector, by demonstrating "value for money" principles.

Vision and strategic planning

Terry Nagov believed that all organisations need to be firmly focused on a visionary objective. He stated that "our (MidShire Health) mission is to deliver health to the people of Midshire and, by that, I don't just mean hospital services for the sick, but a wider vision, where health is a state of complete physical, mental and social well-being and not merely the absence of disease or infirmity".

He believed that this vision could only be achieved through a comprehensive strategic planning process which set objectives, policies and standards at a number of levels in the organisation. In the strategic plan, the high-level objectives and policies of the organisation would be cascaded down to operational levels in a series of lower-level plans, where departments and functions had specific objectives that all contributed to the overall strategic vision. Terry Nagov had successfully implemented such strategic planning systems at previous organisations he had worked for. He believed that centralised, senior management should decide strategy, and that line managers should be given power and responsibility to achieve their defined objectives. This approach had worked well in the heavily automated industries he had worked in, with semiskilled employees closely following standards and procedures defined by senior managers in the organisation.

Terry Nagov believed that a project should be put in place to establish a formal strategic planning system at MidShire Health and that this should be supported by a comprehensive computer-based information system which recorded the outcomes and activities of the organisation. He immediately engaged the commercial IT consultants, Eurotek, to develop and implement this information system using a standard software package that they had originally developed for the banking sector.   The overall strategic planning system project itself would be owned by a small steering group of two senior hospital doctors, two hospital nursing managers and two workers from the health service support sector. Health service support employees provide health services to the wider community in the form of health education and public health information and initiatives. Their inclusion in the steering group was not welcomed by the hospital doctors, but the CEO wanted a wide range of professional input. "Collectively", Terry declared, "the steering group has responsibility for delivering health to the Midshire community".

Initial meeting of the steering group (meeting 1)

The initial meeting of the steering group was not attended by the two senior hospital doctors. In Etopia, it is accepted that hospital doctors, although employed by the health authority on full-time contracts, also have the right to undertake paid private work (practice) where they deliver services for private hospitals to fee-paying patients. This right was negotiated by their professional body, the Institute of Hospital Doctors (IOHD), many years ago. Many of the patients they treat in private practice have paid for private health insurance so that they can be treated quickly and thus avoid the long waiting times associated with the free, public service. The initial meeting of the steering group coincided with a day when both doctors were undertaking private work. In their absence, the steering group approved the overall vision of the CEO and agreed to the initiation of an information system project to generate the detailed planning and control information to support this vision. The exact nature and contents of this information system would be determined by a small multi-disciplinary team reporting to the steering group and referred to as the "implementation team". It was made up of three administrative staff employed by MidShire Health supported by four technical consultants from Eurotek, experienced in implementing their software package solution. The composition of the implementation team and steering group is shown in Figure 1.

Figure 1: Composition of the steering group and the implementation team

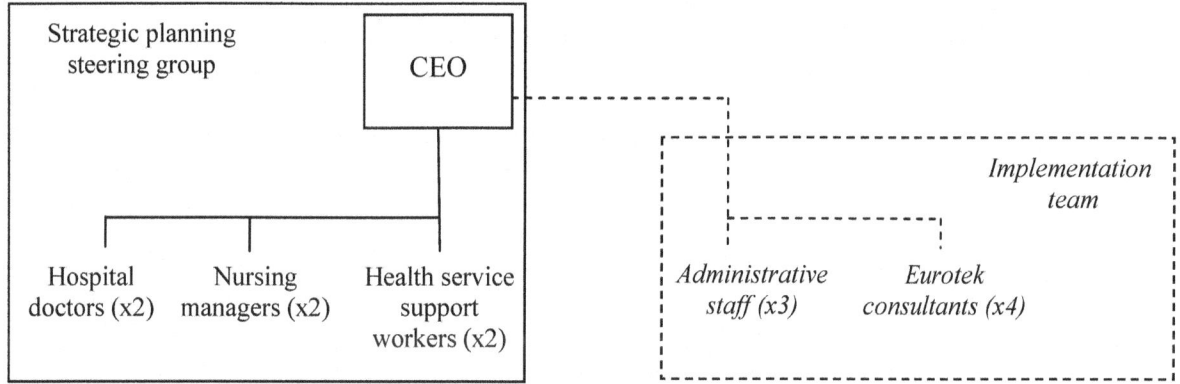

Second meeting of the steering group (meeting 2)

The second meeting was attended by the two senior hospital doctors, but one of the health service support sector workers could not attend. At the start of the meeting, the two hospital doctors questioned the wide definition of health agreed at the previous meeting. One of the hospital doctors suggested that delivering health in this wider context was completely beyond the resources and capabilities of MidShire Health. "You have to realise", he said, "that poor health is often caused by poverty, bad housing and social dislocation. You cannot expect MidShire Health to solve such problems. We can advise and also treat the symptoms, but prevention and cure for these wider issues are well beyond us". The nursing managers, who had previously approved the wider definition of health, now voiced their support for a narrower definition of health and sided with the hospital doctors. One of them commented that "our real work is treating the sick and we must recognise this". The CEO, outnumbered and outmanoeuvred in the meeting, had to agree to a modification of his initial vision, narrowing the overall objective to "effectively and efficiently treating disease". "And, as we all know", stated one of the doctors, "efficiency can only be achieved through giving control and budgets to the doctors, not to the administrators who are an unwanted overhead. This is the very first step we should take." The nursing managers agreed and the meeting came to a slightly acrimonious and early conclusion.

Meeting three of the steering group (meeting 3)

At the third meeting, a presentation was made by the IT consultants, Eurotek, where they demonstrated their software for recording business activities and showed how these activities could be measured against agreed targets. A great deal of discussion took place on the targets that could be set for measuring health efficiency. After a long heated debate, three measures were agreed for hospitals. It was suggested that similar measures should be discussed and developed for health service support services, such as health education. However, at this point, the two senior doctors declared that they had to leave the meeting to "return to our real job of treating patients". The CEO agreed that the health service support workers could establish their own measures before the next meeting. One of these representatives commented that "in my day-to-day job I am confronted by many people who have preventable illnesses. Their problems are due to poor diet and unhealthy habits. Preventing such problems must be better than curing them!" The CEO agreed; this was what he wanted to hear!

Meeting four of the steering group (meeting 4)

The fourth meeting of the steering group began with a discussion of the preventative perspective of health raised by one of the health service support workers at the end of the previous meeting. Both the hospital doctors and nursing managers suggested that this did not come under the revised definition of health used by the steering group, and the CEO quickly agreed. The rest of the meeting was dominated by a discussion of the costs of the Eurotek software solution. A local newspaper had run the headline "spending money on computers – not patients" and it included a number of quotes attributed to one of the hospital doctors on the strategic steering group where he criticised the appointment of Eurotek and the attitude of the MidShire Health CEO. "Running a manufacturing company is very different from running a health service", he said. "We are motivated by service, not products and profit." Terry Nagov, as CEO, openly questioned the ethics of members of the steering group discussing confidential internal matters with the press. The hospital doctors and the nursing managers fiercely defended their right to do so. "You have to understand", they said, "our loyalty is to the profession and to the public. We must act in the public interest." Nevertheless, the CEO raised the possibility of disciplinary action against the hospital doctor. At this point, the senior hospital doctors and the nursing managers left the meeting. The health service support workers stayed and pledged their support to the CEO. They revealed that the autocratic behaviour of hospital doctors often resulted in their work being both unrewarding and unrecognised. One commented, "We have little professional autonomy, we feel controlled by the agenda of the hospital doctors."

Meeting five of the steering group (meeting 5)

The possibility of disciplinary action against the hospital doctor had been published in the press and the Institute of Hospital Doctors (IOHD) had made a formal complaint about the CEO's behaviour to Etopia's health minister. Faced with pressure from within the hospital sector, Terry Nagov was forced to retract his threat of disciplinary action and to issue a public apology, but meeting five was boycotted by the hospital doctors and nursing manager representatives due to "the lack of respect shown by the CEO". Consequently, meeting five was cancelled.

Meeting six of the steering group (meeting 6)

This meeting received a report from the implementation team working on the specification of the information system for MidShire Health. They reported that the software suggested by Eurotek was excellent for time recording, analysis and reporting, but had very few features to aid the planning and control of activities. "I suspected this all along", said one of the hospital doctors. "I think this report shows that you are more interested in finding out what we are doing. The strategic planning exercise is really about cost reduction." It was agreed that Eurotek should be contacted to provide a price for developing a bespoke solution for the information system requirements envisaged by the MidShire implementation team. "I realise", the CEO said, "this will affect the viability of the whole strategic planning project but I ask you all to pull together for the good of MidShire Health and its image within the community."

Just prior to the next planned meeting, the implementation team specifying the information system reported that Eurotek had quoted a price of $600,000 to develop a software solution that integrated planning and control of hospital activities into their software package solution. This was additional to the $450,000 it was charging for the basic software package. The CEO reacted immediately by cancelling the information system project "on cost grounds" and disbanding the steering group. He stated that "from now on, I will personally specify and develop the targets required to bring health to the people of Midshire. I will focus on using the current systems to bring these into place". Emails were sent to the steering committee members informing them of the dissolution of the steering group, stating that no further meetings would be held and no comments were invited. However, the costs of paying penalty charges to Eurotek were soon released to the press and Terry Nagov resigned from his post as CEO of MidShire Health to return to his previous company as chairman. The Institute of Hospital Doctors (IOHD) took the opportunity to issue the following press release:

"Once again, the government has failed to realise that managing public sector services is not the same as managing a private sector profit making company. Money and time have been wasted, and reputations needlessly damaged. Doctors and nurses, people at the cutting edge of the service, know what needs to be done. But time after time our views are disregarded by professional managers and administrators who have little understanding of health care delivery. The public deserve better and we, the IOHD, remain committed to delivering services in the public interest."

Required:

(a)   **(i)**   **Identify and analyse mistakes made by the CEO in the project management process (initiation, conduct and termination) in his attempt to introduce strategic planning, and an associated information system, at MidShire Health.**

(18 marks)

(ii)   **Explain how an understanding of organisational culture and organisational configuration would have helped the CEO anticipate the problems encountered in introducing a strategic planning system, and an associated information system, at MidShire Health.**   (18 marks)

Professional marks will be allocated in part (a) for the clarity, structure and logical flow of your answer.   (4 marks)

(b)   Johnson, Scholes and Whittington identify three strategy lenses: design, experience and ideas.

Evaluate the strategic planning project at MidShire Health through each of these three strategy lenses.   (10 marks)

(50 marks)

Question 4 MACHINESHOP

Arboria is a prosperous industrial country with an established consumer culture that is distinguished by demanding and assertive consumers. Many companies find it difficult to compete successfully in the country but MachineShop is a notable exception. MachineShop sells small electrical machines and tools to both trade (people who use the machines/tools in their work) and domestic customers (people who use the machines/tools at home). For example, it sells a range of paint strippers retailing from $100 to $3,500. These paint strippers are bought by both tradesmen (for example, decorators) and ordinary domestic customers who use them to maintain their own home. It is estimated that 65% of sales are to domestic customers. MachineShop currently has 50 brightly decorated stores throughout Arboria. On average, a further two stores are opened every month. The company has no direct competitors. Most firms offering similar machines only sell them to tradesmen. In many respects MachineShop has defined a new market and it is the only company which, at present, seems to understand the dynamics of this market.

MachineShop is a private company still wholly owned by its directors. The board is headed by Dave Deen, a dynamic entrepreneur who enjoys a high national media profile. He likes the excitement of business and is determined to rapidly grow MachineShop – an ambition shared by his fellow directors. In 2017, on a turnover of $50 million, MachineShop recorded a gross profit margin of 28% and an operating margin of 17%. It delivered a Return on Capital Employed (ROCE) of 17·5%. It currently has a gearing ratio (defined as long-term loans/capital employed) of 15% and an interest cover ratio of 3·5.

Dave Deen has an ambitious growth plan, which he intends to achieve through a combination of internal growth, acquisition and, possibly, strategic alliances. The opening of further stores in Arboria is providing internal (organic) growth. Much of this drive for growth is fuelled by a desire to exploit MachineShop's unique competencies before the idea is copied, both within Arboria and elsewhere in the world. However, the company is having difficulty finding companies to acquire, as there are few equivalent companies to target, either in Arboria or elsewhere in the world. Although MachineShop has never traded outside Arboria, the search for acquisitions is worldwide, with Dave Deen particularly keen to explore international markets in his desire to build a worldwide brand. He has specifically identified the developing country of Ceeland as a potential target, because macroeconomic trends suggest that a consumer society is emerging there, which is similar to the one in Arboria.

Ceeland

The government of Ceeland has spent the last decade building an effective road transport system, supported by low fuel and road taxes which make it cheap to use. The government has also installed a fast digital communication network, providing broadband internet access to all of the population. This is important to MachineShop because internet order placement (either for collection or delivery) is an important part of their business model. The government has also lifted certain restrictions which had been in place under its predecessor. For example, it has removed the need for companies trading in the country to be registered in Ceeland and to have at least one Ceelander citizen on the board. Until recently, there were restrictions on what machines could be used by domestic customers. However, these restrictions have also been removed, as part of a government initiative to encourage the development of light manufacturing in the country. Indeed, one brand of products already stocked by MachineShop is made by a company based in Ceeland.

Fabrique Regle de Garrido (FRG)

Dave Deen has identified Fabrique Regle de Garrido (FRG) as a potential acquisition or strategic partner. FRG currently has 30 depots in Ceeland supplying large machine tools solely to trade customers. It does not sell products to domestic customers. It has an effective distribution network and a sales team which is experienced in selling to Ceeland businesses. MachineShop has the finance (in the form of bank loans and retained earnings) in place for an acquisition or a strategic partnership. Dave Deen has not yet opened up negotiations with FRG, but he has extracted some financial information from the company's most recently filed accounts (see Figure 1). He has also discovered that FRG is a privately owned company, with 30 shareholders, including a local trade union. Dave Deen sees the potential acquisition of FRG as an opportunity to introduce the MachineShop business model into Ceeland. He fully expects the country to become increasingly similar to Arboria and so it will be suitable for the sort of service and products which MachineShop offers. "Achieving quick, substantial growth through acquisition will give us a powerful bargaining position. It will allow us to develop economies of scale, including purchasing in bulk to further drive down product prices. This will help us erect barriers to potential competition", he said.

Figure 1: Extracted financial information for FRG

All figures in $000	*2017*
Revenue	9,000
Cost of sales	(7,500)
Gross profit	1,500
Other expenses	(700)
Finance costs	(300)
Profit before tax	500
Income tax expense	(100)
Profit for the year	400
Non-current liabilities	
Share capital	9,500
Retained profit	400
Long-term loans	2,500

MachineShop acquisitions

MachineShop does have some experience in acquisitions. In 2015 it acquired two companies based in Arboria which still trade as independent companies. The purchase of LogTrans was prompted by the need for MachineShop to have a dedicated and reliable logistics supplier. The post-acquisition performance of the company was spoilt by a dispute between Dave Deen and the senior management of LogTrans. This was due to a personality clash, caused by a different way of doing business. Eventually, the senior management of LogTrans was removed and replaced by people more aligned with the corporate culture of MachineShop. EngSup was also acquired in 2015 to provide an enhanced service facility to people who had purchased machines from MachineShop. Customer feedback showed that many customers were unimpressed by MachineShop's after sales service. EngSup already provided support for many domestic electrical products and so MachineShop bought the company with the intention of using it to provide support for MachineShop's customers. However, initial feedback was negative because EngSup's service engineers provided a poor level of service, coupled with an arrogant approach to the customer. A retraining scheme, together with selected redundancies, has now addressed these problems. Extracts from the current year's figures for both companies, compared with the last full pre-acquisition period of the company, are shown in Figure 2.

Figure 2: Extracted financial information for LogTrans and EngSup

| All figures in $000 | LogTrans | | EngSup | |
Extracted data	2017	2014	2017	2014
Revenue	700	650	350	325
Cost of sales	(575)	(510)	(275)	(250)
Gross profit	125	140	75	75
Other expenses	(60)	(70)	(35)	(30)
Finance costs	(30)	(15)	(10)	(8)
Profit before tax	35	55	30	37
Income tax expense	(15)	(10)	(7)	(10)
Profit for the year	20	45	23	27
Non-current liabilities				
Share capital	500	400	250	100
Retained profit	80	70	40	170
Long-term loans	100	50	30	20

Required:

(a) Internal growth, acquisition and strategic alliances are three methods of pursuing growth.

Explain and evaluate each of these three methods of pursuing growth in the context of MachineShop's development to date and its ambitions for future growth and development. (18 marks)

(b) MachineShop is considering the acquisition of FRG. They have asked you, as a business analyst, to write a report which advises them on this potential acquisition.

Write a report, using the criteria of suitability, acceptability and feasibility, which evaluates the potential acquisition of FRG, concluding with whether you would recommend MachineShop to acquire FRG. (18 marks)

Professional marks will be awarded in part (b) for the structure of the report, the clarity of the analysis and the soundness of the conclusion or recommendation. (4 marks)

(c) Dave Deen has heard about Porter's "diamond" and wants an explanation of the principles, relevance and application of this model.

Explain the principles of Porter's "diamond" and use it to assess the relative attractiveness of Ceeland and Arboria in providing an environment in which MachineShop's growth ambitions could be achieved. (10 marks)

(50 marks)

Question 5 REINK

Eland – the country

Eland is an industrial country with a relatively high standard of living. Most commercial and domestic consumers have computers and printers. However, the economic performance of the country has declined for the last seven years and there are large areas of unemployment and poverty. The economic problems of the country have led to a significant decline in tax revenues and so the government has asked its own departments (and the public sector as a whole) to demonstrate value-for-money in their purchases. The government is also considering privatising some of its departments to save money. The Department of Revenue Collections (DoRC), which is responsible for collecting tax payments in the country, has been identified as a possible candidate for future privatisation.

The people of Eland are enthusiastic about the principles of reuse and recycling. There has been a notable rise in the number of green consumers. Mindful of this, and aware of the economic benefits it delivers, the government is also encouraging its departments (and the economy as a whole) to recycle and reuse products.

The printer consumables market

There is a significant computer printer market in Eland, dominated by Original Equipment Manufacturers (OEMs). Many of these are household names such as Landy, IPD and Bell-Tech. OEMs also dominate the printer consumables market, which is worth about $200m per year. However, there are also independent companies who only supply the printer consumables (printer cartridges and toner cartridges) market, offering prices which significantly undercut the OEMs. The printer and printer consumables markets are both technology driven, with companies constantly looking for innovations which make printing better and cheaper.

The emergence of independent printer consumables suppliers has not been welcomed by the OEMs. They have brought legal actions against the independents in an attempt to make refilling their branded products illegal. However, they have not succeeded. The government in Eland has ruled this to be anti-competitive. However, the OEMs continue to promote their case with political parties, claiming that they need the revenues from printer consumables to fund innovations and advances in printer technology. They also regularly issue statements which worry consumers, claiming that printers may be harmed by using ink which is not from the OEM. Landy has been particularly aggressive in this regard. It continues to pursue legal claims against the independents and has also issued a statement which makes clear that if one of their printers is found to be faulty whilst using non-Landy ink, then the printer's warranty will be void.

It is relatively easy to enter the independent printer consumables market and so companies tend to compete on price. There is little brand loyalty amongst consumers, who regularly change their choice of brand. The independent companies constantly focus on finding technologies which make the print cartridges cheaper to buy and are of better quality. Used print cartridges can be reused for their material alone (recycled), or reused by being refilled with ink. However, there are still printing products on the market which can only be used once, or are expensive to recycle.

ReInk Co

ReInk Co (ReInk) was formed five years ago by Dexter Black, a technology entrepreneur with expertise in printer technologies. He still remains the only shareholder. He set up ReInk to produce and market his designs for reusable ink systems. ReInk is focused primarily on the reuse of printer cartridges by using a process to refill them with ink. Key technical elements of ReInk's innovative process for refilling cartridges have been patented, but in Eland, such patents only last for eight years. The current patent has a further six years to run.

The company was established in a declining industrial town in Eland with high unemployment. Government grants were available for two years to help support hi-tech industry and purpose built factories were cheap, readily available and, initially, rent free. Although the company now pays rent for its factory and offices, the annual rent is relatively low. The area has a good supply of people suitable for administrative and factory jobs in the company. ReInk's location is also close to an attractive area of countryside, which Dexter felt would appeal to the technology experts needed to help him exploit and develop his printer technology ideas. It would help provide a good standard of living and relatively cheap property and so he could attract good staff for modest salaries. His assumption proved correct. He has been able to attract an expert team of technologists who have helped him develop a unique approach to printer cartridge reuse. As one of them commented, "I took a pay cut to come here. But now I can afford a bigger house and my children can breathe fresh country air".

ReInk is an attractive company to work for and the team of technologists are enthusiastic about working with such an acknowledged industry expert, where technical innovation is recognised and rewarded. Both his staff and competitors acknowledge Dexter's technical expertise, but his commercial expertise is less well regarded. Dexter recognised this as a weakness and it was the prime driver behind his decision to recruit two new directors to the company.

To fund the development of the printer refilling technology, ReInk has needed significant bank loans and a substantial overdraft. Although the company has made a small operating profit for the last three years, interest repayments have meant that it has recorded a loss every year. It currently has revenues of $6m per year, 20% of which are derived from a long-term contract with the DoRC. ReInk is not one of the independent companies currently being sued by Landy.

To help him address these continuing financial losses, Dexter recently recruited a sales director to attempt to increase revenue through improved sales and marketing and a human resources (HR) director to review and improve staffing practices. Together with the financial director and Dexter himself, they make up the board of ReInk.

Although both of these recently appointed directors had the commercial expertise which Dexter lacked, neither has been a success. The technologists within the company are particularly scathing about the two new appointments. They claim that the sales director has never really made the effort to understand the market and that "he does not really understand the product we are selling". There has been no evidence so far that he has been able to generate more sales revenue. The HR director upset the whole company by introducing indiscriminate cost cutting and attempting to regrade staff to reduce staff costs. The technologists believe that the HR director "clearly has no experience of dealing with professional staff".

Despite the appointment of the new sales director, ReInk is still not recognised by the majority of the consumers who were surveyed in a recent brand awareness survey. No significant marketing is undertaken outside of the development and promotion of ReInk's website. In search results, it often appears alongside companies which appear to offer similar services and usually have very similar trading names.

ReInk continues to struggle financially, and its bank, Firmsure, in response to its own financial difficulties, has recently reduced ReInk's overdraft facility, creating a cash flow crisis which threatens the company's very existence. At present, it does not have enough cash to meet next month's payroll payments.

The employees of the company are well aware of the company's financial position and although they are proud of the company's technical achievements, they believe that the company may soon go into administration and so many are actively looking for other jobs in the industry or in the area. A combination of poor management (particularly from the new directors) and the company's uncertain financial position has demotivated many of the employees, particularly the technologists who have created the company's vital technical edge over its competitors.

Vi Ventures (VV)

Vi Ventures are venture capitalists who inject money and management expertise into struggling companies, in exchange for a certain degree of control, ownership and dividend reward. They have acknowledged financial and management competencies which they have used in a variety of commercial environments. They are experienced change managers.

VV have been introduced to ReInk by Firmsure and they are considering some form of involvement. Actual arrangements are still under consideration and will only be discussed after they have made their standard assessment of ReInk's strategic position. This standard assessment report contains three elements:

- A SWOT analysis

- An assessment of the contextual factors of strategic change. They need to understand what factors will affect the change which they may need to bring to the company. The framework they use is shown in Figure 1 and is derived from the work of Balogun and Hope Hailey.

- A TOWS matrix analysis to identify strategic options which might be pursued if VV invest in the company.

Figure 1: Contextual features in strategic change

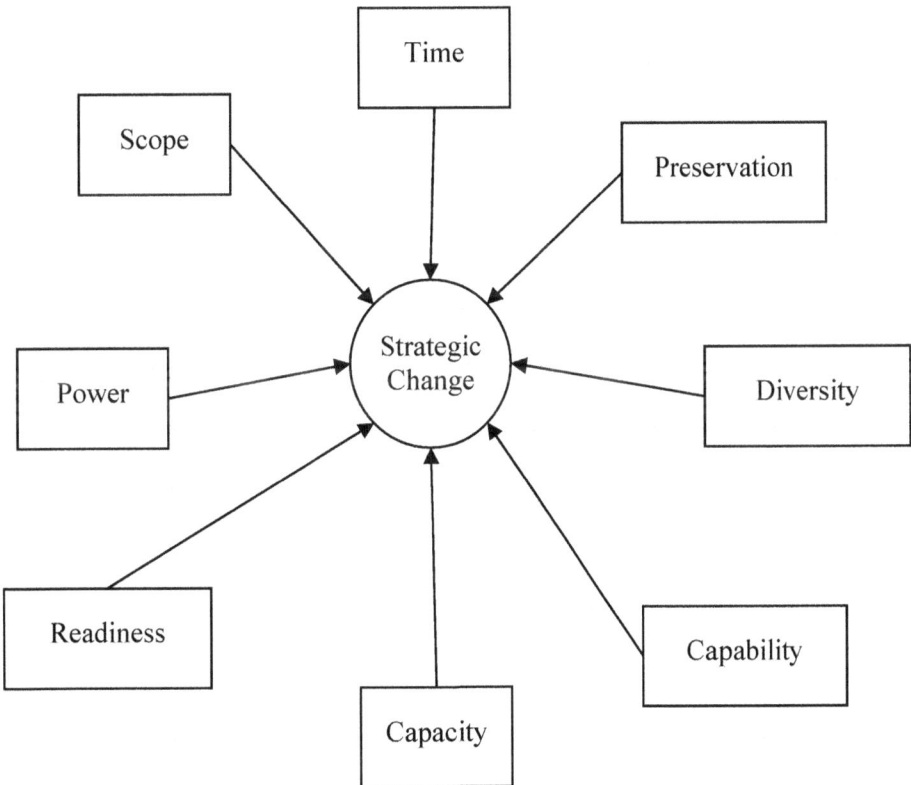

Required:

You have been asked to write the standard assessment report of the strategic position of ReInk required by Vi Ventures. Write a report for Vi Ventures which:

(a)   **Undertakes a SWOT analysis of ReInk Co.**   (20 marks)

(b)   **Evaluates the effect of contextual features on the introduction of strategic change at ReInk Co.**   (14 marks)

(c)   **And, in the light of your analysis above, recommends possible strategic options for each quadrant of a TOWS matrix of ReInk Co.**   (12 marks)

Professional marks will be awarded for the overall quality, construction, fluency and professionalism of the complete standard assessment report required by Vi Ventures.   (4 marks)

(50 marks)

Question 6 IL

Introduction

IL (Independent Living) is a charity that provides living aids to help elderly and disabled people live independently in their own home. These aids include walkers, wheelchairs, walking frames, crutches, mobility scooters, bath lifts and bathroom and bedroom accessories.

IL aims to employ people who would find it difficult or impossible to work in a conventional office or factory. IL's charitable aim is to provide the opportunity for severely disabled people to "work with dignity and achieve financial independence". IL currently employs 200 severely disabled people and 25 able bodied people at its premises on an old disused airfield site. The former aircraft hangars have been turned into either production or storage facilities, all of which have been adapted for severely disabled people.

Smaller items (such as walking frames and crutches) are manufactured here. These are relatively unsophisticated products, manufactured from scrap metal bought from local scrap metal dealers and stored on-site. These products require no testing or training to use and they are packaged and stored after manufacture. IL uses its own lorry to make collections of scrap metal but the lorry is old, unreliable and will soon need replacing.

Larger and more complex items (such as mobility scooters and bath lifts) are bought in bulk from suppliers and stored in the hangars. Delivery of these items to IL is organised by their manufacturers. These products are stored until they are ordered.

When an order is received for such products, the product is unpacked and tested. An IL transfer logo is then applied and the product is re-packaged in the original packing material with an IL label attached. It is then dispatched to the customer. Some inventory is never ordered and last year IL had to write-off a significant amount of obsolete inventory.

All goods are sold at cost plus a margin to cover wages and administrative costs. Prices charged are the same whether goods are ordered over the web or by telephone. Customers can also make a further voluntary donation to help support IL if they wish to. About 30% of customers do make such a donation.

Ordering and marketing

IL markets its products by placing single-sided promotional leaflets in hospitals, doctors' surgeries and local social welfare departments. This leaflet provides information about IL and gives a direct phone number and a web address. Customers may purchase products by ringing IL directly or by ordering over their website. The website provides product information and photos of the products which are supplied by IL. It also has a secure payment facility. However, customers who ring IL directly have to discuss product requirements and potential purchases with sales staff over the phone. Each sales discussion takes, on average, 10 minutes and only one in two contacts results in a sale. 20% of sales are through their website (up from 15% last year), but many of their customers are unfamiliar with the Internet and do not have access to it.

Goods are delivered to customers by a national courier service. Service and support for the bought-in products (mobility scooters, bath lifts) are supplied by the original manufacturer.

Commercial competitors

IL is finding it increasingly difficult to compete with commercial firms offering independent living aids. Last year, the charity made a deficit of $160,000, and it had to sell some of its airfield land to cover this. Many of the commercial firms it is competing with have sophisticated sales and marketing operations and then arrange delivery to customers directly from manufacturers based in low labour cost countries.

Required:

IL fears for its future and has decided to review its value chain to see how it can achieve competitive advantage.

(a)   **Analyse the primary activities of the value chain for the product range at IL.** (10 marks)

(b)   **Evaluate what changes IL might consider to the primary activities in the value chain to improve their competitiveness, whilst continuing to meet their charitable objectives.**
(15 marks)

(25 marks)

Question 7 COOLFREEZE

Introduction

CoolFreeze construct refrigeration systems for supermarkets, food processing plants, warehouses and other industrial premises. It has a sales forecasting committee consisting of the company's sales manager, procurement manager, production manager and the head of administration. The committee produces annual sales forecasts for the company which they review quarterly. Historically, these forecasts have been reasonably accurate.

In the second quarter of 2016 they revised/produced their estimates for the next four quarters. The predicted unit sales volume and prices are given in figure one

Figure one: Sales forecast 2016–2017

Year	Quarter	Predicted sales	Predicted sales price	Revenue
2016	3	81	$1,000	$81,000
	4	69	$1,000	$69,000
2017	1	62	$1,000	$62,000
	2	83	$1,000	$83,000

At the meeting that agreed this forecast the sales manager expressed some doubts about the figures. "My team are telling me that it is very tough out there. Companies are not replacing old equipment or constructing new plants. Furthermore, cheaper foreign products are becoming available – undercutting our prices by 10%". Despite these reservations, the sales manager agreed the sales forecasts produced by the committee.

Actual sales performance

The actual sales for the four projected quarters were as follows (figure two).

Figure two: Actual sales 2016–2017

Year	Quarter	Predicted sales	Actual sales
2016	3	81	82
	4	69	68
2017	1	62	61
	2	83	50

The sudden drop in quarter 2 sales caused consternation in the boardroom, particularly as it was a quarter when high demand and profits were anticipated. An analysis of the quarter 2 trading is shown in figure three.

The managing director of CoolFreeze has called you in to review the forecasting model used by the sales forecasting team. "It must be very flawed to go so badly wrong. I have the feeling that the model is not based on a well-accepted approach". He has obtained a copy of the spreadsheet used by the sales forecasting team (see figure four) to help you in your analysis.

The managing director recognises that the actual quarter 2 performance has to be analysed against the budgeted one. "I think everyone here has made mistakes – the sales manager, procurement manager, production manager, administration manager. They all have to take responsibility. We are in this together and now we must pull together to get out of this mess".

Figure three: Analysis of quarter 2 trading; budget and actual

Quarter 2 – 2017	Budget	Actual
Units	83	50
Revenue	$83,000	$45,000
Raw materials	($29,050)	($15,000)
Labour	($26,975)	($15,750)
Fixed overheads	($18,000)	($18,000)
Operating profit	$8,975	($3,750)

Figure four: Forecasting spreadsheet

A	B	C	D	E	F	G	H	I
Part 1								
Year	Quarter	Units		Trend	Variation	Seasonal	Residual	Check
2013	1	56						
	2	70						
	3	74	524	65.50	8.50	7.35	1.15	74
	4	60	538	67.25	−7.25	−4.73	−2.52	60
2014	1	60	554	69.25	−9.25	−11.65	2.40	60
	2	80	570	71.25	8.75	9.02	−0.27	80
	3	80	582	72.75	7.25	7.35	−0.10	80
	4	70	586	73.25	−3.25	−4.73	1.48	70
2015	1	62	588	73.50	−11.50	−11.65	0.15	62
	2	82	588	73.50	8.50	9.02	−0.52	82
	3	80	586	73.25	6.75	7.35	−0.60	80
	4	70	586	73.25	−3.25	−4.73	1.48	70
2016	1	60	590	73.75	−13.75	−11.65	−2.10	60
	2	84	590	73.75	10.25	9.02	1.23	84
	3	82						
	4	68						

Part 2					
	1	*2*	*3*	*4*	
2013			8.50	−7.25	
2014	−9.25	8.75	7.25	−3.25	
2015	−11.50	8.50	6.75	−3.25	
2016	−13.75	10.25			
Total	−34.50	27.50	22.50	−13.75	
Average	−11.50	9.17	7.50	−4.58	0.58
Adj	0.15	0.15	0.15	0.15	
NewAvg	−11.65	9.02	7.35	−4.73	0.00

Forecast				
2016	3	73.50	7.35	**81**
	4	73.50	−4.73	**69**
2017	1	73.65	−11.65	**62**
	2	74.00	9.02	**83**

Required:

Write a briefing paper for the managing director that:

(a)	**Explains and evaluates the spreadsheet used by the sales forecasting team.**	(12 marks)
(b)	**Analyses the quarter 2 – 2017 performance of CoolFreeze.**	(13 marks)

(25 marks)

Question 8 NESTA

NESTA is a large chain of fixed-price discount stores based in the country of Eyanke. Its stores offer ambient goods (goods that require no cold storage and can be kept at room temperature, such as cleaning products, stationery, biscuits and plastic storage units) at a fixed price of one dollar. Everything in the store retails at this price. Fixed-price discount chains focus on unbranded commodity goods which they buy from a number of small suppliers, for which the dollar shops are the most significant customers. Profit margins on the products they sell are low and overheads are kept to a minimum. The target price is fixed. The products tend to be functional, standardised and undifferentiated.

NESTA has observed the long-term economic decline in the neighbouring country of Eurobia, where a prolonged economic recession has led to the growth of so-called "dollar shops". Three significant dollar shop chains have developed: ItzaDollar, DAIAD and DollaFellas (see Table One). The shops of these three chains are particularly found on the high streets of towns and cities where there is significant financial hardship. Many of these towns and cities have empty stores which are relatively cheap to rent. Furthermore, landlords who once required high rents and long leases are increasingly willing to rent these stores for a relatively short fixed-term lease. The fixed-price dollar shop chains in Eurobia advertise extensively and continually stress their expansion plans. Few weeks go by without one of the chains announcing plans for a significant number of new shops throughout the country.

NESTA has recognised the growth of fixed-price discount retailers in Eurobia and is considering entering this market.

NESTA recently commissioned a brand awareness survey in Eurobia. The survey results showed that NESTA was relatively well-known to respondents who work in the consumer goods retail market. Most of these respondents correctly identified the company as a discount fixed-price company with a significant presence in Eyanke. However, amongst general consumers, only 5% of the respondents had heard of NESTA. In contrast, the three current fixed-price dollar shop discounters in Eurobia were recognised by more than 90% of the respondents.

NESTA itself has revenue of $120,000 million. It has cash reserves which could allow it to lease a significant number of shops in Eurobia and establish a credible market presence. It has recognised competencies in effective supplier selection and management, supported by effective procurement systems. Its logistics systems and methods are core strengths of the company.

There are also many conventional supermarket chains operating in Eurobia. The largest of these has annual revenue of $42,500 million. Supermarkets in Eurobia tend to increasingly favour out-of-town sites which allow the stores to stock a wide range and quantity of products. Customer car parking is plentiful and it is relatively easy for supplying vehicles to access such sites. As well as stocking non-ambient goods, most supermarkets do also stock a very wide range of ambient goods, often with competing brands on offer. However, prices for such goods vary and no supermarkets have yet adopted the discount fixed-price sales approach. In general, the large supermarket chains largely compete with each other and pay little attention to the fixed-price dollar shop discounters. Many supermarkets also have internet-based home ordering systems, offering (usually for a fee of $10) deliveries to customers who are unable or unwilling to visit the supermarket.

Table One shows the relative revenue of the three main discount fixed-price chains in Eurobia.

	2017 $m	2016 $m	2015 $m
ItzaDollar	330	300	275
DAIAD*	310	290	250
DollaFellas	290	235	200
Total	930	825	725

*Don't Ask it's A Dollar

Table One: Revenue of three main discount fixed-price chains in Eurobia

Required:

(a) **Use Porter's five forces framework to assess the attractiveness, to NESTA, of entering the discount fixed-price retail market in Eurobia.** (15 marks)

(b) **Discuss the potential use of scenarios by NESTA's managers as part of their analysis of NESTA's possible entry into the discount fixed-price retail market in Eurobia.** (10 marks)

(25 marks)

Question 9 HELEN BRADSHAW

Helen Bradshaw, a recent graduate with a degree in catering management, has spotted a market opportunity during her first job with a large supermarket chain. She knows there is a growing market for distinctive, quality cakes in the bakery sections of the supermarket chains, as well as in supplying independent individual premium cake shops, and also for catering wholesalers supplying restaurants and hotels.

Helen is very determined to set up her own business under the brand name of "Helen's cakes", and has bought some equipment – industrial food mixers, ovens, cake moulds – and also rented a small industrial unit to make the cakes. Helen has created three sets of recipes – one for the premium cake shop market, one for the supermarkets and one for the catering wholesalers but is uncertain which market to enter first. Each channel of distribution offers a different set of challenges. The premium cake shop market consists of a large number of independent cake shops spread through the region, each looking for daily deliveries, a wide product range and low volumes. The supermarkets are demanding good quality, competitive prices and early development of a product range under their own brand name. The catering wholesalers require large volumes, medium quality and low prices.

Helen has learnt that you are a consultant specialising in start-up enterprises and is looking to you for advice.

Required:

(a) **Discuss the advantages and disadvantages each channel offers and the implications for a successful start-up.** (12 marks)

(b) **Explain how the marketing mix might vary between the three channels Helen is considering using.** (8 marks)

(20 marks)

Question 10 HOUSHAM GARDEN

Housham Garden is a large garden in the country of Euphorbia, where gardening and visiting gardens is a popular pastime. For many years the garden was neglected, until bought by the Popper family who painstakingly restored the garden and four years ago opened it to the public. The garden is now owned and operated by a charitable trust set up by the Popper family – the Housham Garden Trust (HGT) – with initial funding provided by a legacy from the late Clive Popper.

However, HGT is finding it difficult to meet its costs and it is gradually spending the legacy. It is estimated that fixed costs are currently $60,000 per annum. The price of entry into the garden is $5 per visit. At present, there are approximately 1,000 visits per month and the garden is open for eight months a year. It is closed for a period when the weather is usually much colder and few plants are flowering. HGT feels that few people would wish to visit the garden and so they have always closed it for the four "cold" months.

There is a café in the garden and it is estimated that 60% of visitors visit the café and buy drinks and food. However, each purchase is relatively modest. The current trust administrator estimates that the average contribution is $1·25 per visitor using the café.

A recent survey undertaken by a local university revealed that most consumers felt that the admission price for a garden such as Housham was too high. It revealed that the average consumer would be willing to pay an entry fee of $3·25, and indeed similar gardens in Euphorbia charge about this amount.

HGT currently advertises the garden in the monthly magazine "Heritage Gardens". Each display advertisement costs $500 per issue. Adverts have been booked for the next six months, but it is possible to cancel the last three of these without incurring cancellation charges. The advertisements, like HGT's brochure, stress the historical nature of the garden (it is the only surviving garden designed by William Wessex) and the painstaking nature of the restoration. However, these were not factors that figured highly in a recent visitor survey. Table 1 shows the most common primary reasons for visitors visiting the garden. Two hundred visitors were surveyed and they were only allowed to choose one reason for visiting Housham Gardens

Table 1: Primary reasons for visiting the gardens: one day survey

Reason for visiting Housham Garden	Number of respondents
To walk in a peaceful, beautiful, safe environment	100
To enjoy the plants and flowers of the garden	70
To see the restoration work carried out by the trust	20
To visit the café and shop	5
To observe the work of William Wessex	5

Respondents were critical of the food offered by the café. One respondent commented that quality "had gone down since the café was moved into the garden. Really, there is very little choice, and I could not find anything substantial enough for lunch". Her reference to the relocation of the café into the garden refers to the fact that the café used to be in the gatehouse of the garden. At this time, many people just visited Housham to use the café and did not pay for admission into the garden. It was decided that moving the café inside the garden would encourage people to pay for garden entry. However, this has not occurred. It is estimated that the café has lost about 500 visits per month and this has had an adverse effect on staff morale and food quality. The gatehouse area where the café was originally situated is still empty.

In the recent consumer survey, 20% of the respondents said that they would buy an annual (calendar year) ticket giving access to the garden for eight months if it were offered for $9. The customer survey also asked visitors where they had heard of the garden. Table 2 summarises their responses. Again, the 200 respondents were only allowed to make one choice for how they heard about Housham Gardens.

Table 2: How visitors heard about the gardens: one day survey

How did you hear of Housham Gardens?	*Number of respondents*
Personal recommendation from a friend	110
Recent articles in the local newspaper	50
Internet	10
Heritage Gardens magazine	10
Other	20

The reference in Table 2 to recent articles in the local newspaper concerns a series of articles written by the HGT administrator outlining the problems of the trust and the fact that short-term cash flow problems might cause the garden's temporary closure. One visitor commented that "we had never heard of Housham Gardens until then, and we only live four kilometres away".

HGT also has a simple informative web site showing the location of the garden, giving opening times, showing pictures of the restoration and providing a biography of William Wessex.

You are a business analyst who undertakes voluntary work for the trust. You have been asked to suggest immediate short-term changes as well as long-term marketing initiatives for the trust. Short-term changes should be proposals which can be implemented immediately or within three months and will generate quantifiable income or savings.

Long-term marketing initiatives are proposals which will take longer than three months to implement.

Required:

(a)   **Using the data provided, show why HGT is losing money and recommend immediate and other short-term (within three months) changes for HGT, quantifying the increased income or cost savings that these changes should bring.**   (15 marks)

(b)   **Recommend, with justifications, longer-term marketing strategies (longer than three months) for HGT.**   (10 marks)

(25 marks)

Question 11 AUTOFONE

Introduction

AutoFone was established almost 20 years ago at the beginning of the mobile telephone boom. It was formed by a dynamic Chief Executive Officer (CEO) who still remains a major shareholder of the company.

AutoFone brought two new concepts to the market.

(1)   It established retail shops where customers could go and handle the products and discuss mobile phone options with trained sales people. Before AutoFone, all mobile telephones were sold through the customer directly contacting the telephone network provider (like conventional home land line services) and were generally aimed at business rather than leisure users.

(2)   AutoFone sold products and services from all the four major network providers licensed by the government to provide telecommunications services in the country. Previously, customers could only choose products and services from one network provider's range. AutoFone allowed customers to choose products and services across the range of the four providers and reflected this in the company's motto "ethical advice: the customer's choice".

In 1990, AutoFone signed a thirty-year supply contract with each provider. Although, in retrospect, these deals were on commercially favourable terms for AutoFone, the network providers were happy to agree these deals because none of them believed that mobile telephones could be successfully sold through retail shops. However, speaking in 2003, the managing director of one of the networks suggested "that AutoFone had got away with incredible profit margins" when they signed the deals in 1990. The four network providers themselves had re-signed 25-year licence deals with the government in 1995. Under the terms of these deals, licences will be restricted to the four current providers until their renewal date of 2020.

Retail shops Division

AutoFone currently has 415 shops around the country. To reduce costs most shops are on the edge of (but not in) the main shopping area of the town they serve. It is usual for AutoFone to sign a fifty-year shop lease in return for low initial annual rental and a rent-free period at the start of the lease while the company fits out the shop to reflect AutoFone's corporate image. In 1997, AutoFone floated on the country's stock market to assist the funding of further shops and so continue its organic growth. The national coverage of its shops, the publicity generated by its CEO and a successful television advertising campaign culminated, in 2005, with it being rated by consumers as one of the top 20 brands in the country.

The CEO of AutoFone established the retail shops along, in his words, "entrepreneurial lines". He regards each shop as an independent business, having to achieve a profit target but without being closely monitored within these targets. He believes that the company is "about providing opportunity to its employees, providing them with autonomy and responsibility to achieve their goals. It is not about monitoring them every hour of the day, stifling creativity and enthusiasm." To support this approach, sales staff are given a relatively low basic salary with a substantial element of profit-related pay linked to the profit targets of the shop. Commission is also paid to sales staff who successfully sell mobile phone insurance to the customer. Each shop is relatively small, usually employing three or four people.

In recent years the CEO has been increasingly involved in television, sports promotion and charity work. At AutoFone he has established a strategic planning committee of senior headquarters managers to develop and implement the company's business strategy. This committee includes the two longest serving board directors. The strategy still continues to have at its heart the central business idea of giving independent and impartial advice to customers so that they can choose the best equipment and network for their needs.

Marketplace trends

Since AutoFone's arrival into the market, two significant trends have emerged:

(1)   The licensed network providers have opened their own retail stores, usually in city centres. AutoFone has reacted to the opening of these shops by stressing AutoFone's independence and impartiality. Only at AutoFone can impartial advice be received on all four competing networks and their supporting services. The CEO now refers to this as "our central business idea" and, as well as being core to their strategy, it is heavily emphasised in all their promotional material.

(2)   Mobile phones have become more sophisticated. Many now offer integrated cameras, mp3 players, web browsers and e-mail facilities. AutoFone offers these products in both its shops and through its Internet operation. Mobile phones are either purchased outright or provided on monthly contracts. The minimum contract period with the network provider is usually 12 months.

AutoFone has itself established its own Internet division, AFDirect, as a separate division in the group. It has also established an insurance division (AFInsure) offering insurance to cover loss or damage to mobile phones purchased from the company. Revenue earned from each division, analysed by the age of the customer, is shown in table 1.

Table 1: Analysis of AutoFone Sales: 2007 (all figures in $m)

	Age of customer					
	Under 15	15–25	26–40	41–60	Over 60	Total
Division AutoFone retail shops	5	90	60	120	65	340
AFDirect	0	15	20	8	2	45
Total sales of mobile phones						385
AFInsure	0	1	3	7	3	14
Group total						399

Analysts agree that growth in the mobile phone business is slowing down and this is supported by the figures given in table 2 showing revenue from sales (both retail and Internet) for AutoFone and its competitors, the four licensed network providers, for the period 2003–2007.

Table 2: Market Analysis (all figures in $m) of sales of mobile phones

Company	2007	2006	2005	2004	2003
AutoFone	385	377	367	340	320
NetAG	350	348	345	340	305
09Net	390	388	380	365	350
PhoneLine	315	315	315	305	300
NetConnex	295	295	294	290	285
Total	**1,735**	**1,723**	**1,701**	**1,640**	**1,560**

However, while the AFDirect and AFInsure divisions are prospering, there are increasing problems in the retail shops division. Profitability has been declining over the last few years (see table 3) and this has had a demoralising effect on shop employees. One shop manager commented, in his exit interview, that the profit targets were unattainable in the current market. "They might have been appropriate in 1997, but they are not in 2007." Staff are particularly demoralised by spending time explaining a particular product to a customer who then leaves the shop and buys the product cheaper on the Internet. They have to wait for it to be delivered (usually two or three days) but they are prepared to do this to gain the lower prices offered by the direct Internet-based companies, including AFDirect. It is also increasingly common for customers who have bought from AFDirect to take their phones to AutoFone's retail shops for support and service. This activity is not recognised in the shop employee's reward package.

AutoFone's central city branch

Despite the overall decline in the profitability of the shops, one branch has continually met or exceeded its profitability targets and is held up by the CEO as an example of best practice – proof that the company's approach to mobile phone selling can still be profitably applied. This is the central city branch in one of the country's most prosperous cities.

The CEO arranged for three members of the strategic planning committee to visit the shop, posing as customers, to investigate the reasons for the shop's success. They found the staff very friendly and helpful. However, they also found that they were guided towards products and services which had higher profit margins. Further investigation showed this always to be the case and so customers were sold products which were profitable to the shop, rather than those best suited to the customer's needs. On receiving this information, AutoFone's board concluded that this was unethical as it compromised their central business idea which stressed impartial advice to guide the "customer's choice". The manager of the shop was reprimanded and asked to adhere to company policy. He resigned soon afterwards, followed by his two assistants. The shop is currently run by temporary staff and profitability has significantly dropped.

Future strategy

The two longest serving directors on the strategic planning committee are increasingly concerned about the company's decline in profitability (see table 3). They have written an internal paper suggesting that the retail division should be sold off and that AutoFone should re-position itself as an on-line retailer of phones. They believe that the retail shops business model is no longer appropriate. They argue that a company concentrating solely on Internet sales and insurance would be a "smaller but more profitable and focused" business. The CEO is strongly opposed to this suggestion because it was the shop-based approach to selling mobile phones that formed the original business model of the company. He has a strong emotional attachment to the retail business. The two directors claim that this attachment is clouding his judgement and hence he is unable to see the logic of an "economically justifiable exit from the retail business".

Table 3: Extracted Financial Information for AutoFone (retail shops division only)

Extracted Financial Information (all figures in $m)

Extracted from the statement of financial position

	2007	2006	2005	2004	2003
Total non-current assets	143	140	134	128	123
Current assets:					
Inventories	345	340	335	320	298
Trade receivables	1,386	1,258	1,216	1,174	1,120
Cash and cash equivalents	345	375	390	400	414
Total current assets	2,076	1,973	1,941	1,894	1,832
Total assets	**2,219**	**2,113**	**2,075**	**2,022**	**1,955**
Total shareholder's equity	150	155	160	165	169
Non-current liabilities:					
Interest bearing long-term loans	55	50	45	40	35
Other provisions	16	15	13	13	10
Total non-current liabilities	71	65	58	53	45
Total current liabilities	1,998	1,893	1,857	1,804	1,741
Total equity and liabilities	**2,219**	**2,113**	**2,075**	**2,022**	**1,955**

Extracted from the statement of profit or loss

	2007	2006	2005	2004	2003
Revenue	340	337	332	320	305
Cost of sales	250	252	230	220	205
Gross profit	90	85	102	100	100
Wages and salaries	39	38	37	35	33
Other expenses	40	38	35	30	30
Interest expense	4	4	3	3	3
Total	83	80	75	68	66
Profit before tax	7	5	27	32	34
Tax	2	3	5	4	4
Profit after tax	5	2	22	28	30

Extracted from annual reports

	2007	2006	2005	2004	2003
Number of employees	1,400	1,375	1,325	1,300	1,275

Required:

(a) **Using an appropriate model or models analyse the competitive environment of AutoFone's retail shops division.**

        Note: requirement (a) includes 2 professional marks. (20 marks)

(b) AutoFone's CEO is anxious to develop a rational and well-argued case for retaining the retail shops division.

        Write a briefing paper for the CEO to submit to the strategy planning committee explaining why the retail shops division should continue to form a key part of AutoFone's future strategy.

        Note: requirement (b) includes 3 professional marks. (15 marks)

        (35 marks)

Question 12 MOOR FARM

Moor Farm is a large estate in the rural district of Cornaille. The estate covers a large area of forest, upland and farmland. It also includes two villages, and although many of the properties in these villages have been sold off to private homeowners, the estate still owns properties which it rents out. The estate also has a large mansion house set inside a landscape garden designed in the 19th century by James Kent. The garden, although now overgrown and neglected, is the only surviving example of his work in the district. The estate was left as a gift to a charitable trust 10 years ago. The trust is based at the estate. A condition of the gift to the trust was that the upland and forest should be freely accessible to visitors.

The estate has a manager, four full-time staff and 45 volunteers. These volunteers undertake most of the work on the estate, including the continuing excavation of Kent's original garden design. They are happy, the volunteers have become acknowledged experts on land management, through their work on the estate. Government grants for initiatives such as tree planting, protected pasture land and rural employment have been received by the estate in the past. However, a recent change in government means that this funding is unlikely to continue. This will also affect funding for the maintenance of the mansion. It was built almost 80 years ago when the climate of the area was much colder and drier. Recent warm wet winters have caused the fabric of the building to decay and increased the cost of maintaining it.

The estate has appointed a new manager who is due to take over the estate when the current manager retires. She is working alongside the current manager so that she understands her responsibilities and how the estate works. As a one-off project, she has commissioned a stakeholder survey which has requested information on the visitor experience to help with a planned re-design of the estate's website. The website is generally thought to be well structured and presented, but it receives fewer visitors than might reasonably be expected. It provides mainly static information about the estate and forthcoming events but currently users cannot interact with the site in anyway.

Here are some extracts from the survey:

"I live in one of the villages and I am angry about visitors crowding around the village attractions – the tearooms, the craft shops, the souvenir stalls. We feel that we are prisoners in our own village and the traffic is terrible."
Homeowner, from a village on the estate

"We had a good day, but the weather was awful. If we had known it was going to rain all day, then we probably would have postponed the visit until a fine day. It spoilt a family day out."
Visitor with small family

"We were very disappointed, on arrival, to find that the family fun day was fully booked."
Visitor who had travelled 100 kms with two small children to visit a special event

"We all love it here, but we didn't know you had a website!! We almost had to type in the complete website address before we found it! I am sure more people would come if they could only find the website!"

Visitor aged mid-20s

"As usual, we had a great time here and took great photos. It would have been nice to be able to share our pleasure with other people. We would recommend it to anyone who loves the outdoors."

Visitor – family with teenage children

"We met the volunteers who were excavating the buildings in the landscape garden. They were so helpful and knowledgeable. They turned something that looked like a series of small walls into something so much more tangible."

Visitor – elderly couple

"I was disappointed that I was not allowed into the farmland with my dog. As a human being, I have the right to roam. It is a basic human right."

Visitor – elderly female dog-walker

"We are regular visitors and we really want to know what is going on! There are many of us who would like to really be involved with the estate and help it thrive. We need more than just occasional questionnaires."

Visitor – hiking group

"We came out for a nice walk and ended up dodging cyclists. Next time we will go somewhere where they are not welcome."

Visitor – hiking group

"As a farmer, I am appalled with the reckless attitude of some dog walkers. Last week, I lost two sheep, ravaged by dogs that should not have been off their leads."

Farmer – estate tenant

"I'm a volunteer and I love it here. We are a happy, social group of people. I hope the new manager is not going to change things."

Volunteer

Required:

(a) **Evaluate the strategic position of the estate with specific reference to the expectations of stakeholders, to the external environmental factors beyond the control of the estate and to the strategic capabilities of the estate itself.** (15 marks)

(b) **Discuss how the website could be further developed to address some of the issues highlighted in the survey.** (10 marks)

(25 marks)

Question 13 DRB ELECTRONIC SERVICES

DRB Electronic Services operates in a high labour cost environment in Western Europe and imports electronic products from the Republic of Korea. It re-brands and re-packages them as DRB products and then sells them to business and domestic customers in the local geographical region. Its only current source of supply is ISAS electronics based in a factory on the outskirts of Seoul, the capital of the Republic of Korea. DRB regularly places orders for ISAS products through the ISAS website and pays for them by credit card. As soon as the payment is confirmed ISAS automatically e-mails DRB a confirmation of order, an order reference number and likely shipping date. When the order is actually despatched, ISAS send DRB a notice of despatch e-mail and a container reference number. ISAS currently organises all the shipping of the products. The products are sent in containers and then trans-shipped to EIF, the logistics company used by ISAS to distribute its products. EIF then delivers the products to the DRB factory. Once they arrive, they are quality inspected and products that pass the inspection are re-branded as DRB products (by adding appropriate logos) and packaged in specially fabricated DRB boxes. These products are then stored ready for sale. All customer sales are from stock. Products that fail the inspection are returned to ISAS.

Currently 60% of sales are made to domestic customers and 40% to business customers. Most domestic customers pick up their products from DRB and set them up themselves. In contrast, most business customers ask DRB to set up the electronic equipment at their offices, for which DRB makes a small charge. DRB currently advertises its products in local and regional newspapers. DRB also has a website which provides product details. Potential customers can enquire about the specification and availability of products through an e-mail facility in the website. DRB then e-mails an appropriate response directly to the person making the enquiry. Payment for products cannot currently be made through the website.

Feedback from existing customers suggests that they particularly value the installation and support offered by the company. The company employs specialist technicians who (for a fee) will install equipment in both homes and offices. They will also come out and troubleshoot problems with equipment that is still under warranty. DRB also offer a helpline and a back-to-base facility for customers whose products are out of warranty. Feedback from current customers suggests that this support is highly valued. One commented that "it contrasts favourably with your large customers who offer support through impersonal off-shore call centres and a time-consuming returns policy". Customers can also pay for technicians to come on-site to sort out problems with out-of-warranty equipment.

DRB now plans to increase their product range and market share. It plans to grow from its current turnover of $5m per annum to $12m per annum in two years' time. Dilip Masood, the owner of DRB, believes that DRB must change its business model if it is to achieve this growth. He believes that these changes will also have to tackle problems associated with:

- Missing, or potentially missing shipments. Shipments can only be tracked through contacting the shipment account holder, ISAS, and on occasions they have been reluctant or unable to help. The trans-shipment to EIF has also caused problems and this has usually been identified as the point where goods have been lost. ISAS does not appear to be able to reliably track the relationship between the container shipment and the waybills used in the EIF system.

- The likely delivery dates of orders, the progress of orders and the progress of shipments is poorly specified and monitored. Hence deliveries are relatively unpredictable and this can cause congestion problems in the delivery bay.

Dilip also recognises that growth will mean that the company has to sell more products outside its region and the technical installation and support so valued by local customers will be difficult to maintain. He is also adamant that DRB will continue to import only fully configured products. It is not interested in importing components and assembling them. DRB also does not wish to build or invest in assembly plants overseas or to commit to a long-term contract with one supplier.

Required:

(a)   **Draw the primary activities of DRB on a value chain. Comment on the significance of each of these activities and the value that they offer to customers.**   (9 marks)

(b)   **Explain how DRB might re-structure its upstream supply chain to achieve the growth required by DRB and to tackle the problems that Dilip Masood has identified.** (10 marks)

(c)   **Explain how DRB might re-structure its downstream supply chain to achieve the growth required.**   (6 marks)

(25 marks)

Question 14 iCOMPUTE

iCompute was founded twenty years ago by the technology entrepreneur, Ron Yeates. It initially specialised in building bespoke computer software for the financial services industry. However, it has expanded into other specialised areas and it is currently the third largest software house in the country, employing 400 people. It still specialises in bespoke software, although 20% of its income now comes from the sales of a software package designed specifically for car insurance.

The company has grown based on a "work hard, play hard work ethic" and this still remains. Employees are expected to work long hours and to take part in social activities after work. Revenues have continued to increase over the last few years, but the firm has had difficulty in recruiting and retaining staff. Approximately one-third of all employees leave within their first year of employment at the company. The company appears to experience particular difficulty in recruiting and retaining female staff, with 50% of female staff leaving within 12 months of joining the company. Only about 20% of the employees are female and they work mainly in marketing and human resources.

The company is currently in dispute with two of its customers who claim that its bespoke software did not fit the agreed requirements. iCompute currently outsources all its legal advice problems to a law firm that specialises in computer contracts and legislation. However, the importance of legal advice has led to iCompute considering the establishment of an internal legal team, responsible for advising on contracts, disputes and employment legislation.

The support of bespoke solutions and the car insurance software package was also outsourced a year ago to a third party. Although support had been traditionally handled in-house, it was unpopular with staff. One of the senior managers responsible for the outsourcing decision claimed that support calls were "increasingly varied and complex, reflecting incompetent end users, too lazy to read user guides." However, the outsourcing of support has not proved popular with iCompute's customers and a number of significant complaints have been made about the service given to end users. The company is currently reviewing whether the software support process should be brought back in-house.

The company is still regarded as a technology leader in the market place, although the presence of so many technically gifted employees within the company often creates uncertainty about the most appropriate technology to adopt for a solution. One manager commented that "we have often adopted, or are about to adopt, a technology or solution when one of our software developers will ask if we have considered some newly released technology. We usually admit we haven't and so we re-open the adoption process. We seem to be in a state of constant technical paralysis."

Although Ron Yeates retired five years ago, many of the software developers recruited by him are still with the company. Some of these have become operational managers, employed to manage teams of software developers on internal and external projects. Subba Kendo is one of the managers who originally joined the company as a trainee programmer. "I moved into management because I needed to earn more money. There is a limit to what you can earn here as a software developer. However, I still keep up to date with programming though, and I am a goalkeeper for one of the company's five-a-side football teams. I am still one of the boys."

However, many of the software developers are sceptical about their managers. One commented that "they are technologically years out of date. Some will insist on writing programs and producing code, but we take it out again as soon as we can and replace it with something we have written. Not only are they poor programmers, they are poor managers and don't really know how to motivate us." Although revenues have increased, profits have fallen. This is also blamed on the managers. "There is always an element of ambiguity in specifying customers' requirements. In the past, Ron Yeates would debate responsibility for requirements changes with the customer. However, we now seem to do all amendments for free. The customer is right even when we know he isn't. No wonder margins are falling. The managers are not firm enough with customers."

The software developers are also angry that an in-house project has been initiated to produce a system for recording time spent on tasks and projects. Some of the justification for this is that a few of the projects are on a "time and materials" basis and a time recording system would permit accurate and prompt invoicing. However, the other justification for the project is that it will improve the estimation of "fixed-price" contracts. It will provide statistical information derived from previous projects to assist account managers preparing estimates to produce quotes for bidding for new bespoke development contracts.

Vikram Soleski, one of the current software developers, commented that "managers do not even have up-to-date mobile phones, probably because they don't know how to use them. We (software developers) always have the latest gadgets long before they are acquired by managers. But I like working here, we have a good social scene and after working long hours we socialise together, often playing computer games well into the early hours of the morning. It's a great life if you don't weaken!"

Required:

(a) **Analyse the culture of iCompute, and assess the implications of your analysis for the company's future performance.** (13 marks)

(b) iCompute is currently re-considering three high level processes:

   (i)   Advice on legal issues (currently outsourced)
   (ii)   Software support (currently outsourced)
   (iii)   Time recording (in-house, bespoke software development)

   Evaluate, using an appropriate framework or model, the suitability of iCompute's current approach to EACH of these high level processes. (12 marks)

(25 marks)

Question 15 RAMON SILVA

Ramon Silva is a Spanish property developer, who has made a considerable fortune from the increasing numbers of Europeans looking to buy new homes and apartments in the coastal regions of Mediterranean Spain. His frequent contact with property buyers has made him aware of their need for low cost hotel accommodation during the lengthy period between finding a property to buy and when they actually move into their new home. These would-be property owners are looking for inexpensive hotels in the same locations as tourists looking for cheap holiday accommodation.

Closer investigation of the market for inexpensive or budget hotel accommodation has convinced Ramon of the opportunity to offer something really different to his potential customers. He has the advantage of having no preconceived idea of what his chain of hotels might look like. The overall picture for the budget hotel industry is not encouraging with the industry suffering from low growth and consequent overcapacity. There are two distinct market segments in the budget hotel industry; firstly, no-star and one-star hotels, whose average price per room is between 30 and 45 euros. Customers are simply attracted by the low price. The second segment is the service provided by two-star hotels with an average price of 100 euros a night. These more expensive hotels attract customers by offering a better sleeping environment than the no-star and one-star hotels. Customers therefore have to choose between low prices and getting a poor night's sleep owing to noise and inferior beds or paying more for an untroubled night's sleep. Ramon quickly deduced that a hotel chain that can offer a better price/quality combination could be a winner.

The two-star hotels typically offer a full range of services including restaurants, bars and lounges, all of which are costly to operate. The low price budget hotels offer simple overnight accommodation with cheaply furnished rooms and staffed by part-time receptionists. Ramon is convinced that considerable cost savings are available through better room design, construction and furniture and a more effective use of hotel staff. He feels that through offering hotel franchises under the "La Familia Amable" ("The Friendly Family") group name, he could recruit husband and wife teams to own and operate them.

The couples, with suitable training, could offer most of the services provided in a two-star hotel, and create a friendly, family atmosphere – hence the company name. He is sure he can offer the customer two-star hotel value at budget prices. He is confident that the value-for-money option he offers would need little marketing promotion to launch it and achieve rapid growth.

Required:

(a) **Provide Ramon with a brief report, using strategic models where appropriate, showing where his proposed hotel service can add value to the customer's experience.** (12 marks)

(b) **Discuss the advantages and disadvantages of using franchising to develop the La Familia Amable budget hotel chain.** (8 marks)

(20 marks)

Question 16 EXCALIBUR SPORTSWEAR

Excalibur Sportswear is a United Kingdom marketing firm, selling high quality sports clothing within the UK. The firm has been set up by Simon Smith, who until recently was a world-class athlete. Smith, although selling his products exclusively in the UK, is sourcing production overseas, taking advantage of the cheaper labour costs and materials available elsewhere. Smith has used his reputation and his network of contacts to persuade footballers, tennis and golf professionals to wear his products. The logo and brand name of Excalibur are now becoming well known throughout the world as a result of the famous sports personalities being seen on TV wearing the company's products.

Despite this apparent success Excalibur is facing financial difficulties. In order to achieve the favourable exposure the company has spent heavily on advertising. The biggest expenditure has been the payment of promotional expenses to the world-famous sports stars, so that they will be seen wearing the company's products, particularly at events that are likely to be televised throughout the world. Compared with most of its competitors, Excalibur's costs were too high compared with its revenues. The company needed to sell more. The competitors' revenues were higher because they sold their products on a worldwide basis. Smith has decided that his company should look at its market as a global one and not as a national market. Expanding sales should not prove to be a problem for Excalibur. Most of the production is sub-contracted to foreign manufacturers so an expansion of capacity will have minimal financial impact on the marketing company. Similarly as most of the sales are through independent retail outlets there will be few increased costs for Excalibur as a result of the development of sales on a global basis. Naturally marketing costs, in particular those concerned with advertising will rise.

Initial marketing research has confirmed the belief that Excalibur's products will be acceptable in many foreign markets. Many of the issues that can frequently threaten companies who decide to move into foreign markets are seen as favourable or at least benign. Trade barriers on such sports clothing products are relatively low. Although the company has no expertise in selling products overseas the fact that key activities – production and distribution – are outsourced, should make the challenge for Excalibur less testing. Finally, when seeking to establish markets overseas a shortage of finance is often a problem. Excalibur's bank is optimistic about the enterprise and is willing to provide market development finance.

Nevertheless Simon Smith is unhappy about relying on outsiders to provide critical inputs into the organisation. He believes that there is an increased risk of poorer quality and control affecting the company's reputation. Although existing suppliers and distributors have performed adequately he believes that a large expansion of Excalibur's activities, as proposed, might be beyond their capacity and any new suppliers and distributors may be of a lower standard. He is therefore contemplating setting up his own manufacturing facilities and distribution networks.

Required:

(a)   **Evaluate the key factors, which might encourage Excalibur to become involved in overseas marketing and even become a "global" organisation.**   (12 marks)

(b)   **Explain how risk, control and resource commitments might change for Simon Smith's firm as it attempts to take more control of its activities.**   (8 marks)

(20 marks)

Question 17 AMBION

Ambion is the third largest industrial country in the world. It is densely populated with a high standard of living. Joe Swift Transport (known as Swift) is the largest logistics company in Ambion, owning 1,500 trucks. It is a private limited company with all shares held by the Swift family. It has significant haulage and storage contracts with retail and supermarket chains in Ambion. The logistics market-place is mature and extremely competitive and Swift has become market leader through a combination of economies of scale, cost efficiencies, innovative IT solutions and clever branding. However, the profitability of the sector is under increased pressure from a recently elected government that is committed to heavily taxing fuel and reducing expenditure on roads in favour of alternative forms of transport. It has also announced a number of taxes on vehicles which have high carbon emission levels as well as reducing the maximum working hours and increasing the national minimum wage for employees. The company is perceived as a good performer in its sector. Last year's financial results reported a return on capital employed of 18%, a gross profit margin of 17% and a net profit margin of 9·15%. The accounts also showed a current liquidity ratio of 1·55 and an acid test ratio of 1·15. The gearing ratio is currently 60% with an interest cover ratio of 8.

10 years ago the northern political bloc split up and nine new independent states were formed. One of these states was Ecuria. The people of Ecuria (known as Ecurians) traditionally have a strong work ethic and a passion for precision and promptness. Since the formation of the state, their hard work has been rewarded by strong economic growth, a higher standard of living and an increased demand for goods which were once perceived as unobtainable luxuries. Since the formation of the state, the government of Ecuria has pursued a policy of privatisation. It has also invested heavily in infrastructure, particularly the road transport system, required to support the increased economic activity in the country.

The state haulage operator (EVM) was sold off to two Ecurian investors who raised the finance to buy it from a foreign bank. The capital markets in Ecuria are still immature and the government has not wished to interfere with or bolster them. EVM now has 700 modern trucks and holds all the major logistics contracts in the country. It is praised for its prompt delivery of goods. Problems in raising finance have made it difficult for significant competitors to emerge. Most are family firms, each of which operates about 20 trucks making local deliveries within one of Ecuria's 20 regions.

These two investors now wish to realise their investment in EVM and have announced that it is for sale. In principle, Swift are keen to buy the company and are currently evaluating its possible acquisition. Swift's management perceive that their capabilities in logistics will greatly enhance the profitability of EVM. Last year's financial results for EVM are shown in Figure 1. Swift has acquired a number of smaller Ambion companies in the last decade, but has no experience of acquiring foreign companies, or indeed, working in Ecuria.

Joe Swift is also contemplating a more radical change. He is becoming progressively disillusioned with Ambion. In a recent interview he said that "trading here is becoming impossible. The government is more interested in over regulating enterprise than stimulating growth". He is considering moving large parts of his logistics operation to another country and Ecuria is one of the possibilities he is considering.

Figure 1 – Extract from financial results: EVM

Extract from the statement of financial position

	$m	$m
Non-current assets		
Intangible assets		2,000
Property, plant, equipment		6,100
		8,100
Current assets		
Inventories	100	
Trade receivables	900	
Cash and cash equivalents	200	
		1,200
Total assets		9,300
Equity		
Share capital		5,700
Retained earnings		50
Total equity		5,750
Non-current liabilities		
Long-term borrowings		2,500
Current liabilities		
Trade payables	1,000	
Current tax payable	50	
		1,050
Total liabilities		3,550
Total equity and liabilities		9,300

Extract from the statement of profit or loss

	$m
Revenue	20,000
Cost of sales	(16,000)
Gross profit	4,000
Administrative expenses	(2,500)
Finance cost	(300)
Profit before tax	1,200
Income tax expense	(50)
Profit for the year	1,150

Required:

(a)   Assess, using both financial and non-financial measures, the attractiveness, from Swift's perspective, of EVM as an acquisition target.   (15 marks)

(b)   Porter's Diamond can be used to explore the competitive advantage of nations and could be a useful model for Joe Swift to use in his analysis of countries that he might move his company to.

Examine using Porter's Diamond (or an appropriate alternative model/framework) the factors which could influence Swift's decision to move a large part of its logistics business to Ecuria.   (10 marks)

(25 marks)

Question 18 ENVIRONMENT MANAGEMENT SOCIETY

The Environment Management Society (EMS) was established in 2004 by environment practitioners who felt that environmental management and audit should have its own qualification. EMS has its own Board who report to a Council of eight members. Policy is made by the Board and ratified by Council. EMS is registered as a private limited entity.

EMS employs staff to administer its qualification and to provide services to its members. The qualification began as one certificate, developed by the original founding members of the Society. It has since been developed, by members and officers of the EMS, into a four certificate scheme leading to a Diploma. EMS employs a full-time chief examiner who is responsible for setting the certificate examinations which take place monthly in training centres throughout the country. No examinations are currently held in other countries.

If candidates pass all four papers they can undertake an oral Diploma examination. If they pass this oral they are eligible to become members. All examinations are open-book one hour examinations, preceded by 15 minutes reading time. At a recent meeting, EMS Council rejected the concept of computer-based assessment. They felt that competence in this area was best assessed by written examination answers.

Candidate numbers for the qualification have fallen dramatically in the last two years. The Board of EMS has concluded that this drop reflects the maturing marketplace in the country. Many people who were practitioners in environmental management and audit when the qualification was introduced have now gained their Diploma. The stream of new candidates and hence members is relatively small.

Consequently, the EMS Board has suggested that they should now look to attract international candidates and it has targeted countries where environmental management and audit is becoming more important. It is now formulating a strategy to launch the qualification in India, China and Russia.

However, any strategy has to recognise that both the EMS Board and the Council are very cautious and notably risk-averse. EMS is only confident about its technical capability within a restricted definition of environmental management and audit. Attempts to look at complementary qualification areas (such as soil and water conservation) have been swiftly rejected by Council as being non-core areas and therefore outside the scope of their expertise.

Required:

Internal development, acquisitions and strategic alliances are three development methods by which an organisation's strategic direction can be pursued.

(a)   **Explain the principles of internal development and discuss how appropriate this development method is to EMS.**   (8 marks)

(b)   **Explain the principles of acquisitions and discuss how appropriate this development method is to EMS.**   (8 marks)

(c)   **Explain the principles of strategic alliances and discuss how appropriate this development method is to EMS.**   (9 marks)

(25 marks)

Question 19 GRAFFOFF

Emile Gonzalez is an industrial chemist who worked for the government of Pablos for more than 20 years. In his spare time, he continually experimented with formulating a product that could remove graffiti from all surfaces. Graffiti is a particular problem in Pablos and all previous removal methods were expensive, dangerous to apply and did not work on all surfaces. After many years of experimentation, Emile formulated a product that addressed all these issues. His product can be applied safely without protective clothing, it removes graffiti from all surfaces and it can be produced economically in small, as well as large, volumes.

Three years ago, Emile left his government job to focus on refining the product and bringing it to market. He formed a limited liability company, Graffoff, with initial share capital funded by his savings, his family's savings and a legacy from a wealthy relative. He is the sole shareholder in the company, which is based in a factory in central Pablos. The company has filed two years of results (see Figure 1 for extracted information from year (2), and it is expected to return similar net profit figures in its third trading year. Emile takes a significant dividend out of the company each year and he wishes that to continue. He also wishes to remain the sole owner of the company.

Four years ago, Emile was granted a patent for the formula on which his product is based and a further patent on the process used to produce the product. In Pablos, patents are protected for 10 years and so Emile has six further years before his formula becomes available to his competitors. Consequently, he wants to rapidly expand the company and plans to lease premises to create 30 new graffiti removal depots in Pablos, each of which will supply graffiti removing services in its local region. He needs $500,000 to finance this organic growth of his company.

Emile does have mixed feelings about his proposed expansion plan. Despite the apparent success of his company, he prefers working in the laboratory to managing people. "I am just not a people person", he has commented. He is aware that he lacks business experience and, despite the technical excellence of the product, he has failed to build a highly visible brand. He also has particular problems in the accounts receivables department, where he has failed to address the problems of over-worked and demotivated employees. Emile dislikes conflict with customers and so he often offers them extended payment terms to the dismay of the accounts receivables section, who feel that their debt collecting effectiveness is being constantly undermined by his concessions. In contrast, Graffoff pays bills very promptly, due to a zealous administrator in accounts payable who likes to reduce creditors. Emile is sanguine about this. "I guess we have the money, so I suppose we should pay them."

In Pablos, all goods are supplied to customers on 30 days credit. However, in the services sector that Graffoff is trading in, the average settlement period for payables (creditors) is 40 days. One supplier commented that "Graffoff is unique in its punctuality of payment".

Emile is currently reviewing how to finance his proposed organic growth. He is unwilling to take on any further external debt and consequently he has also recently considered franchising as an alternative to organic growth. In his proposed arrangement, franchisees would have responsibility for leasing or buying premises to a specification defined in the franchise agreement. The franchise would have exclusive rights to the Graffoff product in a defined geographical region.

The Equipment Emporium has 57 superstores throughout the country selling tools and machines such as air compressors, generators and ventilation systems. It is a well-recognised brand with a strong marketing presence. It focuses on selling specialist products in bright, well-lit superstores. It has approached Graffoff to ask whether it can sell the Graffoff product through its superstores. Emile has rejected this suggestion because he feels that his product requires proper training if it is to be used efficiently and safely. He sees Graffoff as offering a complete service (graffiti removal), not just a product (graffiti removal equipment) and so selling through The Equipment Emporium would be inappropriate.

Figure 1: Extracted financial data for Graffoff's second year of trading, reported at 31 December 2017

Extract from the statement of financial position   *Extracts from the statement of profit or loss*

All figures in $000:		All figures in $000:	
ASSETS		**Revenue**	1,600
Non-current assets		Cost of sales	(1,375)
Property, plant and equipment	1,385	Gross profit	225
Intangible assets	100	Administrative expenses	(100)
Total non-current assets	1,485	Finance costs	(15)
Current assets		Profit before tax	110
Inventories	100	Income tax expense	(20)
Trade receivables	260	Profit for the period	90
Cash and cash equivalents	30		
Total current assets	390		
Total assets	1,875		
EQUITY AND LIABILITIES			
Share capital	1,500		
Retained earnings	30		
Total equity	1,530		
Non-current liabilities			
Long-term borrowings	250		
Total non-current liabilities	250		
Current liabilities			
Trade and other payables	75		
Current tax payable	20		
Total current liabilities	95		
Total liabilities	345		
Total equity and liabilities	1,875		

Required:

(a) **Evaluate the franchising option being considered by Graffoff, highlighting the advantages and disadvantages of this approach from Emile's perspective.** (10 marks)

(b) Johnson, Scholes and Whittington have identified franchising as a form of strategic alliance.

Evaluate how other forms of strategic alliance might be appropriate approaches to strategy development at Graffoff. (7 marks)

(c) A consultant has suggested that Graffoff should be able to completely fund its proposed organic expansion (at a cost of $500,000) through internally generated sources of finance.

Evaluate this claim. (8 marks)

(25 marks)

Question 20 SENSATIONAL SOUNDS

Sensational Sounds (SS) manufactures high quality headphones. These can be used with any devices such as MP3 players, laptop computers and smartphones. The products are designed and manufactured in Homeland, but are sold around the world through carefully selected retailers. They are also sold online through the company's web site.

The company targets two particular customer groups, and has a range of products to satisfy each. The first group is young adults with plenty of disposable income who always have the latest high tech gadgets. They consider SS headphones to be a must have fashion accessory. The second group is serious music listeners, who love listening to music, and demand high quality sound. This group is mainly middle aged and affluent.

Historically the company has relied on traditional approaches to market research such as focus groups and questionnaires to determine the company's sales and marketing strategy. A new marketing manager, Lucio Sanchez, has expressed dismay at the failure of the company to make greater use of Big Data. He believes that there is valuable potential marketing information available from the company's own management information systems and from social networks.

Lucio wants to invest in a business intelligence system that would enable all the data from the company's existing systems to be extracted and uploaded onto a database from which it can be analysed using sophisticated query and reporting tools. The existing systems contain much useful data but do not have the capability to provide the reports that Lucio wants. "If I want to have information about sales of a particular range of headphones in a particular location, the information has to be extracted manually and entered onto a spreadsheet," Lucio told you. He added, "I need to know who is buying which headphones today, not yesterday! This market is fast changing. If we can't predict the changes, we can't give our customers what they want."

Lucio also wants to buy a package that can analyse conversations on social media networks such as Facebook and Twitter. "I need to listen and become involved in the conversation!" he said. "I need to know who is saying what about our products and our competitors' products."

John Boycott, the finance director of SS, is sceptical about the benefits that these systems would bring to the company and has asked you for your opinion.

Required:

(a)   **Explain the potential benefits to SS of the business intelligence system that Lucio wants.**
(10 marks)

(b)   **Explain how organisations such as SS use and analyse social media networks to improve their strategic performance.** (15 marks)

(25 marks)

Question 21 PHARMACY SYSTEMS INTERNATIONAL

Introduction

Retail pharmacies supply branded medicinal products, such as headache and cold remedies, as well as medicines prescribed by doctors. Customers expect both types of product to be immediately available and so this demands efficient purchasing and stock control in each pharmacy. The retail pharmacy industry is increasingly concentrated in a small number of nationwide pharmacy chains, although independent pharmacies continue to survive. The pharmacy chains are increasingly encouraging their customers to order medicinal products online and the doctors are being encouraged to electronically send their prescriptions to the pharmacy so that they can be prepared ready for the patient to collect.

Pharmacy Systems International

Pharmacy Systems International (PSI) is a privately owned software company which has successfully developed and sold a specialised software package meeting the specific needs of retail pharmacies. PSI's stated objective is to be a "highly skilled professional company providing quality software services to the retail pharmacy industry". Over the last three years PSI has experienced gradual growth in turnover, profitability and market share (see Figure 1).

Figure 1: PSI Financial information

	20Y2	20Y1	20Y0
Turnover ($000)	11,700	10,760	10,350
Profits ($000) (pre-tax)	975	945	875
Estimated market share	26%	24%	23%
Number of employees	120	117	115

PSI has three directors, each of whom has a significant ownership stake in the business. The chief executive is a natural entrepreneur with a past record of identifying opportunities and taking the necessary risks to exploit them. In the last three years he has curbed his natural enthusiasm for growth as PSI has consolidated its position in the market place. However, he now feels the time is right to expand the business to a size and profitability that makes PSI an attractive acquisition target and enables the directors to realise their investment in the company. He has a natural ally in the sales and marketing director and both feel that PSI needs to find new national and international markets to fuel its growth. The software development director, however, does not share the chief executive's enthusiasm for this expansion.

The chief executive has proposed that growth can best be achieved by developing a generic software package which can be used by the wider, general retail industry. His plan is for the company to take the current software package and take out any specific references to the pharmaceutical industry. This generic package could then be extended and configured for other retail sectors. The pharmaceutical package would be retained but it would be perceived and marketed as a specialised implementation of the new generic package.

This proposed change in strategic direction is strongly resisted by the software development director. He and his team of software developers are under constant pressure to meet the demands of the existing retail pharmacy customers. On-line ordering of medicinal products and electronic despatch of prescriptions are just two examples of the constant pressure PSI is under from their retail customers to continuously update its software package to enable the pharmacies to implement technical innovations that improve customer service.

Ideally, the software development director would like to acquire further resources to develop a more standardised software package for their current customers. He is particularly annoyed by PSI's salesmen continually committing the company to producing a customised software solution for each customer and promising delivery dates that the software delivery team struggle to meet. Frequently, the software contains faults that require expensive and time-consuming maintenance. Consequently, PSI is being increasingly criticised by customers. A recent user group conference expressed considerable dissatisfaction with the quality of the PSI package and doubted the company's ability to meet the published deadline for a new release of the software.

Required:

(a) The proposal to develop and sell a software package for the retail industry represents a major change in strategy for PSI.

Analyse the nature, scope and type of this proposed strategic change for PSI. (10 marks)

(b) The success of any attempt at managing change will be dependent on the context in which that change takes place.

Identify and analyse, using an appropriate model, the internal contextual features that could influence the success or failure of the chief executive's proposed strategic change for PSI. (15 marks)

(25 marks)

Question 22 COUNTRY CAR CLUB

Introduction

The Country Car Club (3C) was established fifty years ago to offer breakdown assistance to motorists. In return for an annual membership fee, members of 3C are able to phone for immediate assistance if their vehicle breaks down anywhere in the country. Assistance is provided by "service patrol engineers" who are located throughout the country and who are specialists in vehicle repair and maintenance. If they cannot fix the problem immediately then the vehicle and its occupants are transported by a 3C recovery vehicle back to the member's home address free of charge.

Over the last 15 years 3C has rapidly expanded its services. It now offers vehicle insurance, vehicle history checks (to check for previous accident damage or theft) as well as offering a comprehensive advice centre where trained staff answer a wide range of vehicle-related queries. It also provides route maps, endorses hotels by giving them a 3C starred rating and lobbies the government on issues such as taxation, vehicle emissions and toll road charging. All of these services are provided by permanent 3C employees and all growth has been organic culminating in a listing on the country's stock exchange three years ago.

However, since its stock market listing, the company has posted disappointing results and a falling share price has spurred managers to review internal processes and functions. A Business Architecture Committee (BAC) made up of senior managers has been charged with reviewing the scope of the company's business activities. It has been asked to examine the importance of certain activities and to make recommendations on the sourcing of these activities (in-house or outsourced). The BAC has also been asked to identify technological implications or opportunities for the activities that they recommend should remain in-house.

First review

The BAC's first review included an assessment of the supply and maintenance of 3C's company vehicles. 3C has traditionally purchased its own fleet of vehicles and maintained them in a central garage. When a vehicle needed servicing or maintenance it was returned to this central garage. Last year, 3C had seven hundred vehicles (breakdown recovery vehicles, service patrol engineer vans, company cars for senior staff, etc) all maintained by thirty staff permanently employed in this garage. A further three permanent employees were employed at the garage site with responsibility for the purchasing and disposal of vehicles. The garage was in a residential area of a major town, with major parking problems and no room for expansion.

The BAC concluded that the garage was of low strategic importance to the company and, although most of the processes it involved were straightforward, its remoteness from the home base of some vehicles made undertaking such processes unnecessarily complicated. Consequently, it recommended outsourcing vehicle acquisition, disposal and maintenance to a specialist company. Two months ago 3C's existing vehicle fleet was acquired by AutoDirect, a company with service and repair centres nationwide, which currently supplies 45,000 vehicles to companies throughout the country. It now leases vehicles back to 3C for a monthly payment. In the next 10 years (the duration of the contract) all vehicles will be leased from AutoDirect on a full maintenance basis that includes the replacement of tyres and exhausts. 3C's garage is now surplus to requirements and all the employees that worked there have been made redundant, except for one employee who has been retained to manage the relationship with AutoDirect.

Second review

The BAC has now been asked to look at the following activities and their supporting processes. All of these are currently performed in-house by permanent 3C employees.

■ *Attendance of repair staff at breakdowns* – currently undertaken by permanent "service patrol engineers" employed at locations throughout the country from where they attend local breakdowns.

■ *Membership renewal* – members must renew every year. Currently renewals are sent out by staff using a bespoke computer system. Receipts are processed when members confirm that they will be renewing for a further year.

■ *Vehicle insurance services providing accident insurance which every motorist legally requires.*

■ *Membership queries handled by a call-centre. Members can use the service for a wide range of vehicle-related problems and issues.*

■ *Vehicle history checks.* These are primarily used to provide "peace of mind" to a potential purchaser of a vehicle.

The vehicle is checked to see if it has ever been in an accident or if it has been stolen. The check also makes sure that the car is not currently part of a loan agreement.

Required:

(a) The Business Architecture Committee (BAC) has been asked to make recommendations on the sourcing of activities (in-house or outsourced). The BAC has also been asked to identify technological implications or opportunities for the activities that they recommend should remain in-house.

Suggest and justify recommendations to the BAC for each of the following major process areas:

(i)   **Attendance of repair staff at breakdowns;**
(ii) **Membership renewal;**
(iii) **Vehicle insurance services;**
(iv) **Membership queries; and**
(v)   **Vehicle history checks.**   (15 marks)

(b) **Analyse the advantages that 3C will gain from the decision to outsource the purchase and maintenance of their own vehicles.**   (10 marks)

(25 marks)

Question 23 FLEXIPIPE

Introduction

Flexipipe is a successful company supplying flexible pipes to a wide range of industries. Its success is based on a very innovative production process which allows the company to produce relatively small batches of flexible pipes at very competitive prices. This has given Flexipipe a significant competitive edge over most of its competitors whose batch set-up costs are higher and whose lead times are longer. Flexipipe's innovative process is partly automated and partly reliant on experienced managers and supervisors on the factory floor. These managers efficiently schedule jobs from different customers to achieve economies of scale and throughput times that profitably deliver high quality products and service to Flexipipe's customers.

A year ago, the Chief Executive Officer (CEO) at Flexipipe decided that he wanted to extend the automated part of the production process by purchasing a software package that promised even further benefits, including the automation of some of the decision-making tasks currently undertaken by the factory managers and supervisors. He had seen this package at a software exhibition and was so impressed that he placed an order immediately. He stated that the package was "ahead of its time, and I have seen nothing else like it on the market".

This was the first time that the company had bought a software package for something that was not to be used in a standard application, such as payroll or accounts. Most other software applications in the company, such as the automated part of the current production process, have been developed in-house by a small programming team. The CEO felt that there was, on this occasion, insufficient time and money to develop a bespoke in-house solution. He accepted that there was no formal process for software package procurement "but perhaps we can put one in place as this project progresses".

This relaxed approach to procurement is not unusual at Flexipipe, where many of the purchasing decisions are taken unilaterally by senior managers. There is a small procurement section with two full-time administrators, but they only become involved once purchasing decisions have been made. It is felt that they are not technically proficient enough to get involved earlier in the purchasing lifecycle and, in any case, they are already very busy with purchase order administration and accounts payable. This approach to procurement has caused problems in the past. For example, the company had problems when a key supplier of raw materials unexpectedly went out of business. This caused short-term production problems, although the CEO has now found an acceptable alternative supplier.

The automation project

On returning to the company from the exhibition, the CEO commissioned a business analyst to investigate the current production process system so that the transition from the current system to the new software package solution could be properly planned. The business analyst found that some of the decisions made in the current production process were difficult to define and it was often hard for managers to explain how they had taken effective action. They tended to use their experience, memory and judgement and were still innovating in their control of the process. One commented that "what we do today, we might not do tomorrow; requirements are constantly evolving".

When the software package was delivered there were immediate difficulties in technically migrating some of the data from the current automated part of the production process software to the software package solution. However, after some difficulties, it was possible to hold trials with experienced users. The CEO was confident that these users did not need training and would be "able to learn the software as they went along". However, in reality, they found the software very difficult to use and they reported that certain key functions were missing. One of the supervisors commented that "the monitoring process variance facility is missing completely. Yet we had this in the old automated system". Despite these reservations, the software package solution was implemented, but results were disappointing. Overall, it was impossible to replicate the success of the old production process and early results showed that costs had increased and lead times had become longer.

After struggling with the system for a few months, support from the software supplier began to become erratic. Eventually, the supplier notified Flexipipe that it had gone into administration and that it was withdrawing support for its product. Fortunately, Flexipipe were able to revert to the original production process software, but the ill-fated package selection exercise had cost it over $3 million in costs and lost profits. The CEO commissioned a post-project review which showed that the supplier, prior to the purchase of the software package, had been very highly geared and had very poor liquidity. Also, contrary to the statement of the CEO, the post-project review team reported that there were at least three other packages currently available in the market that could have potentially fulfilled the requirements of the company. The CEO now accepts that using a software package to automate the production process was an inappropriate approach and that a bespoke in-house solution should have been commissioned.

Required:

(a) **Critically evaluate the decision made by the CEO to use a software package approach to automating the production process at Flexipipe, and explain why this approach was unlikely to succeed.** (12 marks)

(b) The CEO recommends that the company now adopts a formal process for procuring, evaluating and implementing software packages which they can use in the future when a software package approach appears to be more appropriate.

Analyse how a formal process for software package procurement, evaluation and implementation would have addressed the problems experienced at Flexipipe in the production process project. (13 marks)

(25 marks)

Question 24 CHEMICAL TRANSPORT

Chemical Transport (CT) is a specialist haulage company providing transport services for several chemical wholesalers. Despite these wholesalers being in competition with each other, many of them have outsourced their distribution to CT, recognising the company's expertise in this area and its compliance with stringent and emerging legislation. This legislation is at both national and international level and concerns the transportation and handling of chemicals, as well as the maintenance of trucks and trailers and the health, competencies, safety and driving hours of drivers. There are also chemical wholesalers in the country who either organise their own distribution or outsource to one of CT's competitors.

CT handles the distribution of chemicals from either the port of importation or point of production to the wholesaler's depots or directly to the end customers of the wholesaler. The chemical wholesalers are increasingly attempting to minimise their own storage costs, so many of CT's deliveries are now directly from the point of production (or port of importation) to the end customer. Most of these end customers are manufacturing companies with limited chemical storage capacity.

The complex and changing nature of legislation has led to CT engaging a specialist legal consultancy to provide it with advice. They have found this advice to be both useful and proactive. The consultancy has identified the potential effect of employment, tax and health and safety legislation in advance and has notified CT of its likely implications. CT has benefited from this advice but it is concerned that it is expensive and it is considering employing a full-time legal expert, instead of using the legal consultancy.

The chemical wholesalers have asked CT to provide an internet-based system which would allow them to request and track deliveries. CT does currently have a website, but it only contains information about the company: its structures, history, key contacts and case studies. CT has agreed to provide such a system because it is aware that failure to do so will lead to wholesalers looking for an alternative distributor.

CT does have an internal IT capability with some expertise in building web-based systems. The internal IT team have also developed a bespoke payroll system. Drivers at CT are rewarded with basic pay, together with a complex set of bonuses and deductions which have been developed and enhanced over the last few years. There are bonuses for certain skills and attainments and deductions for missed or delayed deliveries or mistakes. The drivers themselves find the pay arrangements very confusing. One commented that "we find it almost impossible to check if we have been paid correctly and it confuses us rather than motivates us!" Changes in national tax legislation are also continually affecting the payroll calculation. Indeed, recent changes in legislation led to the IT team being fully occupied for three months, developing and testing the required modifications to the payroll system.

(a)   Three significant business process areas have been identified in the scenario: (1) payroll, (2) legal advice and (3) an enhanced web service allowing wholesalers to request and track deliveries.

Required:

Use Harmon's process-strategy matrix to analyse the characteristics of each of the three process areas defined above and suggest how each should be sourced and implemented at CT. (15 marks)

(b)   Requesting and tracking information could be the first part of a comprehensive customer relationship management (CRM) system

Required:

Evaluate how CT could use a CRM system to acquire and retain customers. (10 marks)

(25 marks)

Question 25 BRIDGE

Introduction

The following is an interview with Mick Kazinski, a senior marketing executive with Bridge Co, a Deeland-based construction company. It concerns their purchase of Custcare, a Customer Relationship Management (CRM) software package written by the Custcare Corporation, a software company based in Solland, a country some 4,000 km away from Deeland. The interview was originally published in the Management Experiences magazine.

Interviewer: Thanks for talking to us today Mick. Can you tell us how Bridge Co came to choose the Custcare software package?

Mick: Well, we didn't choose it really. Teri Porter had just joined the company as sales and marketing director. She had recently implemented the Custcare package at her previous company and she was very enthusiastic about it. When she found out that we did not have a CRM package at Bridge Co, she suggested that we should also buy the Custcare package as she felt that our requirements were very similar to those of her previous company. We told her that any purchase would have to go through our capex (capital expenditure) system as the package cost over $20,000. Here at Bridge Co, all capex applications have to be accompanied by a formal business case and an Invitation to Tender (ITT) has to be sent out to at least three potential suppliers. However, Teri is a very clever lady. She managed to do a deal with Custcare and they agreed to supply the package at a cost of $19,995, just under the capex threshold. Teri had to cut a few things out. For example, we declined the training courses (Teri said the package was an easy one to use and she would show us how to use it) and also we opted for the lowest level of support, something we later came to regret. Overall, we were happy. We knew that Custcare was a popular and successful CRM package.

Interviewer: So, did you have a demonstration of the software before you bought it?

Mick: Oh yes, and everyone was very impressed. It seemed to do all the things we would ever want it to do and, in fact, it gave us some ideas about possibilities that we would never have thought of. Also, by then, it was clear that our internal IT department could not provide us with a bespoke solution. Teri had spoken to them informally and she was told that they could not even look at our requirements for 18 months. In contrast, we could be up and running with the Custcare package within three months. Also, IT quoted an internal transfer cost of $18,000 for just defining our requirements. This was almost as much as we were paying for the whole software solution!

Interviewer: When did things begin to go wrong?

Mick: Well, the implementation was not straightforward. We needed to migrate some data from our current established systems and we had no-one who could do it. We tried to recruit some local technical experts, but Custcare pointed out that we had signed their standard contract which only permitted Custcare consultants to work on such tasks. We had not realised this, as nobody had read the contract carefully. In the end, we had to give in and it cost us $10,000 in fees to migrate the data from some of our internal systems to the new package. Teri managed to get the money out of the operational budget, but we weren't happy.

We then tried to share data between the Custcare software and our existing order processing system. We thought this would be easy, but apparently the file formats are incompatible. Thus we have to enter customer information into two systems and we are unable to exploit the customer order analysis facility of the Custcare CRM.

Finally, although we were happy with the functionality and reliability of the Custcare software, it works very slowly. This is really very disappointing. Some reports and queries have to be aborted because the software appears to have hung. The software worked very quickly in the demonstration, but it is painfully slow now that it is installed on our IT platform.

Interviewer: What is the current situation?

Mick: Well, we are all a bit deflated and disappointed in the package. The software seems reasonable enough, but its poor performance and our inability to interface it to the order processing system have reduced users' confidence in the system. Because users have not been adequately trained, we have had to phone Custcare's support desk more than we should. However, as I said before, we took the cheapest option. This is for a help line to be available from 08.00 hours to 17.00 hours Solland time. As you know, Solland is in a completely different time zone and so we have had to stay behind at work and contact them in the late evening. Again, nobody had closely read the terms of the contract. We have taken legal advice, but we have also found that, for dispute resolution, the contract uses the commercial contract laws of Solland. Nobody in Bridge Co knows what these are! Our solicitor said that we should have asked for this specification to be changed when the contract was drawn up. I just wish we had chosen a product produced by a company here in Deeland. It would have made it much easier to resolve issues and disputes.

Interviewer: What does Teri think?

Mick: Not a lot! She has left us to rejoin her old company in a more senior position. The board did ask her to justify her purchase of the Custcare CRM package, but I don't think she ever did. I am not sure that she could!

Required:

(a)   **Suggest a process for evaluating, selecting and implementing a software package solution and explain how this process would have prevented the problems experienced at Bridge Co in the Custcare CRM application.** (15 marks)

(b)   The CEO of Bridge Co now questions whether buying a software package was the wrong approach to meeting the CRM requirements at Bridge Co. He wonders whether they should have commissioned a bespoke software system instead.

Explain, with reference to the CRM project at Bridge Co, the advantages of adopting a software package approach to fulfilling business system requirements compared with a bespoke software solution. (10 marks)

(25 marks)

Question 26 VIVA ESPANA

"Viva Espana!" (VE) is an established Spanish language school with branches in several major capital cities across the world. The school specialises in Spanish courses for business people and provides a range of courses from beginner through to advanced levels. The school also prepares students to sit recognised exams in Spanish as a foreign language. The school has a good reputation internationally and its client base includes several large companies.

Three years ago, the company launched online courses to provide services to students who are not able to attend live classroom courses. Online courses include books, online webinars, tests and interactive e-books that can be downloaded and used on mobile devices or laptop computers. Customers order these products through VE's website and pay for them by credit card or other online payment methods.

Rafael Sanchez has recently joined the company as the director responsible for online products. Having previously worked for an online retailer, Rafael is aware of the security risks of doing business online and is concerned about the adequacy of VE's systems controls. He has identified three areas of concern:

(1)   VE stores information about its online customers, including their credit card payment information in its application systems. This information is not encrypted.

(2)   Controls over access to materials appear to be lacking. Students can login to the student portal to access their e-learning course immediately after receiving a welcome e-mail. Students are encouraged to change their password once they login; but they are not required to do so. Students can login from any computer connected to the internet. A student who logs in from a computer at the school and forgets to logout can still log in using the same account information from a home computer or internet café. Materials can be downloaded an unlimited number of times and the same user name and password can be used to log onto a webinar several times.

(3)   Controls to prevent unauthorised access to the application systems and data ("hacking") are poor.

Rafael also believes that the company's e marketing is not very effective and wishes to increase the visibility of the company's web site to acquire new customers.

Required

(a)   **Explain the potential risks of the three areas of concern identified by Rafael.**   (6 marks)

(b)   **For each area of concern, describe two controls that could be implemented to mitigate the risk.**   (12 marks)

(c)   **Describe three methods that VE could use to acquire more customers to its online products.**   (7 marks)

(25 marks)

Question 27 THE MANAGEMENT PRESS

Introduction

TMP (The Management Press) is a specialist business publisher; commissioning, printing and distributing books on financial and business management. It is based in a small town in Arcadia, a high-cost economy, where their printing works were established fifty years ago. 60% of the company's sales are made through bookshops in Arcadia. In these bookshops TMP's books are displayed in a custom-built display case specifically designed for TMP. 30% of TMP's sales are through mail order generated by full-page display advertisements in magazines and journals. Most of these sales are to customers based outside Arcadia. The final 10% of sales are made through a newly established website which offers a restricted range of books. These books are typically very specialised and are rarely featured in display advertising or stocked by general bookshops. The books available on the website are selected to avoid conflict with established supply channels. Most of the online sales are to customers based in Arcadia. High selling prices and high distribution costs makes TMP's books expensive to buy outside Arcadia.

Business changes

In the last decade costs have increased as the raw materials (particularly timber) used in book production have become dearer. Paper is extremely expensive in Arcadia and the trees used to produce it are becoming scarcer. Online book sellers have also emerged who are able to discount prices by exploiting economies of scale and eliminating bookshop costs. In Arcadia, it is estimated that three bookshops go out of business every week. Furthermore, the influential journal "Management Focus", one of the journals where TMP advertised their books, also recently ceased production. TMP itself has suffered three years of declining sales and profits. Expenditure on marketing has been reduced significantly in this period and further reductions in the marketing budget are likely because of the weak financial position of the company. Overall, there is increasing pressure on the company to increase profit margins and sales.

Despite the poor financial results, the directors of TMP are keen to maintain the established supply channels. One of them, the son of the founder of the company, has stated that "bookshops need all the help they can get and management journals are the heart of our industry".

However, the marketing director is keen for the company to re-visit its business model. He increasingly believes that TMP's conventional approach to book production, distribution and marketing is not sustainable. He wishes to re-examine certain elements of the marketing mix in the context of the opportunities offered by e-business.

A young marketing graduate has been appointed by the marketing director to develop and maintain the website. However, further development of the website has not been sanctioned by the Board. Other directors have given two main reasons for blocking further development of this site. Firstly, they believe that the company does not have sufficient expertise to continue developing and maintaining its own website. It is solely dependent on the marketing graduate. Secondly, they feel that the website will compete with the established supply channels which they are keen to preserve.

However, the marketing director is convinced that investing in e-business is essential for the survival of TMP. "We need to consider what unique opportunities it offers for pricing the product, promoting the product, placing the product and providing physical evidence of the quality of the product. Finally, we might even re-define the product itself." He feels if the company fails to grasp these opportunities, then one of its competitors will, and "that will be the end of us".

Required:

(a)   Determine the main drivers for the adoption of e-business at TMP and identify potential barriers to its adoption.

(5 marks)

(b)   Evaluate how e-business might help TMP exploit each of the five elements of the marketing mix (price, product, promotion, place and physical evidence) identified by the marketing director.

(20 marks)

(25 marks)

Question 28 CRONIN AUTO RETAIL

Cronin Auto Retail (CAR) is a car dealer that sells used cars bought at auctions by its experienced team of buyers. Every car for sale is less than two years old and has a full service history. The company concentrates on small family cars and, at any one time, there are about 120 on display at its purpose-built premises. The premises were acquired five years ago on a 25-year lease and they include a workshop, a small cafe and a children's playroom. All vehicles are selected by one of five experienced buyers who attend auctions throughout the country. Each attendance costs CAR about $500 per day in staff and travelling costs and usually leads to the purchase of five cars. On average, each car costs CAR $10,000 and is sold to the customer for $12,000. The company has a good sales and profitability record, although a recent economic recession has led the managing director to question "whether we are selling the right type of cars. Recently, I wonder if we have been buying cars that our team of buyers would like to drive, not what our customers want to buy?" However, the personal selection of quality cars has been an important part of CAR's business model and it is stressed in their marketing literature and website.

Sales records show that 90% of all sales are to customers who live within two hours' drive of CAR's base. This is to be expected as there are many competitors and most customers want to buy from a garage that they can easily return the car to if it needs inspection, a service or repair. Consequently, CAR concentrates on display advertising in newspapers in this geographical area. It also has a customer database containing the records of people who have bought cars in the last three years. All customers receive a regular mail-shot, listing the cars for sale and highlighting any special offers or promotions. The company has a website where all the cars are listed with a series of photographs showing each car from a variety of angles. The website also contains general information about the company, special offers and promotions, and information about its service, maintenance and repair service.

CAR is keen to expand the service and mechanical repair side of its business. It would particularly like customers who have purchased cars from them to bring them back for servicing or for any mechanical repairs that are subsequently required. However, although CAR holds basic spare parts in stock, it has to order many parts from specialist parts companies (called motor factors) or from the manufacturers directly. Mechanics have to raise paper requisitions which are passed to the procurement manager for reviewing, agreeing and sourcing. Most parts are ordered from regular suppliers, but there is an increasing backlog and this can cause a particular problem if the customer's car is in the garage waiting for the part to arrive. Customers are increasingly frustrated and annoyed by repairs taking much longer than they were led to expect. Another source of frustration is that the procurement manager only works from 10.00 to 16.00. The mechanics work on shifts and so the garage is staffed from 07.00 to 19.00. Urgent requisitions cannot be processed when the procurement manager is not at work. The backlog of requisitions is placing increased strain on the procurement manager who has recently made a number of clerical mistakes when raising a purchase order.

Requests for stationery and other office supplies also go through the same requisitioning process, with orders placed with the office supplier who is offering the best current deal. Finding this deal can be time consuming and so employees are increasingly submitting requisitions earlier so that they can be sure that new supplies will be received in time.

The managing director is aware of the problems of the requisitioning system but is reluctant to appoint a second procurement manager because he is trying to keep staff overheads down during a difficult trading period. He is keen to address "more fundamental issues in the marketing and procurement processes". He is particularly interested in how the "interactivity, intelligence, individualisation and independence of location offered by e-marketing media can help us at CAR".

Required:

(a) **Evaluate how the principles of interactivity, intelligence, individualisation and independence of location might be applied in the e-marketing of the products and services of CAR.** (16 marks)

(b) **Explain the principles of e-procurement and evaluate its potential application at CAR.**
(9 marks)

(25 marks)

Question 29 BA TIMES

The country of Umboria has two professional business analysis associations, both running certification examination schemes for business analysts worldwide. These are the Association of Benefits Consultants (ABC) and the Institute of Consultants, Finance and Commerce (ICFC). Many private and public sector learning providers run accredited training courses to prepare candidates for the examinations. Some learning providers provide courses for both associations, whilst others focus on niche markets. Umboria itself is a wealthy country with high labour costs and property prices, particularly in the capital city of Ambosium.

Victor is the editor of the *BA Times*, a subscription magazine, published once a month, which provides news and articles preparing students for the examinations of both business analysis associations. The magazine is edited and printed in offices and an adjoining factory in Ambosium. The offices and factory are leased and the magazine currently employs 20 people, all of whom live close to the offices. It is the only independent magazine in the sector. Each association has its own magazine and website, but relatively tight control is maintained over their editorial policy. Victor was the editor of the ABC magazine (Business Analysis Today) for 16 years before establishing the *BA Times* nine years ago. Because of its independence, the *BA Times* can be a little more controversial and provocative than its rivals and it is popular with students and well respected by the profession.

However, despite such recognition, the magazine is currently unprofitable due to increased production, distribution and office costs, falling subscriptions and reduced advertising. Changing reading habits in Umboria, particularly amongst the young, has led to less reading of printed media. All of the traditional media providers are experiencing financial problems. The sales of printed magazines and the profits of publishers are both falling dramatically throughout Umboria. Furthermore, advertisers are increasingly unconvinced about the effectiveness of advertising in printed magazines and so the advertising revenues of these magazines are also falling.

The *BA Times* currently has a website but its role is to convince the visitor to order the printed magazine. The website offers extracts of news and articles, often with provocative headlines, which may only be read in full in the printed magazine.

Recent survey

A recent survey of people who had decided not to renew their *BA Times* subscription revealed the following comments:

I am studying the ABC syllabus and so in-depth articles on ICFC topics and examinations are not relevant to me. I quite enjoy reading the news parts, but not the in-depth analysis of examinations that I am not taking. *ABC student*

I have reached the final stage of my examinations. I do not want to read articles about the stages I have already passed. I reckon only about 15% of *BA Times* is relevant to me now. *ABC Final Stage student*

Some of the readers' letters are really irritating or just plain wrong, but the editor seldom makes a comment! It really annoys me! *ICFC student*

I became a business analyst to get a job, not just to sit examinations and read about examining bodies. *ICFC student*

The examinations are getting more demanding and Victor is under pressure to increase the number of technical examination articles in the magazine, despite the fact that this will make the magazine longer and heavier and so increase print and distribution costs.

Victor is aware that new technology and new media offer opportunities for changing the business model and the financial performance of the *BA Times*. However, he likes the physical, tactile feel of printed magazines and he feels that some of his subscribers do as well. Also, he cannot see how harnessing new technology will make him money, particularly if it leads to decreasing sales of the printed magazine. He is also concerned about how his subscribers and advertisers will react to technological change. He feels that some subscribers will not have access to online technology and that many advertisers would prefer to continue with display advertisements in a printed magazine.

Required:

(a)   **Analyse how the principles of interactivity, individualisation, intelligence and independence of location offered by the internet and other new media could be exploited by Victor in his development of a new business model for the *BA Times*.**   (15 marks)

(b)   **Write a short report which addresses the specific concerns Victor has about the effect of any potential technology or media change on his subscribers, on his advertisers and on the financial viability of his company.**   (10 marks)

(25 marks)

Question 30 ASW

ASW is a software house which specialises in producing software packages for insurance companies. ASW has a basic software package for the insurance industry that can be used immediately out of the box. However, most customers wish ASW to tailor the package to reflect their own products and requirements. In a typical ASW project, ASW's business analysts define the gap between the customer's requirements and the basic package. These business analysts then specify the complete software requirement in a system specification. This specification is used by its programmers to produce a customised version of the software. It is also used by the system testers at ASW to perform their system tests before releasing it to the customer for acceptance testing.

One of ASW's new customers is CaetInsure. Initially CaetInsure sent ASW a set of requirements for their proposed new system. Business analysts from ASW then worked with CaetInsure staff to produce a full system specification for CaetInsure's specific requirements. ASW do not begin any development until this system specification is signed off. After some delay (see below), the system specification was eventually signed off by CaetInsure.

Since sign-off, ASW developers have been working on tailoring the product to obtain an appropriate software solution. The project is currently at week 16 and the software is ready for system testing. The remaining activities in the project are shown in figure 1. This simple plan has been put together by the project manager. It also shows who has responsibility for undertaking the activities shown on the plan.

The problem that the project manager faces is that the plan now suggests that implementation (parallel running) cannot take place until part way through week 28. The original plan was for implementation in week 23. Three weeks of the delay were due to problems in signing off the system specification. Key CaetInsure employees were unavailable to make decisions about requirements, particularly in the re-insurance part of the system. Too many requirements in this module were either unclear or kept changing as users sought clarification from their managers. There have also been two further weeks of slippage since the sign-off of the system specification.

The CaetInsure contract had been won in the face of stiff competition. As part of securing the deal, the ASW sales account manager responsible for the CaetInsure contract agreed that penalty clauses could be inserted into the contract. The financial penalty for late delivery of the software increases with every week's delay. CaetInsure had insisted on these clauses as they have tied the delivery of the software in with the launch of a new product. Although the delay in signing off the system specification was due to CaetInsure, the penalty clauses still remain in the contract. When the delay was discussed with the customer and ASW's project manager, the sales account manager assured CaetInsure that the "time could be made up in programming".

The initial planned delivery date (week 23) is now only seven weeks away. The project manager is now under intense pressure to come up with solutions which address the project slippage.

Required:

(a)   **Evaluate the alternative strategies available to ASW's project manager to address the slippage problem in the CaetInsure project.**   (10 marks)

(b)   **As a result of your evaluation, recommend and justify your preferred solution to the slippage problem in the CaetInsure project.**   (6 marks)

(16 marks)

Figure 1: Project Plan – ASW: CaetInsure Contract

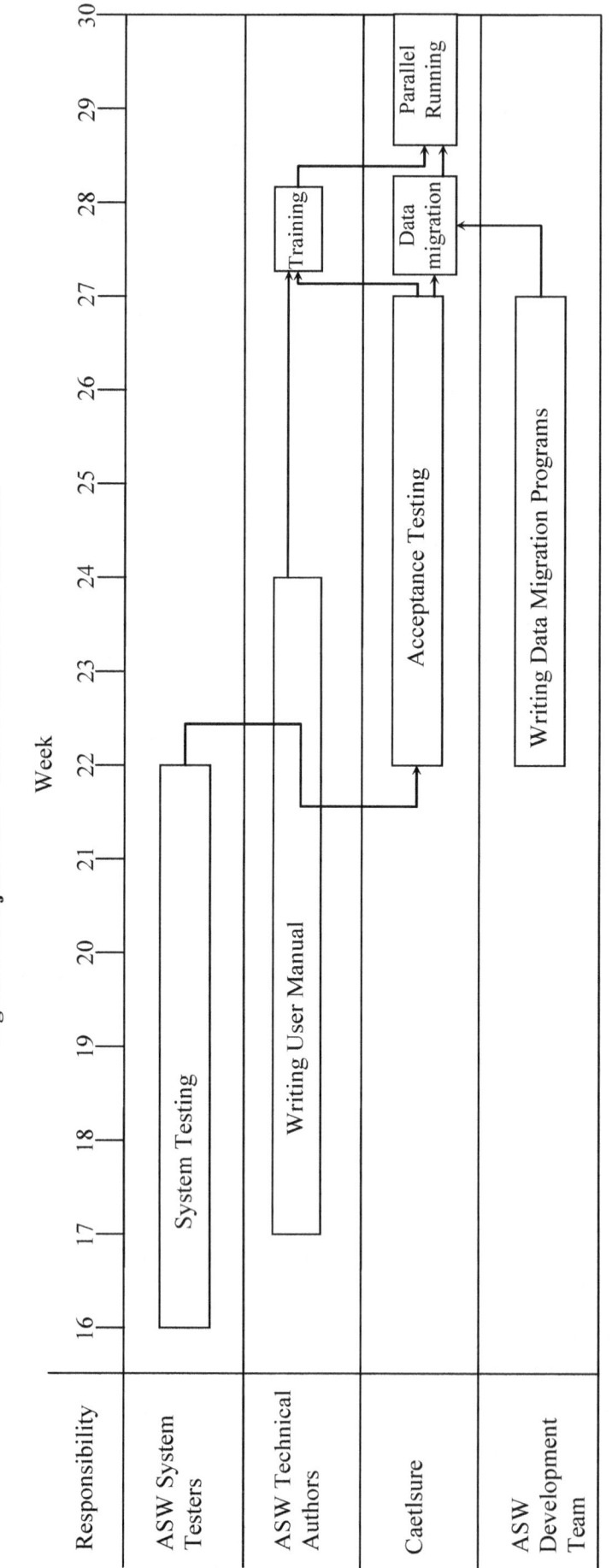

Question 31 MAHEM

Introduction

The country of Mahem is in a long and deep economic recession with unemployment at its highest since the country became an independent nation. In an attempt to stimulate the economy the government has launched a Private/Public investment policy where the government invests in capital projects with the aim of stimulating the involvement of private sector firms. The building of a new community centre in the industrial city of Tillo is an example of such an initiative. Community centres are central to the culture of Mahem. They are designed as places where people can meet socially, local organisations can hold conferences and meetings and farmers can sell their produce to the local community. The centres are seen as contributing to a vibrant community life. The community centre in Tillo is in a sprawling old building rented (at $12,000 per month) from a local landowner. The current community centre is also relatively energy inefficient.

In 2017 a business case was put forward to build a new centre on local authority owned land on the outskirts of Tillo. The costs and benefits of the business case are shown in Figure 1. As required by the Private/Public investment policy the project showed payback during year four of the investment.

All figures in $	Year 1	Year 2	Year 3	Year 4	Year 5
Costs: Initial	600,000				
Costs: Recurring	60,000	60,000	60,000	60,000	60,000
Benefits: Rental savings	144,000	144,000	144,000	144,000	144,000
Benefits: Energy savings	30,000	30,000	30,000	30,000	30,000
Benefits: Increased income	20,000	20,000	70,000	90,000	90,000
Benefits: Better staff morale	25,000	25,000	25,000	25,000	25,000
Cumulative net benefits	(441,000)	(282,000)	(73,000)	156,000	385,000

Figure 1: Costs and benefits of the business case for the community centre at Tillo

New buildings built under the Private/Public investment policy must attain energy level targets and this is the basis for the estimation, above, of the energy savings. It is expected that the new centre will attract more customers who will pay for the centre's use as well as increasing the use of facilities such as the cafeteria, shop and business centre. These benefits are estimated, above, under increased income. Finally, it is felt that staff will be happier in the new building and their motivation and morale will increase. The centre currently employs 20 staff, 16 of whom have been with the centre for more than five years. All employees were transferred from the old to the new centre. These benefits are shown as *better staff morale* in Figure 1.

Construction of the centre 2017–2020

In October 2017 the centre was commissioned with a planned delivery date of June 2018 at a cost of $600,000 (as per Figure 1). Building the centre went relatively smoothly. Progress was monitored and issues resolved in monthly meetings between the company constructing the centre and representatives of the local authority. These meetings focused on the building of the centre, monitoring progress and resolving issues. Most of these issues were relatively minor because requirements were well specified in standard architectural drawings originally agreed between the project sponsor and the company constructing the centre. Unfortunately, the original project sponsor (an employee of the local authority) who had been heavily involved in the initial design, suffered ill health and died in April 2018. The new project sponsor (again an employee of the local authority) was less enthusiastic about the project and began to raise a number of objections. Her first concern was that the construction company had used sub-contracted labour and had sourced less than 80% of timber used in the building from sustainable resources. She pointed out the contractual terms of supply for the Private/Public policy investment initiatives mandated that sub-contracting was not allowed without the local authority's permission and that at least 80% of the timber used must come from sustainable forests. The company said that this had not been brought to their attention at the start of the project. However, they would try to comply with these requirements for the rest of the contract.

The new sponsor also refused to sign off acceptance of the centre because of the poor quality of the internal paintwork. The construction company explained that this was the intended finish quality of the centre and had been agreed with the previous sponsor. They produced a letter to verify this. However, the letter was not counter-signed by the sponsor and so its validity was questioned. In the end, the construction company agreed to improve the internal painting at their own cost. The new sponsor felt that she had delivered "value for money" by challenging the construction company. Despite this problem with the internal painting, the centre was finished in May 2018 at a cost of $600,000. The centre also included disability access built at the initiative of the construction company. It had found it difficult to find local authority staff willing and able to discuss disability access and so it was therefore left alone to interpret relevant legal requirements. Fortunately, their interpretation was correct and the new centre was deemed, by an independent assessor, to meet accessibility requirements.

Unfortunately, the new centre was not as successful as had been predicted, with income in the first year well below expectations. The project sponsor began to be increasingly critical of the builders of the centre and questioned the whole value of the project. She was openly sceptical of the project to her fellow local authority employees. She suggested that the project to build a cost-effective centre had failed and called for an inquiry into the performance of the project manager of the construction company who was responsible for building the centre. "We need him to explain to us why the centre is not delivering the benefits we expected", she explained.

Required:

(a)   The local authority has commissioned the independent Project Audit Agency (PAA) to look into how the project had been commissioned and managed. The PAA believes that a formal "terms of reference" or "project initiation document" would have resolved or clarified some of the problems and issues encountered in the project. It also feels that there are important lessons to be learnt by both the local authority and the construction company.

Analyse how a formal "terms of reference" (project initiation document) would have helped address problems encountered in the project to construct the community centre and lead to improved project management in future projects.   (13 marks)

(b)   The PAA also believes that the four sets of benefits identified in the original business case (rental savings, energy savings, increased income and better staff morale) should have been justified more explicitly.

Draft an analysis for the PAA that formally categorises and critically evaluates each of the four sets of proposed benefits defined in the original business case.   (12 marks)

(25 marks)

Question 32 INSTITUTE OF INDEPENDENT ANALYSTS

The Institute of Independent Analysts (IIA), an examining body, is considering replacing its conventional assessment process with computer-based assessment which produces instant results to the candidate. A business case has been developed for the computer-based assessment project. Figure 1, extracted from the business case, shows the financial appraisal of the project. It uses a discount rate of 8%. The NPV of the project is $10,925.

All figures in $000s

Year	0	1	2	3	4	5	6	7
Costs								
Initial software	200	200						
Software maintenance			40	40	40	40	40	40
Question bank	50	50	5	5	5	5	5	5
Security			20	20	20	20	20	20
Disruption		15	15					
Total costs	250	265	80	65	65	65	65	65
Income/Savings								
Marker fees			125	125	125	125	125	125
Admin saving		20	30	30	30	30	30	30
Extra income			10	20	30	30	40	40
Total benefits		20	165	175	185	185	195	195
Benefits – costs	(250)	(245)	85	110	120	120	130	130
Discount factor	1	0.926	0.857	0.794	0.735	0.681	0.630	0.583
Present value	(250)	(226.870)	72.845	87.340	88.200	81.720	81.900	75.790
NPV								10.925

Figure 1: Financial cost/benefit of the computer-based assessment project

An explanation of the costs and benefits is given below.

Initial software – refers to the cost of buying the computer-based assessment software package from the vendor. The software actually costs $375,000, but a further $25,000 has been added to reflect bespoke changes which the IIA requires. These changes are not yet agreed, or defined in detail. Indeed, there have been some problems in actually specifying these requirements and understanding how they will affect the administrative processes of the IIA.

Software maintenance – This will be priced at 10% of the final cost of the delivered software. This is currently estimated at $400,000; hence a cost of $40,000 per annum.

Question bank – refers to the cost of developing a question bank for the project. This is a set of questions which the software package stores and selects from when producing an examination for an individual candidate. Questions will be set by external consultants at $50 for each question they successfully deliver to the question bank. It is expected that further questions will need to be added (and current ones amended) in subsequent years.

Security – refers to security provided at computer-based assessment centres. This price has already been agreed with an established security firm who have guaranteed it for the duration of the project.

Disruption – refers to an expected temporary decline in IIA examinations staff productivity and staff morale during the implementation of the computer-based assessment solution.

Marker fees – manual marking is undertaken in the current conventional assessment process. There will no longer be any requirement for markers to undertake this manual marking. All examinations will be automatically marked.

Admin saving – concerns reduction in examinations staff at IIA headquarters. The actual savings will partly depend on the detailed requirements currently being discussed with the software package provider. It is still unclear how this will affect the administrative process.

Extra income – the IIA expects candidates to be attracted by the convenience of computer-based assessment. Other competing institutions do not offer this service. The extra income is the IIA's best guess at the amount of income which will result from this new assessment initiative.

The IIA is also putting in place a benefits management process for all projects. The IIA director is concerned that project managers are just moving on to other projects and not taking responsibility for the benefits initially established in the business case.

Required:

(a)   **Critically evaluate the financial case (cost/benefit) of the computer-based assessment project.**   (15 marks)

(b)   Benefit owners, benefits maps and benefits realisation are important concepts in benefits management process.

        Explain each of these concepts and their potential application to the computer-based assessment project.   (10 marks)

(c)   The business change process can be analysed into a series of steps called the business change lifecycle. A typical business change lifecycle includes the following steps: alignment, definition, design, implementation and realisation.

        Explain each of these steps, illustrating how each might be applied to the change in the assessment process at IIA.   (15 marks)

                                                                                                  (40 marks)

Question 33 8-HATS PROMOTIONS

8-Hats Promotions was formed 20 years ago by Barry Gorkov to plan, organise and run folk festivals in Arcadia. It soon established itself as a major events organiser and diversified into running events for the staff and customers of major companies. For example, for many years it has organised launch events, staff-reward days and customer experiences for Kuizan, the car manufacturer. 8-Hats has grown through a combination of organic growth and acquiring similar and complementary companies. Recently, it purchased a travel agent (now operated as the travel department of 8-Hats) to provide travel to and from the events that it organised.

Barry Gorkov is himself a flamboyant figure who, in the early years of the company, changed his name to Barry Blunt to reflect his image and approach. He calls all the events "jobs", a terminology used throughout the company. A distinction is made between external jobs (for customers) and internal jobs (within 8-Hats itself). The company is organised on functional lines. The sales and marketing department tenders for external jobs and negotiates contracts. Sales managers receive turnover-related bonuses and 8-Hats is known in the industry for its aggressive pricing policies. Once a contract is signed, responsibility for the job is passed to the events department which actually organises the event. It is known for its creativity and passion. The operations department has responsibility for running the event (job) on the day and for delivering the vision defined by the events department. The travel department is responsible for any travel arrangements associated with the job. Finally, the finance department is responsible for managing cash flow throughout the job, raising customer invoices, paying supplier invoices and chasing any late payments.

However, there is increasing friction between the departments. The operations department is often unable to deliver the features and functionality defined by the events department within the budget agreed by the sales manager. Finance is unaware of the cash flow implications of the job. Recently, an event was in jeopardy because suppliers had not been paid. They threatened to withdraw their services from the event. Eventually, Barry Blunt had to resolve friction between finance and other departments by acquiring further funding from the bank. The event went ahead, but it unsettled Kuizan which had commissioned the job. The sales and marketing department has also complained about the margins expected by the travel department, claiming that they are making the company uncompetitive.

There has been a considerable amount of discussion at 8-Hats about the investment appraisal approach used to evaluate internal jobs. The company does not have sufficient money and resources to carry out all the internal jobs that need doing. Consequently, the finance department has used the Net Present Value (NPV) technique as a way of choosing which jobs should be undertaken. Figure 1 shows an example comparison of two computer system applications that had been under consideration. Job One was selected because its Net Present Value (NPV) was higher ($25,015) than Job Two ($2,090).

"I don't want to tell you about the specific details of the two applications, so I have called them Job One and Job Two" said Barry. "However, in the end, Job One was a disaster. Looking back, we should have gone with Job Two, not Job One. We should have used simple payback, as I am certain that Job Two, even on the initial figures, paid back much sooner than Job One. That approach would have suited our mentality at the time – quick wins. Whoever chose a discount rate of 8% should be fired – inflation has been well below this for the last five years. We should have used 3% or 4%. Also, calculating the IRR would have been useful, as I am sure that Job Two would have shown a better IRR than Job One, particularly as the intangible benefits of improved staff morale appear to be underestimated. Intangible benefits are just as important as tangible benefits. Finally, we should definitely have performed a benefits realisation analysis at the end of the feasibility study. Leaving it to after the project had ended was a ridiculous idea."

Job One

		Year 0	Year 1	$000s Year 2	Year 3	Year 4	
Costs							
	Hardware costs	50	0	0	0	0	
	Software costs	50	0	0	0	0	
	Maintenance costs	10	10	10	10	10	
	Total	110	10	10	10	10	
Benefits	Staff savings	0	40	5	0	0	
	Contractor savings	0	20	10	10	10	
	Better information	0	0	0	20	30	
	Improved staff morale	0	0	10	20	30	
	Total	0	60	25	50	70	
	Cash Flows	−110	50	15	40	60	
	Discount Factor at 8%	1·000	0·926	0·857	0·794	0·735	NPV
	Discounted CF	−110·000	46·300	12·855	31·760	44·100	25·015

Job Two $000s

Costs		Year 0	Year 1	Year 2	Year 3	Year 4	
	Hardware costs	50	0	0	0	0	
	Software costs	30	10	10	0	0	
	Maintenance costs	10	10	10	10	10	
	Total	90	20	20	10	10	
Benefits	Staff savings	0	30	10	5	0	
	Contractor savings	0	30	15	15	15	
	Better information	0	0	0	10	10	
	Improved staff morale	0	0	10	10	10	
	Total	0	60	35	40	35	
	Cash Flows	–90	40	15	30	25	
	Discount Factor at 8%	1·000	0·926	0·857	0·794	0·735	NPV
	Discounted CF	–90·000	37·040	12·855	23·820	18·375	2·090

Figure 1: NPV calculation for two projects at 8-Hats (with a discount rate of 8%)

Required:

(a)   Barry Blunt has criticised the investment appraisal approach used at 8-Hats to evaluate internal jobs. He has made specific comments on payback, discount rate, IRR, intangible benefits and benefits realisation.

Critically evaluate Barry's comments on the investment appraisal approach used at 8-Hats to evaluate internal jobs. (15 marks)

(b)   **Discuss the principles, benefits and problems of introducing a matrix management structure at 8-Hats.** (10 marks)

(25 marks)

Question 34 HOMEDELIVER

HomeDeliver is a nationwide company that sells small household goods to consumers. It produces an attractive, comprehensive catalogue which it distributes to staff known as catalogue supervisors. There are 150 of these supervisors in the country. Each supervisor has approximately 30 part-time home-based agents, who then deliver the catalogue to consumers in their homes. Agents subsequently collect the catalogue and any completed order forms and forward these forms to their supervisor. Payment is also taken when the order is collected. Payment is by cash or cheque and these payments are also forwarded to the supervisor by the agent. At the end of the week the supervisor returns completed order forms (and payments) to HomeDeliver. Order details are then entered into a computer system by order entry administrators at HomeDeliver and this starts an order fulfilment process that ends with goods being delivered directly to the customer. The supervisors and the agents are all self-employed. HomeDeliver rewards supervisors on the basis of how many agents they manage. Agents' reward packages are based on how many catalogues they deliver and a commission based on orders received from the homes they have collected orders from.

In August 20Y0 HomeDeliver decided to replace the physical ordering system with a new electronic ordering system. Agents would be provided with software which would allow them to enter customer orders directly into the computer system using their home personal computer at the end of each day. Payments would also be paid directly into a HomeDeliver bank account by agents at the end of each day.

The software to support the new ordering system was developed in-house to requirements provided by the current order entry administrators at HomeDeliver and managers concerned with order fulfilment and invoicing. The software was tested internally by the order entry administrators. At first, both the specification of requirements and initial software testing progressed very slowly because order administrators were continuing with their normal operational duties. However, as project delays became more significant, selected order administrators were seconded to the project full-time. As a result the software was fully acceptance tested by the end of July 20Y1, two months behind schedule.

In August 20Y1 the software was rolled out to all supervisors and agents. The software was claimed to be easy to use, so no formal training was given. A large comprehensive manual with colour screenshots was attached as a PDF to an email sent to all supervisors and agents. This gave detailed instructions on how to set up and use the software.

Unfortunately, problems began to appear as soon as the agents tried to load and use the software. It was found to be incompatible with one particular popular browser, and agents whose computers used that browser were advised to use an alternative browser or computer. Agents also criticised the functionality of the software because it did not allow for the amendment of orders once they had been submitted. It emerged that customers often contacted agents and supervisors to amend their order prior to it being sent to HomeDeliver. This was no longer possible with the new system. Many agents also claimed that it was not possible to enter multiple orders for one household. However, HomeDeliver confirmed that entering multiple orders was possible; it was just not clear from the software, or from the instructions provided, how this could be achieved.

Most of the agents were reluctant to print off the manual (preferring to read it on screen) and a significant number claimed that they did not receive the email with the manual attachment. Agents also found quite a number of spelling and functionality errors in the manual. At certain points the software did not perform in the way the manual stated that it would.

Internal standards at HomeDeliver require both a post-project and a post-implementation review.

Required:

(a)   **Explain the purpose of each of the following: a post-project review, a post-implementation review and a benefits realisation review.**   (6 marks)

(b)   **Evaluate the problems and the lessons that should be learned from a post-project review and a post-implementation review of the electronic ordering system at HomeDeliver.**
                                                                                      (12 marks)

(c)   HomeDeliver does not have a benefits management process and so a benefits realisation review is inappropriate. However, it does feel that it would be useful to retrospectively define the benefits to HomeDeliver of the new electronic ordering system.

         Identify and discuss the potential benefits to HomeDeliver of the new electronic ordering system.   (7 marks)

                                                                                      (25 marks)

Question 35 iTTRAIN

For 11 years, Marco was a senior salesman at AQT, a company specialising in IT certification courses. During that time, AQT became the most successful and dominant training provider in the market.

Marco has now left AQT and established his own training company, iTTrain, aimed at the same IT certification market as his former employers. He wishes to offer premium quality courses in a high quality environment with high quality teaching. He has selected a number of self-employed lecturers and he has agreed a daily lecturing fee of $450 per day with them. He has also selected the prestigious CityCentre training centre as his course venue. It has a number of training rooms which hold up to nine delegates. Each training room costs $250 per day to hire. There is also a $10 per day per delegate charge for lunch and other refreshments. Although not a lecturer, Marco is an IT expert and he has already produced the relevant documentation for the courses iTTrain will run. He sees this as a sunk cost and is not concerned about recovering it. However, printing costs mean that there is also a $20 cost for the course manual which is given to every course delegate.

Marco has scheduled 40 courses next year, as he is limited by the availability of lecturers. Each course will have a maximum of nine delegates (determined by the room size) and a minimum of three delegates. Each course is three days long.

iTTrain has been set up with $70,000 of Marco's own money. He currently estimates that fixed annual costs will be $65,000 (which includes his own salary) and he would like the company to return a modest profit in its first year of operation as it establishes itself in the market.

Marco is currently considering the price he wishes to charge for his courses. AQT charges $900 per delegate for a three-day course, but he knows that it discounts this by up to 10% and a similar discount is also offered to training brokers or intermediaries who advertise AQT courses on their own websites. Some of these intermediaries have already been in touch with Marco to ask if he would be prepared to offer them similar discounts in return for iTTrain courses being advertised on their websites. There are also a number of cheaper training providers who offer the same courses for as little as $550 per delegate. However, these tend to focus on self-financing candidates for whom price is an issue. These courses are often given in poor quality training premises by poorly motivated lecturers. Marco is not really interested in this market. He wants to target the corporate business market, where quality is as important as price and the course fee is paid by the delegate's employer. He is currently considering a price of $750 per delegate.

During his employment at AQT, Marco collected statistics about courses and delegates. Figure 1 shows the data he collected showing the attendance pattern over 1,000 courses.

Number of delegates attending the course	Number of courses
3	150
4	210
5	250
6	190
7	70
8	80
9	50
Total	1,000

Figure 1: Analysis of attendance at 1,000 AQT courses

Required:

(a)   **Suggest a pricing strategy for iTTrain, including an evaluation of the initial price of $750 per delegate suggested by Marco. Your strategy should include both financial and non-financial considerations.**   (16 marks)

(b) Physical evidence, people and process are three important elements of the marketing mix for services.

Analyse the contribution each of these three elements could make to the success of iTTrain's entry into the IT certification market. (9 marks)

(25 marks)

Question 36 GREEN SOCKET

You have recently been appointed CFO of Green Sockett, a company that invests in renewable energy production. The company is based in Homeland, where it owns two solar energy plants, three wind farms and a biofuel production plant. The solar plants and wind farm produce electricity which is sold to the government-owned electricity distribution company. The biofuel plant produces bio diesel which is sold to local councils who use it to fuel their buses. The government of Homeland is keen to encourage the use of renewable energy and Green Sockett benefits from generous subsidies.

Electricity output from the solar and wind farms is largely unpredictable since it depends on weather conditions, while the costs of operating the farms are largely fixed. Biodiesel is made using vegetable oils such as rape seed oil. The industry is growing due to concerns about the shortage of non-renewable fossil fuels. Costs of producing biodiesel are relatively high, but research into production methods is identifying new ways of production that are leading to cost savings. Green Sockett spends considerable amounts on such research.

The company is keen to make more acquisitions, buying up small, specialist companies in Homeland, and expanding into several neighbouring countries. Green Sockett is a private company, but three years ago it raised finance from a venture capital fund which now owns 20 percent of the company. It is hoped that the company will be floated on the stock exchange of Homeland in the next five years.

The finance department is centralised at head office. It consists of a chief accountant, a payroll clerk, two purchase ledger clerks and a sales ledger clerk who is responsible for booking invoices and collecting cash from customers. The outgoing CFO spent a few days explaining the job to you, and told you that he spent most of time on the following areas:

- Managing the accounting staff;
- Performing investment appraisals of new acquisitions;
- Dealing with the mountain of queries and reports required by the venture capital investor;
- Ensuring compliance with regulations, such as health and safety; and
- Preparing cash flow forecasts for the bank.

The chief accountant is responsible for managing the bookkeeping, preparing the annual financial statements and preparing monthly management accounts. You have reviewed the monthly management accounts. They include monthly comparisons of actual costs and revenues against a flexed budget and some commentary to explain large variances.

You have just had a discussion with Mr Swartz, the founder and CEO of Green Sockett. He has been reading about the changing role of the finance department in many companies where the finance department acts as a business partner, which provides commercial advice and plays an active part in strategic management. He said, "I am interested to hear your views about this, as I believe that our own finance department is rather old fashioned". He has asked, "Can you put together some ideas for me about how you could transform our finance department here at Green Sockett?"

Required:

(a)   Discuss ways in which the role of the finance department at Green Sockett could be transformed to improve business performance. (13 marks)

(b)   Evaluate the use of budgets in support of strategic planning and decision making at Green Sockett. (12 marks)

(25 marks)

Question 37 GIFT DESIGNS

David Silvester is the founder and owner of a recently formed gift packaging company, Gift Designs. David has spotted an opportunity for a new type of gift packaging. This uses a new process to make waterproof cardboard and then shapes and cuts the card in such a way to produce a container or vase for holding cut flowers. The containers can be stored flat and in bulk and then simply squeezed to create the flowerpot into which flowers and water are then put. The potential market for the product is huge. In the UK hospitals alone there are 200,000 bunches of flowers bought each year for patients. David's innovative product does away with the need for hospitals to provide and store glass vases. The paper vases are simple, safe and hygienic. He has also identified two other potential markets; firstly, the market for fresh flowers supplied by florists and secondly, the corporate gift market where clients such as car dealers present a new owner with an expensive bunch of flowers when the customer takes delivery of a new car. The vase can be printed using a customer's design and logo and creates an opportunity for real differentiation and impact at sales conferences and other high profile PR events.

David anticipates a rapid growth in Gift Designs as its products become known and appreciated. The key question is how quickly the company should grow and the types of funding needed to support its growth and development. The initial financial demands of the business have been quite modest but David has estimated that the business needs $500,000 to support its development over the next two years and is uncertain as to the types of funding best suited to a new business as it looks to grow rapidly. He understands that business risk and financial risk is not the same thing and is looking for advice on how he should organise the funding of the business. He is also aware of the need to avoid reliance on friends and family for funding and to broaden the financial support for the business. Clearly the funding required would also be affected by the activities David decides to carry out himself and those activities better provided by external suppliers.

Required:

(a)   Provide David with a short report on the key issues he should take into account when developing a strategy for funding Gift Designs' growth and development. (10 marks)

(b)   Using models where appropriate, identify the likely critical success factors (CSFs) as the business grows and develops. (10 marks)

(20 marks)

Question 38 ONEENERGY

OneEnergy supplies over half of the electricity and gas in the country. It is an expanding, aggressive company which has recently acquired two smaller, but significant, competitors.

Just over a year ago, OneEnergy purchased the RitePay payroll software package from RiteSoftware. The recently appointed Human Resources (HR) director of OneEnergy recommended the package because he had used it successfully at his previous employer – a major charity. His unreserved recommendation was welcomed by the board because the company was currently running three incompatible payroll systems. The purchase of the RitePay payroll system appeared to offer the opportunity to quickly consolidate the three separate payroll systems into one improved solution. The board decided to purchase the software without evaluating alternative solutions. It was felt that payroll rules and processes were relatively standard and so there was no need to look further than a package recommended by the HR director. The software was purchased and a project initiated for converting the data from the current systems and for training users in the features and functions of the new software.

However, it soon became apparent that there were problems with the suitability of the RitePay software package. Firstly, OneEnergy had a wide variety of reward and pay schemes to reflect previous employment in the acquired companies and to accommodate a wide range of different skills and grades. Not all of these variations could be handled by the package. Consequently, amendments had to be commissioned from the software house. This led to unplanned costs and also to delays in implementation. Secondly, it also became clear that the software was not as user-friendly as the previous systems. Users had problems understanding some of the terminology and structure of the software. "It just does not work like we do", commented one frustrated user. Consequently users made more errors than expected and training costs exceeded their budget.

Three months ago, another set of amendments was requested from RiteSoftware to allow one of the acquired companies in OneEnergy to pay bonuses to lorry drivers in a certain way. Despite repeated requests, the amendments were not received. Two weeks ago, it was announced that RiteSoftware had filed for bankruptcy and all software support was suspended. Just before this was announced the HR director of OneEnergy left the company to take up a similar post in the public sector.

OneEnergy has engaged W&P consultants to advise them on the RitePay project. An interim report from W&P suggests that OneEnergy should abandon the RitePay package. "It is clear to us that RitePay never had the functionality required to fulfil the variety of requirements inevitable in a company the size of OneEnergy." They also commented that this could have been avoided if the project had followed the competitive procurement policy defined in company operating procedures.

W&P also reports that:

■ The procurement department at OneEnergy had requested two years of accounts from RiteSoftware. These were provided (see Figure 1) but not interpreted or used in the selection process in any way. W&P concluded "that there were clear signs that the company was in difficulty and this should have led to further investigation".

■ They discovered that the former HR director of OneEnergy was the brother of the managing director of RiteSoftware.

Figure 1: RiteSoftware Accounts

Extract from the statement of financial position	$000	$000
Assets		
Non-current assets	*20Y2*	*20Y1*
Property, plant and equipment	30	25
Goodwill	215	133
	245	158
Current assets		
Inventories	3	2
Trade receivables	205	185
	208	187
Total assets	453	345
Liabilities		
Current liabilities		
Trade payables	257	178
Current tax payable	1	2
Bank overdraft	10	25
	268	205
Non-current liabilities		
Long-term borrowings	80	35
Total liabilities	348	240
Equity		
Share capital	105	105
Total equity and liabilities	453	345

Extract from the statement of comprehensive income		
Revenue	2,650	2,350
Cost of sales	(2,600)	(2,300)
Gross profit	50	50
Other costs	(30)	(20)
Finance costs	(10)	(4)
Profit before tax	10	26
Income tax expense	(1)	(2)
Profit for the year	9	24
Extract from the annual report		
Number of staff	90	70

Required:

(a) W&P concluded in their report "that there were clear signs that the company (RiteSoftware) was in difficulty and this should have led to further investigation".

Assess, using the financial information available, the validity of W&P's conclusion.

(13 marks)

(b) **Examine FOUR ways in which OneEnergy failed to follow a proper evaluation procedure in the selection of the RitePay software package. Include in your examination a discussion of the implication of each failing.** (12 marks)

(25 marks)

Question 39 DESPARD

Despard manufactures and sells a single product. The following data have been extracted from the current year's budget:

Sales and production (units)	5,000
Variable cost per unit	$50
Fixed cost per unit	$70
Contribution to sales ratio	75%

The selling price per unit for next year is to be 8% above the current year's budgeted figure, whereas both the variable cost per unit and the total fixed costs are forecast to increase by 12% above their budgeted level in the current year.

The target for next year is that total profit should remain the same as that budgeted for the current year.

Required:

(a) **Calculate for the current year the budgeted:**

    (i)   **contribution per unit;**
    (ii)   **total profit.** (3 marks)

(b) **Calculate the number of units which the company should produce and sell next year in order to achieve the target level of profit.** (4 marks)

(c) **Explain, with an example, the term semi-variable (mixed) cost and how such a cost would be dealt with in undertaking the analysis in (a).** (3 marks)

(10 marks)

Question 40 WORLD ENGINES

World Engines (WE) is one of the largest producers of aircraft and ship engines in the world. It has assets in excess of $600 billion. It is currently considering improvements to its marine engine production facilities. These improvements include the introduction of specialist hardware and software engine testing technology. Two companies have been shortlisted for supplying this technology.

Amethyst is a well-established company whose product provides sophisticated testing facilities and costs $7 million. The software that supports the product is written in a conventional programming language. The solution is widely used, but it is relatively inflexible and it has an out-of-date user interface. Amethyst has been trading profitably for 20 years and currently has an annual turnover of $960 million.

Topaz is a relatively new company (formed three years ago) whose product is more expensive ($8 million) but it offers significant advantages in high volume performance and stress testing. It has a modular software design that allows it to be easily maintained and upgraded. It is written in a relatively new powerful programming language and it also has an attractive and contemporary user interface. Topaz currently has a turnover of $24 million per year. Some WE executives are concerned about purchasing from such a young, relatively small company, although externally commissioned credit reports show that Topaz is a profitable, liquid and lightly geared company.

On a recent evaluation visit to Amethyst, WE's complete evaluation team of five people, including the financial specialist, were killed when their aircraft crashed on its approach to landing. It was a small, 12 seat commuter aircraft that was flying the WE team on a short 100 km flight from the international airport to a small rural airport close to Amethyst's base. It later emerged that small commuter airlines and aircraft were subject to less stringent safety procedures than larger aircraft used by established airlines.

Later that year, one of the divisional directors of WE was given responsibility for picking up and running the testing technology evaluation project. He has found the following table (Figure 1) produced by the financial specialist in the evaluation team who was killed in the air crash. The divisional director recalls that these returns were based on "tangible benefits resulting from the two options. The returns reflect the characteristics of the two products. Topaz produces better returns if demand for testing is high, but is less effective in low demand circumstances. This is a reflection of the fact that the two solutions differ slightly in terms of their functional scope and power".

Figure 1: Expected returns for three demand and supplier combinations.

Option	Supplier	IF High demand	IF Low demand
A	Amethyst	$3m per annum	$0·5m per annum
B	Topaz	$4m per annum	$0·1m per annum

The divisional director also recalls a workshop convened to consider future market demand.

"Demand in the marine industry is currently affected by global economic uncertainty and it is increasingly difficult to predict demand. I remember that we were also asked to estimate demand for our marine products for the next six years. We eventually came up with the following figures, although it was relatively hard to get everyone to agree and debate at the workshop became a little heated."

- High demand for six years: probability p = 0·4
- Low demand for six years: probability p = 0·4
- High demand for three years, followed by low demand for three years: probability p = 0·2

These figures are confirmed by a document also recovered from the air crash site. "As I recall", said the divisional director, "the financial specialist intended to develop a decision tree to help us evaluate the Amethyst and Topaz alternatives. However, there is no evidence that he ever constructed it, which is a pity because we could have taken the procurement decision on the basis of that decision tree".

Required:

(a)   **Develop a decision tree from the information given in the scenario and discuss its implications and shortcomings.**

   Ignore the time value of money in your analysis.   (9 marks)

(b)   The divisional director suggests that the procurement decision could have been taken on the evidence of the decision tree.

   Discuss what other factors (not considered by the decision tree analysis) should also be taken into consideration when deciding which option to select.   (6 marks)

(c)   World Engines executives are concerned about the risk of Topaz, as a relatively new company, going out of business. They have also expressed concern about the loss of the evaluation team in a fatal accident and they believe that this should lead to a review of the risks associated with employee travel.

   Discuss how EACH of the above risks (supplier business failure and employee travel) might be avoided or mitigated.   (10 marks)

                                                                                     (25 marks)

Question 41 ATD

ATD is a medium-sized engineering company providing specialist components for the marine engineering market. The sales manager is currently under pressure from the other departmental managers to explain why his sales revenue forecasts are becoming increasingly unreliable. Errors in his forecasts are having consequential effects on production, inventory control, raw materials purchasing and, ultimately, on the profitability of the company itself. He uses a "combination of experience, intuition and guesswork" to produce his sales forecast, but even he accepts that his forecasts are increasingly inaccurate.

Consequently, he has asked a business analyst to investigate more rigorous, appropriate ways of forecasting. The business analyst has suggested two possible alternatives. The first (summarised in Figure 1) is least squares regression. The second (summarised in Figure 2) is time series analysis. The actual sales figures in both of these examples are for ATD, so the company is currently in quarter 3 – 2017. However, the business analyst has left the company before completing and explaining either the basis for, or implications of, these two alternative approaches to forecasting.

Figure 1: Least squares analysis

Year/quarter	Quarter Sales ($000)				
	x	y	x^2	xy	y^2
2014 quarter 1	1	110	1	110	12,100
2014 quarter 2	2	160	4	320	25,600
2014 quarter 3	3	155	9	465	24,025
2014 quarter 4	4	96	16	384	9,216
2015 quarter 1	5	116	25	580	13,456
2015 quarter 2	6	160	36	960	25,600
2015 quarter 3	7	153	49	1,071	23,409
2015 quarter 4	8	100	64	800	10,000
2016 quarter 1	9	128	81	1,152	16,384
2016 quarter 2	10	180	100	1,800	32,400
2016 quarter 3	11	169	121	1,859	28,561
2016 quarter 4	12	99	144	1,188	9,801
2017 quarter 1	13	137	169	1,781	18,769
2017 quarter 2	14	180	196	2,520	32,400
		1,943	1,015	14,990	281,721
	b	1·84			
	a	125·022			
	r	0·253			

The equation of a straight line is y = a + bx

Figure 2: Time series analysis

Quarter	Sales ($000)	Trend	Deviation	Svar (1)	Residual	Sadj (2)
2014 quarter 1	110					124·70
2014 quarter 2	160					127·77
2014 quarter 3	155	131·00	24·00	22·55	1·45	132·45
2014 quarter 4	96	131·75	−35·75	−40·08	4·33	136·08
2015 quarter 1	116	131·50	−15·50	−14·70	−0·80	130·70
2015 quarter 2	160	131·75	28·25	32·23	−3·98	127·77
2015 quarter 3	153	133·75	19·25	22·55	−3·30	130·45
2015 quarter 4	100	137·75	−37·75	−40·08	2·33	140·08
2016 quarter 1	128	142·25	−14·25	−14·70	0·45	142·70
2016 quarter 2	180	144·13	35·88	32·23	3·64	147·77
2016 quarter 3	169	145·13	23·88	22·55	1·33	146·45
2016 quarter 4	99	146·25	−47·25	−40·08	−7·17	139·08
2017 quarter 1	137					151·70
2017 quarter 2	180					147·77

	1	2	3	4	
Analysis of seasonal variation			24·00	−35·75	
	−15·50	28·25	19·25	−37·75	
	−14·25	35·88	23·88	−47·25	
Totals	−29·75	64·13	67·13	−120·75	
Average	−14·88	32·06	22·38	−40·25	−0·69
Adjustment	0·17	0·17	0·17	0·17	
Svar (1)	−14·70	32·23	22·55	−40·08	

Note 1: Svar: seasonal variation

Note 2: Sadj: seasonally adjusted figures

The failure of the company to meet sales targets for quarters 1 and 2 of 2017 has prompted the Chief Executive Officer (CEO) to put into place a broad cost-cutting policy. He has banned business travel, cancelled a number of marketing initiatives and introduced a complete freeze on recruiting for posts which become vacant on the resignation of the current post holder. He claims that "our failure to meet sales targets means we must ruthlessly cut costs". However, many of the departmental managers are critical of such an indiscriminate approach and believe that the measures might be counter-productive.

This cost-cutting has particularly demotivated the production manager and the inventory manager, who both blame the sales director for setting unrealistic targets. The production manager has commented that, "I am working tirelessly to keep costs down, but my only reward is that I cannot replace one of my best purchasing administrators who left last month". In general, departmental managers at the company feel "powerless and undervalued".

The company currently does not have a formal budgeting process in place. The production manager is sure that such a process, particularly if senior managers were involved in the budget setting process, would help address issues around forecast reliability, the low morale of departmental managers and the seemingly indiscriminate cost-cutting of the CEO.

Required:

(a)   **Explain and analyse the data in the least squares regression and time series analysis spreadsheets (Figures 1 and 2) left by the business analyst and evaluate the appropriateness of both techniques to sales forecasting at ATD.**   (15 marks)

(b)   **Analyse how introducing a formal budgeting process would address the issues of inaccurate forecasting, low morale and indiscriminate cost cutting at ATD.**   (10 marks)

(25 marks)

Question 42 RICK HEIN

This scenario summarises the development of a company called Rock Bottom through three phases, from its founding in 1965 to 2008 when it ceased trading.

Phase 1 (1965–1988)

In 1965 customers usually purchased branded electrical goods, largely produced by well-established domestic companies, from general stores that stocked a wide range of household products. However, in that year, a recent university graduate, Rick Hein, established his first shop specialising solely in the sale of electrical goods. In contrast to the general stores, Rick Hein's shop predominantly sold imported Japanese products which were smaller, more reliable and more sophisticated than the products of domestic competitors. Rick Hein quickly established a chain of shops, staffed by young people who understood the capabilities of the products they were selling. He backed this up with national advertising in the press, an innovation at the time for such a specialist shop. He branded his shops as "Rock Bottom", a name which specifically referred to his cheap prices, but also alluded to the growing importance of rock music and its influence on product sales. In 1969, 80% of sales were of music centres, turntables, amplifiers and speakers, bought by the newly affluent young. Rock Bottom began increasingly to specialise in selling audio equipment.

Hein also developed a high public profile. He dressed unconventionally and performed a number of outrageous stunts that publicised his company. He also encouraged the managers of his stores to be equally outrageous. He rewarded their individuality with high salaries, generous bonus schemes and autonomy. Many of the shops were extremely successful, making their managers (and some of their staff) relatively wealthy people.

However, by 1980 the profitability of the Rock Bottom shops began to decline significantly. Direct competitors using a similar approach had emerged, including specialist sections in the large general stores that had initially failed to react to the challenge of Rock Bottom. The buying public now expected its electrical products to be cheap and reliable. Hein himself became less flamboyant and toned down his appearance and actions to satisfy the banks who were becoming an increasingly important source of the finance required to expand and support his chain of shops.

Phase 2 (1989–2002)

In 1988 Hein considered changing the Rock Bottom shops into a franchise, inviting managers to buy their own shops (which at this time were still profitable) and pursuing expansion though opening new shops with franchisees from outside the company. However, instead, he floated the company on the country's stock exchange. He used some of the capital raised to expand the business. However, he also sold shares to help him throw the "party of a lifetime" and to purchase expensive goods and gifts for his family. Hein became Chairman and Chief Executive Officer (CEO) of the newly quoted company, but over the next 13 years his relationship with his board and shareholders became increasingly difficult. Gradually new financial controls and reporting systems were put in place. Most of the established managers left as controls became more centralised and formal. The company's performance was solid but unspectacular. Hein complained that "business was not fun anymore". The company was legally required to publish directors' salaries in its annual report and the generous salary package enjoyed by the Chairman and CEO increasingly became an issue and it dominated the 2002 Annual General Meeting (AGM). Hein was embarrassed by its publication and the discussion it led to in the national media. He felt that it was an infringement of his privacy and civil liberties.

Phase 3 (2003–2008)

In 2003 Hein found the substantial private equity investment necessary to take Rock Bottom private again. He also used all of his personal fortune to help re-acquire the company from the shareholders. He celebrated "freeing Rock Bottom from its shackles" by throwing a large celebration party. Celebrities were flown in from all over the world to attend. However, most of the new generation of store managers found Hein's style to be too loose and unfocused. He became rude and angry about their lack of entrepreneurial spirit. Furthermore, changes in products and how they were purchased meant that fewer people bought conventional audio products from specialist shops. The reliability of these products now meant that they were replaced relatively infrequently. Hein, belatedly, started to consider selling via an Internet site. Turnover and profitability plummeted. In 2007 Hein again considered franchising the company, but he realised that this was unlikely to be successful. In early 2008 the company ceased trading and Hein himself, now increasingly vilified and attacked by the press, filed for personal bankruptcy.

Required:

(a)   **Analyse the reasons for Rock Bottom's success or failure in each of the three phases identified in the scenario. Evaluate how Rick Hein's leadership style contributed to the success or failure of each phase.**   (18 marks)

(b)   Rick Hein considered franchising the Rock Bottom brand at two points in its history – 1988 and 2007.

        Explain the key factors that would have made franchising Rock Bottom feasible in 1988, but would have made it "unlikely to be successful" in 2007.   (7 marks)

(25 marks)

Question 43 ACADEMIC RECYCLING COMPANY

Ten years ago Sully Truin formed the Academic Recycling Company (ARC) to offer a specialised waste recycling service to schools and colleges. The company has been very successful and has expanded rapidly. To cope with this expansion, Sully has implemented a tight administrative process for operating and monitoring contracts. This administrative procedure is undertaken by the Contracts Office, who track that collections have been made by the field recycling teams. Sully has sole responsibility for obtaining and establishing recycling contracts, but he leaves the day-to-day responsibility for administering and monitoring the contracts to the Contracts Office. He has closely defined what needs to be done for each contract and how this should be monitored. "I needed to do this", he said, "because workers in this country are naturally lazy and lack initiative. I have found that if you don't tell them exactly what to do and how to do it, then it won't get done properly." Most of the employees working in the Contracts Office like and respect Sully for his business success and ability to take instant decisions when they refer a problem to him. Some of ARC's employees have complained about his autocratic style of leadership, but most of these have now left the company to work for other organisations.

A few months ago, conscious that he was a self-taught manager, Sully enrolled himself on a week's course with Gapminding, a training consultancy which actively advocates and promotes a democratic style of management. The course caused Sully to question his previous approach to leadership. It was also the first time, for three years, that Sully had been out of the office during working hours for a prolonged period of time. However, each night, while he was attending the course, he had to deal with emails from the Contracts Office listing problems with contracts and asking him what action they should take. He became exasperated by his employees' inability to take actions to resolve these issues. He discussed this problem with his course tutors. They suggested that his employees would be more effective and motivated if their jobs were enriched and that they were empowered to make decisions themselves.

On his return from the course, Sully called a staff meeting with the Contracts Office where he announced that, from now on, employees would have responsibility for taking control actions themselves, rather than referring the problem to him. Sully, in turn, was to focus on gaining more contracts and setting them up. However, problems with the new arrangements arose very quickly. Fearful of making mistakes and unsure about what they were doing led to employees discussing issues amongst themselves at length before coming to a tentative decision. The operational (field) recycling teams were particularly critical of the new approach. One commented that "before, we got a clear decision very quickly. Now decisions can take several days and appear to lack authority." The new approach also caused tensions and stress within the Contracts Office and absenteeism increased.

At the next staff meeting, employees in the Contracts Office asked Sully to return to his old management style and job responsibilities. "We prefer the old Sully Truin", they said, "the training course has spoilt you". Reluctantly, Sully agreed to their requests and so all problems are again referred up to him. However, he is unhappy with this return to the previous way of working. He is working long hours and is concerned about his health. Also, he realises that he has little time for obtaining and planning contracts and this is severely restricting the capacity of the company to expand.

Required:

(a)   Analyse Sully Truin's leadership style before and immediately after the training course and explain why the change of leadership style at ARC was unsuccessful.   (15 marks)

(b)   Describe the principles of job enrichment and evaluate its potential application in the Contracts Office at ARC.   (10 marks)

(25 marks)

DECEMBER 2014

Question 1 ROAM GROUP CO

Roam Group Co (The Roam Group) was formed in 2012 when the owners of Stuart Roam Road Transport decided to create a group structure to facilitate the acquisition of companies. The CEO of The Roam Group is Sir John Watt, a highly experienced businessman and he has a financial director and an operations director to assist him. The objectives of The Roam Group is to acquire companies which fit well with its existing companies, which would benefit from being part of the Group and which would also bring benefits to companies already in the Group. The Roam Group is a very lean operation. Besides the three full-time directors, it only has two full-time administrative employees. There are currently three operating companies in the Group: Stuart Roam Road Transport, Stuart Roam Warehousing and Stuart Roam Rail. The managing directors of all three operating companies also sit on the board of The Roam Group. Each of these operating companies has significant autonomy within the Group.

The Roam Group, like all the operating companies in the Group, has the majority of its shares owned by the Roam family. Financial information for the operating companies is given in Table One. The Roam Group and its operating companies are all based in the country of Meeland.

Stuart Roam Road Transport

Stuart Roam Road Transport (SRRT) was founded in 1959 by Stuart Roam. It has grown to be the largest road freight company in Meeland, with over 2,000 trucks. It specialises in the haulage of consumer food and drink and it has significant contracts with most of the large supermarket chains. There are no toll roads in Meeland. Taxes for roads are levied through a fuel tax and an annual road fund licence. The managing director of SRRT is Stuart Roam junior, who was originally employed by his father as a driver. He still drives a truck for one day every month, so that "he never loses touch with the business". SRRT's distinctive red and white trucks are seen all over the country, and all carry the company's catchphrase "All roads lead to Roam". They have attracted a fan club, whose members spot the trucks on the road and record their movements on a dedicated internet site. These so-called "New-Roamantics" have themselves become famous and, partly as a result of this, Stuart Roam has become a household name and is the most recognisable brand in the road transport industry. To maintain a modern fleet, SRRT replaces its trucks every three years. It wants to ensure that they are reliable, efficient and that they project a modern image which is attractive to their customers.

Stuart Roam Warehousing

The growth of company outsourcing and consumer internet purchasing made it increasingly clear that SRRT's customers wanted an integrated transport and storage solution. The Roam Group acquired a number of warehouses from its customers who wished to divest themselves of this part of their operations. In 2012, it consolidated these, together with a number of small warehousing companies it had acquired, into a company called Stuart Roam Warehousing (SRW). The 2013 figures shown in Table One represent the first year that the company traded in its current form. Nationwide, it owns 4 million square metres of warehousing, with its warehouses painted red and white and prominently displaying the Stuart Roam logo. The warehouses are efficient and highly automated. However, development land for warehouses is getting more difficult to find and acquisition costs of the land are also increasing. The average price for warehouse development land in Meeland is now $20,000 per hectare. A hectare is 10,000 square metres.

Stuart Roam Rail

Increasing fuel costs, increasing road congestion and concern about the environmental consequences of road transport caused The Roam Group to look at opportunities offered by rail transport.

In 2013 The Roam Group purchased the Freight Direct Rail Company (FDRC). FDRC was formed in 2002 when the government of Meeland privatised the rail freight business. FDRC had struggled to survive in a business dominated by two large companies who shared the lucrative bulk freight contracts (coal, iron ore and oil) between them. The FDRC board welcomed The Roam Group acquisition and the locomotives were quickly painted in the red and white corporate colours and FDRC was renamed Stuart Roam Rail. However, despite experienced managers being transferred into the company from other companies in the Group, Stuart Roam Rail (like FDRC) has struggled to make a significant impact in the rail freight sector. Most of its customers are at locations which are not directly accessible by rail. Furthermore, the lucrative bulk rail freight contracts (coal, iron ore and oil) are in products which companies within The Roam Group have no experience in. It is still unclear whether the movement of consumer food and drink to multiple locations (The Roam Group's core business) is suited to rail transport. Furthermore, it has also been difficult for The Roam Group's senior management to understand the culture and economics of the rail freight business. The railway tracks, which are still owned by the state, are subject to very close control and monitoring and Stuart Roam Rail's use of these tracks is directly charged. There has also been a failure to recognise that train driving requires far greater skills and training than truck driving.

However, on the positive side, Stuart Roam Rail has developed an innovative mini-container system which can easily transfer goods between trucks and trains and it also effectively uses warehouse space. Furthermore, most of the supermarkets, attracted by a green image, are very supportive of the rail initiative and wish to be associated with it.

	2016		2015		2014		2013		2012	
	Roam	Industry	Roam	Industry	Roam	Industry	Roam	Industry	Roam	Industry
Stuart Roam Road Transport										
Revenue	575	2,050	565	2,025	550	2,015	520	2,050	500	2,000
Operating profit	10·80%	9·98%	10·75%	9·95%	10·80%	9·93%	10·45%	9·50%	10·25%	9·57%
ROCE	12·25%	11·50%	12·15%	11·45%	12·05%	11·45%	11·95%	11·30%	11·95%	11·35%
Stuart Roam Warehousing										
Revenue	315	3,200	275	3,010	270	3,050	255	2,950	250	2,850
Operating profit	14·55%	14·50%	14·25%	14·15%	14·20%	14·25%	14·00%	14·25%	13·85%	14·15%
ROCE	14·50%	14·15%	14·25%	14·10%	14·15%	14·10%	13·95%	13·90%	13·95%	13·85%
Stuart Roam Rail										
Revenue	112	3,150	110	3,000	105	2,850	105	2,650	105	2,500
Operating profit	4·75%	12·45%	4·50%	12·35%	4·85%	12·25%	4·95%	12·75%	5·15%	12·85%
ROCE	3·50%	8·75%	3·65%	8·55%	3·75%	8·55%	3·85%	8·35%	3·85%	8·25%

Table One: Financial data for operating companies in The Roam Group

The performance of the company is shown under the columns headed Roam. Industry averages (provided by Freight Line International) are shown under the columns headed Industry. All revenue figures are in $million.

Note 1: Stuart Roam Warehousing first traded in 2013. The 2012 figure is compiled from companies which were consolidated into Stuart Roam Warehousing.

Note 2: Stuart Roam Rail was formed after the takeover of FDRC. 2014 was the first reporting period for Stuart Roam Rail. The 2012 and 2013 figures are for FDRC.

Note 3: The standard payment terms in Meeland is payment within 30 days of the invoice date.

Godiva airport

The Godiva airport is situated on the outskirts of Boleyn town where SRRT already has three transport depots and warehouses. The airport occupies a site of 450 hectares and it has two tarmac runways, four hangers and a small terminal/flying club facility. The airfield is exclusively used by private flyers and two flying clubs. The airport is adjacent to the motorway which connects North and South Meeland.

Financial information for Godiva airport is given in Table Two.

All figures in $000s	
Assets	
Non-current assets	
Property, plant and equipment	6,000
Goodwill	250
Total non-current assets	6,250
Current assets	
Inventory	550
Trade receivables	80
Cash	370
Total current assets	1,000
Total assets	7,250
Equity and liabilities	
Share capital	2,550
Retained earnings	250
Total equity	2,800
Non-current liabilities	
Long-term borrowings	4,050
Current liabilities	
Trade payables	120
Short-term borrowings	250
Current tax payable	30
Total current liabilities	400
Total liabilities	4,450
Total equity and liabilities	7,250
Statement of profit or loss	
Revenue	975
Cost of sales	(700)
Gross profit	275
Administrative expenses	(125)
Finance costs	(100)
Profit before tax	50
Tax expense	(10)
Profit for the period	40

Table Two: Godiva airport – extracts from financial statements – 2016

The Roam Group has recently issued the following press release from Sir John Watt:

The Roam Group is pleased to announce that it has signed an initial agreement to purchase Godiva airport from the Godiva Airport Company for the sum of $7m, funded from retained profits from within the Group. We see this as a natural extension of our transport capabilities. Road, rail and air have long been complementary forms of transport and we are pleased to be able to offer our customers all three, using our innovative mini-container system as an effective transhipment method between transport modes. We also hope to attract a no-frills airline to the airport, encouraged by low landing fees and a population of over 150,000 people living within 20 miles of the airport. Godiva Airport Company will become an operating company within The Roam Group, and renamed Stuart Roam Air.

In a critical article on the proposed airport acquisition in the financial press, an independent aviation consultant has provided national performance statistics for airports of a similar size and type to Godiva airport (see Table Three).

Operating profit Margin	Return on Capital Employed	Current ratio	Acid test ratio	Gearing ratio
17·5%	8·5%	2·25	1·50	40%

Table Three: Average national performance figures for medium-sized light aviation airports: 2016

He has also cast doubt on Sir John Watt's statement about attracting a no-frills airline to the airport. He says that a local regional population of at least 500,000 people is required to make such a service attractive. He believes that the population of the Boleyn area is much too small to make passenger services economical.

Required:

(a) **Write an independent report which:**

(i) **Evaluates the current performance and contribution of each of the three current operating companies in The Roam Group portfolio and assesses their relative significance in its future strategy.** (21 marks)

(ii) **Evaluates the proposed acquisition of Godiva airport.** (15 marks)

Professional marks will be allocated in part (a) for the clarity, structure, logical flow and appropriate tone of your answer. (4 marks)

(b) A Business Analysis research student has suggested that Stuart Roam Road Transport (SRRT) pursues a hybrid strategy of offering a price lower than its competitors, whilst simultaneously attempting to achieve differentiation.

Required:

Discuss how both elements of this route to competitive advantage (price and differentiation) might be achieved by Stuart Roam Road Transport. (10 marks)

(50 marks)

Question 2 STELLA ELECTRONICS

Stella Electronics (SE) owns a chain of electrical retail stores throughout the country of Arborium. The company sells to the general public through its stores and website. It has outsourced three areas of a business process to Terra Call Generale (TCG), a call centre specialist based overseas. They handle, on behalf of SE, the following calls:

- Customers requesting service contracts;
- Customers requesting refunds for goods purchased from the SE website;
- Customers with technical queries about the products they have bought.

The business process for handling these calls is given in Figure 1.

SE is currently reviewing the renewal of the TCG contract in the light of customer complaints about:

- The time taken to complete a query;
- The frustration caused by the need to provide a reference number and password;
- The problem of understanding the accents of the people in the call centre.

Unemployment is rising in Arborium and there is increased resistance to services being outsourced and offshored to companies such as TCG. SE is aware of the growing hostility of customers to such arrangements.

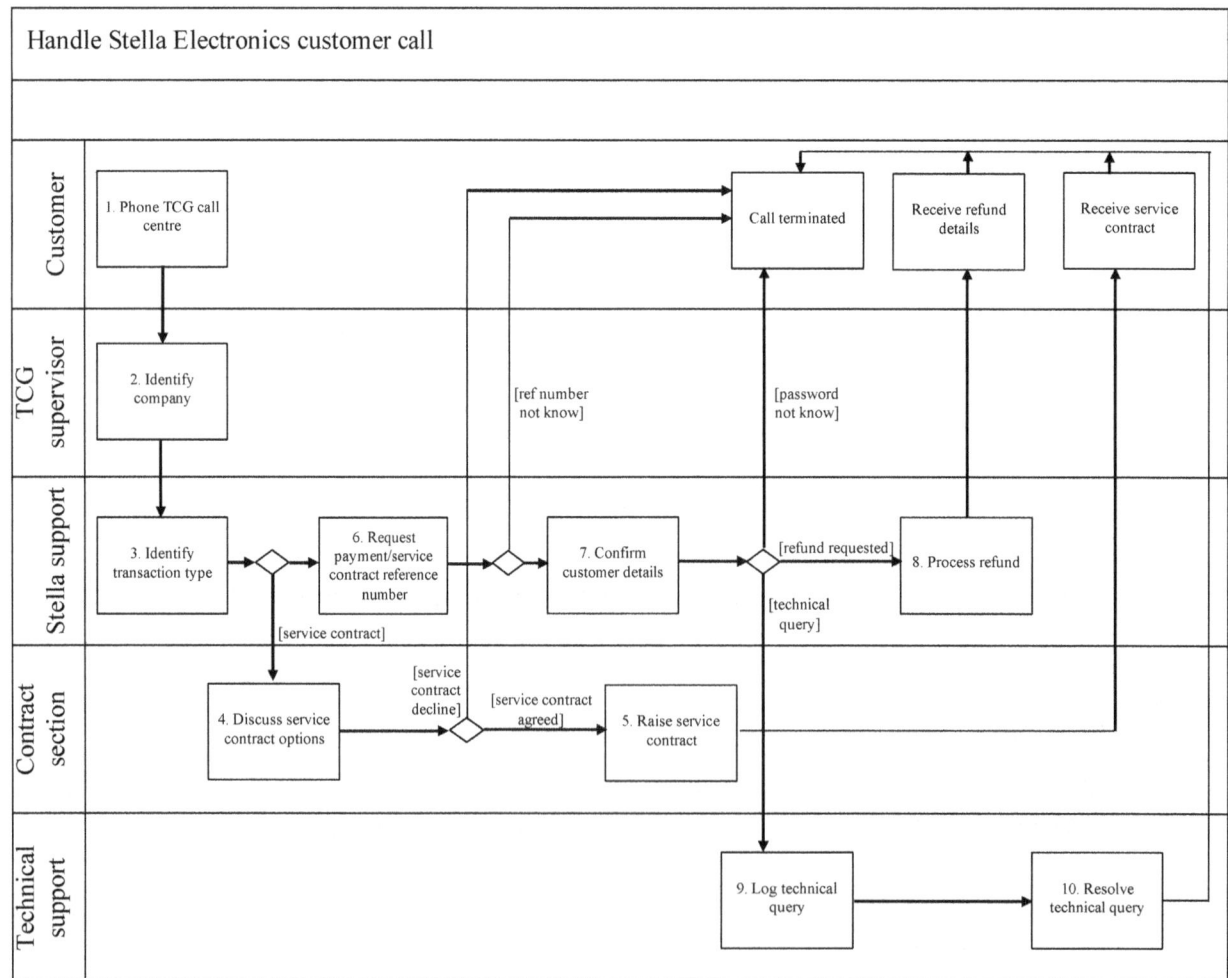

Figure 1: Business process for handling a Stella Electronics customer call

Call centre processing (TCG) – to be read in conjunction with Figure 1

(1)   The process is initiated by a customer phoning the TCG call centre.

(2)   TCG offers call centre services to a number of companies. The supervisor asks the customer which company they are phoning about. Calls for SE are routed to Stella support. Calls for other companies are routed to other support teams (not shown here).

(3)   The TCG support operator asks the customer what their call is about. Three transaction types are possible.

(4)   Callers who wish to discuss a service contract are passed immediately to the contracts section. Service contract options are discussed and if the caller decides to buy a service contract, then this is raised in the next activity in the process (5: Raise service contract).

(5)   Raise service contract and details are emailed to the customer. If the caller decides not to have a service contract, then the call is terminated.

(6)   For all other transaction types, Stella support asks the customer for their payment reference number or service contract reference number. If the customer cannot supply either of these, then the call is terminated. If the reference number is provided, then the support team member enters it into the computer system.

(7)   The computer system retrieves customer details and these are confirmed by the support team member with the customer. These details include a password which the customer has to give. Failure to give the correct password leads to the call being terminated.

(8)   If the password is correct and the customer requires a purchase refund, then the refund is processed and details emailed to the customer and the call is terminated.

(9)   If the password is correct and the customer has a technical query, then the call is passed to technical support who log and then resolve (process 10) the query before terminating the call.

Further information

■   TCG provides a 24 hour/7 days per week service. There are 600 calls per 24 hours from SE customers.

■   60% are technical queries, 25% are requests for refunds and 15% are for service contracts.

■   30% of customers do not know their payment/service reference number.

■   5% of customers who do know their payment/service reference number are unable to remember their password.

■   TCG charges SE $1 for every call they take (so, typically $600 per day).

■   TCG has 10 staff dedicated to SE: six in technical support, one in the contracts section and three in SE support.

■   SE has calculated that it would cost $50 to employ one equivalent employee in Arborium for an eight hour shift.

Required:

(a)   **Evaluate the current process for handling SE's customer calls at TCG and suggest improvements to that process at TCG.**   (15 marks)

(b)   **Discuss whether SE should continue outsourcing its customer call handling process to TCG or should it bring the process in-house.**   (10 marks)

(25 marks)

Question 3 TKP

This information was taken from an internal newsletter of The Knowledge Partnership LLP (TKP), a company which offers project and software consultancy work for clients based in Zeeland. The newsletter, dated 2 November 2017, describes two projects currently being undertaken by the partnership.

Project One

In this project, one of our clients was just about to place a contract for a time recording system to help them monitor and estimate construction contracts when we were called in by the Finance Director. He was concerned about the company supplying the software package. "They only have an annual revenue of $5m", he said, "and that worries me". TKP analysed software companies operating in Zeeland. It found that 200 software companies were registered in Zeeland with annual revenues of between $3m and $10m. Of these, 20 went out of business last year. This compared to a 1% failure rate for software companies with revenues of more than $100m per year. We presented this information to the client and suggested that this could cause a short-term support problem. The client immediately re-opened the procurement process. Eventually they bought a solution from a much larger well-known software supplier. It is a popular software solution, used in many larger companies.

The client has now asked us to help with the implementation of the package. A budget for the project has been agreed and has been documented in an agreed, signed-off, business case. The client has a policy of never re-visiting its business cases once they have been accepted; they see this as essential for effective cost control. We are currently working with the primary users of the software – account managers (using time and cost data to monitor contracts) and the project support office (using time and cost data to improve contract estimating) – to ensure that they can use the software effectively when it is implemented. We have also given "drop in" briefing sessions for the client's employees who are entering the time and cost data analysed by the software. They already record this information on a legacy system and so all they will see is a bright new user interface, but we need to keep them informed about our implementation. We are also looking at data migration from the current legacy system. We think some of the current data might be of poor quality, so we have established a strategy for data cleansing (through offshore data input) if this problem materialises. We currently estimate that the project will go live in May 2018.

Project Two

In this project, the client is the developer of the iProjector, a tiny phone-size projector which is portable, easy to use and offers high definition projection. The client was concerned that their product is completely dependent on a specialist image-enhancing chip designed and produced by a small start-up technology company. They asked TKP to investigate this company. We confirmed their fears. The company has been trading for less than three years and it has a very inexperienced management team. We suggested that the client should establish an escrow agreement for design details of the chip and suggested a suitable third party to hold this agreement. We also suggested that significant stocks of the chip should be maintained. The client also asked TKP to look at establishing patents for the iProjector throughout the world. Again, using our customer contacts, we put them in touch with a company which specialises in this.

We are currently engaged with the client in examining the risk that a major telephone producer will launch a competitive product with functionality and features similar to the iProjector.

The iProjector is due to be launched on 1 May 2018 and we have been engaged to give advice on the launch of the product. The launch has been heavily publicised, a prestigious venue booked and over 400 attendees are expected.

TKP have arranged for many newspaper journalists to attend. The product is not quite finished, so although orders will be taken at the launch, the product is not expected to ship until June 2018.

Further information

TKP only undertakes projects in the business culture which it understands and where it feels comfortable. Consequently, it does not undertake assignments outside Zeeland.

TKP has $10 million of consultant's liability insurance underwritten by Zeeland Insurance Group (ZIG).

Required:

(a)   **Analyse how TKP itself and the two projects described in the scenario demonstrate the principles of effective risk management.**   (15 marks)

(b)   **Describe the principle of the triple constraint (scope, time and cost) on projects and discuss its implications in the two projects described in the scenario.**   (10 marks)

(25 marks)

Question 4 NOBLE PETS

Noble Pets is one of four companies which dominate the pet food market in the country of Brellia. Between them, these four companies share 90% of the market. Noble Pets was established in 1932 in the market town of Milton. Its factory (plant) was updated in 1972 with new canning and labelling technology. However, further developments and expansion to the factory site were prevented by the rapid growth of housing in Milton. The factory, which was once on the edge of the town, is now surrounded by modern housing development. The town is also relatively remote from the motorway network which has been developed in Brellia since 1962. Trucks transporting goods in and out of the plant have to negotiate relatively minor rural roads and also have to pass through the town centre of Milton, which is often very congested. Furthermore, the large 44 tonne trucks which Noble Pets and its competitors use, wherever possible, to distribute cans of pet food to wholesalers and supermarket distribution centres are banned from the centre of the town. Thus distribution out of the Milton plant is undertaken with smaller 36 tonne trucks, which are less cost-effective. However, residents find even this size of truck too large, complaining that they keep them awake at night.

The Milton plant is solely concerned with the production of moist pet food. Raw foodstuff and empty unlabelled cans are brought into the plant, where the foodstuff is cooked and put into cans which are then labelled and distributed to wholesalers or supermarket distribution centres. Many of these distribution centres, like Noble Pets' competitors, are now located on or near the motorway network. Although the recipe for the pet food is very similar to its competitors, Noble Pets has a reputation for producing a quality product. This quality has been promoted ever since the company's formation by clever marketing campaigns which stress the importance of giving your pet good food, and the superior nature of Noble Pets' products to its competitors. This has traditionally been supported by free fact guides and information promoting responsible pet ownership and nutrition. The company now has a website dedicated to giving advice and guidance. This advice appears to be unbiased, although recommended solutions to pet problems often involve Noble Pets' products.

Noble Pets is currently reviewing its operations and has asked external consultants to assess the Milton plant from a value chain perspective. It has provided the following table (Table One) to help in that analysis. Average figures for its competitors are also provided.

Production cost of a six can pack All figures in $	*Milton factory*	*Competitor A*	*Competitor B*	*Competitor C*
Raw foodstuff costs	0·10	0·10	0·09	0·15
Cost of cans	0·05	0·10	0·06	0·05
Direct labour costs	0·25	0·25	0·30	0·24
Production costs	0·30	0·25	0·20	0·26
Transport costs (good inward)	0·15	0·10	0·10	0·12
Transport costs (good outward)	0·10	0·05	0·05	0·08
Sales price (to customer)	1·25	1·15	1·10	1·20

Table One: Direct costs of the Milton plant compared to major competitors

Dry pet food is an alternative to moist pet food. It is packaged in bags and it is in the form of a biscuit. Many people who buy pet food prefer the dry food because it does not smell and can be left in the pet's bowl for longer. Noble Pets also produces dry pet food, but not at its Milton plant. It would like to reduce costs at Milton but it is concerned that the demand for moist pet food will not justify such investment. Consequently, it has also asked the consultants to look at the pet food market as a whole and to forecast demand for moist pet food for the next three years (2017, 2018 and 2019). It is aware that new technology is available (and is already being used by its competitors) which offers more efficient and reliable canning, but it is not sure that it is worth investing in.

The consultants have identified the following information provided by the Pet Food Industry Group.

Years	Year (x)	Moist pet food (000s tonnes) (y)	Dry pet food (000s tonnes)
2010	1	370	292
2011	2	350	307
2012	3	331	321
2013	4	325	329
2014	5	315	341
2015	6	310	351
2016	7	310	359

Table Two: Production of pet food (2010–2016)

A linear regression analysis has been conducted for the moist food production. Time (years) is represented as x (the independent variable) and moist pet food volume as y. The linear regression analysis has identified the following values of a, b and r for the relationship between time and moist pet food production.

a	b	r
369·5714	–9·86	–0·94432

Noble Pets currently has a market share of 30% of the moist food market, a share which has remained unchanged since 2009. It has three sites. As well as the Milton plant it has two other plants. These two plants combined have an annual maximum capacity of 40,000 tonnes of moist pet food.

Required:

(a)   **Evaluate the strengths and weaknesses of the Milton plant from the perspective of the primary activities of a value chain analysis.** (15 marks)

(b)   (i)   **Analyse trends in the pet food industry;** (5 marks)

        (ii)   **Forecast demand for moist pet food for the next three years, as required by Noble Pets, using the regression formula given and comment on the validity and implications of that forecast.** (5 marks)

(25 marks)

Answer 1 NATIONAL MUSEUM

(a) PESTEL analysis

The PESTEL framework may be used to explore the macro-environmental influences that might affect an organisation. There are six main influences in the framework: political, economic, social, technological, environmental and legal. However, these influences are inter-linked and so, for example, political developments and environmental requirements are often implemented through enacting legislation.

Tutorial note: *Candidates will be given credit for identifying the main macro-environmental influences that affect the NM, whether or not they are classified under the same influences as the examiner's model answer.*

Political

Monitoring, understanding and adapting to the political environment are absolutely essential for NM. It is currently very reliant on government funding and so is significantly affected by the recently elected government's decision to gradually reduce that funding. The implications of this were recognised by the Board of Trustees and led to the appointment of a new Director General. Unfortunately, senior staff at the museum did not share this perception of the significance of the funding changes. Their opposition to change, which culminated in the Director General's resignation, has led to further political ramifications. The government is now threatening heavier funding cuts and further political trustee appointments. Furthermore, it does appear that the political context has changed for the foreseeable future. The government has only just been elected and the opposition also agrees that the reliance of museums on government funding has to be reduced.

The political appointment of two (and possibly more) trustees is also important to NM. It was significant that it was the two trustees appointed by the government who supported the Director General and his proposed changes. Finally, the continued funding of the government will now largely depend on performance measures which have been determined by a political agenda (e.g. accessibility). The museum must strive to meet these objectives even if they are not shared by senior staff. The old ways – built around an assessment of Heritage Collections – appear to have gone forever and senior staff members need to recognise this.

Economic

Up to now NM has been largely sheltered from the economic environment. It has been funded by the government, not the marketplace, and that funding has been largely determined by stable internal factors (e.g. artefacts in the Heritage Collection). Evidence from the scenario and Figure 1, suggests that this funding is stable, increasing on an annual basis to reflect inflation. However, the progressive reduction of government funding will mean that the museum will be exposed to economic realities. It will have to set realistic admission charges. Resources will also have to be used effectively and new opportunities identified and exploited for increasing income. The Director General included a number of these ideas in his proposals. However, it will be difficult to set a charge that will attract sufficient customers to cover the museum's costs, particularly as visitors have been used to paying only a nominal entry charge.

Social

The social environment is important to the museum from at least two different perspectives:

(1)   Social inclusion is an important part of the government's targets. The government is committed to increasing museum attendance by both lower social classes and by younger people who they feel need to be made more aware of their heritage. The visitor information shown in Figure 3 suggests that not only are visitor numbers declining in total, but the average age of these visitors is increasing. The percentage of visitors aged 22 and under visiting the NM has decreased from 19% of the total visitors (in 20X8) to just over 12% in 20Y1. The museum needs to identify what it needs to do to attract such groups to the museum. The Director General had suggested free admission. This could be combined with popular exhibitions (perhaps tied in with television programmes or films) and "hands-on" opportunities. It appears that the immediate neighbourhood of the museum now houses many of the people the government would like as visitors and so, from this angle, the location of the museum is an advantage. However, the comment of the Director of Art and Architecture about popularity and historical significance hardly bodes well for the future.

(2)   The decay of the neighbourhood and the increased crime rate may also deter fee-paying visitors. The museum is becoming increasingly isolated in its environment, with many of its traditional middle-class customers moving away from the area and reluctant to visit. The extensive reporting of a recent assault on a visitor is also likely to deter visitors. The museum needs to react to these issues by ensuring that good and safe transport links are maintained to the museum and by improving security both in the museum and in its immediate vicinity. Visitors need to feel safe and secure. If the museum believes this to be unachievable, then it might consider moving to a new site.

Technological

It is estimated that only 10% of the museum's collection is on view to visitors. Technology provides opportunities for displaying and viewing artefacts on-line. It provides an opportunity for the museum to become a virtual museum – allowing visitors from all over the world access to images and information about its collections. Indeed, such an approach should also help the museum achieve some of its technology and accessibility targets set by the government. Technology can also be used to increase marketing activity, providing on-line access to products and allowing these products to be bought through a secure payment facility. The appropriate use of technology frees the museum from its physical space constraints and also overcomes issues associated with its physical location.

Environmental

It can be argued that all contemporary organisations have to be aware of environmental issues and the impact their activities have on the environment. These are likely to be exacerbated by the museum being located in an old building which itself requires regular maintenance and upgrading to reflect government requirements. It is also very unlikely that such an old building will be energy efficient and so heating costs are likely to be high and to continue to increase. The museum needs to adopt appropriate policies on recycling and energy conservation, but it may be difficult to achieve these targets in the context of an old building. Consequently, environmental issues may combine with social issues to encourage the consideration of the possible relocation of the museum to a modern building in a more appropriate location. However, the museum building is also of architectural importance, and so some acceptable alternative use for the building might also have to be suggested.

Legal

Legal issues affect the museum in at least two ways:

(1)   There is already evidence that the museum has had to adapt to legal requirements for disability access and to reflect health and safety requirements. Some of these requirements appear to have required changes in the building which have been met with disapproval. It is likely that modifications will be expensive and relatively awkward, leading again to unsightly and aesthetically unpleasing modifications to the building. Further tightening of legislation might be expected from a government with a mandate for social inclusion. For example, it might specify that all documentation should be available in Braille or in different languages. Legislation concerning fire safety, heating, cooking and food preparation might also exist or be expected.

(2)   The museum is run by a Board of Trustees. There are legal requirements about the behaviour of such trustees. The museum must be aware of these and ensure that their work is properly scoped and monitored. Trustees have, and must accept, ultimate responsibility for directing the affairs of the museum, ensuring that it is solvent, well-run, and meeting the needs for which it has been set up. The museum is a charity and it is the responsibility of the trustees to ensure that its operation complies with the charity law of the country.

(b)   Cultural web analysis for NM

The underlying cultural issues that would explain the failure of the Director General's strategy at NM can be explored using the cultural web. It can be used to understand the behaviours of an organisation – the day-to-day way in which the organisation operates – and the taken-for-granted assumptions that lie at the core of an organisation's culture.

Tutorial note: *The question suggests that it was a lack of understanding of NM's culture that lay at the heart of the Director General's failure. In this suggested answer the cultural web is used as a way of exploring the failure of the Director General's strategy from a cultural perspective. However, other appropriate models and frameworks that explore the cultural perspective will also be given credit.*

A cultural web for NM is suggested in Figure 1. The cultural web is made up of a set of factors that overlap and reinforce each other.

Symbols

The symbols explore the logos, offices, titles and terminology of the organisation. The large offices, the special dining room and the dedicated personal assistants are clear symbols of hierarchy and power in the museum. Furthermore, the language used by directors in their stories (see below) suggests a certain amount of disdain for both customers and managers. The status of professor conferred on section heads with Heritage Collections also provides relative status within the heads of collection sections themselves. The proposal of the Director General to close the heads' dining room and to remove their dedicated personal assistants would take away two important symbols of status and is likely to be an unpopular suggestion.

Power

The power structures of the organisation are significant. Power can be seen as the ability of certain groups to persuade or coerce others to follow a certain course of action. At present, power is vested in the heads of collection sections, reflected by their dominance on the Board of Directors. Three of the five directors represent collection sections. Similarly the Board of Trustees is dominated by people who are well-known and respected in academic fields relevant to the museum's collections.

The power of external stakeholders (such as the government) has, until the election of the new government, been relatively weak. They have merely handed over funding for the trustees to distribute. The Director General of the museum has been a part-time post. The appointment of an external, full-time Director General with private sector experience threatens this power base and his suggestion for the new organisation structure takes away the dominance of the collection heads. On his proposed board, only one of six directors represents the collection sections.

Organisational structure

The organisational structure is likely to reflect and reinforce the power structure. This appears to be the case at the museum. However, it is interesting to note that the collections themselves are not evenly represented. Both the Director of Industrial Art and the Director of Media and Contemporary Art represent five collection sections. However, only two collection areas are represented by the Director of Art and Architecture. This imbalance, reinforced by different symbols (professorships) and reflected in stories (see later) might suggest a certain amount of disharmony between the collection heads, which the Director General might have been able to exploit. Management at the museum are largely seen as administrators facilitating the museum's activities. This is reinforced by the title of the director concerned; Director of Administration.

Controls

The controls of the organisation relate to the measurements and reward systems which emphasise what is important to the organisation. At NM the relative budget of each section has been heavily influenced by the Heritage Collections. These collections help determine how much the museum receives as a whole and it appears (from the budget figures) that the Board of Trustees also use this as a guide when allocating the finance internally. Certainly, the sections with the Heritage Collections appear to receive the largest budgets. Once this division has been established the principle of allocating increases based on last year's allocation, plus a percentage, perpetuates the division and indeed accentuates it in real financial terms. Hence, smaller sections remain small and their chance of obtaining artefacts for them to be defined a Heritage Collection becomes slimmer every year. Again, this may suggest a potential conflict between the larger and smaller collection sections of the museum. Finally, up until the election of the new government, there appears to have been no required measures of outputs (visitor numbers, accessibility, etc). The museum was given a budget to maintain the collections, not to attract visitors. The proposal of the Director General to allocate budgets on visitor popularity disturbs the well-established way of distributing budgets in a way that reinforced the current power base.

Routines and rituals

The routines and rituals are the way members of the organisation go about their daily work and the special events or particular activities that reinforce the "way we do things around here". It is clear from the scenario that it is not thought unacceptable for directors to directly lobby the Board of Trustees and to write letters to the press and appear on television programmes to promote their views. In many organisations issues in the boardroom remain confidential and are resolved there. However, this is clearly not now the case at NM. The scenario suggests that there are certain *rites of challenge* (exemplified by the new Director General's proposals) but equally there are strong *rites of counter-challenge*, resistance to the new ways of doing things. Often such rites are limited to grumbling or working-to-rule, but at NM they extend to lobbying powerful external forces in the hope that these forces can be combined to resist the suggested changes.

Stories

Stories are used by members of the organisation to tell people what is important in the organisation. The quotes included in the scenario are illuminating both in content and language. The Director of Art and Architecture believes that Heritage Collections have a value that transcends popularity with the "undiscerning public". He also alludes to the relative importance of collections. He suggests that fashion may not be a suitable subject for a collection, unlike art and architecture. Similarly, the anonymous quote about lack of consultation, that includes a reference to the new Director General as "an ex-grocer", attempts to belittle both management and commerce.

Paradigm

In the centre of the cultural web is the *paradigm* of NM. This is the set of assumptions that are largely held in common and are taken for granted in the organisation. These might be:

■   The museum exists for the good of the nation;
■   It is a guardian of the continuity of the nation's heritage and culture;
■   What constitutes heritage and culture is determined by experts;
■   The government funds the purchase and maintenance of artefacts that represent this heritage and culture.

There are two important elements of the Director General's proposals that are missing from this paradigm; visitors and customers. Changing the current paradigm may take considerable time and effort.

Figure 1: Possible cultural web for the National Museum

Symbols
- Head of section has large office, special dining room, dedicated PA
- National Collection confers status of professor
- Disdain for customers, managers and colleagues

Power
- Department based, largely reflects the head of section structure
- Board of trustees dominated by academics relevant to museum's collections
- Traditionally very little influence from external stakeholders
- New government beginning to exert power

Stories
- Value of National Collections
- People are transient, collections have established worth
- Belittle management and commerce

- Exists for the good of the nation
- Funded by government
- Guardians of the continuity of nation's heritage and culture
- What constitutes heritage and culture is determined by experts

Routines and Rituals
- Lobbying of external organisations
- Limited role of Board of Trustees

Organisational Structure
- Within collections, art and architecture appears to have disproportionate representation
- Administrative role of management reinforced by title: Director of Administration

Controls
- Annual budget decided on last year's figures and a percentage for inflation
- Budget division heavily influenced by 'National Collections'
- Traditionally, 90% funded by government
- New government changing funding basis

Tutorial note: *Candidate answers which considered the cultural web from a perspective of how it might have helped the Director General develop and implement proposals are also acceptable.*

Alternative cultural web analysis

For example:

■   He may have considered deferring one or both of the proposals to remove the head of collection sections' dining room and their dedicated personal assistants. These are important symbols of their status and the financial gains from removing them seem unlikely to outweigh the consequences of their removal.

■   He might have considered simply adding directors to the organisational structure, rather than inviting conflict by removing two of the collection directors. For example, replacing the current Director of Administration with the four new directors of his proposed structure (Finance, Visitor Services, Resources and Information Systems) might then have been more acceptable. The actual number of collection related directors remains the same (three), but their relative power in the board would have been decreased.

■   An analysis of the cultural web identifies a possible conflict between the collection section heads that could have been exploited. A significant number of sections are not designated as Heritage Collections and so are not headed by professors. These sections are also less well represented on the board and they receive less money, which is allocated in a way that accentuates and perpetuates the relative wealth of the powerful sections. Published stories and deriding fashion, reinforces this division. The Director General could have identified proposals that could have brought the heads of certain sections "on side" and so destroy the apparently harmonious position of the collection heads.

■   He also needed to recognise the structure of the Board of Trustees. Their current composition meant that there was little chance that they would support his proposals.

■   Finally, he would have benefited from understanding the paradigm of NM and how at odds this paradigm is with his own vision and with the vision of the incoming government. In this context the cultural web has important implications for the heads of collection sections. Both the *power* and *controls* elements of the cultural web are undergoing significant change. The new government is exploiting its position as a major stakeholder and insisting on new controls and measures that reflect their paradigm. Although the heads of collection sections have successfully lobbied for the removal of the Director General, they are very unlikely to change the government's policy. Indeed the sacking of the Director General has strengthened the government's action and resolve. The sacking of the Director General may have been a *pyrrhic victory* and a much worse defeat now awaits the heads of collection sections.

(c)   **Strategy lenses analysis for NM**

Design lens

The design lens views strategy as the deliberate positioning of an organisation as the result of some "rational, analytical, structured and directive process". Through the design lens it is the responsibility of top management to plan the destiny of the organisation. Lower levels of management carry out the operational actions required by the strategy. The design lens is associated with objective setting and a plan for moving the organisation towards these objectives. In the context of the scenario, the government is now significantly involved in objective setting and tying funding to those objectives. The Director General has responsibility for defining and delivering a strategy within these objectives. There is evidence that he has gone about this in a "top-down" way and not sought advice from current employees. On the television programme, employees were particularly critical of a lack of consultation; "these proposals have been produced with no input from museum staff. They have been handed down from on-high". In many ways, the approach taken at NM under the new Director General represents the design lens view of strategy. Such an approach is not unusual in public sector organisations, where elements of strategy are dictated by government manifestos.

Experience lens

Strategy as experience provides a more adaptive approach to strategy, building on and changing the existing strategy. Changes are incremental as the organisation adapts to new opportunities and threats in the environment. The experience lens views strategy development as the combination of individual and collective experience together with the taken-for-granted assumptions of cultural influences. However, it has to be recognised that the assumptions and practices of the organisation may become so ingrained that it is difficult for people to question or change them. This certainly appears to be true for the heads of collection sections at NM. The museum is now facing a fundamental change in the way it will be funded and the increased influence of the government suggests a change in the paradigm of the organisation. It seems unlikely that people with a vested interest in the current arrangement and perpetuating that current arrangement will come up with the change in strategy that is now required. The "taken-for-granted" behaviour of people in organisations is one of the major barriers to developing innovative strategies. Strategy as experience seems innately conservative. It could work well when a small incremental change is required in a stable environment. However, this does not appear to be the situation at NM and so developing strategy as experience may not seem a possible way forward and perhaps this is why the Director General explicitly rejected this approach.

Ideas lens

Strategy as ideas has a central role for innovation and new ideas. It sees strategy as emerging from the variety and diversity in an organisation. It is as likely to come from the bottom of the organisation as from the top. Consequently, the organisation should foster conditions that allow ideas to emerge and to be considered for inclusion in a "mainstream strategy". Certain conditions, such as a changing and unpredictable environment, foster ideas and innovation. It could be argued that the macro-environmental conditions for adopting this lens are present at NM. Political, social and environmental influences might lead to new ideas (e.g. the relocation of the museum and the exploitation of on-line access to resources creating a virtual museum). The museum is undergoing a fundamental change in priorities and funding and the consequences of these changes is unpredictable. On the other hand, the museum is a long-established conservative organisation with many symbols of hierarchy and deference. There is no evidence in the scenario of a group of people generating conflicting ideas and encouraged to compete with each other in an open and supportive environment. NM seems to be dominated by powerful individuals protecting their own interests. Finally, a key factor in the selection of ideas is the marketplace. NM is currently operating in a protected economic environment, although this is set to change.

Summary

There is plenty of evidence to suggest that it is difficult to change strategies in a hierarchical or deferential structure. At NM the Director General decided to pursue a designed strategy. In many ways this appeared to be the natural lens to adopt given the objectives set by the newly elected government that was beginning to exert its power. This strategy may have worked if he had been more sensitive to the cultural web and, also, if he had not asked for the backing of the Board of Trustees. This was always unlikely to be forthcoming given its composition. The paradigm change means that it is unlikely that the experience lens would have proved fruitful. However, it may have been possible to exploit strategy as ideas if the Director General had carefully selected heads of collection sections who were relative losers under the current system.

Answer 2 EA GROUP

(a)   **Analysis of the four companies and their future contribution to EA Group's portfolio**

Power of the Sun (POTS)

The growth of the EA Group (EA) was largely made possible by the profits produced by POTS in the decade 2000–2010. It provided the funding for such acquisitions as ENCOS and Neach Glass. Since 2010, the company has become steadily less profitable. Gross profit has fallen in each of the last four reported periods (from 25% to 21%). Net profit has fallen in line (from 11·04% to 7·00%) and is now less than half that of the company's heyday. Market growth has slowed considerably as alternative forms of energy have become available. However, POTS market share remains high as many of its competitors have either ceased business or scaled down their operations. In the last two years, when the market has grown by only 0·5%, the company has increased its market share from 25% to 30%. In Boston Box terms, POTS is probably a cash cow, with its high market share and presence meaning that it should be able to maintain unit costs below that of its competitors. However, there is concern within the Group that the company is being neglected and this is being reflected in its profitability. The best managers have been taken out of the company to work in new acquisitions and this has had a demoralising effect within the company. There is also evidence that the brand has grown tired and is not well recognised or respected. This is probably one of the problems with the cash cow. How can managers in the company be motivated when they see their hard-earned profits invested elsewhere in the Group? If EA is still committed to solar energy as an important energy source, then it would probably be beneficial for it to revisit the brand, review its operation and publically reaffirm its commitment to it.

Neach Glass

Neach Glass was an important supplier of POTS in the latter's formative years. The managing director, Kevin Neach, became a close personal friend of Ken Nyg, the managing director of POTS (and later the CEO of EA Group). When Neach was on the brink of going into administration it was purchased by EA to preserve the supply of high quality glass. It also allowed Ken Nyg to help out a personal friend. However, in the past five years substantial financial investment and the transfer of some of POTS' best managers have failed to improve performance. Although market share has increased in the last four years (from 7% to 9%), Neach remains a relatively small player in a declining market (reduced by 2% in the last year). Gross and net profit margins are improving (gross profit from 16·98% to 18·26%; net profit from 7·14% to 9·07%) but, in terms of performance within the Group, they remain stubbornly low. Despite using some of the Group's best managers, net profit has risen less than 2% since acquisition. In Boston Box terms the company is probably a dog. It seems to have inherent problems which the EA Group cannot solve. It was understandable that EA bought the company to preserve the supply line.

But, in retrospect, this should have been a short-term response whilst POTS found a new supplier and the company should have then been sold. There are no obvious similarities between energy management and glass manufacture. Divesting this company from the portfolio remains the most appropriate response.

ENCOS

Acquiring ENCOS appeared to make sense. It was clear that other renewable alternatives to solar energy were becoming more common and that a more rounded approach to alternative energy management was required. ENCOS had expertise in energy control systems, but had little marketing expertise and lacked contacts with the large public sector organisations that were seeking to install such systems. EA could bring this knowledge to the company, together with more experienced managers and a higher profile. The acquisition appears to have been successful. It has an increasing market share (19% to 25·93%) in a growing market (15·71% growth in the four years under consideration). Furthermore, the growth of the company is outstripping the growth of the market. Gross and net profit margins are both growing (net profit margin up from 12·41% to 15·95% in the four years under consideration, gross profit up from 19·17% to 23·81%). In absolute terms, these returns are the highest of the companies considered here and net profitability continues to grow disproportionately, suggesting that operating costs appear to be falling. In Boston Box terms the company is a potential star, although further information would be required to confirm this. It has clear synergy with POTS and EA appear to have brought significant competencies to bear. It could be argued that it is performing much better under EA's guidance than it would have as an independent company.

Steeltown Information Technology (Steeltown IT)

If the industry Steeltown IT is competing in is defined as "public sector technology", then it seems reasonable to suggest that the potential market growth is relatively high. The present government is committed to privatising non-core services, so it can be expected that many councils will follow the example of Steeltown City Council (Steeltown CC) and outsource information technology. It could be argued that Steeltown IT enjoys a very high market share in this new sector, so again potentially qualifying (in Boston Box terms) as a star. No conventional financial figures are available and although the cost plus contract agreed with the council does mean that profits will be reported for, at least, the last five years, these will be relatively modest. The real question with this acquisition is whether it makes sense. EA does have experience of gaining contracts within the public sector, but in energy and control technology, not information technology and systems. It has no experience of acquiring a public sector organisation and creating the degree of change required to move its culture to a profit-driven private sector company. Overall, EA is trying to broaden its product base, and the acquisition of Steeltown IT is its vehicle for pursuing this strategy. Acquisition is an acknowledged way of entering a new market, but usually the acquired company is established in that market, which is not the case with the newly formed Steeltown IT. Whether the perceived synergies with ENCOS will emerge is debateable. The two companies work in different markets. ENCOS is focused on technical control systems in the energy sector. In comparison, Steeltown IT develops commercial information processing systems in a public sector environment. The drivers are quite different. ENCOS is focused on complex mathematical algorithms with little user intervention. Steeltown IT deals with developing systems for end users who have difficulty in both defining and implementing the systems they commission.

(b)   **Analysis of contextual factors on strategic change at Steeltown IT**

The issues explored in this question are four of the eight contextual factors, identified by Balogun and Hope-Hailey, which significantly influence strategic change.

Time refers to the amount of time available for EA to implement the changes at Steeltown IT. In some circumstances, time is a very critical factor, because the perilous financial nature of the organisation requires action to be taken quickly to arrest a decline in turnover or profitability, or indeed just to ensure its short-term financial viability. This was the situation at Neach Glass when it was acquired by EA. However, at Steeltown IT the 10-year contract with the city council, only reviewed after five years, means that there is no obvious need for the speedy implementation of change. Sufficient profitability is guaranteed for the next five years to maintain present levels of resources at Steeltown IT and this, potentially, gives EA a long elapsed period to implement the changes that they envisage.

The *Scope* of change can be considered as either largely realignment, or largely transformational. Realignment can usually be accommodated within the current culture of the organisation, whilst transformational change requires a significant cultural shift. It seems reasonable to suggest that the change at Steeltown IT will be transformational. Current work is inwardly focused, budget rather than profit-driven, run by managers with little experience of the private sector. There will have to be a fundamental change in the core assumptions of the organisation. Fortunately, there is no need to quickly implement these changes and so an *incremental* approach to change can be adopted. In the Balogun and Hope Hailey model (adapted by Johnson, Scholes and Whittington) this suggests an *evolutionary* approach to change, where paradigm change is required, but over a relatively long time period.

Capability refers to what experience there is of managing change in the organisation. Does the organisation have managers who have successively managed change in the past? Is the workforce used to change and have they readily accepted changes in their work practices? In the context of Steeltown IT, evidence suggests that employees have little experience of change. In fact, established work practices written into trade union agreements have tended to restrict change and this is one of the reasons why the city council decided that they wanted to separate off the information technology department. Employees have been very concerned and anxious throughout the whole process of outsourcing, from the initial decision, through tender evaluation, to agreeing the sale of the organisation to EA. On the other hand, EA does have experience of implementing change in the organisations that they have acquired. This is probably one of the competencies it perceives that it is bringing to Steeltown IT. However, it has to be recognised that this capability has not appeared to be successful at Neach Glass and so some concern might be expressed about the validity of such a claim.

Readiness for change concerns the organisation's attitude towards change. Is it likely to embrace it or is there widespread opposition to change within the organisation or, indeed, do significant pockets of resistance exist? There is little doubt that, initially, there is evidence that there was considerable opposition to change. However, once the proposal was agreed and the sale made to EA, there appears to have been a greater acceptance of the need for change. Perhaps it is best illustrated by the manager who stated that "he was against outsourcing in principle, but now the sale has been agreed, let's get on with it". The resignation of the IT director and his deputy has removed a significant pocket of resistance to change and it should make EA's task easier.

(c)   **Benchmarking at Steeltown IT**

Benchmarking is an attempt to assess the relative performance of an organisation. It is understandable that EA wants to benchmark Steeltown IT. Although the contract with the city council is guaranteed for at least the first five years, it is important for EA to understand the performance of the organisation it has bought and the opportunity for driving out improvements and, hence, profitability.

There has been a tendency for organisations to increasingly attempt to benchmark themselves against the industry or sector they compete in, rather than against their historical performance. However, such historical benchmarking was traditionally used when Steeltown IT was part of the City Council. Examples given in the scenario are the reliability of software as measured by reported faults and the satisfaction of users as measured by internally developed and analysed questionnaires. This evidence suggests that the software produced by the organisation is becoming more reliable. However, this may reflect the fact that fewer new systems were developed in the past two years as the council arranged for the technology department's transition to the private sector. Established software tends to have fewer faults than recently released software. Furthermore, the measure is an absolute one, not a relative one. The apparent improvements in user satisfaction may also reflect the hiatus associated with the transition from public to private sector. Furthermore, the overall figures do not seem very high even though the questions were set, collected and analysed by the technology department. In general, externally measured satisfaction surveys are to be preferred.

Benchmarking against competitors is problematic in the context of Steeltown IT because of choosing what sector to compare it with. It is possible to make comparisons, using published government statistics, with other public sector organisations and indeed it seems to compare relatively well, reporting greater user satisfaction and software reliability. However, again these figures have to be treated with care. Did the user satisfaction surveys in the other councils use the same assessment criteria? Now that it has been privatised, the uniqueness of the Steeltown IT experiment makes it almost impossible to find IT companies providing exclusive services to a public sector client against which it might be benchmarked. EA has suggested benchmarking it against the performance of ENCOS. However, the technology it provides and the nature of the client it serves make such comparisons very tenuous. The focus of development has been quite different. ENCOS reports on profit per contract, but Steeltown IT currently only has one contract and is unlikely to have any relevant data, as profitability was not an objective of the organisation. In any case, a major concern with such industry comparisons is that the whole industry might be performing badly and, in some circumstances, losing out to industries or technologies that can satisfy customers' needs in a different way. For example, poor performing companies providing bespoke software solutions may lose out to an organisation providing a standard off-the-shelf software package solution.

The shortcomings of industry norm comparisons have encouraged organisations to seek best practice wherever it can be found. Johnson, Scholes and Whittington comment that "the real power of this approach is ... shaking managers out of the mind-set that improvements in performance will be gradual as a result of incremental changes in resources or competencies". They give an example of a police force studying a call centre as a way of improving their response to emergency telephone calls. However, software development is quite specific and it will be difficult to think of any appropriate, innovative comparisons.

Finally, benchmarking can be criticised for the following reasons:

- It can lead to a situation where you get what you measure, which may not have been the intended strategic outcome. If the strategy is flawed, then the benchmarking will encourage the organisation to continue, perhaps even accelerate, in the wrong direction. For example, a focus on measuring the certification of staff is only valid if there is a proven causal link between certification and software quality.

- Since benchmarking compares inputs, outputs or outcomes, it does not, itself, identify the reasons for good or poor performance. The benchmark does not directly compare competencies. As mentioned earlier, improvements may be due to external environmental factors, not directly linked to what the organisation is striving to achieve.

Although benchmarking seems superficially attractive, it appears quite difficult to use effectively at Steeltown IT. EA might be better focused, in the short term, on successfully implementing change and improving employee motivation and processes rather than trying to establish and measure sensible benchmarks.

Answer 3 MIDSHIRE HEALTH

(a)   **Introduction of strategic planning and information system**

   (i)   *Mistakes in the project management process*

It is good practice to establish a Project Initiation Document (PID) or Terms of Reference (ToR) at the start of the project defining the objectives, scope, constraints, authority (owner, sponsor) and resources of the project. In the context of the case study scenario, there appears to be confusion around the objectives, scope and ownership of the project.

Project objectives and project scope: what is the project?

The objectives and scope of the project appear to be at different levels. The project might be "to establish a formal strategic planning system at MidShire Health", or, it might be more restricted to the development of a "comprehensive computer-based information system recording the outcomes and activities of the organisation". Certainly the implementation team set up to undertake the detailed work appears to be primarily concerned with the functionality of the software package and the presence of Eurotek support consultants would tend to support this focus. The assertion from the CEO that the objective of the steering group is "to deliver health to the Midshire community" adds further confusion. Although this objective is amended later in the project, restricting it to "effectively and efficiently treating disease", both of these objectives really concern the organisation as a whole, not a specific project within that organisation. It is preferable that the project objectives should be more restricted.

The immediate employment of consultants with a potential software solution will inevitably skew the project towards a particular technical solution designed to support the planning system. There needs to be a distinction at the initiation of the project between the **business objectives** of the project and the **technical objectives** of the software system required to support those business objectives. The CEO confuses the two, a confusion accentuated by the early selection of a technical solution, before the business requirements have been defined (see later).

A failure to define a consistent achievable objective often results in projects lacking focus, leading to confusion amongst the project participants about what they are supposed to be doing. Terry Nagov really needed to establish a proper project objective within a formal Project Initiation Document.

The role of the steering group: who owns the project?

All projects should have a sponsor or authority that makes decisions about the project and supports it throughout its lifecycle. Ideally, this should be one person. It is possible for a group of people to play this role, but it is important that they promote a united front. Even if the objectives and scope of the project can be defined (see previous paragraph), the steering group is disunited in the context of project sponsorship. There are clear conflicts within the group and some of these have been made public. Projects without a well-defined committed sponsor are likely to be unsuccessful as they lack clear leadership and support. Furthermore, if the sponsor is a group, then the focus of the project will veer to reflect changes in interest and power in the make-up of the group. The sponsor (owner) role should have been given more thought at the start of the project and responsibility should have been documented in the Project Initiation Document.

Conduct of the project

Two aspects in the conduct of the project deserve scrutiny:

(1)   the procurement process; and
(2)   group and stakeholder management.

(1)   Procurement process

The Eurotek solution was selected before the requirements of the strategic planning process had been defined. Once these requirements had been developed, it became clear that the software package was a poor fit and that a considerable amount of bespoke work was needed to make it fit-for-purpose. The cost of these developments effectively led to the end of the project. This was a poor process. The information system requirements of the strategic planning process should have been developed before a potential software package solution was selected. The selection process should have involved more than one company and should have been transparent, so that the reasons for selecting a particular solution were documented and auditable. It is unclear from the scenario why the Eurotek solution was selected so early in the process, particularly as their expertise appeared to lie in the banking industry, rather than health care. Most public sector organisations have to follow strict procurement guidelines and it is surprising that these were not in place at MidShire Health.

(2)   Group and stakeholder management

Terry Nagov appears to believe that the three employee sets within the steering group (senior hospital doctors, hospital nursing managers and health service support staff) are equally powerful within the project context. However, this is clearly not the case. The hospital doctors resent the inclusion of the health service support staff in the steering group. The hospital nursing managers side with the hospital doctors at key points. The objectives of the health service support staff appear to be aligned with those of Terry Nagov, but this support is not as effective as it may appear because it comes from the weakest set within the steering group. In Tuckman and Jenson's terms the group is fractional, stuck in a storming stage. Differences in power and culture will make it extremely difficult for the group to move beyond this stage. However, the person who could make it happen (Terry Nagov) undermines possible progress by choosing to openly question the ethics of one of the hospital doctors. This appears to destroy the possibility of group harmony and also brings into play a significant actor (Etopia's health minister) who, although very powerful, had hitherto had no obvious interest in the project.

Project cancellation procedures

The CEO did not explore opportunities for negotiating the $600,000 quoted development cost or look for alternatives. Eurotek might have been flexible on price, particularly if the developed software could have potentially been used in other health authorities. In such circumstances, MidShire Health might have negotiated a royalty fee, to help them recoup their investment. Perhaps this was also the point when alternative suppliers could have been sought, providing solutions which were closer to the requirements of the organisation. This would have led to the investment in Eurotek being written off, but this was also a consequence of project cancellation. No post-project review was conducted, and lessons learned were not fed back into the project management process. In fact, the email sent to the steering group members specifically stated that there would be no further meetings. As someone once wrote, the "only unforgiveable failure was the failure to learn from failure".

(ii)   *Organisational culture*

Johnson, Scholes and Whittington (JS&W) suggest that the culture of an organisation consists of four layers:

(1)   *Values* which are often written down as statements of the organisation's mission. The visionary objective of the CEO might be an example of a value. The "mission is to deliver health to the people of Midshire and, by that, I don't just mean hospital services for the sick, but a wider vision, where health is a state of complete physical, mental and social well-being and not merely the absence of disease or infirmity".

(2)   *Beliefs* are more specific and concern issues which people in the organisation can talk about. The hospital doctors appear to firmly believe that the visionary objective of the CEO is unobtainable. "You have to realise that poor health is often caused by poverty, poor housing and social dislocation. You cannot expect MidShire Health to solve these problems. We can advise and also treat the symptoms, but prevention and cure for these wider problems are well beyond us."

(3)   *Behaviours* are the day-to-day way in which the organisation operates. Certain aspects of these become clear in the scenario describing the strategic planning project.

(4)   *Taken-for-granted assumptions* that are at the core of an organisation's culture. In the scenario there is a contrast between the CEO's vision of delivering health and the perception of hospital doctors and nursing staff that the real work is really about treating the ill.

The *behaviours* of the organisation can be explored further through selected facets of the cultural web.

The *stories* told by the hospital doctors are primarily concerned with belittling the role of the professional administrator. "As we know", stated one of the doctors, "we all agree that efficiency can only be achieved through giving control and budget to the doctors, not to the administrators *who are an unwanted overhead*. This is the first step we should take." We can assume that the chief administrator (the CEO) present at the meeting could not have missed this slight. Secondly, the planning process does not appear to be perceived as real work. During one of the meetings the hospital doctors stated that they had to leave to get back to their *real job of treating patients*. It almost appears that the hospital doctors have agreed to participate in the planning process as a damage limitation exercise, trying to protect their power and status, rather than because they have any real interest or belief in the planning process and its goals.

A definite hierarchy in the *power structures* appears to exist during meetings. When the senior hospital doctors are present, the nursing representatives side with them and provide a powerful block to any of the initiatives proposed by the CEO. When the hospital doctors are not present, the nursing representatives appear to be more conciliatory, agreeing to actions and objectives that they renege on in subsequent meetings. The opinions of the support staff are clearly not valued by the hospital doctors. The hospital doctors showed their disdain by leaving one of the meetings when the objectives and role of the support staff were discussed. Their ideas, for example for preventative care, are quickly dismissed by the powerful coalition of the hospital doctors and the nursing managers.

The activities of MidShire Health are affected by the hospital doctors who, through their powerful professional organisation, have negotiated very favourable terms of employment. Not only do they enjoy high salaries for full-time positions, but they also have the right to undertake private practice where they deliver services for private hospitals to fee-paying patients.

1014

This almost unprecedented degree of freedom is tolerated by the government and is a parameter that the CEO has to work within. As Mintzberg observed, such organisations are "the one place in the world where you can act as if you were self-employed yet regularly receive a pay check (cheque)". Such flexibility does not seem to stretch to the nursing staff, but long-term loyalties seem to bond them to the hospital doctors. In contrast, the support workers appear to work under difficult circumstances, expected to serve the whims of professionals, but with little recognition of their contribution and little autonomy in undertaking their work. Probably as a result of this, they appear to be the most receptive group to the changes proposed by the CEO.

The lack of *control* the organisation has over the powerful hospital doctors is shown by the fact that one of the doctors perceives that it is perfectly acceptable to criticise his employer in public, disclosing private information from meetings to the press. This behaviour is excused as being in the "public interest" and the doctor receives support from his colleagues. The CEO, although appalled by the behaviour, cannot pursue any disciplinary action because of threats from nurses and doctors.

Organisational configuration

Organisations tend to *configure* in a number of ways. The attributes or building blocks of the organisation relate to each other in different ways.

Terry Nagov was formerly the CEO of a company making mobility appliances. As well as having a profit motive (unlike MidShire Health), the company developed its business strategy through a centralised management structure, with line managers given the power and responsibility to achieve defined objectives and targets. Production itself was heavily automated, administered and controlled through semiskilled employees who followed standards and procedures defined by senior managers. In terms of Mintzberg's configurations, the company appears to exhibit many aspects of a *machine bureaucracy*. The work it undertook appears to be routine, with much of it being simple and repetitive, allowing the company to establish efficient highly standardised processes. Within machine bureaucracies much of the power resides with the managers at the top of the organisation.

To outsiders such organisations can often appear to be an example of a focused, structured organisation which, as Mintzberg himself concedes, "can be enormously efficient and provide an unmatchable reliability of service". To a government struggling with rising costs in an economic recession, such organisations contrast starkly with, as the government minister put it, "the anarchy of the health service". To an outside agency, such as the government, appointing a CEO such as Terry Nagov to bring order and control must have seemed an attractive step. Nagov had an excellent record in the private sector and bringing such skills to the public sector would seem to have self-evident benefits.

In Mintzberg's terms, MidShire Health is probably a *professional bureaucracy*. Although the work is still relatively standardised, its complexity means that judgements are usually required. The type of work undertaken in the professional bureaucracy is quite different to that of the machine bureaucracy. Considerable discretion is required in the application of skills that have been gained over years of training. MidShire Health depends on its professional staff and, consequently, like all professional bureaucracies, gives them considerable control over their own work. A machine bureaucracy generates its own standards internally and enforces them through its line managers. This is the approach that the CEO is familiar with. However, in contrast, the standards for a professional bureaucracy originate from self-governing associations that the professionals belong to. Hence the intervention of the Institute of Hospital Doctors (IOHD) would be viewed legitimately by the hospital doctors, who believe that authority comes through expertise, not through a management hierarchy.

In questioning the legitimacy of such advice, the CEO failed to recognise the central role that professional associations play in such bureaucracies. It was bound to cause offence to the professional staff on the working party.

A recognition of MidShire Health as a professional bureaucracy should also have helped the CEO predict the hospital doctors questioning the value of having support staff on the working party. In such organisational configurations, such employees are seen as largely subservient to the professionals delivering the fundamental activities of the organisation. In fact, many support staff are managed in a machine, top-down way, and so their enthusiasm for the formal planning initiative might be expected. It closely matches their experience, as well as providing an opportunity to potentially undermine what they consider to be the comfortable, capricious existence of the powerful professionals.

Similarly, the request of the CEO for the doctors to consider the "good of MidShire Health and its image within the community" is likely to fall on "deaf ears". As Mintzberg comments, "most professional focus their loyalty on their profession, not on the place where they happen to practice it".

The problem of introducing change in professional bureaucracies is explicitly considered by Mintzberg. He states that "change in the professional organisation does not sweep in from new administrators taking office to announce wide reforms or from government officials intent on bringing the professional under technocratic control". This, of course, exactly describes the situation at MidShire Health. Rather, he sees change as seeping in through a slow process of changing the professionals themselves, through altering recruitment policies and training. In the short term, he would probably suggest that the government would be better off placing pressure on the professional associations that influence their member (e.g. the IOHD), rather than tamper with the professional bureaucracies directly.

Finally, it has to be recognised that MidShire Health is a public sector organisation funded by general taxation, rather than by its specific users or customers. In principle the provider of the funds (government) provides resource inputs into a service that is competing with other services funded by general taxation (e.g. national security). Thus health services, in principle, need to show that they are providing value for money so that politicians support further funding. Such an approach appears to give the government a lot of power. However, the existence of powerful professions and the willingness of press and public to defend health service principles dilute this power, leading to the kind of frustration explicitly articulated in the case study scenario.

(b) **Analysis of strategic planning at Midshire using strategy lenses**

The approach to strategy suggested by the CEO is essentially *strategy by design*, based on a logical process whereby senior management devises a clear strategic direction and a system is then put in place to implement this direction throughout the organisation. The overall mission of the organisation is pursued through increasingly specific objectives cascaded down through the organisation, so that all layers of management are pursuing objectives defined and aligned to the determined strategy. This is probably the most popular perception of how strategy is developed. Although it has its critics, such an approach *appears* to be used by many organisations. Perhaps the relatively simple manufacturing environment of the CEO's former company made a rational planned approach a feasible way of managing strategy. Certainly such order often appeals to politicians, as in the case study scenario, particularly when the provided service is funded out of general taxation and where politicians define the resource inputs – how much money is to be spent on health, compared with competing claims of defence, education etc. Politicians increasingly look for *value for money*, and a designed strategy appears to be an orderly and controlled way of delivering such value.

Strategy as experience is based on the premise that organisational strategy is largely based on the adaptation of past strategies. This adaptation is a reflection of the experience of managers and others working within the organisation. As JS&W suggest, this is "strongly driven by the taken-for-granted assumptions and ways of doing things embedded in the culture of the organisation". This is largely the approach of the senior hospital doctors and nursing managers on the steering committee. Strategy as experience resolves different views and expectations through a process of bargaining and negotiation. By participating in the steering group, these two powerful interest groups were increasingly able to negotiate a vision of health care and health care delivery that matched their perceptions. The powerful position of professions in a public bureaucracy and the relative weakness of professional managers and administrators make it unlikely that large shifts in strategy will happen. Such organisations as the IOHD are clearly willing to publicly undermine the value of professional managers and administrators in a public service. They do this by alluding to "public interest", rather than self-interest and appear to have little problem in rallying public support. The CEO is unlikely to have experienced this in previous posts and so would have been relatively inexperienced in developing strategy from a coalition of vested interests.

Strategy as ideas largely concerns the issues of innovation. This strategic lens emphasises the importance of diversity and variety in and around the organisation which can be harnessed to produce new ideas. Strategy emerges from people working within the organisation who are faced with challenges and issues in their everyday work. Senior management provides the context for strategy, selecting and promoting ideas originally emanating from lower down in the organisation. Elements of this can be seen in one of the health support members of the steering committee stressing a strategy that encourages problem prevention rather than problem treatment. However, even within the constraints of the steering committee, these ideas were quickly dismissed by a powerful coalition of the hospital doctors and nursing managers. It is likely that the CEO will have experienced suggestions from employees in the past. Ideas would have probably emanated from production operators for reducing waste and from sales managers suggesting new pricing ideas and new products. However, the current culture of MidShire Health seems unlikely to nurture many ideas and innovations. Powerful vested interests are in a position to smother innovations that reflects "thinking outside the box". Certainly such ideas would need special protection, something that the CEO fails to offer even within the closed environment of the steering committee.

JS&W see the three strategy lenses as complementary. A certain perspective may fail to see important issues raised by using a different lens. In the context of the case study scenario, the CEO would perhaps be better to develop strategy through experience, perhaps supplemented by new ideas and innovation. The strategy by design appears flawed, particularly given the divergent views on the mission of the organisation. However, despite this, strategy by design is the approach that the CEO appears to prefer and adopt.

Answer 4 MACHINESHOP

(a) Methods of growth

Internal growth, sometimes called organic growth, takes place when the company grows by building on and developing its own existing competencies. This is how MachineShop has grown to date. The frequent opening of new stores represents its organic growth. The company appears to be comfortable and successful in this approach.

As well as being familiar with this approach, internal growth has a number of other advantages for MachineShop.

- MachineShop is the only company which really understands the market that it has positioned itself in. Consequently, there are no equivalent companies or competitors to target for acquisition and so there is no clear alternative to organic growth.

This market knowledge is a core competence, creating and reinforcing competitive advantage.

- Although the final cost of developing through organic growth may be greater than through acquisition, the spread of cost may be easier to bear. Acquisitions usually require a major expenditure at a certain point in time. A slower rate of change, associated with more gradual expenditure and sustainable growth, may also minimise disruption to other activities within the company. Acquisition can be a significant distraction and it could easily prevent the directors from continuing their successful expansion of the MachineShop stores.

- In some circumstances, internal growth may be the only realistic option available to an organisation. This may be the case at MachineShop. It acknowledges that it is having difficulty in identifying companies to acquire or with which to pursue a strategic alliance. FRG (analysed in depth in the part (b)) is the best fit that MachineShop can find, yet it is a business which primarily deals with trade customers and larger machines and it has no experience of selling to domestic consumers.

- Internal development avoids the political and cultural problems arising from post-acquisition integration and coping with the different traditions and expectations of the acquired company. MachineShop has already experienced such problems with LogTrans and EngSup.

However, international expansion is often very difficult to achieve with internal growth. This can be due to government restrictions. For example, the government of Ceeland required, until recently, that firms trading in Ceeland were registered in that country and had at least one Ceelander director. Cultural differences also inhibit organic growth. The company will have little understanding of how business is done in the country, the expectations of stakeholders or the way that business transactions are agreed and executed.

An *acquisition* takes place when ownership is taken of another organisation. A compelling reason to develop by acquisition is the speed of entry it apparently provides into a new product or geographical market. This speed of entry is often associated with scale. MachineShop is considering the purchase of a company which already has revenues of $9 million. It would take a long time to build a company of that size. One of the concerns of Dave Deen is that the MachineShop concept will be adopted by emerging competitors in countries where it does not have a presence. A prime motive for considering the acquisition of FRG is that it has a depot network, distribution and sales team already in place. FRG is also familiar with the organisational and social culture of Ceeland. It is aware of its laws and corporate responsibilities, tax and legislative regimes. If MachineShop tried to grow organically in Ceeland, it would be starting from scratch in a country where it had no experience of trading.

The acquisition may provide an opportunity for MachineShop to exploit its core competencies in a new market, as well as satisfying Dave Deen's desire for continuing growth and high profile business activity.

Rapid growth through acquisition may also offer immediate economies of scale. This is one of the attractions to Dave Deen. As the company grows larger, it should be able to reduce product costs, allowing it to raise the barriers to market entry, reducing the attraction of the market to potential competitors. Growth through acquisition is a quick way of delivering the scale and cost efficiency of operations required to deter potential competitors from entering the market that it understands and dominates.

Finally, acquisition may provide an opportunity for an organisation to address a lack of resources or competencies in certain areas. This is what prompted MachineShop's two acquisitions in 2015. LogTrans was bought to provide the company with internal logistics capacity and EngSup was purchased to assist in post-sales support.

Strategic alliances take place when two or more organisations share resources and activities to pursue a given strategy. Both companies seek to gain benefits through co-operation. In the context of MachineShop and FRG, the prime motive would be what Johnson, Scholes and Whittington (JS&W) term "co-specialisation". An alliance would be used to enter a new geographical market where an organisation needs local knowledge and expertise. One of the features of strategic alliances is the range of alliances that might be pursued. Some alliances are very formal, others involve informal networking between organisations with no shareholding or common ownership involved.

A *joint venture* is an arrangement where a newly created organisation is jointly owned by the parents. In this instance, a new company could be created in Ceeland with the local company providing labour, local expertise and countrywide knowledge. MachineShop would provide the products, marketing expertise and finance. At the other end of the spectrum, MachineShop could consider a looser network arrangement where FRG would provide space in their stores for a MachineShop franchise to operate. In this way, MachineShop would gain depot space which they could use to build their own market. This would be an ideal way of prototyping the MachineShop concept in Ceeland to see if the market really does exist and that parallels with Arboria are not unrealistic. In return, FRG would receive a franchise fee which would help it improve its financial position, as well as it potentially benefiting from cross-purchases by customers attracted to the store by the MachineShop facility. Such a loose arrangement could be put in place very quickly, compared to any formal joint venture, acquisition or organic expansion.

One of the main problems of strategic alliances is the ability of the initiator to find an appropriate partner. It is not known if the company which is currently being targeted (FRG) would be interested in a strategic alliance. Hence a search for a partner would have to take place, which could prove difficult and time-consuming. There may also be a concern, at MachineShop, that once the partner understands the dynamics of the market, they will steal the idea and promote it as their own. Networking also offers a relatively modest and low profile approach to expansion and this may not give Dave Deen and his fellow directors the visible growth they seek. It may be too conservative and not exciting enough.

Summary

A case could be made for adopting any of these three distinct approaches and this is recognised by MachineShop itself. This is probably why it believes that growth will be achieved through a combination of organic growth, acquisition and strategic alliance. The latter two are really quite problematic given MachineShop's internal competencies and the market that it is in.

In the context of risk, a loose strategic alliance with a foreign agent seems an attractive route. However, the company would have to find a suitable partner and the approach may not deliver the visible growth required by the directors. An acquisition is risky, particularly in countries where MachineShop has no experience of trading. Furthermore, MachineShop's limited experience of acquisition to date has not been particularly successful, despite both acquired companies being based in Arboria. Organic growth offers the advantages of being proven and familiar. However, it may be difficult to achieve the rapid growth demanded, and is particularly risky to pursue in countries where the company has little understanding of trading arrangements, organisational and social culture and stakeholder expectations.

(b) **Report**

> **From:** **Business analyst**
> **To:** **The Board of MachineShop**

Introduction

This brief report looks at the potential acquisition of FRG by MachineShop. It uses the criteria of suitability, acceptability and feasibility, which is a standard framework for evaluating potential acquisitions. It concludes with my recommendation.

Suitability

Suitability is concerned with whether a strategy addresses the circumstances in which an organisation is operating, the strategic position. In the context of MachineShop, does an acquisition make sense and, in the narrower context, does the acquisition of FRG make sense? JS&W, noted authors on business strategy, have suggested that an acquisition makes particular sense if speed to market is vital. This appears to be the case at MachineShop, where the board wants the company to grow quickly whilst there are no direct competitors. In terms of capabilities, the delivery of economies of scale is also important and this has already been identified as a key benefit of the acquisition, further raising a barrier to entry to potential competitors. Finally, in terms of growth, acquisition appears to largely avoid the cultural problems that are bound to arise by trying to organically grow a company in a foreign land. Expansion in Ceeland is seen as an *opportunity* for rapid growth, exploiting important *strengths*, in particular the internal competencies of MachineShop. Acquisition, particularly in Ceeland, appears to offer the rapid growth which the company seeks.

Acceptability

Acceptability is concerned with the expected outcomes of a strategy. These can be seen in context of stakeholder reactions, risk and return. In the context of MachineShop, the primary stakeholders, the board, are likely to be excited by a foreign acquisition. It provides you with the high profile and the business excitement that you enjoy. However, in financial performance, the potential purchase of FRG looks less attractive. Any financial ratios calculated for FRG cannot really be compared with MachineShop, because the nature of the customers is quite different, with 65% of MachineShop's sales being made to domestic consumers, and so is the country and culture that the two companies operate in. However, whilst acknowledging this limitation, an analysis of the latest financial figures (Table 1) does not appear to paint a particularly attractive picture. FRG has gross profit and operating margins well below that of MachineShop. FRG also has a relatively low Return on Capital Employed (ROCE) of 6·45%, compared to 17·5% for MachineShop. The gearing ratio is higher (20·16%) and the interest cover is lower (2·67) than MachineShop.

Table 1: Comparison of MachineShop and FRG

	Calculation	*MachineShop*	*FRG*
Gross profit margin	Gross profit/revenue	28·00%	16·67%
Operating margin	Operating profit/revenue	17·00%	8·89%
ROCE	Operating profit/capital employed	17·50%	6·45%
Gearing ratio	Long-term loans/capital employed	15·00%	20·16%
Interest cover ratio	Operating profit/finance charges	3·5	2·67

Tutorial note: *Alternative acceptable definitions of ratios would be credited.*

Improving the financial performance of FRG might be seen as an opportunity for MachineShop, except that the post-acquisition performance has actually worsened at the two companies it acquired in Arboria and these were also marred by management and labour disputes. At present, improving the financial performance of acquired companies does not appear to be a core competence of MachineShop. MachineShop also has no experience of acquiring a foreign company and the scale of the acquisition is much greater than its two acquisitions to date. FRG has a turnover of $9 million, almost nine times the combined revenue of the two Arborian companies which MachineShop acquired in 2015.

Feasibility

Feasibility is concerned with whether an organisation has the resources and competencies to deliver a strategy. Financial resources are in place to fund an acquisition through a combination of loans and retained profit. However, no negotiations have yet been opened with FRG. As a result, no comment on the financial feasibility of the acquisition can yet be made. However, the difficulty of satisfactorily valuing a private company suggests that many months of negotiation might lie ahead, particularly given the number and composition of the shareholders of FRG. Trade unions may require certain post-acquisition guarantees about labour retention and reward. Such protracted negotiations would partly nullify, at least, the speed of growth that acquisition appears to offer.

Overall, acquisitions have a poor record in delivering business success. There are usually problems of integration and cultural fit. MachineShop has experienced this to some extent with both LogTrans and EngSup. At LogTrans, the directors had to be removed post-merger because of personality clashes. At EngSup, there was a problem in instilling in service engineers the need for appropriate customer service.

The post-financial performance of the two acquired companies has also been disappointing. Since acquiring LogTrans, gross profit, operating margin and ROCE have fallen and the company is more highly geared than it was before the merger with a reduced interest cover ratio. The same is true at EngSup. Table 2 summarises the data. MachineShop has to review its competencies in acquisitions, not just its competencies in its market. It must also recognise that both these acquisitions took place in Arboria, a country where it understands the culture, laws and regulations. It might be reasonable to expect that the acquisition of a foreign company would be even less successful.

Table 2: Performance analysis, LogTrans and EngSup (2014–2017)

	LogTrans – 2017	LogTrans – 2014	EngSup – 2017	EngSup – 2014
Gross profit margin	17·86%	21·54%	21·43%	23·08%
Operating margin	9·29%	10·77%	11·43%	13·85%
ROCE	9·56%	13·46%	12·50%	15·52%
Gearing ratio	14·71%	9·62%	9·38%	6·90%
Interest cover ratio	2·17	4·67	4·00	5·63

It also has to be recognised that FRG is not a complete match to MachineShop. FRG is experienced in the business market, but has no experience of selling to domestic customers, a service that accounts for 65% of MachineShop's sales.

Conclusion

In theory, an acquisition would appear to be a suitable growth strategy given MachineShop's strategic position and objectives. However, whether the acquisition of FRG is appropriate is more doubtful. FRG does not appear to be financially performing particularly well and it has no experience of selling to domestic customers. Furthermore, MachineShop has no experience of acquiring a company outside Arboria or, indeed, a company as large as this one. Its two previous acquisitions were within Arboria and were relatively modest in size.

Both acquired companies should have represented relatively good "fits" within the supply chain of MachineShop. However, performance post-acquisition has been disappointing, with both companies reporting drops in profitability. MachineShop would have to improve their competencies in managing acquisitions.

Overall, the proposed purchase of FRG appears to be very risky and MachineShop might be better looking elsewhere for a more suitable acquisition. It might also consider entering into a dialogue with FRG about a strategic alliance of some sort (perhaps followed by acquisition), which might offer an attractive alternative to immediate purchase of the company.

(c) **Porter's diamond**

Michael Porter developed his diamond to explore the determinants of national competitive advantage. Its primary use is at a national and regional level as a framework for exploring the competitiveness of a nation (or region) and as a framework for determining policy initiatives. However, it might also be used in this context to analyse, in a more structured way, the competitive nature of Ceeland, the country which MachineShop is keen to expand into, and also to understand factors that might have contributed to MachineShop's success in Arboria. The diamond has four principal determinants:

(1) *Factor conditions* are the inputs necessary to compete in any industry (e.g. labour, land, natural resources, capital and infrastructure). The case study scenario suggests that the transportation system in Ceeland is cheap and effective and ease of distribution is one of the factors which attracted MachineShop to the country. Furthermore, the country has a well-established digital communications structure, and as MachineShop expects to make extensive use of internet order placement, this is also important. Both of these are examples of *advanced factors* which offer more sustainable advantages than basic factors (e.g. natural resources and unskilled labour) and they would make Ceeland attractive to MachineShop. However, both these factors are also *generalised factors* which do not provide as decisive and sustainable a basis for competitive advantage as other more *specialised factors*.

(2) *Demand conditions* concern the nature of home demand for an industry's product or service. This appears particularly significant in the context of MachineShop. Porter argues that the home market usually has a disproportionate impact on a firm's ability to perceive and interpret buyer needs. One of the reasons for this is the attention the home market requires. Product development usually takes place in the home market. Pride and ego focus attention on succeeding in this market. Pressure from buyers is immediate and the proximity and cultural similarity of these buyers mean that their needs are well understood.

MachineShop has reaped the benefits of supplying a vigorous, growing and demanding home market in Arboria which, it believes, may allow it to anticipate buyer needs in other countries. Dave Deen believes that macroeconomic factors suggest that Ceeland is quickly beginning to resemble Arboria. MachineShop has to hope that his perception is correct and that consumers' needs are not just idiosyncratic to Arboria. Further research needs to be undertaken to ensure that Ceeland's cultural and social values will really lead to the changes in consumer behaviour that the economic trends are suggesting. If they do, then MachineShop will have definitely benefited from demands placed on it from the sophisticated and demanding buyers in Arboria.

(3) *Related and supporting industries* concern the presence in the nation of supplier industries or related industries which are internationally competitive. There is some evidence of this in the scenario (MachineShop already buy from a Ceeland supplier), although the government (see later) is encouraging the production of light engineering and so related, supporting industries may eventually develop in Ceeland.

(4) *Firm strategy, structure and rivalry.* Porter suggests that there is a strong association between vigorous domestic rivalry and the creation and persistence of competitive advantage in an industry. This has not really been a major factor in the success of MachineShop because it has no obvious rivals in the market in Arboria, particularly for domestic customers. A similar situation is likely to occur in Ceeland and so vigorous domestic rivalry will be lacking.

Porter also considers the nature of chance and the role of the government. The role of government is particularly significant in this scenario and it influences elements of the diamond. For example, it has:

■ Invested heavily in transportation systems and information technology (factor conditions);

■ Lifted regulations on what type of machine can be used by an unqualified operator (demand conditions);

■ Removed the requirement for all companies trading in Ceeland to be registered in that country and to have at least one Ceelander director (firm strategy, structure and rivalry);

■ Encouraged the production of light engineering (related and supporting industries).

So, although Porter's diamond is probably more relevant to understanding industries and countries, it does provide a framework for understanding the national competitive structure that individual firms compete within. Ceeland appears to be relatively attractive from the perspective of factor and demand conditions. However, the stimulus experienced by a company operating in a country where there are internationally competitive suppliers or related industries, or where there is a great degree of rivalry between competitors, will be missing.

Answer 5 REINK

(a) SWOT analysis

Introduction

This first section of the required report analyses the internal competencies of ReInk (in terms of its strengths and weaknesses) and the external environment which the company currently operates in. This environment creates opportunities for, and threats to, the organisation.

Strengths

Technological expertise is a significant strength of the company. It has successfully developed an innovative process for cheaply and successfully refilling ink cartridges. The technical elements of this process have been patented, which gives the company a further six years protection. The technical expertise of Dexter Black is acknowledged by his staff and his competitors. Many of the senior technical employees have been attracted to ReInk by the opportunity to work with an acknowledged expert in the field. Most of the skilled, experienced staff still remain at ReInk, although many are now seeking job opportunities elsewhere (see weaknesses).

The long-term contract with the government Department of Revenue Collections (DoRC) is an important asset. As well as providing 20% of the company's revenues, it also helps promote the legitimacy of ReInk as a significant and reliable supplier. Selling into other government departments may be a significant opportunity (see opportunities)

Location: Although ReInk is a high technology company, its operations are in a declining industrial town and are relatively cheap. Indeed, Dexter was originally attracted to the town by government grants and a rent-free period. Although this has now expired, the rent remains low. Furthermore, property prices in the area are also cheap, and the area offers a good standard of living. This means that staff can be attracted by relatively modest salaries, as one commented, "I took a pay cut to come here. But I can now afford a bigger house and my children can breathe fresh country air". In a market place where companies primarily compete on price, low production costs are important.

Weaknesses

The major weakness which has to be immediately addressed is the *financial state of the company*. Although ReInk is making a small operating profit, it is undermined by the need to service a considerable debt. The recent decision by Firmsure bank to reduce the company's overdraft facility has created a cash flow crisis which threatens the continued existence of the company. Capital needs to be injected into the company so that it can meet next month's payroll obligations.

Weak management team: The technological expertise of Dexter has been acknowledged. However, he has little commercial expertise or experience and the directors he has appointed to address this weakness have failed to deliver. The technologists at the company also have little faith in their management team, claiming that the sales director "does not really understand the product" and the HR director "clearly has no experience in dealing with professional staff". The overall competence of the management team can be classified as a company weakness.

Demotivated staff: The employees are proud of their achievements and respect the technological expertise of Dexter. However, the attitude of senior management and the obvious financial problems of the company have combined to demotivate and demoralise them. A poorly thought out programme of cost cutting and staff regrading has compounded this attitude, and many are resigned to the company failing and are actively looking for other jobs.

The final weakness concerns *poor brand awareness*. Although ReInk is a technological leader, the public has little knowledge of its services and capabilities. Marketing has focused on the website, to the detriment of all other channels, where the company is up against competitors who appear to offer similar services and also have very similar trading names.

Opportunities

The continued decline of the economy provides a significant opportunity for ReInk. Both domestic and commercial users will be looking to reduce their printing costs and so the market place should be growing. Indeed, ReInk will have to monitor the economy to detect any upturn which could adversely affect the demand for its product.

Increased awareness of the need to reuse and recycle products should also provide the company with significant sales opportunities. The number of "green consumers" is growing within the country. These consumers may have particular concerns about using printer cartridges which can only be used once, or which are expensive to recycle.

Government contracts: The economic problems in the country have accentuated the need for government departments to show value-for-money, as well as demonstrating excellent reuse and recycling practices.

Threats

Legal threats: It is important for the organisation to continually scan the legal environment to identify potential threats. Original Equipment Manufacturers (OEMs) have failed in their attempts to make refilling their products illegal. However, they continue to lobby political parties to change the law, citing their need for income from printer consumables to fund their investment in advances in printer technology. The company also has to be aware of threats to their patented process, or indeed to patents which might threaten their competitive edge.

Technical threats: Threats will continue to emerge from new technology. These threats might be to produce reusable ink services at a lower cost, or indeed to remove the need for ink replacement all together. The printer industry is very technology driven and ReInk will have to continuously monitor new innovations and product announcements to see if its services and products are threatened.

Competitive rivalry: The print consumables industry is very competitive. Entry costs into the industry are relatively low, and companies largely compete on price. This is partly why OEMs, with their higher costs, find it difficult to compete in this market. Consequently, they largely compete on quality and the generation of fear amongst consumers that unauthorised products could damage their printers, and, if they do, their printer warranty will be invalid. Thus it is an extremely competitive environment, with relatively low brand loyalty. If the potential damage to printers is overlooked, then there are no switching costs in moving to a different consumables supplier.

Finally, the *government is considering privatising the DoRC.* This could jeopardise the continuation of the contract to supply this department with reusable ink products and services, on which ReInk is highly dependent as it contributes 20% of its revenue.

In summary, the company is operating in a very competitive industry where OEMs also compete aggressively on non-price criteria. However, economic and environmental issues provide ReInk with opportunities for growth if they can properly harness their strengths and address the financial and management weaknesses of the company.

(b) **Effect of contextual features on the introduction of strategic change**

Introduction

The second part of this report looks at the contextual features which will have to be taken into consideration if strategic change is to be successfully implemented at ReInk.

Time: refers to the amount of time available to implement change. An organisation which faces immediate problems has a quite different context for change than one which is stable enough to be able to plan carefully for incremental change over a number of years. ReInk has pressing financial problems and so Vi Ventures (VV) will have to move quickly to make their investment. However, once that investment is made, VV will then have some time to make the changes necessary to address the financial performance of ReInk. For example, investing in initiatives to increase brand awareness and increase sales which will increase the company's operating profit.

Preservation: In most change situations there is a need to preserve some elements of the current organisation. In particular, the change will have to safeguard the competencies which are vital if the change is to succeed. In the case of ReInk, these are the skills and experience of the technologists.

These employees are key to the success of the company, but have become demotivated and restless, and some are actively looking for other jobs. If VV makes their proposed investment in ReInk, then they must move swiftly to reassure the senior technical staff and dissuade them from leaving the company.

Diversity: Diversity refers to *diversity of experience*. Change can be assisted by a significant degree of diversity of experience, views and opinions within the organisation. It is hampered by a homogenous view, formed from pursuing the same strategy for years. The latter seems more likely at ReInk. The focus has been on technical excellence and innovation. There are no clear groups offering a different perspective. If the proposed investment does take place, then VV can expect some resistance to change as they bring in new ideas and directions.

Capability: Capability concerns the experience the organisation has in managing change. Some organisations have experience of effectively managing change and also have a workforce which has readily accepted and implemented these changes. At ReInk, the opposite appears to apply. The management team has been unable to formulate any changes which have improved the financial performance of the company. Moreover, the changes they have implemented have not been accepted by the workforce and indeed have led to a fall in staff motivation. VV's experience of implementing change will be an important capability which they will bring to ReInk.

Capacity: Change programmes require management and financial resources. Capacity for change is concerned with whether the organisation has sufficient resources to effect the required change. In some circumstances, the organisation might have the capability to undertake the change, but they do not have the resources (capacity) to carry it out. At ReInk, the current management do not have the capability or the capacity. VV will have to invest financial and management resources to successfully implement strategic change.

Readiness: Readiness for change refers to how changes will be welcomed in the organisation. There may be certain employee groups who are resistant to change and will hamper the progress of change programmes. This appears unlikely at ReInk. The technologists are likely to positively embrace change as they are very disillusioned with the expertise of the current management team. VV should have little problem in convincing this group about the need for change, particularly as VV will be anxious that their competencies are *preserved* within the company. The most difficult group might be the current management team. Except for Dexter, it seems unlikely that they will have a role in the future. VV should be aware of this and ensure that the acquisition takes place in a way which does not alienate this group. Otherwise, the investment may not go ahead, as the management team protect their position, even if this is at the long-term detriment of the company.

Power: For change to be successful there has to be someone in the organisation who has the power to effect the desired changes. This again will influence the terms associated with VV's proposed investment. Given the situation, they need to be in a position in ReInk where they have such power, unencumbered by the current managing director or current members of the management team. They have to have an appropriate shareholder structure in place as part of the investment agreement, otherwise they may not be in a position to bring in the changes which their competencies and finances should allow.

Scope: A proposed change may just need to realign the organisation within the current organisational beliefs or assumptions. Alternatively, it may require fundamental transformational change. *Transformational change* is usually associated with an elemental change in strategic direction. The scope of change is often associated with the nature of change. *Incremental change* takes place over a longer period of time, *"big bang"* takes place very quickly, and is typically needed when the organisation is facing crisis or needs to change direction very quickly.

The scope and nature of change can be represented in the following table:

		Scope of the change	
Nature of the		Realignment	Transformation
change	Incremental	Adaptation	Evolution
	Big Bang	Reconstruction	Revolution

VV probably needs to implement *Reconstruction* change at ReInk. This type of change is rapid and usually brings about a great deal of upheaval, but it does not fundamentally change the paradigm of the organisation. It is typical of a turnaround situation where there is a need for major structural changes to deal with a decline in financial performance.

In summary

VV needs to be aware of the context of change at ReInk before it finalises its investment and the terms of that investment. It needs to ensure that it has the *power* to speedily implement the required changes and *preserve* the competencies of the company. It will bring important *capabilities, capacity and diversity* of experience to a company which lacks them. In return, it will find a company which generally is *ready for change* and should welcome it, although vested interests in the current management team will have to be carefully considered during negotiations on the terms of the proposed investment. Finally, it will need to *reconstruct* ReInk, quickly implementing the required changes, but not fundamentally changing the nature and direction of the business.

(c)   **Possible strategic options**

Introduction

This final section of the report uses a TOWS matrix to generate strategic options. Each quadrant of the matrix is used to identify options which address a different combination of internal factors (strengths and weaknesses) and external factors (opportunities and threats).

		Internal factors	
		Strengths (S)	Weaknesses (W)
External factors	Opportunities (O)	SO	WO
	Threats (T)	ST	WT

TOWS analysis of ReInk

SO – this quadrant is used to generate options which use the strengths of the business to take advantage of identified opportunities. The government of the country is committed to environmental policies and demonstrating value-for-money. ReInk has a product which fulfils both of these criteria and it also has a track record in the sector, through its contract with the DoRC. A strategy of focusing on a market niche of government and public sector organisations may be very lucrative and generate good short-term results. It will take time to address the weakness of brand awareness (see WO), but focusing sales and marketing on a well-defined business-to-business sector should be much easier.

WO – is concerned with options which take advantage of opportunities by overcoming weaknesses in the organisation. The growth of the green consumer has been recognised as an opportunity. In general, individual consumers are increasingly keen to recycle products, particularly if it also brings economic benefits, as they are likely to be affected by living in a country which is experiencing continuing economic decline. ReInk can offer reusability and cost savings. However, its brand awareness is low. Addressing this weakness should allow it to take advantage of the opportunities offered by the green consumer movement. Like many WO options, this is a medium-term initiative.

ST – this quadrant is used to generate options which use strengths to avoid or counter threats. One of the threats which affect ReInk is the continual technology development from an industry which is committed to deliver better and cheaper technology. Continual research of the technical environment, combined with internal innovation, reinforces the need for a strategy which is committed to continual product development. It particularly needs to ensure that new patented processes are in place when its current patent runs out. Like many ST options, this is a medium-term initiative.

WT – is concerned with generating options which minimise weaknesses or avoid threats. These are primarily defensive, aiming to avoid threats and the impact of weaknesses. To a large extent, the weaknesses identified in the SWOT analysis are being addressed by inviting investment and participation from Vi Ventures. However, it is unlikely that the company will ever have the financial strength and brand awareness of the large OEMs which it is competing with. One of these companies (Landy) is aggressive in its statements about warranty and is litigious. Avoiding this company in the marketplace, by not offering refills for its products, could be a reasonable defensive strategy.

In summary, there are viable strategic options in all quadrants of the TOWS matrix. In many respects, the investment of money and expertise by VV represents a reasonable initial strategy in the WT quadrant. The WO and ST quadrants seem to both offer medium-term initiatives. However, the analysis of the SO quadrant, focusing sales and marketing on a well-defined business sector (government and public sector organisations), appears to offer achievable short-term success which would help address the profitability of the company and offer VV early rewards for its investment in ReInk.

Answer 6 IL

(a)   **Value chain components**

IL supplies both manufactured products (crutches, walking frames) and bought-in products (mobility scooters, bath lifts). The value chain for these two sets of products is different and this is reflected in the following analysis. The primary activities of the value chain are:

Inbound logistics

These are activities associated with receiving, storing and disseminating inputs to the product. Typical examples are materials handling, warehousing and inventory (stock) control.

For manufactured products this concerns collection of material from scrap merchants and the storage of that material prior to use. For bought-in products, inbound logistics is handled by the supplying manufacturers. Products are stored in the warehouse.

Operations

This is concerned with transforming inputs into the final product. This includes machining, assembly, testing and packaging. In the context of manufactured products this covers the production of crutches and walkers (and other simple aids), their testing and packaging. For bought-in products, operations is concerned with the careful opening of packaging, the addition of an IL transfer logo, the testing of the equipment and the re-packaging of the product into its original packaging.

Outbound logistics

These are activities associated with storing and then physically distributing the product to buyers. Finished goods warehousing, order processing and delivery is considered here.

At IL, both manufactured and bought-in products need to be stored prior to delivery. Distribution is undertaken by a national courier company. Orders are placed by telephone or through the website.

Marketing and sales

These are activities by which customers can learn of the existence of and then purchase the products. It includes advertising, promotion, sales and pricing. At IL this covers leaflets in hospitals and surgeries, a website catalogue and order taking and the giving of advice.

Service

These are activities associated with providing a service to enhance or maintain the value of the product. It includes installation, repair, training, parts' supply and product adjustment. The simple nature of the manufactured products means that service is inappropriate. For bought-in product, service is undertaken by the original manufacturer.

(b)   **Value chain changes to increase competitiveness**

The value chain is used as a basis for answering the question. Many of the potential re-structuring suggestions produce cost reductions. However, it must be acknowledged that the charity also has the objective of providing jobs for severely disabled people. Suggestions for change have to reflect this fact. It is also clear from the scenario that some customers are prepared to pay price premiums for the goods by making donations to the charity as part of their purchase of these goods.

Inbound logistics

For manufactured products, IL could explore the possibility of reducing scrap metal storage costs by requesting dealers to store the metal until it is required. Furthermore, dealers may also be able to offer competitive delivery costs. This would remove the need for IL to maintain (and eventually replace) the lorry it uses for collection of this material. For bought in products, IL could explore the cost of using a specialist logistics company to carry out both its inbound and outbound logistics. This should produce economies of scale leading to reduced costs. Many of these logistics companies also offer storage facilities. However, IL already has storage at an airfield site and the employment of severely disabled labour is one of its objectives.

Operations

It seems vital that IL retains its manufacturing capability to help achieve its goal of providing work and income for severely disabled people. It could probably gain cost savings by outsourcing manufacture to cheaper countries (like its commercial competitors) but this would not meet its core objective. IL marketing could stress the location of the manufacture as an important differentiator. Customers might then perceive it as an ethical choice.

The operations part of the value chain for bought-in products is relatively labour intensive (see later notes) and could be simplified in two ways.

(1)   Asking manufacturers to affix the IL logo and label prior to despatch to IL. The testing of the products could also be delegated to the manufacturer as they provide post-delivery support.

(2)   Reducing inventory by arranging for bought in goods to be supplied to the customer directly by the manufacturer. Not only would this cut delivery costs but it would also reduce inventory costs, and eliminate the costly write-off of obsolete purchased inventory.

Employees in the warehouse could be reallocated to order processing and other administrative tasks.

Outbound logistics

The ordering of products through the website appears to be extremely effective. The site includes a product catalogue and a secure payment facility. However, although use of the website is growing, most orders are still placed by telephone. IL might consider ways of encouraging further use of the website, for example by offering discounts, cheaper prices and a wider range of products. It might also consider how it could make its website more available to potential consumers, perhaps by placing dedicated terminals in hospitals and surgeries.

The telephone ordering process is currently too complex because sales staff have to describe the products available and also provide purchasing advice and guidance. IL needs to consider ways of making details of their product range available to customers before they place the order (see below).

Marketing and sales

Relatively little sales and marketing takes place at IL which is probably due its charitable status. Charities are usually very keen to minimise their overhead costs. Traditional marketing appears to be very limited, restricted to leaflets in hospitals and surgeries. IL could consider replacing its current leaflets (which just give a phone number and a website) with a leaflet that effectively doubles as a catalogue, showing the products on offer. This should help improve the efficiency of the telephone ordering service. Display advertising in magazines and newspapers with coupons to request a catalogue would also increase the profile of the brand.

Many charities use Customer Relationship Management (CRM) systems to manage their donors. IL should explore the potential of this. It already has records of purchasers and also those purchasers that have made extra donations.

All sales and marketing material needs to stress the charitable status of the organisation. This effectively differentiates it from commercial competitors. There is already evidence that some customers are willing to reflect this by increasing the price they pay for goods by including a donation to support the charity.

Service

Because of the nature of the product, little direct support is required. However, IL could expand its website to give general support and advice on mobility problems and independent living.

Answer 7 COOLFREEZE

Briefing paper

I have had the opportunity to analyse the spreadsheet that you provided. My analysis suggests that the forecasting team used moving averages to help them analyse past sales and forecast the future. This is a well-established technique of analysing a time series and you are incorrect in your assumption that it is "not based on a well-accepted approach".

(a) **Spreadsheet construction**

Explanation

The technique is based on averaging figures in the time series. For example, column D is calculated by adding up the first four figures (56,70,74,60) and then adding this total to the total moved on by one quarter (70, 74,60,60). This value is than divided by 8 (the number of values in the total calculation) to give the average value in column E. This represents the trend of the time series.

The figures in column F are the variation of the trend from the actual sales figures. These variations are analysed in part 2 where a seasonal variation is calculated.

This seasonal variation is then subtracted from the total variation of each quarter to determine the random or residual variation (column H).

The author of the spreadsheet has checked that the total of the trend plus seasonal plus random variation comes to the original sales figure (column I).

It is difficult to identify where the forecast figures come from. They are roughly in line with the observed trends and represent a very modest increase on the previous year (less than 1% growth). The forecasting group probably thought they were being very realistic.

Evaluation

Time series analysis is based on past data. It cannot be used to predict sudden changes in the marketplace. The sales manager had expressed reservations when the forecasts were agreed. His sales staff had already reported that customers were less optimistic about the future because of a weakening economy and the availability of cheap foreign imports. In retrospect, a greater consideration of the external environment should have been included in the overall forecasting approach. Perhaps a number of scenarios should have been considered that took into account changes in the external marketplace.

However, even without such consideration it is clear from the trend figures that growth had been weakening. The growth from 2013 to 2014 (based on the quarter 3 trend figure) was about 11%. In contrast the growth from quarter 2 of 2015 to quarter 2 of 2016 (again based on the trend values) was less than 1%. The final two actual sales figures for 2016 were, in total, exactly the same as the previous year (150 units). This weakening was reflected in the cautious forecasts put forward by the forecasting team. However, there appears very little in the statistical data that suggests that the rapid decline in sales experienced in quarter 2 of 2017 could have been anticipated from the data alone.

The forecasting team might have given further consideration to the sudden increase in random variations in the last three analysed quarters. These might have suggested that the external environment was changing and that other factors were beginning to influence the marketplace. The absolute random variation reported in the last three quarters is greater than that reported in total in the preceding six quarters.

One of the weaknesses of the approach used by the forecasting team is that data from four years ago is given as much weight as much more recent data. This could have been addressed by using exponential smoothing that uses a smoothing constant to reduce the influence of early data considered in the time series. This method uses a series of weights with higher weights given to the most recent data.

Overall, time series analysis is a well-documented way of analysing past data and using it to forecast the future. However, it is suited to a relatively stable situation where historical data is representative. The concerns of the sales manager should have been taken into consideration. Changes in the external environment meant that a technique that had worked well in the past produced optimistic forecasts that could not be achieved.

(b) **Quarter 2 – 2017 performance**

The budgeted sales volume for the second quarter of 2017 was 83 units. Except for warnings from the sales manager, there was no evidence that this would not be achieved. The actual sales for the previous three quarters had been in-line with the forecast and so there was no clear case for the budgeting committee to change its sales forecast.

Flexing the budget allows us to look at the consequences if the planned level of output had been 50 (actual sales) rather than 83 (planned sales).

This flexed budget is presented below:

Output (sales)	50 units
Sales revenue	$50,000
Raw materials	($17,500)
Labour	($16,250)
Fixed overheads	($18,000)
Operating profit (loss)	($1,750)

The table below compares budget, actual and the flexed budget.

Budget	*Budget*	*Actual*	*Flexed budget*
Units	83	50	50
Price	$1,000	$900	$1,000
Revenue	$83,000	$45,000	$50,000
Raw materials	($29,050)	($15,000)	($17,500)
Labour	($26,975)	($15,750)	($16,250)
Fixed overheads	($18,000)	($18,000)	($18,000)
Operating profit	$8,975	($3,750)	($1,750)

A number of conclusions can be drawn.

Sales volume

The sales volume variance for quarter 1 is an adverse variance. The sales manager should be held accountable for this. However, in fairness to him, he had warned of weakening demand at the meeting of the planning committee that set the targets for the four quarters. The reasons appear to be associated with changes in the external environment. Customers are reluctant to invest in new machines or replace old machinery in times of difficult trading conditions. Cheaper foreign imports have also been identified.

Sales price variance

The sales price variance for quarter 1 is also an adverse variance. This is due to lower prices being charged. The sales manager is again accountable for this. He has probably discounted prices to compete with cheaper foreign imports. He warned in the scenario of cheaper foreign imports undercutting prices by about 10%. It appears that the sales manager has had to match these prices, as the sales unit price fell to $900 in this quarter.

Materials variance

The materials variance is a favourable variance because actual costs ($15,000) are less than the flexed budget $17,500. There may be at least two reasons for this:

(1)   The production manager may have been able to reduce the amount of raw material used in the manufacture of the equipment. This may be possible, although with such a well-established product this seems unlikely.

(2)   It is more likely that the procurement manger has been able to negotiate lower prices for raw materials. CoolFreeze has had to reduce its prices (reflected in the sales price variance) but this has been partly offset by obtaining lower prices from suppliers.

Labour variance

The labour variance is again favourable because actual labour costs were less than the flexed budget. The variance is relatively small; $500. There may, be two possible reasons for this:

(1)   Labour costs have been reduced by paying lower rates. This would be the responsibility of the personnel department. This may be possible; perhaps some employees have left and have been replaced by cheaper employees.

(2)   Perhaps the number of hours required to produce each unit has been reduced. This would be the responsibility of the production manager.

Further information is needed to come to a firm conclusion.

Overhead costs

Fixed overheads have remained as per the original budget.

Summary

Your assertion that "we have all made mistakes" seems rather sweeping. The main problems to be addressed appear to be in sales volume and sales price. These are the responsibility of the sales manager. In contrast, raw materials and labour costs have been well controlled with positive variances achieved by the production and procurement managers. Similarly, overheads have been maintained at their budgeted value.

Answer 8 NESTA

(a)   Analysis of market using Porter's five forces model

NESTA has identified the growth of discount fixed-price stores in Eurobia and is considering entering the marketplace. The long economic recession in Eurobia has led to the increased popularity of these so-called "dollar shops", where all goods and products are priced at $1·00. Most of these shops are on the high streets of towns and cities where there is particular financial hardship. NESTA has expertise in running such shops in Eyanke. The company is well-known within the retail trade of Eurobia, but it is largely unknown to the domestic consumers of the country. Only 5% of those polled recognised the NESTA brand.

The bargaining power of NESTA appears to be very strong. There are several factors that contribute to this:

- The products supplied by the supplier earn a relatively low profit margin for the buyer. Low profits provide a great incentive to buyers to pursue lower purchasing costs.

- Switching costs are relatively low as the products are largely unbranded commodity goods. The buyer should find it relatively easy to switch supplier.

- The purchased products are standard and undifferentiated. Buyers should always find it relatively easy to find alternative suppliers and can play companies off against each other in their search for better prices and other terms of supply.

- The products purchased from suppliers represent a significant fraction of the buyer's cost. Buying is price sensitive and the company is likely to spend a great deal of effort trying to ensure the best terms of supply.

- Purchasing companies are fewer and larger than potential suppliers. Suppliers may have alternative customers but their scope is limited. In contrast, the buying companies have many smaller supplying companies competing for their business.

Supplying companies are fragmented and the fixed-price discount channel represents a significant customer group. None of the suppliers appears to offer a credible threat of *forward integration* whereby they might become competitors of their current customers. From NESTA's perspective their high bargaining power is an attractive aspect of the discount fixed-price channel in Eurobia. Furthermore, effective purchasing systems, supplier selection and excellent logistics are perceived as core strengths of NESTA. There is a good match between the nature of the market and the core competencies of NESTA.

Within Eurobia there are currently three dominant competitors. The three fixed-price discount chains compete on profit margins (the target price is fixed at $1), on brand name and on expanding the number of outlets in the chain. The *intensity of the rivalry amongst existing competitors* is largely caused by their ambitious expansion plans. Apparently, few weeks go by without one of the companies announcing plans to extend their chain of shops. It is likely that a new arrival into the market will be resisted, particularly when it is a potential entrant as well-known (in the retail market) as NESTA. Resistance will probably be through tightened supplier contracts (better prices, agreement not to supply competitors), increased marketing and rapid store expansion. However, evidence from Table One also suggests that the market sector is continuing to grow. Year on year growth in the last two years has been around 13%, in an economy that is in recession. In such circumstances, companies competing in the market can continue to improve their results simply by keeping up with industry performance. It gives all competitors greater breathing space. Furthermore, perhaps the arrival of NESTA in the market may help grow the market (by giving it greater legitimacy) and by NESTA exploiting geographical areas not yet comprehensively served by existing competitors.

The main *barriers to entry* to any potential entrant is the capital required to rent, stock and staff the number of stores required to realise the required economies of scale and to establish a credible market presence. It appears that NESTA has both the capital and expertise, particularly as the economic recession has led to reduced shop rents and greater shop availability. Furthermore, possible *exit costs* have also been reduced by the willingness of landlords to consider short fixed-term leases. NESTA's main problem could be quickly establishing a brand name in a country where it is relatively unknown (5% awareness), and competing with three incumbents who are very well known. The survey showed that all three established brands were recognised by more than 90% of the consumers in Eurobia. Finally, there may also be barriers to entry erected by the government to prevent foreign companies opening stores in Eurobia. This will have to be investigated.

The threat of *substitute products* is probably best considered in terms of alternative channels of supply. The scenario notes that the large supermarkets do supply ambient goods, but have so far resisted competing on price. They are differentiating through product (a wider range of branded goods) and through place (providing the convenience of purchasing a wide range of other goods, including food, in one location). Their sheer scale may mean that they have been willing to overlook the discount fixed-price market niche up to now. The largest discount fixed-price company has revenue of $330 million, a fraction of the size of the largest supermarket group ($42,500 million). However, the arrival of NESTA, an established global player, in the market may change the dynamic and cause the established supermarkets to take another look.

The supply of ambient goods is also well-suited to the internet and the growth of internet-based competitors has to be considered. The current market is firmly based around high street shopping. The internet might be a substitute channel, and indeed might be considered by NESTA as a way of differentiating itself on its entry into the market. The current internet home delivery service offered by the supermarkets is unlikely to be much of a threat as long as they continue to charge a significant fee for using it. It is clearly aimed at a different market segment.

(b)   **Use of scenarios to analyse possible entry into discount fixed-price retail market**

When the business environment is highly uncertain, it may be impossible to develop a single view of how environmental influences might impact on an organisation's strategy. Thus it might be useful for managers to envisage a number of alternative futures. These alternative futures are described in scenarios.

Scenarios are detailed and plausible views of how the business environment might develop in the future, based on different assumptions about key environmental influences and drivers for change within the industry or market itself. It is helpful if the number of influencing factors is *limited to a few significant ones*, so that the analysis does not become too complex. It is also preferable to focus on factors *which are largely out of the control of the organisation*. The organisation can influence its own behaviour and expertise. However, macroeconomic forces in a country are normally well beyond its scope of control. It can react to changes, but not influence them. Indeed, it has been recommended that managers should develop contingency plans (strategies) for each unfolding scenario. Johnson, Scholes and Whittington have also suggested that "sharing and debating these scenarios improves organisational learning by making managers more perceptive about the forces in the business environment and what is really important".

In NESTA, scenarios might be developed around four significant factors:

(1)   The continued economic recession in Eurobia. The growth of discount fixed-price shops appears to depend upon continued economic problems. Recovery may lead to consumers shunning such shops. Scenarios might consider the economic situation remaining the same, improving and getting worse.

(2)   The response of established companies in the market-place to NESTA's entry. The response of the incumbents is very difficult to predict. Scenarios might consider a neutral response. The current companies are, after all, relatively small (in retail terms) and inexperienced. A muted response might also be considered (increased marketing, tying in suppliers, more shops) and, alternatively, an aggressive response, perhaps leading to consolidation within the market sector due to takeovers or mergers.

(3)   The attitude of the established supermarkets to the discount, fixed-price market. The conventional supermarkets are currently not competing on price against the discount fixed-price shops. They may continue to do this or they may wish to compete, perhaps by setting up specialised branded outlets or by acquiring one or more of the current significant players, and they have the relative size and economic power to do so.

(4)   The implications of channel change, with customers preferring to shop via the internet. This has been a significant factor in many retail markets.

Scenarios would consider combinations of these factors. For example: economic recovery combined with a muted response from incumbents, together with established supermarkets continuing to ignore the discount, fixed-price niche. The attractiveness of entering the Eurobia market could be considered for each scenario, together with strategies for implementing any proposed entry in to the market.

Statistical information might be used to define and evaluate scenarios. For example, published economic data might assist the managers to define the likelihood of each of the three economic outcomes. Consumer data might help establish a statistical relationship between spending in the market sector and defined economic indicators. This would help managers predict product demand in different scenarios. NESTA is experienced in the sector (although not in Eurobia) and so managers should have some understanding of the costs and margins of running such shops. This should give them some insight into the likelihood and effect of any responses of the firms currently competing in the Eurobia market.

Scenarios may be underpinned by models which predict the outcome of different scenarios. Random selection methods (Monte Carlo simulations) might be used to generate some of the input data to these models.

Answer 9 HELEN BRADSHAW

(a)   Advantages and disadvantages of each channel

Entry strategies for "Helen's cakes"

The choice of market entry strategy is a crucial one for Helen and one that will have significant consequences for the operational side of the business. Her choice of distribution channel will determine the customers she reaches, the volume of sales she will achieve and ultimately the level of profitability attained. Key questions will include – is there a market for her cakes, how big is this market, what segments of the market will she reach and is this the most appropriate channel for accessing her customers? Answers to these questions will influence her marketing strategy and its implementation through the marketing mix detailed below. This choice of channel will effectively position her cakes in the market.

Her intention to produce "distinctive quality cakes" suggests that she is intent on differentiating her cakes from those of her competitors. An assessment of the implications of choosing a particular entry strategy is set out below. Each entry strategy has a different combination of costs and benefits and involves different levels of risk. Although she will be supplying basically the same product into each market, each market is very different and will require a different marketing approach.

Premium cake market

Here there is the opportunity to establish her brand and develop her reputation for meeting the demands of discerning customers. There is also the opportunity to obtain premium prices based on the exclusivity of her cakes. New quality brands are likely to be welcomed by the specialist cake shops and cafes and there is the advantage of relatively few brands with which she has to compete. Entry barriers are therefore relatively low and the product range can be developed in a planned way. Volumes, at least initially, are likely to be low and her existing capacity should be able to cope. However, entry into this premium market may have some disadvantages. Clearly, for a premium product, commanding premium prices, quality is an absolute must. Therefore, rigorous quality systems must be in place to ensure customer satisfaction. Equally, the demand will be for fresh cakes with a short shelf-life and this again will require small batch production and careful scheduling and planning. Her distributors are likely to want many varieties of cakes, but in small volumes, which again has cost implications, and her ability to make-to-order may be an important factor in generating sales. As she is likely to be supplying a large number of outlets spread over a wide area, this is likely to lead to high distribution costs per unit sold. Opportunity should be taken to supply cakes to any chains of cake shops or cafes and thus lower the costs of distribution. She will clearly have to work out the break-even position for each customer so as to avoid having large numbers of small customers who order insufficient quantities to cover costs.

Supermarkets

Here there is the advantage of generating high volume sales and achieving some economies of scale. Equally, if she is able to convince the buyers to stock her product using her brand this will gain her excellent exposure in the market. The fact that she is supplying to a small number of large customers will also have a beneficial effect on her distribution costs.

Supplying the supermarkets with her cakes will bring some problems however. Here the attention to quality will be considerable and the product must be consistent to prevent product rejection. She is likely to have to meet demands for recipe change and price variations may also be required. Above all, the buying power of the supermarkets will put extreme pressure on her prices and is likely to result in small profit margins. Equally important is the likely pressure to make cakes to be sold under the supermarkets' own label brands. Again the pressure on costs is likely to be intense and there is no opportunity to develop her brand. Getting space on the supermarket shelves is likely to be expensive – she may be under pressure to reduce prices to support in-store promotions. Also, the power of electronic point-of-sale equipment means that underperforming products are soon deleted from the product list and removed from the shelves. Overall this is a high volume/low margin market entry and getting her product accepted may take considerable time and effort.

Catering market

Here, typically, supplying catering wholesalers who in turn supply catering establishments. Volumes are likely to be significant, with large bulk orders being placed. The product range is likely to be less extensive than with the other two markets and there will be less need to offer recipe variations. This market is likely to be less quality conscious provided the cakes meet the demands of the caterers. There is less pressure to produce cakes under the caterer's own brand and therefore the opportunity to build her own brand. Barriers to entry would be relatively low with the caterers having little brand or supply loyalty. Batches of cakes are likely to be large with lower production costs as a result. Distribution costs are also likely to benefit from delivery to a few large wholesalers.

The downside of supplying this market segment is meeting the particular demands of the caterers – they may be more interested in products that can be stored as opposed to being fresh. As wholesalers operate on narrow margins, there will be pressure on prices. The volume demands will also place pressure on her ability to deliver the right sort of cakes from the limited capacity at her disposal. Also, having her brand associated with a mass catering market with its modest reputation for quality may limit her ability to move the brand into higher quality segments of the market.

From the above analysis she can see that each distribution channel has particular demands. It is unlikely that in starting her business she will be able to supply all three outlets. It is important that she choose her distribution policy carefully with a view to where she wants to be in the future. Each route to market will have a significant impact on the whole of the company and place different demands on her.

(b) **Variances in the marketing mix**

The analysis of each of the market entry strategies has begun the process of identifying how the marketing mix of product, price, place and promotion will vary significantly between the three outlets.

Product – here the nature of the product in terms of recipes and product range can be varied reasonably easily to meet the demands of the outlet.

Price – again this will vary in significance between the three outlets with the greatest pressure coming from the supermarkets and catering wholesalers. Margins may come under pressure with the supermarkets looking for a contribution to sales promotions.

Promotion – here the issue of brand development is a crucial factor. Using her own brand, Helen can develop the product range and extend the outlets she sells through.

Place – this is largely covered in the earlier analysis of the advantages and disadvantages of each outlet.

Product		*Premium market*	*Supermarket*	*Catering*
Product	variety	multiple	multiple	simple
	volumes	small	large	medium
	quality	important	important	average
price		less important	important	important
promotion		brand development	private v own brand	less important
place		multi-site high cost	widespread low cost	low cost

Overall, the marketing mix shows the choices open to Helen in looking to implement her marketing strategy. It should be remembered that this marketing effort is intended to result in sales generating revenue and profit. Some writers have argued for sales and sales management to be added to the elements of the marketing mix. Clearly, on setting up the business, Helen must decide where she is best employed in the business. Success will bring a need to decide who carries out the key marketing activities in the company.

Answer 10 HOUSHAM GARDEN

(a)   **Reasons for loss and short term changes recommended**

Tutorial note: Any short-term strategy which produces reasonably justifiable income increases or cost savings (in the context of the scenario) would be acceptable.

A simple analysis of the financial data shows why the trust is currently running at a loss.

The annual fixed costs are $60,000. Monthly visitor figures are 1,000 per month. The gardens are only open for eight months per year. So, as a result, 8,000 visits generate $40,000 direct income. The contribution from café sales is estimated at $1·25 per visitor. Only 60% of visitors use the café, generating an annual contribution of $6,000. This leaves an annual financial shortfall of $14,000 per year, which explains why the trust is gradually using up the legacy left by Clive Popper.

Immediate actions that might be considered

Reduce the admission fee to the price consumers are willing to pay. Surveys have suggested that the price that consumers are willing to pay is $3·25. Reducing the admission price to this level would mean that a breakeven visitor volume would be 15,000, assuming that 60% of these visitors still use the café and the contribution from café sales remains $1·25. This assumes that the contribution from each admission would be $3·25, as the scenario does not identify any variable cost associated with each visit. Here are the workings, where n is the required number of visitors:

$0·6n \times 1·25 + 3·25n = 60,000$
$0·75n + 3·25n = 60,000$
$4n = 60,000$, so $n = 15,000$

15,000 visits $\times$ 3·25 = $48,750 admittance revenue

15,000 visits $\times$ 0·6 $\times$ 1·25 = $11,250 profit from café sales, giving a total revenue of $60,000

Obviously the trust will have to consider the likelihood of such a dramatic increase in visitor numbers (from the current 8,000 per year). If visitor numbers do not increase as significantly as a result of reducing the price to $3·25, then overall contribution towards fixed costs may actually fall. In fact, reducing the price to $3·25 would require an increase in visitors of ($4n = 14,000$) 3,500 from the previous level not to make the financial performance of HGT any worse than it is currently.

Introduce a season's membership card. Evidence suggests that 20% of visitors would consider purchasing an annual membership card, if it were priced at $9. This would have the advantage of providing a short-term boost to cash flow. However, the actual income is difficult to estimate. There are 8,000 visits per year, but the scenario does not specify how many individual visitors there are. It seems likely that some people are likely to make more than one visit in a year. However, if an estimate of 6,000 individual visitors is used, then this would give a relatively immediate income of 6,000 $\times$ 0·2 $\times$ 9 = $10,800 which could be used to meet short-term cash flow problems. Obviously, income from future visits will be lost, but it could be argued that the promise of subsequent free admission will encourage people to visit more, leading to more use of, and income from, the café.

Short-term actions that might be considered

Relocate the café. The café was much more popular when it was located in the gatehouse, where café users were not required to pay an admission fee for the garden. Moving the café inside the garden may have seemed like a good idea at the time, but takings have reduced considerably. It should be relatively easy to relocate the café to the gatehouse because the site it previously occupied is still empty. There will be some costs associated with removal and refurbishment, but if the café returns to its previous levels of use, then profit from this source should be $625 per month (500 visitors × $1·25 contribution), or $5,000 over the eight-month season (8 × $625).

Increase revenues from the café. There have been some criticisms that the café menu is limited in scope and does not offer substantial lunches. Perhaps the limited nature of its menu means that revenue is unnecessarily low and that better, more appealing drinks and food may be offered at a higher contribution. There may also be scope for reducing supply costs. A more attractive menu may also lead to an improvement in the take up of customers. Currently, only 60% of garden visitors actually use the café. For example, an increase in contribution to $1·75 per visit and an increase to a 75% take up of customers would lead to an increase of $4,500 in revenue ((8,000 × 0·75 × 1·75) – 6,000) over the eight-month season, based on current visitor numbers.

Reduce display advertising

Tutorial note: *Although the savings from cancelling the subscription is long term (greater than three months), the action to cancel has to be implemented immediately. However, credit would be given whether included in part (a) or part (b).*

There is always concern that reducing advertising expenditure is an inappropriate instinctive response to financial problems. However, evidence from the consumer survey suggests that the display advertisements are not effective and although six months of advertisements have been booked, three of these can be cancelled without penalty. The survey suggests that 5% of visitors heard about the garden through the Heritage Gardens magazine. Even if all visits represented individual visitors, this would only lead to 50 visits per month (1,000 × 0·05), producing an income of $287·50 per month ($250·00 (admittance fee: 50 × $5) and $37·50 spent at the café (50 × 0·6 × 1·25)). So, the monthly cost of $500 per advert is only generating $287·50 in income. Furthermore, it has to be recalled that the survey only asked respondents for one choice about how they heard about the gardens. Respondents who heard about the garden through the Heritage Gardens magazine might have also heard about it through other media.

(b)   Recommended longer term marketing strategies

Tutorial note: *There is considerable scope around all the "Ps" of the marketing mix in this question. The applicability of some of these could be interpreted as either short or long-term strategies. For example, although reducing the price to the target price could be made immediately, it could also be considered as a longer-term strategy. Furthermore, the effect of cancelling the subscriptions might also be included in this section as its effect will not be felt until three months' time. This model answer focuses on product and promotion. However, answers centred, for example, on physical evidence and price would be given as much credit as long as they are relevant to the scenario.*

In the long term, HGT needs to reflect more on what product it actually offers to the consumer. Most of the marketing is currently focused on the historical importance of the garden and the efforts that have been made to restore it. HGT stresses the restoration effort and the importance of William Wessex as a garden designer. This is very much the trust's perception of what is important, with a focus on history and restoration.

However, whether this is the focus of visitors is open to question. To them, the garden offers an *experience*, and HGT needs to understand what that experience is. Perhaps it is the opportunity to wander around in a peaceful, safe, attractive environment, enjoying the plants and flowers. Certainly, the consumer survey suggests that this is the motivation of 85% of visitors. Perhaps this should be the main basis of the marketing message.

In understanding this experience, HGT might also be able to augment the product to help visitors enjoy the gardens and to increase visitor numbers. For example, more visitors with young children might be attracted if a supervised play area were provided well away from the garden. HGT might also consider selling appropriate supporting products in the café. HGT needs to think more widely about the product: what it is from a customer's perspective and what can be done to improve their experience of the product. For example, it might consider selling plants.

HGT has also just focused on the private visitor. Businesses might also benefit from running events in the garden environment, particularly those with products aimed at well-being or gardening. The definition of the customer may also require re-definition.

Finally, the product is constrained by its opening season – eight months. HGT has assumed that there will be fewer visitors in the four months when the weather is colder. However, this assumption has never been tested and it could be argued that the garden offers walking "in a peaceful, beautiful, safe environment" the whole of the year. Indeed, the reason given by 65% of the respondents for visiting the garden arguably remains relevant in the colder period. Perhaps special events can be organised to compensate for the relative scarcity of flowering plants in this season. The effect of extending the opening season on fixed costs will also have to be evaluated.

Promotion has focused on display advertising. Perhaps these display advertisements have the wrong message (heritage and restoration) and are placed in the wrong magazine (Heritage Gardens). Evidence from the survey supports this. Only 5% of visits were prompted by the expensive advertisements in the Heritage Gardens magazine. Again, focusing on heritage rather than a peaceful garden experience might be the fundamental issue here. HGT needs to reconsider its message and how it can be effectively communicated.

Publicity and public relations have been particularly poor. The work in the garden has not been recorded in the local press. Consequently, many of the people in the local area are not aware of the garden. HGT needs to actively engage with local newspapers, local radio and tourist agencies to raise its profile. The recent articles written by the trust's administrator have been one of the main reasons prompting visits to the garden. However, it has taken a crisis within the trust to prompt it to use this relatively simple form of promotion.

The internet also has many possibilities. At present the site is relatively static, concentrating again on the restoration of the gardens and stressing their historical importance. There is no interaction with the user. HGT should reconsider the design and content of the site. Again it needs to ensure that the message about the experience is relevant. There is also an opportunity to use the internet to build a community to support the gardens and perhaps this can be part of the service offered to those taking up annual membership, introduced in the short-term suggestions. The internet also provides an opportunity to:

- Reconsider the pricing structure. Perhaps discounts could be given for pre-booking. Pricing may be differentiated by age. Currently there is one price per visit. Lower prices could be offered to the elderly, children and those on state support benefits.

- Providing *physical evidence* – showing visitors through webcams and videos the type of experience that they will get by visiting the garden.

- Improving the process of purchasing tickets, particularly in applying for an annual membership.

Answer 11 AUTOFONE

(a)   **Competitive environment analysis**

Introduction

One possible approach to answering this question is provided by using Michael Porter's five forces framework. The framework is designed to analyse "the structure of an industry and its competitors" (Porter). There are five inter-connecting forces in the framework; potential entrants (the threat of entry), the bargaining power of suppliers, the bargaining power of buyers, the threat of substitutes and the competitive rivalry that exists amongst existing organisations in the industry. Each of these is now considered in turn in the context of AutoFone, focusing on those factors that have a significant effect on their industry.

Tutorial note: Other models might have been used in framing this answer and credit would be given for using appropriate models in the context of the AutoFone retail shops division.

Potential entrants (the threat of entry)

New entrants into an industry bring new capacity and resources with which they aim to gain market share. Their entry may lead to price reductions, increased costs and reduced profitability for organisations already in that market. Potential entrants may be deterred by high barriers to entry and by the threat of aggressive retaliation from existing competitors in the industry. In the context of AutoFone's retail sales business, the following barriers appear to be the most significant:

Access to supply channels

The retail outlets of AutoFone were established before the network providers developed their own retail outlets. At the time, the network providers were sceptical that mobile phones could be sold through shops. Consequently, AutoFone was able to negotiate favourable long-term supply deals. It now seems unlikely that the network providers would sign such deals (because the new entrant will be a competitor of their own retail business) and, if they did, any deals would be at less favourable terms. As the managing director of one of the networks suggested, "AutoFone had got away with incredible profit margins" when they signed the original deals. Improved supply terms would be attractive to the network provider and phone manufacturers (who would increase their profitability on each unit sold) but it would also cause profitability problems for the new entrant. Furthermore, the provision of networks is currently highly regulated, with licences still having 13 years to run. It seems unlikely that public policy restricting the number of network providers allowed to provide services will change in the foreseeable future and so access to supply channels will remain a very significant barrier to entry.

Economies of scale

Economies of scale deter entry by forcing the new entrant to come in at such a large scale that they risk strong reaction from existing firms in the marketplace. In the context of AutoFone, these economies of scale are associated with purchasing, service and distribution of products through a large scale retail network of 415 shops. Any new entrant would have to enter at a scale that would incur relatively significant capital investment. Furthermore, evidence suggests that the AutoFone brand is well known in the market place, with consumers having identified it as one of the "top 20" brands in the country. New entrants would not only have to fund a large number of retail outlets, they would also have to support their entry by investing heavily in "un-recoverable up-front advertising" (Porter). Capital will also be required for establishing significant inventories in the large number of retail shops required to achieve the required economies of scale.

Bargaining power of suppliers

Suppliers exert bargaining power over participants in an industry by raising prices or reducing the quality of their goods and services. Suppliers tend to be powerful when the industry is dominated by a few companies. This is the case with the mobile phone industry where the supply of networks is dominated by relatively few suppliers. The potential role of suppliers restricting the supply channel has already been recognised as a barrier to entry. However, when supplier power is high, there is a possibility that the suppliers themselves will seek forward integration, with "suppliers competing directly with their buyers if they do not obtain the prices, and hence the margins that they seek" (Johnson, Scholes and Whittington). This is exactly the situation affecting AutoFone, with network suppliers now running their own retail outlets.

There are two further elements of the retail phone market which encourage the supplier group to exert significant power. These are:

■ The supplier group does not have to contend with other substitute products for sale to the industry. There are few direct substitutes for the mobile phone (see below).

■ The supplier's product is an important input to the buyer's business. In AutoFone's situation it is a vital input into the business.

Hence the bargaining power of suppliers is extremely high in AutoFone's retail industry, although this is reduced by AutoFone's long-term supply contracts.

Bargaining power of buyers

Buyers attempt to obtain lower prices or seek to get increased or better quality services or products. They do this by playing competitors off against each other. Under certain conditions a buyer group can have considerable influence. Many of these conditions only arise when the buyer itself is an organisation, not an individual consumer. For example, Porter suggests that buyer power is high when there is a credible threat of the buyer integrating backwards into the market place and so becoming a competitor. Such conditions do not appear to apply to the retail phone industry which is largely aimed at individual consumers.

However, some of the circumstances of significant buyer bargaining power do appear to exist in the industry. For example: *the products which buyers are purchasing are standard or undifferentiated.* Buyers are always sure that they can find an alternative supplier and so they can play one supplier off against another. This is the case for sale of mobile phones as a whole, not just the retail sector. Furthermore, *buyers face few switching costs.* The only real lock-in is the term of the contract, currently 12 months long, after which buyers can switch to a competitor without penalty.

Threat of substitutes

Substitute products are usually products that can perform the same *function* as the product of the industry under consideration. The threat to the mobile phone industry is largely from other products that support mobile communication, such as tablet computers. However, the . products offered by AutoFone include mostly smart phones that are also mp3 players, radios, cameras and allow email and web access. Hence the industry appears to be relatively free of potential substitutes.

Competitive rivalry in the industry

Rivalry normally always takes place in an industry. Rivals jockey for position by reducing prices, launching advertising campaigns and improving customer service or product warranty. In the context of the retail mobile phone industry, the intensity of the rivalry is fuelled by:

Equally balanced competitors. The information in Table 2 suggests that the retail sales market is relatively equally divided between the five main suppliers. Evidence suggests this creates instability in the market because the companies are "prone to fight each other and have the resources for sustained and vigorous retaliation" (Porter).

Lack of differentiation or switching costs. Mobile phones are largely perceived by customers as commodities. In such circumstances buyer choice is based on price and service, and this results in intense pressure for price and service competition.

Slowing industry growth. Evidence from Table 2 also suggests that industry growth is slowing considerably. There was less than 1% growth last year. This means that competitors will increasingly pursue growth by increasing market share. This will intensify the rivalry between the competitors.

(b) **Support for retaining retail shops division**

The two longest serving directors of AutoFone have suggested that the retail business should be divested and that AutoFone should re-position itself as an on-line retailer of phones. They argue that an organisation concentrating solely on Internet sales and insurance would be a "smaller but more profitable" organisation. The CEO is vehemently opposed to such a strategy because it was the shop-based approach to selling mobile phones that formed the original basis of the company. He has strong emotional attachment to the retail business. The two directors claim that this attachment is clouding his judgement and hence he is unable to see the logic of an "economically justifiable exit from the retail business".

Tutorial note: *This question asks the candidate to draft a supporting case for the CEO's position, so that his response is not just seen to be based on emotional attachment. The briefing paper should challenge the suggestion of the two directors and provide a reasoned case for opposing the divestment of the retail sales business. Of course, divestment might be the best option. The four network providers might pay a handsome price to remove AutoFone from the market. However, this is not the focus of the question!*

Briefing paper

Introduction

This paper begins by looking at the basis of the directors' suggestion and claims that they have not interpreted the business situation correctly. It then goes on to examine the exit barriers that AutoFone must consider if they are to seriously consider moving out of the retail sales market.

Product and industry life cycles

It has to be recognised that industries and products move through life cycles. The slowdown in market growth documented in table 2 suggests that, in the context of the product life cycle model, the mobile phone market appears to be in either the shake-out or maturity stage. This means that buyers will be increasingly selective and that for many buyers the purchase will be a repeat event affected by previous experience. Companies in the market will have to fight to gain market share and the emphasis will increasingly be on efficiency and low cost.

Similarly, industries pass from rapid growth into the more modest growth associated with industry maturity. Like most infant industries the mobile phone industry experienced rapid growth as it developed. However, evidence from table 2 and table 3 suggests that both growth and profits are now reducing as the industry matures. Slowing growth in the industry means that there is more competition for market share as companies seek to maintain their own growth at the expense of others. The transition to maturity usually means that the old "way of life" of the company has to change. It is significant that the idea for divestment has come from the two longest serving directors. They can recall the excitement associated with rapid growth and, in the case of AutoFone, the pioneering of a business idea. In many ways the current expansion of AFDirect recalls the early period of AutoFone and so operating in the growing Internet market appeals to them.

Financial analysis

An analysis of Table 3 shows how profitability has fallen. The ROCE has steadily declined from over 18% five years ago to just over 5% last year. Net profit margin has fallen from just over 12% to just over 3% over the same period. Gross profit margins have not fallen quite as much as this. However, liquidity has remained almost constant during this period and so the ability of the company to meet its short term financial obligations has not been impaired by the fall in profitability. Gearing has risen during the period, from just over 21% to just over 32% and this reflects increased dependence on borrowed money. However, the absolute level of gearing should probably not be a cause for concern.

Porter suggests that one of the issues of the transition to a mature market is that directors have to scale down their expectations of financial performance. "If managers try to meet the old standards, they may take actions that are extremely dysfunctional for the long-term health of the company." The concern is that the two directors are pursuing such a policy, giving up too quickly and sacrificing a market and market share in favour of a course of action that they believe will deliver short-term profits. Divestment means that they are avoiding the challenges of taking a business like AutoFone into its mature stage.

Industry structure

Evidence from the analysis of AutoFone's competitive position (part a) suggests that AutoFone is in a retail industry dominated by powerful suppliers. Customer bargaining power is also relatively strong and reduced growth in the industry has led to relatively fierce competition. However, there is little threat from substitutes or new entrants because of the high entry barriers. Consequently, AutoFone is in a unique position based on its early entry into the market before the network providers became aware of the potential of retail sales. Furthermore, the company's uniqueness is enhanced by the fact that it is the only retail outlet to offer genuinely independent advice. The two directors appear to wish to carry on in the old way rather than changing strategy and expectations to reflect the maturing of the product and the industry. The real challenge for the board is to exploit AutoFone's unique market position in this changing landscape.

Exit barriers

Exit barriers are economic, strategic and emotional factors that keep companies competing in industries in which they are earning low or even negative returns. These are the barriers concerned with preventing the company from leaving the industry. In the context of AutoFone there are at least two potential non-emotional exit barriers which need to be considered.

Costs associated with leaving the industry

- The high cost of terminating shop leases. AutoFone achieved low start-up costs by taking on very long leases. These leases are often in areas just outside the main shopping areas and so may be difficult to re-let.

- The high cost of staff redundancies and the liquidation of stock. There are currently 1,400 employees in the retail shops division.

Loss of strategic interrelationship with other parts of the company

The divestment of the retail shops business is likely to have an important effect on the two remaining divisions (AFDirect and AFInsure) in at least two ways.

Reduced brand perception. Research has shown that AutoFone is a well-recognised brand. However, most of this brand awareness was built by the retail shops division. The brand is also being constantly reinforced by consumers seeing and visiting these shops. Removing these will lose this reinforcement. Indeed if shops lie empty (because of the difficulty of re-letting shops with long leases) it could harm the brand. Customers may perceive that AutoFone is a company in trouble (or indeed has ceased trading altogether) and so the Internet and insurance arms suffer as a result.

Reduced sell-on into related businesses. Evidence (from table 2) suggests that most insurance sales are in the age bands which predominantly purchase from the retail shops. Hence it seems likely that most insurance sales result from the sales of mobile phones in the retail sales operation. There are probably two reasons for this:

(1)   Retail sales are mainly to customers in a certain age group. These customers are less confident in their purchase (which is why they are visiting the shop) and as a result can be guided in the purchase of insurance.

(2)   Sales assistants giving this advice are given commission incentives to sell insurance. Consequently, the closing of the shops may have a major effect on the income of the insurance business.

There is also the issue of the cross-selling benefits between the retail sales and Internet sales business. There is evidence to suggest that some customers visit a retail branch to physically see the phones and to get advice before ordering on the Internet. This is currently an issue for staff in the shops who spend time explaining the features of a particular phone only to see the potential customer leave and order the same item on the Internet. Of course not all of these Internet orders are made through AFDirect because customers may take advantage of better offers from rival suppliers. However, a percentage of those sales must be as a result of a shop visit and the company potentially loses the benefit of these goodwill sales as a result of closing their shops. There is also evidence that Internet customers value the option of visiting a shop to get after-sales service for a product bought from AFDirect over the Internet. Although sales staff currently dislike offering this service, removing it may again hit Internet sales.

Conclusion

The company needs to recognise that the mobile phone market has matured and this has implications for both growth and profits. However, AutoFone remains in good shape to exploit the opportunities of a maturing market place (e.g. repeat buying). Although profitability has declined, liquidity has remained constant. Gearing has increased but it has not risen to a figure which would cause concern. There are significant exit barriers to leaving the market place. The most significant of these is the loss of a strategic interrelationship with other parts of the company. The Internet division could suffer significantly if AutoFone closed its retail shops division.

Answer 12 MOOR FARM

(a)   **Evaluation of the strategic position of the estate**

Many issues will need to be considered in the formulation of a strategy for the estate. However, in the context of the scenario, special attention will have to be paid to the expectations of stakeholders, to external environmental factors beyond the control of the estate and to the strategic capabilities of the estate itself. These are now considered in turn.

Expectations of stakeholders

Any proposed strategy will have to take into account the expectations of many stakeholders, some of which have conflicting objectives. From an internal perspective, the strategy has to take into account the objectives of volunteers who make up 90% of the workforce. Any strategy that alienates volunteers may leave the charity unable to maintain the estate or meet its basic operational obligations. Volunteers have different objectives to a paid workforce and these needs have to be understood. Replacing volunteers is not as straightforward as replacing a paid workforce, where scarce labour can be attracted through improved pay and conditions.

Most organisations have relatively straightforward relationships with their customers. Providing a service or product to one customer rarely conflicts with offering a service or product to another. Where it does conflict, for example in providing audit and consultancy services, a supplier can usually elect not to supply the customer, who then looks elsewhere for a similar service. In the case of Moor Farm, potential customers do conflict. There are documented examples of cyclists clashing with walkers and dog walkers with farmers. Access to the land is free (a stipulation of the charitable bequest) and so it is difficult to exclude potential customers. Consequently, a strategy has to be developed that is sensitive to the conflicting needs of customers, within the constraints of the charitable bequest.

Finally, the Moor Farm estate also surrounds two villages where private homeowners are angry about the increasing number of visitors to certain parts of the estate. Attractions have been created, causing traffic problems. As well as having a moral responsibility to these homeowners, the estate also depends, to some extent, on rental income from some of the houses in these villages. Again, residents need to be considered in the definition of the estate's strategy.

External environmental issues

The estate needs to continually scan the external environment to identify issues that might affect its situation. Strategy may have to be developed to either exploit or reflect these external changes, most of which are outside the control of the estate. At best, it can only lobby those responsible for creating these influences.

In the scenario, mention is made of a changed political landscape where government funding is to be reduced on initiatives such as tree planting, protected pasture land and rural employment. This will affect the income of the estate. Changes in weather patterns are also causing problems for the mansion that is situated in the estate. Built originally to resist cold dry weather typical of the time, it has proved susceptible to the warmer, wetter winters now experienced in this part of the country. This is causing long-term maintenance issues as the fabric of the mansion deteriorates.

Finally, the population of the country is increasingly vocal about the "rights" of individuals. The survey suggests that individuals believe that they have a "right to roam" on private land, even when this violates the "rights" of others (e.g. farmers and other land users). The estate has to take into account this social trend and potential stakeholder conflicts in its planned strategy.

Strategic capability

Finally, the strategy has to take into account the internal resources and competencies of the estate. The estate has significant tangible resources (e.g. land and property). It also has a unique resource, the only landscape garden developed by James Kent in the district. This is a unique resource which the strategy should aim to exploit. There are also other internal capabilities that should be recognised. A happy, motivated volunteer workforce must be properly utilised by any strategic change, not alienated. Amongst these are volunteers with exceptional skills in land management which could be used to exploit other opportunities on similar estates in the country. Leadership style also needs to be considered. The previous manager was well-liked and successful. Any sudden change in style may cause disruption and a fall in morale. The new leader has to be sensitive to her predecessor's leadership style, whilst building on the success of the previous leader by improving the visitor experience.

The estate has valuable and, in some cases, unique resources, which it needs to exploit with a varied set of stakeholders who sometimes come into conflict with each other. A stakeholder analysis, leading to appropriate stakeholder management policies, seems key here, and may provide some insights into how the website might be improved (see part (b)). One of these stakeholders, the government, needs to be particularly monitored, as their policies threaten the funding of the trust.

(b)   Development of the website

There is little point in having a well-designed website if it is difficult to find. The role of search engines is significant here. Moor Farm needs to be near the top of the search engine listings for search terms that are directly relevant. The estate needs to discuss what these terms might be. "Moor Farm" is an obvious one, but searches such as "walking in rural Cornaille" may bring in visitors who are not aware of the estate's existence. There is conflicting advice on how to structure a website to achieve a high position in a search engine listing. One fool-proof way is to buy sponsored links which are shown as such at the top of the displayed page. Some commercial organisations are dubious about the value of such links, but they seem completely appropriate in the context of a charitable estate.

Although the website is well regarded and well presented, it does not appear to have weather feeds that would avoid people coming on days when the weather was so poor that it might be dangerous, or, as in the quote, when it might spoil a family's enjoyment. The website may have a weather forecast, a feed on current conditions, and perhaps webcams showing the actual weather at a number of agreed locations. Of course, these feeds and webcams will also show good weather conditions as well, perhaps enticing people to the estate who were prevaricating about their visit.

The website currently shows information about events, but it does not allow customers to book these events. The interactivity of the site has to be improved, allowing customers to book and pay in advance, so that they can be sure that they will be able to attend the event and avoid the disappointment of the family who travelled 100 km only to find the event fully booked. Such a facility also has advantages for the estate. For example, it has some feel about the popularity of the event before it is run, so that the scale of the event can be altered to reflect the likely demand. Furthermore, payment is received in advance, thus improving cash flow.

Feedback from satisfied customers can be an important factor in attracting new customers. At present the site does not appear to allow visitors to post comments, photographs and recommendations. This means that an effective marketing tool, unsolicited recommendations, do not appear on the site. Comment has also been made about the enthusiasm and knowledge of the volunteers. This could be harnessed on the site by asking volunteers to write blogs, explaining what they are doing and what is going on. This could be linked through to Twitter and other social networking sites.

Finally, there is obviously a group of regular visitors to Moor Farm who wish to become more involved. As the quotation suggests "we really want to know what is going on!". The website can be used to develop a community that supports and promotes the estate. This could be achieved by asking users to register with their email address. They will then receive newsletters, special offers and information about forthcoming events. Special events can be offered to this community and part of the website can be set aside for members of this community. Not only will this provide the estate with valuable resource, it will also allow them to build up a marketing profile of likely visitors and, through surveys and questionnaires, continue to understand what different types of visitor want from the estate.

Answer 13 DRB ELECTRONIC SERVICES

(a)   **Primary activities of DRB**

On a value chain

Handling and storing inbound fully configured equipment Quality inspection	Re-branding of products Re-packaging of products	Customer collection Technician delivery and installation	Local advertising Web-based enquiries	On-site technical support Back to base support
Inbound logistics	**Operations**	**Outbound logistics**	**Marketing and sales**	**Service**

Significant and value

Inbound logistics: Excellent quality assurance is required in inbound logistics. This is essential for pre-configured equipment where customers have high expectations of reliability. As well as contributing to customer satisfaction, high quality also reduces service costs.

Operations: This is a relatively small component in the DRB value chain and actually adds little value to the customer. It is also being undertaken in a relatively high cost country. DRB might wish to re-visit the current arrangement.

Outbound logistics: Customer feedback shows that this is greatly valued. Products can be picked up from stock and delivery and installation is provided if required. Most of the company's larger competitors cannot offer this service. However, it is unlikely that this value can be retained when DRB begins to increasingly supply outside the geographical region it is in.

Marketing and sales: This is very low-key at DRB and will have to be developed if the company is to deliver the proposed growth. The limited functionality of the website offers little value to customers.

Service: Customer feedback shows that this is greatly valued. Most of the company's competitors cannot offer this level of service. They offer support from off-shore call centres and a returns policy that is both time consuming to undertake and slow in rectification. However, it is unlikely that this value can be retained when DRB begins to increasingly supply outside the geographical region it is in.

(b)   **Restructuring upstream supply chain**

DRB has already gained efficiencies by procuring products through the supplier's website. However, the website has restricted functionality. When DRB places the order it is not informed of the expected delivery date until it receives the confirmation email from ISAS. It is also unable to track the status of their order and so it is only when it receives a despatch email from ISAS that it knows that it is on its way.

Because DRB is not the owner of the shipment, it is unable to track the delivery and so the physical arrival of the goods cannot be easily predicted. On occasions where shipments have appeared to have been lost, DRB has had to ask ISAS to track the shipment and report on its status. This has not been very satisfactory and the problem has been exacerbated by having two shippers involved. ISAS has not been able to reliably track the transhipment of goods from their shipper to EIF, the logistics company used to distribute their products in the country. Some shipments have been lost and it is time-consuming to track and follow-up shipments which are causing concern. Finally, because DRB has no long term contract with ISAS, it has to pay when it places the order through a credit card transaction on the ISAS website.

DRB has stated that it wishes to continue importing fully configured products. It is not interested in importing components and assembling them. It also does not wish to build or invest in assembly plants in other countries. However, it may wish to consider the following changes to its upstream supply chain:

- Seek to identify a wider range of suppliers and so trade through other sell-side websites. Clearly there are costs associated with this. Suppliers have to be identified and evaluated and financial and trading arrangements have to be established. However, it removes the risk of single-sourcing and other suppliers may have better systems in place to support order and delivery tracking.

- Seek to identify suppliers who are willing and able to re-brand and package their products with DRB material at the production plant. This should reduce DRB costs as this is currently undertaken in a country where wage rates are high.

- Re-consider the decision not to negotiate long-term contracts with suppliers (including ISAS) and so explore the possibility of more favourable payment terms. DRB has avoided long-term contracts up to now. It may also not be possible to enter into such contracts if DRB begins to trade with a number of suppliers.

- Seek to identify suppliers (including ISAS) who are able to provide information about delivery dates prior to purchase and who are able to provide internet-based order tracking systems to their customers. This should allow much better planning.

- Consider replacing the two supplier shippers with a contracted logistics company which will collect the goods from the supplier and transport the goods directly to DRB. This should reduce physical transhipment problems and allow seamless monitoring of the progress of the order from despatch to arrival. It will also allow DRB to plan for the arrival of goods and to schedule its re-packaging.

DRB might also wish to consider two other procurement models; buy-side and the independent marketplace.

In the buy-side model DRB would use its website to invite potential suppliers to bid for contract requirements posted on the site. This places the onus on suppliers to spend time completing details and making commitments. It should also attract a much wider range of suppliers than would have been possible through DRB searching sell-side sites for potential suppliers. Unfortunately, it is unlikely that DRB is large enough to host such a model. However, it may wish to prototype it to see if it is viable and whether it uncovers potential suppliers who have not been found in sell-side websites searches.

In the independent marketplace model, DRB places its requirements on an intermediary website. These are essentially B2B electronic marketplaces which allow, on the one hand, potential customers to search products being offered by suppliers and, on the other hand, customers to place their requirements and be contacted by potential suppliers. Such marketplaces promise greater supplier choice with reduced costs.

They also provide an opportunity for aggregation where smaller organisations (such as DRB) can get together with companies that have the same requirement to place larger orders to gain cheaper prices and better purchasing terms. It is also likely that such marketplaces will increasingly offer algorithms that automatically match customers and suppliers, so reducing the search costs associated with the sell-side model. The independent marketplace model may be a useful approach for DRB. Many of the suppliers participating in these marketplaces are electronics companies.

(c) **Restructuring downstream supply chain**

DRB's downstream supply chain is also very simple at the moment. It has a web-site that shows information about DRB products. Customers can make enquiries about the specification and availability of these products through an e-mail facility.

Conventional marketing is undertaken through local advertising and buyers either collect their products or they are delivered and installed by a specialist group of technicians. DRB could tune its downstream supply chain by using many of the approaches mentioned in the previous section. For example:

- Developing the website so that it not only shows products but also product availability. Customers would be able to place orders and pay for them securely over the website. The site could be integrated with a logistics system so that orders and deliveries can be tracked by the customer. DRB must recognise that most of its competitors already have such systems. However, DRB will have to put a similar system in place to be able to support its growth plans.

- Participating in independent marketplace websites as a supplier. DRB may also be able to exploit aggregation by combining with other suppliers in consortia to bid for large contracts.

- DRB may also consider participating in B2C marketplaces such as e-bay. Many organisations use this as their route to market for commodity products.

DRB may also wish to consider replacing its sales from stock approach with sales from order. In the current approach, DRB purchases products in advance and re-packages and stores these products before selling them to customers. This leads to very quick order fulfilment but high storage and financing costs. These costs will become greater if the planned growth occurs. DRB may wish to consider offering products on its website at a discount but with specified delivery terms. This would allow the company to supply to order rather than supply from stock.

Answer 14 iCOMPUTE

(a) **Analysis of the culture**

The culture of an organisation can be explored from a variety of perspectives and through a number of frameworks and models. No specific model or framework is required by the question so a variety of appropriate approaches are acceptable. This model answer uses selected elements of the cultural web.

Stories are told by employees in an organisation. These often concern events from the history of the organisation and highlight significant issues and personalities. In the context of iCompute, there is evidence of stories that celebrate the earlier years of the organisation when founder Ron Yeates had an important role. "Ron used to debate responsibility for requirements changes with the customer." In contrast modern management is perceived as weak, giving in too easily in negotiations with customers. Not only is this perceived weakness affecting morale, but it also appears to be affecting profit margins and this is an important consequence for the organisation.

Symbols include logos, offices, cars, titles and the type of language and terminology commonly used within the organisation. The language and symbols of technology appear to dominate at iCompute. Software developers constantly scan the horizon for new technological opportunities. They embrace these technologies and solutions and, as a result, continually distract the organisation. As soon as a technical direction or solution is agreed, or almost agreed, a new alternative is suggested causing doubt and delay. One of the managers claimed that the company was "in a state of constant technical paralysis". This paralysis has implications. Furthermore, technological objectives can quickly outweigh business and financial objectives, to the detriment of the company as a whole.

The perceived inability of managers to effectively participate in technological discussions is derided by software developers who suggest that they are technically out of touch. Ownership and understanding of up-to-date mobile phones is perceived to be important, particularly by the software developers who are an important and powerful group within the organisation.

Finally, the language of the manager who suggested that support should be outsourced is very illuminating. Support calls are not from customers but from "incompetent end users, too lazy to read user guides". Re-focusing managers on customers appears to be long overdue.

Routines and rituals concern the "way we do things around here". At iCompute this involves long working hours and after-work social activities such as football, socialising and playing computer games. The latter of these reinforces the technical focus (discussed in symbols) of employees. The routines and rituals of the organisation are largely male-oriented (football, computer games) and would probably exclude most females. This would almost certainly contribute to the company's inability to recruit and retain women employees. Furthermore, long working hours and after-work activities will also alienate employees who have to get home to undertake family commitments or simply do not wish to be "one of the lads". This must contribute to almost one-third of all employees leaving within their first year at the company. The consequence of this culture is an expensive recruitment and training process.

The *control systems* of the organisation include measurement and reward systems. Within iCompute technical expertise is only rewarded to a certain organisational level. To earn more, technically adept employees have to become managers. Evidence appears to suggest that many are unsuited to management, unable to deal appropriately with their former peers. These managers also seem anxious to show that their technical expertise is not diminishing, emphasising the importance of technology as a symbol within the organisation. Consequently, they often try to demonstrate this expertise (e.g. through programming) but are unaware that this brings derision rather than respect. The absence of measurement systems has recently been recognised by management within the company. This has led to the initiation of an in-house project to improve time recording. However, software developers within the company see this as an unwelcome initiative.

Paradigm and discussion

Initially, iCompute was an entrepreneurial organisation with a significant work ethic based on long hours, technical innovation and competitive management. Although the organisation has superficially matured, the stories told by employees and the recruitment and retention of similarly minded people, has led to the continuation of a male-oriented, technologically focused workforce managed by unprepared and unsuitable managers. Managers' reaction to conflict is to avoid it (agreeing with customers over requirements), outsource it (software support) or put in formal computer systems to control it (the implementation of a time recording system). The failure to recruit and retain female staff appears to be a direct consequence of the organisational culture of iCompute. The "work hard, play hard work ethic" is only suitable for employees with certain objectives, characteristics and minimal childcare responsibilities. This culture needs to change if the company is to employ a more balanced and representative workforce that is focused on business rather than technological objectives.

(b) **Suitability of approach to high level processes**

The question does not suggest an appropriate framework to use in the candidate's answer. This model answer uses the Harmon process-strategy grid as its reference point. However, credit would be given for any appropriate alternative framework.

The primary purpose of the Harmon process-strategy matrix is to ensure that organisations focus their process redesign efforts in the most appropriate areas. The grid has two axes. One is concerned with process complexity and the other with strategic importance. For each quadrant of the grid Harmon suggests appropriate solution options. For example, straightforward commodity processes with low process complexity and low strategic importance should be either outsourced or automated, using a commercial off-the-shelf software package. Elements of this grid can be applied to the three high level process applications identified at iCompute.

Advice on legal issues Bespoke systems development is risky. There is evidence in the scenario of litigation between iCompute and two of its customers. Contracts have to be carefully worded and advice taken to head off or manage legal disputes. Although iCompute is considering moving this process in-house, it seems unlikely that it will be able to afford, attract or motivate an internal legal team. Advice on legal issues could be classified as a process of high complexity and low strategic importance on the process/strategy matrix. Consequently, it seems that continuing the outsourcing arrangement should be the preferred option. The current supplier employs experts who keep up-to-date in an increasingly complex field. They can also advise on employee legislation.

Software support is provided by the company to support both its bespoke and package solutions. This used to be organised in-house, but was outsourced a year ago. Subsequent customer feedback has been poor, but even without this feedback, it could be argued that outsourcing was a poor decision. Service is one of the primary activities of Porter's value chain. It directly influences the customer's perception of the supplier and the likelihood of a repeat purchase. In the context of iCompute, feedback from end users to their managers is likely to influence future software purchasing decisions. Consequently, not only is support relatively complex (as acknowledged by the manager who made the outsourcing decision) but it is also of strategic importance to iCompute. This suggests that iCompute should bring support back in-house, perhaps by the use of an automated system.

Time recording The management of iCompute requires much more detailed time recording information, showing how long employees have worked on certain tasks and projects. Some contracts are on a time and materials basis and time recording data is required for accurate and prompt billing. However, most contracts are on a fixed price basis and better internal information is required on which to build quotes for this type of work. The company has decided to develop software in-house to support this high level process. This appears to be a questionable decision for at least three reasons.

(1)   It uses resources which could be employed on external fee-earning contracts.

(2)   Accurate time recording is a key requirement in many professions (lawyers, accountants, etc) and it seems highly likely that a range of off-the-shelf packages would be available to fulfil their needs.

(3)   It could be argued that the application is a relatively simple low-value process in the process-strategy matrix and so should be carried out either through a software package or an outsourced solution.

Answer 15 RAMON SILVA

(a)   **Competitive advantage through differentiation**

> To: Ramon Silva
> From:

Value innovation in La Familia Amable hotel chain

In strategic terms you are looking to create a competitive advantage over existing hotels based on a cost focus strategy. Although, the success of this niche marketing strategy will depend on your ability to attract customers from the existing providers, there does seem a gap to exploit. In many ways you have an advantage in that you are not constrained by previous experience in the hotel industry and this has enabled you to look to deliver a significantly different value proposition to your customers and not simply look to marginally improve on what currently is on offer. One particular study on innovation drew attention to five dimensions of strategy where innovators can significantly outperform existing companies. This is important, as the industry does not look particularly attractive with low growth and overcapacity – a recipe for low profitability.

Industry assumptions – here existing companies take the competitive conditions as given whereas innovators are looking to influence and change those conditions.

Strategic focus – simply benchmarking against the current hotel providers may not create any real advantage, innovators are seeking to provide a step change in the experience given to the customer.

Customers – the route to success may not be through ever increasing segmentation and customisation but by actually looking to focus on the shared attributes of the service that customers value – a good night's sleep for a low price being a prime example.

Assets and capabilities – rather than looking to leverage existing assets and capabilities the innovator looks to ask what would we do if we were starting a new business.

Product and service offering – existing competitors may again be constrained in their thinking by the existing boundaries of the industry and the innovator by identifying new customers and services that take them outside this boundary may offer a "total solution" that transforms the industry. The "no frills", low cost budget airlines are a good example of such thinking.

In the hotel business "location, location, location" is argued to be at the heart of a successful strategy. Clearly this will be your choice and is affected by the customer groups you are looking to attract. Establishing a brand name and reputation is an important marketing strategy and this will be facilitated by growing the chain rapidly and giving customers easy access to your hotels. In value chain terms the company infrastructure looks to be lean with a reliance on trained husband and wife teams to deliver the service. Franchising would also seem to be a route to grow the business that will place reduced strain on company headquarters. The creation of a chain should lend itself to significant buying and procurement advantages, right from the design of the hotels which will focus on the core value you are providing – namely quiet and cost. One French hotel chain was able to cut in half the average cost of building a room, its "no frills" service cut staff costs from between 25% and 35% of sales – the industry average – to between 20% and 23%.

Good design will therefore affect the quality of service that the operations side of the value chain delivers to the customer. This may be a simpler service to that provided by its competitors – simpler, more basic rooms, no expensive restaurants or lounge areas all impact on the cost of operations and consequently the price charged. Marketing, as previously referred to above, is much more effectively done through satisfied customers' recommendations than by expensive advertising. Many hotel chains have used technology to create customer loyalty schemes of questionable benefit to the customer. You will certainly have to seriously consider the value of such an after sales service. The established competitors often make assumptions as to what a customer wants and typically this is offering more and more services that are expensive to provide. Your entry into a "mature" industry such as this, allows you to really challenge these assumptions and deliver a price/value combination that is hard to beat.

Yours,

(b) **Franchising**

Franchising is typically seen as a quick and cost effective way of growing the business but Ramon should be aware of both the advantages and disadvantages of using it as the preferred method of growth. Franchised chains are argued to benefit from the sort of brand recognition and economies of scale not enjoyed by independent owner/managers. When combined with the high levels of motivation normally associated with owner/managed businesses, franchises can be argued to get the best of both worlds.

Franchising is defined as "a contractual agreement between two legally independent companies whereby the franchisor grants the right to the franchisee to sell the franchisor's product or do business under its trademarks in a given location for a specified period of time. In return, the franchisee agrees to pay the franchisor a combination of fees, usually including an up-front franchise fee, royalties calculated as a percentage of unit revenues, and an advertising contribution that is also usually a percentage of unit sales."

Ramon is considering a type of franchising called "business-format franchising", where the franchisor sells a way of doing business to its franchisees. Business-format franchising is a model frequently found in the fast food and restaurant industry, hotels and motels, construction and maintenance and non-food retailing. Often these franchises are labour intensive and relatively small-scale operations.

Franchising is seen as a safer alternative to growing the business organically, so while this may be true of well-established global franchises, failure rates among franchised small businesses were greater than those of independent businesses (in one US study a 34.7% failure rate for franchises as opposed to 28.0% for independents over a six or seven-year period). Often it is the failure of the franchisor that brings down its franchisees. Failure stems from the franchisee not only having to rely on their own skills and enthusiasm but also the capacity of the franchisor and other franchisees to make the overall operation work.

The advantages to the franchisee are through gaining access to a well-regarded brand name that will generate a higher level of demand and use of a tried and tested business model that should reduce the franchisee's operating costs. Both of these benefits stem from being a member of a well-established franchised system. Yet La Familia Amable along with many other franchises will be new and small. These smaller franchises tend to be regional in scope and fairly unknown outside their regional market. This has a significant effect on what the franchisees can expect to gain from their franchisors and their prospects of success. Both parties need to carefully assess the strengths and weaknesses of the system. Companies growing via franchises need to take the time to understand their business model thoroughly and determine how franchising fits with their long-term strategy. Care must be taken with the franchise agreement that creates a genuine partnership with the right balance between freedom and control over the franchisees.

Answer 16 EXCALIBUR SPORTSWEAR

(a)   **Factors encouraging Excalibur to export or become an international organisation**

In order to appreciate why Excalibur might wish to become firstly an exporting company and ultimately a global company, involving itself in the ownership of manufacturing and distribution facilities overseas, it might be beneficial to adapt *Kenichi Ohmae's "3Cs* model".

(1)   *Customer*

It is apparent that Excalibur products appeal to a transnational market segment – probably young sports-aware consumers. This global interest is heightened by the use of world-renowned sporting personalities to promote the products. This approach typifies that of a geocentric company whereby products tend to be standardised because of a commonality of customer tastes. It is demand driven. This is unlike the polycentric style company which, believing every market to be different, customises its products to meet the different market demands. It is also different from the ethnocentric style company which standardises its products only for manufacturing savings and because it does not really understand the foreign markets. These companies can be considered to be supply-driven. Simon Smith understands the need for products with universal appeal. His products have an attraction throughout the world and there is a minimal need for change in the specifications. This approach also brings the company another advantage.

(2)   *Company*

By selling almost identical products into a wider array of markets Excalibur will be able to spread its fixed costs – promotion in particular – over a larger volume of sales. This will lower its costs and make it much more price competitive and allow the company to compete with other rivals more effectively. Any move that lowers its cost base has to be seen as an incentive for Excalibur to seek markets on a more global basis.

(3)   *Competition*

This is also an inducement to become more global in approach. If other competitors are developing a worldwide appeal it is important that Excalibur should also follow this strategy. It must not be seen as a parochial player. This could degrade the image that Smith has attempted to develop for his company. Furthermore, Smith may now have to consider some of his competitors as strategic allies. It is unlikely that his company can manufacture a total spread of sports clothing products alone. It will need to work in partnership with these rivals so that they can complement each other's product range. Consequently this is another inducement for Excalibur to consider involving itself in a global strategy. If Smith's close competitors are there, he will be expected to follow.

The above factors apply to many companies seeking to be involved in overseas marketing. The factors below relate more specifically to globally oriented companies.

The volatility of international currency movements may necessitate Smith setting the company up as a global company as distinct from an exporting company. By manufacturing and distributing from wholly or partially owned (as part of a joint venture) foreign subsidiaries Excalibur will minimise the problems that may be caused by changing currency exchange rates. A small and adverse movement in the exchange rate can have an inordinate impact upon profit margins. By paying for and selling goods at stable currency levels the company can avoid potential losses in this area.

Finally by being more economically active in particular countries Excalibur may obtain a number of benefits. The company may access cheaper labour and raw materials so improving its cost position. It may even be given access to cheaper development finance. Furthermore, by being resident in certain countries, it can be seen as an "insider". This image of being local can help Excalibur (despite there being few or no trade barriers) as frequently customers often prefer buying from suppliers who appear to be local or who at least have committed resources to their "home" market.

Tutorial note: *Although candidates may not choose to follow the Ohmae model the main criteria included above are likely be presented in any answer (i.e. transnational segmentation, the spreading of fixed costs, minimising currency volatility, accessing cheaper resources, appearing to be a local company).*

(b) **Changes to risk and resource requirements**

As Smith's firm, Excalibur, attempts to take more control of its activities by setting up wholly owned manufacturing and distribution facilities it alters its profile of both risk and resource commitment. Generally it is assumed that risk and resource commitment are positively correlated with control.

In this scenario Smith is hoping to increase his control over Excalibur by owning his own manufacturing and distribution facilities so controlling more closely the quality, delivery and marketing aspects of the value chain. In doing so he has reduced the risk of poor performance hindering his progress in these markets. He has also reduced the risk of losses resultant from adverse currency movements in those countries. However, conversely he has also increased other risks. He has now established more fixed assets in foreign markets. These are at risk if the market fails to expand as has been anticipated. There is also a slight risk of assets being expropriated in areas where military and political conflict may not be unknown. There is also a risk of a loss of reputation if the products do not meet the consumers' needs. In the former circumstances most of these losses would have been borne by the independent distributors, whereas now Excalibur will rightly be more closely associated with its products.

There is also a risk that this large increase in expenditure might overstretch Smith's financial resources. His known expertise is in design and promotion. By moving into manufacturing and distribution he could be moving out of his core competences. This may be an expansion too far. There are other ways of achieving growth without taking on the risks associated with organic development. A judicious use of strategic alliances might be preferable but this will raise another set of different risks. Whichever way Smith uses to grow he will encounter a new profile of risks. He has to judge which set will be the least threatening.

Consequently although Simon Smith will have greater control in some areas – he will be able to ensure that the quality, stock levels, presentation and marketing of his products are up to his required and expected standards – he will be less dependent upon other peoples' efforts – he will also discover that in some circumstances he will have less control. By generating supplies overseas he will have to rely on events and circumstances outside of his control. Environmental influences can be notoriously unpredictable. Smith is now going to have to depend upon issues such as economic and political conditions over which he has negligible control. Paradoxically his attempt to obtain increased control can effectively result in reduced control.

This proposed expansion into the new areas of manufacturing and distribution would inevitably require a greater commitment of resources from Excalibur. This commitment will be in a number of areas. As has already been discussed, there will be a need for an increased commitment of finance for the expansion of the enterprise. We know from the case scenario that this is likely to be forthcoming. However Excalibur has no expertise in these expanding areas and this must be acquired. Staff with a knowledge and understanding of these matters must be employed, so demonstrating an increased commitment to this expansion. As the business becomes more complex, control systems must be initiated and managed, requiring even more resources and attention.

What has not really been considered yet is the amount of extra time Smith and his staff must spend on these new activities. Although difficult to measure, this increased commitment in the time needed to set up and run the overseas enterprises may prove to be critical. There is a danger that this extra commitment might distract the company's attention from the current core business, so worsening aggregate performance.

Although Simon Smith's proposed strategy might provide his business with growth potential, the associated growth in risk and the widening of commitment, in all its forms, may not be acceptable nor even be advisable for Excalibur to contemplate. Such an expansion may promise high rewards rather quickly but at the expense of security which may, however, be maintained with a more conservative strategy.

Answer 17 AMBION

(a)   **Attractiveness to Swift of EVM as an acquisition target**

> **Tutorial note:** *The acquisition of EVM can be analysed using the success criteria of suitability, acceptability and feasibility.*

Suitability is concerned with whether a strategy addresses the issues identified when considering the strategic position of the company. In general terms the acquisition appears to make sense. The market is mature and competitive in Ambion, pushing down margins. These margins are further eroded by a government that is hostile to road transport resulting in high taxation on fuel, road taxes linked to carbon emission and restricted working practices. The acquisition of EVM provides an opportunity for Swift to exploit their core competencies in a different geographical market where demand is rising, the national government is investing in road infrastructure and competition is immature. The increased size of the group will further allow Swift to exploit economies of scale when purchasing trucks and other equipment.

Concerns around suitability surround the potential clash of cultures between Swift and EVM. Swift has no experience of acquiring or running foreign companies. It has no experience of trading in Ecuria. Furthermore, although EVM is now in private hands, it may be possible that the work practices and expectations of employees may still reflect the time when they were working for the central government. Although altering these practices may give scope for even greater profitability, it may lead to labour disputes that harm the service and reputation of the company. Swift wishes to acquire this company and adopt the practices, principles and technology of the Ambion operation. This may lead to conflict that they may find hard to resolve.

Acceptability is concerned with the expected performance of a strategy in terms of return, risk and stakeholder reactions.

Return: EVM delivers a very similar (18%) Return on Capital Employed (ROCE) to Swift Transport. This appears to be a strong performance for the sector, and should certainly be acceptable to the Swift shareholders. The gross profit margin (20%) is higher than Swift, but the net profit margin (7.5%) is lower. This may support some of the concerns discussed under suitability. The company may still be carrying high costs from its days as a nationalised company. Swift presumably believes that it can improve the net profit margin by implementing competences gained in the Ambion market.

Risk: Both the current liquidity ratio (1.14%) and the acid test ratio (1.05%) are lower than the Swift equivalents and Swift will need to look at this. The introduction of Swift's practices may help reduce trade payables. The gearing ratio (30%) for EVM is much lower than Swift and perhaps reflects a more conservative approach to long-term lending and a reflection of the fledgling capital markets in the country. However, the interest cover ratio (5) is half that of Swift, perhaps reflecting lower profitability and higher business taxation.

Stakeholders: Joe Swift and his family are the major stakeholders in what is still a family-run private limited company. It is unlikely that there will be any opposition to the acquisition from shareholders. However, stakeholders such as drivers might be wary of this strategy and also the government, outspokenly criticised by Joe, may also respond in some way (e.g. by imposing taxation on foreign investment).

Feasibility is about whether an organisation has the resources and competencies to deliver the strategy. It appears that Swift does, as funds are in place and the competences are what are partly driving the acquisition.

(b)   **Factors which could influence Swift's decision**

In his book *The Competitive Advantage of Nations*, Michael Porter suggests that there are inherent reasons why some nations are more competitive than others, and also why some industries within nations are more competitive than others. He suggests that the national home base of the organisation plays an important role in creating international advantage, something that will be very important to Joe Swift. He identifies four main determinants of national advantage and arranges these as a diamond, with each of these determinants interacting with and reinforcing each other. Two further determinants, chance and government, are discussed outside of the diamond in terms of how they influence and interact with the determinants inside the diamond.

Tutorial note: *This answer uses Porter's diamond as its basis. However, credit would also be given for alternative appropriate frameworks or models.*

The four main determinants are:

(1)   The nation's position in *factor conditions*, such as skilled labour or infrastructure, necessary for firms to compete in a given industry. The acknowledged work ethic of the people and the investment in transport infrastructure by the government are significant factor conditions in Ecuria.

(2)   The nature of the home *demand conditions* for the industry's product or service. Home demand influences economies of scale, but it also shapes the rate and character of improvement and innovation. In Ecuria, the move to a market economy has stimulated a rapid growth in the transport of goods. The Ecurian people are traditionally demanding in their standards. They have a passion for precision and promptness and this has shaped the operations of EVM.

(3)   The presence or absence of *related and supporting industries* that are internationally competitive. Competitive advantage in certain industries confers potential advantages on firms in other industries. Porter suggests that the "Swiss success in pharmaceuticals was closely connected to previous international success in the dye industry". There is no evidence in the case study that Ecuria has internationally competitive industries related to logistics. Hence, it is the absence of these that is significant when considering this determinant.

(4)   *Firm strategy, structure and rivalry* concerns the conditions in the nation governing how companies are created, organised and managed. It also considers the nature of domestic rivalry. EVM was created by nationalising the state-run haulage system. For the first few years of operation it had few competitors. The nature of the capital markets makes it very difficult to raise finance in Ecuria. Consequently, most of EVM's competitors are small, family-run companies who offer a local service. Porter suggests that there is a strong relationship between vigorous domestic rivalry and the creation and persistence of competitive advantage in an industry. There is little evidence of this emerging in Ecuria.

Porter also recognises the influence of chance and government. Chance events are developments outside the control of firms and the nation's government. Wars, external political developments and a reduction in foreign demand are all examples of chance factors. Government, in effect, helps shape the diamond by enacting policies that influence each of the determinants. In Ecuria, the government's approach to infrastructure investment and policies towards capital markets has affected factor conditions and impacted on firm structure and rivalry.

Answer 18 ENVIRONMENT MANAGEMENT SOCIETY

Context

The decline in the number of people taking the qualification appears to be a reflection of the maturity of the marketplace. The large pool of unqualified environmental managers and auditors that existed when the qualification was launched has now been exploited. There are now fewer candidates taking the examinations and fewer members joining the EMS. The organisation's response to this has been to look for international markets where it can promote the qualifications it currently offers. It hopes to find large pools of unqualified environmental managers and auditors in these markets.

The scenario suggests that EMS currently has relatively limited strategic ambitions. There is no evidence that EMS plans to develop new qualifications outside its current portfolio. Indeed, attempts to look at complementary qualifications (such as soil and water conservation) have been rejected by Council. Hence, expansion into new strategic business markets does not appear to be an option.

Strategy development

(a)   *Internal development*

Internal development takes place when strategies are developed by building on or developing the organisation's own capabilities. It is often termed organic growth. This is how EMS has operated up to now. The original certificates were developed by the founders of the Society. Since then, additional certificates have been added and the Diploma programme developed at the instigation of members and officers of the Society.

In many ways this type of organic growth is particularly suited to the configuration of the organisation, one where there is a risk-averse and cautious culture. The organic approach spreads cost and risk over time and growth is much easier to control and manage. However, growth can be slow and indeed, as in the case of EMS, may have ceased altogether.

Growth is also restricted by the breadth of the organisation's capabilities. For example, EMS has not been able to develop (or indeed even consider developing) any products outside of its fairly restricted product range. Furthermore, although internal development may be a reasonable strategy for developing a home market it maybe an inappropriate strategy for breaking into new market places and territories. This is particularly true when, as it appears in the case of the EMS, internal resources have no previous experience of developing products in overseas markets.

In summary, internal growth has been the method of strategy development at EMS up to now, based on a strategic direction of consolidation and market penetration. There is no evidence that EMS is considering developing new products to arrest the fall in qualification numbers. However, the Board has suggested developing new markets for the current qualification range and India, China and Russia have been identified as potential targets. It seems unlikely that internal development will be an appropriate method of pursuing this strategic direction.

(b)   *Mergers and acquisitions*

A strategy of acquisition is one where one organisation (such as EMS) takes ownership of other existing organisations in the target countries. One of the most compelling reasons for acquisition is the speed it allows an organisation to enter a new product or market area. EMS might look to acquire organisations already offering certification in its target markets. These organisations would then become the mechanism for launching EMS qualifications into these markets. In addition, it is likely that these organisations will have qualifications that the EMS does not currently offer. These qualifications could then be offered, if appropriate, in EMS's home market. This arrangement would provide EMS with the opportunity to quickly offer its core competences into its target markets, as well as gaining new competencies which it could exploit at home.

However, acquisitions usually require considerable expenditure at some point in time and evidence suggests that there is a high risk that they will not deliver the returns that they promised. It is unlikely that the EMS will have enough money to fund such acquisitions and its status as a private limited entity means that it cannot currently access the markets to fund such growth. Any acquisitions will have to be funded from its cash reserves or from private equity investment groups. Furthermore, acquisitions also bring political and cultural issues which evidence suggests the organisation would have difficulty with. Under achievement in mergers and acquisitions often results from problems of cultural fit. This can be particularly problematic with international acquisitions, which is exactly the type of acquisition under consideration here. So, although acquisitions are a popular way of fuelling growth it is unlikely that EMS will have either the cash or the cultural will to pursue this method of strategy development. There is no evidence that EMS has any expertise in acquiring organisations in its home market and so such acquisitions overseas would be extremely risky.

(c)   *Strategic alliances*

A strategic alliance takes place when two or more organisations share resources and activities to pursue a particular strategy. This approach has become increasingly popular for a number of reasons. In the context of EMS it would allow the organisation to enter into a marketplace without the large financial outlay of acquiring a local organisation. Furthermore, it would avoid the cultural dislocation of either acquiring or merging with another organisation. The motive for the alliance would be co-specialisation with each partner concentrating on the activities that best match their capabilities. Johnson, Scholes and Whittington suggest that co-specialisation alliances "are used to enter new geographic markets where an organisation needs local knowledge and expertise". This fits the EMS requirement exactly.

The exact nature of the alliance would require much thought and indeed different types of alliance might be forged in the three markets targeted by EMS.

■ A joint venture is where a new organisation is set up jointly owned by the parents. This is a formal alliance and will obviously take some time to establish. EMS will have to contribute cost and resources to the newly established company, but such costs and resources should be much less than those incurred in an acquisition. However, joint ventures take time to establish and it may be not be an option if EMS wants to quickly move into a target marketplace to speedily arrest its falling numbers.

■ A licence agreement could be an alternative where EMS licenses the use of its qualification in the target market. This could be organised in a number of ways. For example, a local organisation could market the EMS qualification as its own and pay EMS a fee for each issued certificate and diploma. Alternatively, the qualification may be marketed by the local organisation as an EMS qualification and EMS pays this organisation a licence fee for every certificate and diploma it issues in that country. This requires less commitment from EMS but it is likely to bring in less financial returns, with less control over how the qualification is marketed. Furthermore, if the qualification is successful, there is the risk that the local organisation will develop its own alternative so that it gains all the income from the transaction, not just a percentage of the transaction fee.

At first sight, the strategic alliance appears very appropriate to EMS's current situation. The licensing approach is particularly attractive because it seems to offer very quick access to new markets without any great financial commitment and without any cultural upheaval within EMS itself. However, the uptake of the qualification is unpredictable and the marketing and promotion of the qualification is outside the control of EMS. EMS may find this difficult to accept. Furthermore, the EMS will only be receiving a fraction of the income and so it must ensure that this fraction is sufficient to fuel growth expectations and service the newly qualified members in other countries. Finally, there is often a paradox in organisations where internal development has been the strategic method adopted so far. An organisation used to internal development and control often finds it difficult to trust partners in an alliance. Yet trust and cooperation is probably the most important ingredient of making such strategic alliances work.

Answer 19 GRAFFOFF

(a)   **Evaluation of franchising option at Graffoff**

Johnson and Scholes have identified franchising as a form of strategic alliance in their classification of methods of strategy development. In this approach, franchises are independently run businesses that would enter into a licence agreement with Graffoff to purchase training, equipment and materials in return for an exclusive geographical franchise area. The proposal is that the franchisee would buy or lease appropriate premises, not Graffoff as in Emile's organic expansion plan. Most franchises are required to make a large up-front payment, which would provide Emile with significant funds for investment or, indeed, for further dividend payments. There are also a number of avoided costs as franchisees usually pay for all the operating costs of the franchise.

Running their own business is usually sufficient to motivate the franchise owners and the motivation of any staff they employ is also their responsibility. Emile has already acknowledged that he is not a people person and so franchising neatly sub-contracts this issue. Thus, Emile could continue running Graffoff more or less as it is currently and he would avoid the problem of raising significant finance and managing a difficult period of expansion.

However, it is possible (but not inevitable) that the long-term returns to Graffoff might be lower than through directly owned or leased depots. Franchisees will take most of the profits and Graffoff will be dependent for income from materials supply and, usually, from a relatively small percentage of the franchise's annual sales specified in the licence contract. There are also important issues to consider in the appropriate selection and control of franchises. Although the initial fee will be received by Graffoff irrespective of the franchise's success, continuing income (and brand awareness) is dependent upon the success of the franchise. Graffoff has no experience in selecting appropriate franchisees, neither is there any evidence that it has systems in place to control quality and audit performance. These would be needed to ensure that the product is being used correctly and that the correct percentage of sales is being paid to Graffoff. Such systems will need investment and development and need to be in place before the franchise scheme is launched.

Furthermore, the success of franchises is often determined by the visibility of the brand. Emile himself recognises that Graffoff has a very low profile and he acknowledges that he has very little expertise in this area. Also, it would be obvious to potential franchisees that it may be difficult to maintain sales volumes once the patent has expired. Thus, there may be problems in attracting franchisees, particularly those willing to invest a significant amount for a product which, they may consider, has a relatively short lifetime and whose brand awareness is low. Emile could address the first of these issues by employing marketing expertise and launching vigorous campaigns. He might also address the patent issue by looking at improving the product. Thus focusing on product development (what he is good at) and not business expansion, where he has little experience and interest.

Although franchising appears to reduce financial risk, it is unlikely to produce the financial returns as quickly as the internal growth option. Emile must not underestimate the time taken to draw up the licence agreement, develop systems to support the franchise and recruit and appoint franchisees. He must also accept that some franchises are likely to fail and that returns will be low in the early years of operation as the fledgling franchises seek to establish themselves as viable independent companies.

(b)   **Evaluation of other types of strategic alliance at Graffoff**

> **Tutorial note:** *A range of strategic alliances could be considered. Two are explicitly evaluated in the model answer. However, appropriate alternatives would be given credit.*

Strategic alliances take place where two or more organisations share resources and activities to pursue a strategy. Many organisations recognise that they need to acquire materials, skills, innovation, finance or access to markets, and increasingly recognise that these may be more readily obtained through cooperation rather than ownership. The franchising option is a type of alliance, and Emile sees it as a way of funding his expansion without incurring employee motivational and management issues that he is not confident in addressing.

In terms of Graffoff, the motivation for an alliance is likely to be *co-specialisation*, where each partner concentrates on activities that best match their capabilities. Graffoff specialises in product design and product development. Its weaknesses, in the context of the planned expansion, appear to lie in marketing, retail and finance. Franchising has already been considered as a type of alliance. Another type of alliance that Emile might consider is a *joint venture*, where a new organisation is set up jointly owned by its parents. It is often used by companies to enter a new geographical market where one of the companies provides the expertise and the other local knowledge and labour. This is not the case here, where expansion is within the country. Furthermore, there is no obvious candidate for a joint venture and, even if a partner could be found, it would take time to establish a contractual relationship. Emile, as an entrepreneur, might also find it difficult to work within a framework of a joint venture where he would need to cede a certain amount of control.

In a *network arrangement*, two or more organisations work in collaboration without a formal relationship. The Equipment Emporium already has 57 superstores in the country selling tools and machines. Emile rebuffed their initial advance offering to sell his product in the store, because of the need for mandatory product training. However, he might return to them and offer to set up small in-store outlets where his product could be demonstrated and its services sold. The Equipment Emporium would be paid a fee, but such an approach would, in essence, be the same as his organic growth plan but without the need for large scale capital investment. Furthermore, the locations already exist and are backed up by significant marketing expertise and high brand awareness. This kind of *opportunistic alliance* is a quick way of achieving the expansion that Emile requires and it draws on both partners' expertise. There is a concern in such a loose arrangement that one partner might steal the other's ideas or products, but that seems unlikely here. Graffoff is not interested in becoming a general machine superstore and The Equipment Emporium is primarily focused on products not services. From Emile's perspective, this *opportunistic alliance* provides a potential way of piloting his proposed organic growth expansion strategy before moving into dedicated premises or, indeed, offering the outlets to franchisees.

(c)   **Evaluation of consultant's claim regarding internal funding of investment**

The consultant has suggested to Emile, that the company has internal sources of finance it can exploit to fully meet its required funding for organic growth. Typical sources of internal finance are retained profits, tighter credit control, reduced inventory and delayed payment to creditors. Given that Emile is committed to high dividend payments and that no information is given about inventory, two of these are relevant here.

Tightening up credit control makes it possible to release money for funding. The average settlement period for receivables can be calculated as (trade receivables/sales revenue) × 365. For the second year trading this is 59 days (260 ÷ 1,600 × 365 = 59·3). Thus, customers take, on average, 59 days to pay their debts, despite agreeing to a 30 day payment term.

Reducing this to the agreed 30 days would realise about $128,500, which could be used to invest in the business. Reducing it to 40 days (the sector-wide standard) would realise approximately $84,500.

However, these gains would only be achieved through implementing better procedures in accounts receivable. Emile realises that this section is poorly motivated and under-staffed. Thus some of the proposed savings may be offset by increased staffing costs. He is also very sensitive to upsetting his customers and so the need to strictly adhere to payment terms may create initial difficulties and strain customer relations. He will have to refrain, in future, from intervening in the debt collection process, and not offer the generous terms of payment that currently undermine the debt collection efforts of the accounts receivable department.

This approach might be allied to delaying payments to creditors. Given the limited information, a crude estimate of the average settlement period for payables (creditors) can be calculated by (trade payables/cost of sales) × 365. In this instance this is 20 days (75 ÷ 1,375 × 365 = 19·9). Thus Graffoff pays its creditors within 20 days, whilst 40 days is common in this sector. Bringing the company in line with this practice would realise up to a further $75,500 which again could be used for investment. There is no suggestion that this will cause a problem. The current fast payment of invoices seems to reflect the zeal of the administrator in accounts payable, rather than any policy of the company. If Graffoff elects to pay within 30 days (the normal credit terms for the country), this will still realise about $38,000.

This means that up to approximately $204,000 could be raised by Graffoff if customers adhered to payment terms and suppliers accepted sector-wide practice. This would result in a short-term, one-off acceleration of cash inflow.

Finally, the acknowledged problems with credit control might also cause Emile to consider factoring the company invoices. Debt factoring involves a third party taking over the businesses debt collection. Most factoring companies are willing to pay 80% of approved trade receivables in advance. At current values, this should lead to an immediate cash input of $208,000 and this might be an attractive alternative to trying to manage receivables internally. It might also address the problems of motivation and staffing in the accounts receivables section. Factoring might be very valuable in a period of expansion, improving cash flow and removing, from the company, responsibility for credit investigation and debt chasing.

Whichever options are chosen, internal finance resources cannot completely raise the $500,000 required for the organic growth plan and so the consultant is incorrect in his assertion. Emile would have to seek external sources of finance to make up the shortfall. However, the amount raised through internal sources may be sufficient to effectively finance either the franchising option or the building of an opportunistic alliance with The Equipment Emporium.

Answer 20 SENSATIONAL SOUNDS

(a)   **Benefits of business intelligence systems**

Business intelligence systems analyse transactional data – that is data held on the organisation's existing systems, such as the ERP and accounting systems. Parise, Iyer and Vesset suggest that there are two strategies that can be used for such data:

(1)   Performance management – which involves querying the data to measure performance of various aspects of the business. This might be sales by country, sales by retailer or sales by product line for example. Such information can be used to identify which parts of the business are under performing so that action can be taken.

(2)   Data exploration – this involves using the data to predict future behaviour of customers so that the company can react accordingly.

In terms of performance measurement, the obvious information that might become available would be sales, analysed by country, retailer or salesman. This might help to identify sales staff who are underperforming, or countries that need more support.

Based on the comments of Lucio, it seems that he is mostly interested in using the system for data exploration purposes, since he has mentioned the need to predict changes in what customers are buying. Detailed analysis of sales using business intelligence systems may identify trends. Since many of the customers of the headphones are young, fashion conscious adults, it is likely that their tastes may change fairly quickly. Being able to predict these changes can have the following advantages:

■   Improving the accuracy of sales forecasts means that production schedules can be aligned with demand. If demand for a particular product is falling, for example, then production can be reduced to avoid excess or obsolete inventory. If demand is growing quickly, production can be increased to take advantage of higher demand and avoid stock outs. This would lead to higher sales and lower inventory waste.

■   Analysis of sales may identify particular countries where sales are growing at a higher rate. This would enable the company to take advantage of this by focussing more marketing effort on these countries.

■   Valuable marketing intelligence might be gained by analysis of sales by gender, age, income bracket and so on. If the company is more aware of which market segments are buying its products, it can better direct its marketing strategy (e.g. by better use of the 4Is).

It is clearly difficult to evaluate the financial impact of these, but it should be clear that the business intelligence has the potential to make a significant improvement in the sales of the company over the longer term.

(b) **Analysis of social media**

Parise, Iyer and Vesset suggest two strategies relating to analysis of social media:

(1)   Social analytics measures the exposure that the organisations achieve on social networks. In this sense, the network is being used as an advertising tool for publicising the company's products and services.

(2)   Decision science, which "listens to the conversation" and aims to discover what people are saying about the organisation's products and services.

To use social analytics, SS would have a company presence on social media (e.g. a page on Facebook or a Twitter account). This online presence is a way of advertising the company and its products to users of social media by posting information (e.g. about new products) or simply posting messages to keep users aware of the products. Analytics would then measure how effective the campaigns have been. This might be in terms of how many users have re-posted or shared the company's messages or, more importantly, how many have led to visits to the company's web site, or even to online orders.

The advantage of social analytics is that the link between the popularity on social media and increased sales can be measured, so it is possible to see the financial benefits.

The explosive growth in social media networks in recent years means that many people have more conversations online. These conversations may contain commercially valuable information to an organisation such as SS, including information about the company's own products and those of its competitors. Decision science aims to tap into these conversations to obtain this information.

The information could be used in various ways by SS:

■   It could find out what customers like and do not like about SS's products. These findings can be taken into account when new ranges of the headphones are designed. It is mentioned that many of the younger users consider headphones to be a fashion accessory, so monitoring such conversations may give insights into changes in tastes and trends.

■   Finding out what customers like and dislike about competitors' products. This information can be fed back to the design teams so future product updates can take these opinions into account.

■   Understanding better who the customers are. When people discuss the product, find out as much as possible about them from other information held in their profile. This can provide valuable information about the market segments that the headphones are sold to. This can be used to improve marketing campaigns and promotions.

■   Knowing what people are interested in at the present moment. This can lead to opportunities for a focussed campaign online. If people are discussing a video released by a pop artist, for example, and that video includes shots of the artist using a pair of headphones from SS, this would be an excellent opportunity for an online advertising campaign.

■   Where people are complaining about products, their comments can be passed on to the customer services department who can contact them to try to rectify the problem. This might then lead to more positive posts commenting on the company.

The information from analysis of social media can be used to better understand who the company's customers are and give them what they want.

A difficulty with decision science is that the tools used to analyse text are not completely accurate and it may be necessary to manually check much of it, which is time consuming. It may also be difficult to see the link between understanding what is happening on the social networks and how that leads to actual sales.

Answer 21 PHARMACY SYSTEMS INTERNATIONAL

(a) **Strategic change analysis**

The proposal to develop and sell a software package for the general retail industry represents a major strategic decision for PSI. Up till now it has been relatively successful in identifying and servicing the software needs of a specialist niche market – the retail pharmacy market. In Michael Porter's terms it is currently a focused differentiator. Its proposed entry into the general retail market represents both a new product and a new market and so, using the perspective of Ansoff's growth matrix, it is a diversification strategy with high levels of risk. The proposal would lead to significant strategic change and, perhaps not surprisingly, is meeting resistance from the software development director who is responsible for a key activity in this change.

Johnson, Scholes and Whittington argue that there is a danger in believing that there is "only one way, or one best way, to change organisational strategies". They believe that most strategies are profoundly influenced by earlier strategies and their success or failure. Consequently, strategies are often incremental in nature, adding to or adapting, previous or existing strategy. Rarely is the proposed change so fundamental that it challenges the existing business model and the processes and activities that support it.

JSW make use of a model developed by Balogun and Hope Hailey, which identifies four types of change which have very different degrees of impact. It is suggested that there are two key measures of change.

(1)   The *nature of change* – how big is it? *Incremental* or "step-by-step" change does not challenge the existing way of doing things and may indeed reinforce the organisation's processes and culture. It is therefore likely to meet less resistance than *Big Bang* or quantum change, which represents significant change to most or all the organisation. Often this *Big Bang* change is necessary to respond to a crisis facing the firm, such as a major fall in profitability and/or the appointment of a new chief executive.

(2)   The *scope* of change process is important – how much of the firm's activities are to be changed? If the change does not alter the basic business model (or "paradigm" in JSW's terms) then it is regarded as "a *realignment of strategy* rather than a fundamental change in strategic direction" (JSW). However, if the proposed change is a radical challenge to the existing business model or paradigm then it is regarded as a *transformational* change.

The consideration of the two key measures of change enables the identification of four types of change.

Tutorial note: *These four types are used in this answer but other models and approaches would be acceptable.*

	Scope of change	
Nature of Change	*Realignment*	*Transformation*
Incremental	Adaptation	Evolution
Big Bang	Reconstruction	Revolution

Adaptation

Adaptation is a change that can be made in the current business model (realignment) and it occurs incrementally. JSW argue this is the most common form of change in organisations.

Reconstruction

Reconstruction represents significant change in the organisation, often prompted by a crisis, such as an unwelcome takeover bid, but it does not require a fundamental change to the business model. Turnaround strategies where the aim is to rapidly reduce costs or increase revenues to ensure business survival may affect the whole organisation, but not change the basic business model.

Evolution

Evolution is a change in strategy, which requires the business model to be significantly changed over a period of time. The perceived need for "transformation" may be as result of careful business analysis leading to a planned evolutionary change. Alternatively, change may take place through an emergent process where the scope of change only becomes apparent once it is completed.

Revolution

Revolution affects the whole of the organisation and the scope of change requires a fundamental shift in the business model – the way the firm chooses to compete.

Viewed dispassionately, it appears that PSI's proposed move into the general retail market represents an evolutionary change. It is incremental because it will build on the skills, routines and beliefs of those in the organisation. However, it is transformational because the proposed move away from the current market niche to a market which requires a generic solution is a fundamental change in strategic direction. It is likely that internal processes and activities will need to significantly change for the company to successfully develop and sell the new packages. In PSI's case, the evolution is driven top-down, by the chief executive's desire to create a company which is an attractive acquisition, at which point he can realise some or all of his investment in the company.

Interestingly, the three directors may not all perceive the change as evolutionary. The entrepreneurial chief executive and the sales and marketing director may see the proposal as adaptive change, realigning the company to take advantage of a business opportunity which will lead to realising their personal goals. Indeed they may see the current product as just the specific implementation of a generic retail software solution. In contrast, the software development director is more likely to agree with our assessment of the change as evolutionary.

(b)   Strategic change influences

JSW argue that successfully managing change depends on context. This context is made up of a number of factors or contingencies particular to the organisation under consideration. How change is managed in a relatively small privately owned firm like PSI is very different to how it might be managed in a large international firm of accountants with hundreds of partners.

JSW again use the work of Balogun and Hope Hailey to consider the contextual features that need to be taken into account in deciding how a strategic change programme should be managed.

Tutorial note: *These features are shown in the diagram below and are used in the model answer. However candidates could adopt other models and approaches.*

Contextual features and their influence on strategic change programmes

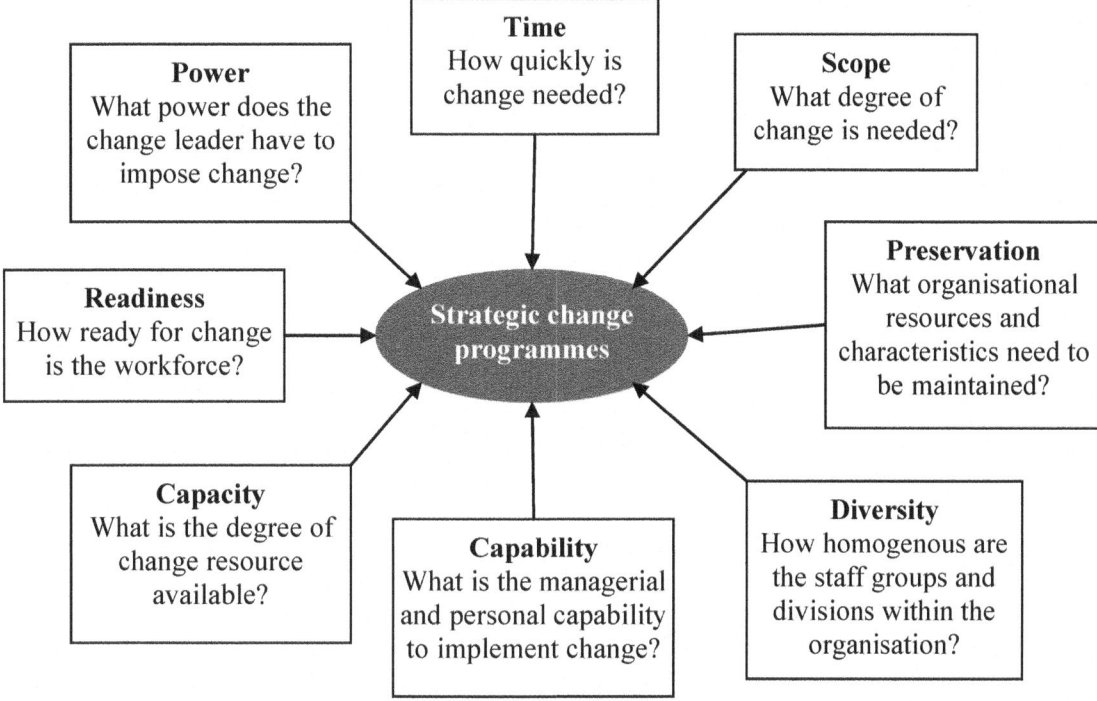

Source: Johnson, Scholes and Whittington

In the context of PSI, the following observations could be made.

Time

The company is not facing any immediate financial or business problems and so there is no apparent need for rapid change. Figure 1 suggests a company that is slowly consolidating in its market place. There is no evidence of a crisis that requires urgent remedial action. It is likely that it will take a relatively long time to develop the new generic software package, particularly when the current pressures on the software development team are taken into account. They are already having problems meeting deadlines for the current product. The only urgency is that injected by the impatience of the chief executive who may want to quickly introduce change to achieve the objectives of realising his investment in the company. The natural inclination of the software team and their director will be to use any available time to consolidate the current product and to improve its quality. In contrast, the chief executive will want to use available time to produce the new generic product. This will almost certainly lead to conflict, both in the organisation and with customers pressurising the software team for fault rectification and new requirements. The increased concentration of pharmacies into nationwide chains may also increase the power of certain customers.

Scope

The degree of change should not be underestimated in a relatively small firm like PSI. Supplying a clearly defined segment supported by a vertical marketing strategy is very different to the horizontal marketing strategy required for the proposed move into the general retail market. The company has built up expertise in a niche market. It is unlikely that it will have comparable expertise in the generic retail market as well as in the other niche retail markets that it intends to target with its configurable software package.

Preservation

Software development skills are a crucial resource and capability and must be preserved to enable the proposed strategic change. The retention of the software team's expertise and motivation is essential. If they are upset by the proposed change and disturbed by the further pressures it is likely to create then it is unlikely that they will support it. The agreement of the software development director to the change is also vital and some way of securing this must be explored. Although the proposed change is largely based on the competency of current personnel, it is likely that they will be disturbed by the increased pressure imposed on them and so there is a high probability that key employees will leave the company.

Diversity

Change may be helped if there is a diversity of experience. However, change may be hampered if the organisation has followed a particular strategy for a number of years. The relative stability of the last three years and the company's stated objective to be a "highly skilled professional company providing quality software services to the retail pharmacy industry" seem at odds with the chief executive's vision of expansion. There is also evidence to suggest that the goals of the sales force and those of the software developers are already conflicting and there seems even more opportunity for this to occur in the context of a generic retail software package. Change will be hampered by the current conflict between sales and development.

Capability

The chief executive and sales and marketing director are entrepreneurial in outlook and want change to fuel growth and their personal aspirations. The software development director is much less enthusiastic as he can clearly see the implications of the proposed change in strategic direction. Furthermore, over the last three years the workforce has been relatively settled and has not been subject to much significant change. In some ways the small size of the business may make change easy to facilitate (see power), but there may also be significant barriers to change. The software development director and his staff control and implement the key activity of the new strategy. It may be difficult to overcome their lack of enthusiasm for the proposed change.

Capacity

Capacity is concerned with resources such as people, finance and information. More detailed analysis will be necessary to see if PSI has the necessary resources to implement the proposed change. However, evidence from the scenario is not encouraging. For example, the company has recently been criticised at a user group conference for failing to meet its proposed release deadlines. The acquisition of necessary resources will take both time and money. There is no evidence that the company has the finances to support the acquisition of new resources. It is a private company and so it will not be able to raise money through the stock market. It will rely on further investments from the current shareholders (and the software development director may be reluctant to participate in this) or on bank finance. Furthermore, it usually takes a long time to integrate software developers into a business. There is a long learning curve during which they have to learn not only how the product works, but how it is designed.

Hence they are unlikely to be productive until several months after appointment and this lack of progress might again clash with the impatience of the chief executive.

Readiness

There is no evidence that the organisation is ready for the type of change proposed by the chief executive. In fact the current pressure on the software development team suggests that they may not welcome the proposed new strategy. What they might be ready for is a strategy that leads to a consolidation of the pharmaceutical product so that faults are fixed and new requirements released on time.

Power

The chief executive has the ultimate power in this organisation, reinforced by (through combining with the sales and marketing director) ownership of the majority of the shares. However he must secure the co-operation of the software development director to make progress. The fact that he has power may lead to him forcing through a strategy which is essentially wrong for the organisation.

Conclusion

Overall, an analysis of the context for change at PSI should provide warning signs to the chief executive. Although the chief executive has the power to impose change, there are concerns about the scope and capacity for change which may make it very difficult for the company to preserve its current resources and competencies. There is a real concern that these will actually be destroyed by the proposed change and this will lead to major difficulties in their current market. There is already evidence of this from the scenario. The company has been criticised at a user group conference for quality failures and there are doubts about whether planned new features will be released on time. The product is fundamental to the efficient purchasing and stock control required in contemporary pharmacies. Customers may switch to a competitor if they feel that their emerging requirements are not met with sufficient promptness and quality.

The workforce is neither ready for change nor diverse enough to welcome change. There are current conflicts between sales and development which are likely to be escalated by the proposed strategic change. Finally, there are also grave doubts about the capacity of the company to deliver the proposed change within the likely time scale required by the chief executive.

There is a concern that the chief executive will rely on managing change through coercion, which "is the imposition of change or the issuing of edicts about change". This is not unusual in small firms where the chief executive also has a large ownership stake in the business. It is most appropriate in crisis situations where time is of the essence and clear direction is imperative. However, PSI does not appear to be in a crisis situation. Unfortunately, however, it looks like the chief executive is about to create one!

Answer 22 COUNTRY CAR CLUB

(a)   **Process analysis and recommendations**

Tutorial note: *Although the question does not explicitly ask for it, the process-strategy matrix suggested by Paul Harmon would provide an appropriate context for the answer to this question. However, other appropriate models or frameworks could be used by candidates to answer this part of the question.*

The process-strategy matrix

The process-strategy matrix has two axes. The vertical axis is concerned with process complexity and dynamics. At the base of the vertical axis are simple processes often with simple procedures while at the top are complex processes which may require negotiation, discussion and complicated design. On the horizontal axis is the strategic value of these processes. Their importance increases from left to right with low-value processes concerned with things that must be done but which add little value to products or services. On the extreme right of this axis are high-value processes which are very important to success and add significant value to goods and services. From these two axes, Harmon categorises four quadrants and makes suggestions about how processes should be tackled in each quadrant.

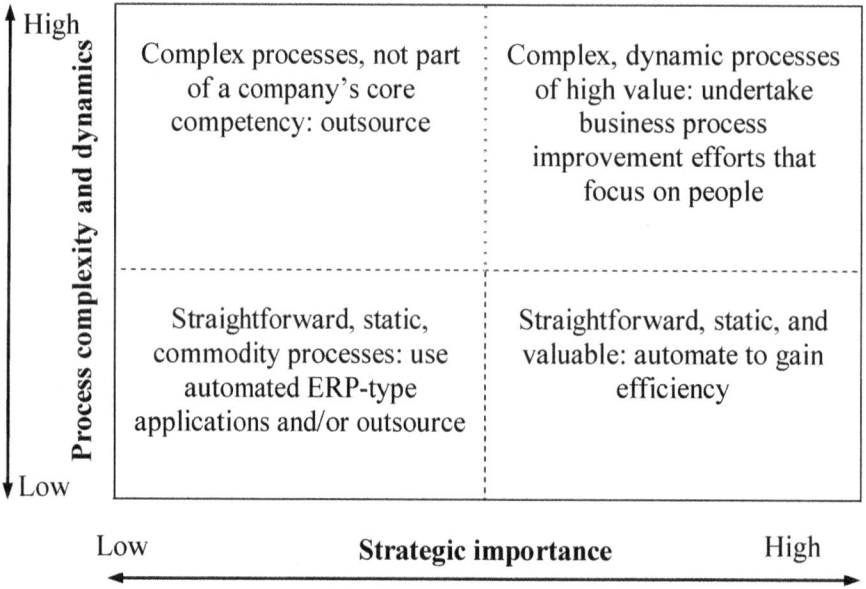

Low strategic importance, low process complexity and dynamics

This quadrant contains relatively straightforward stable processes which add little business value. They are processes that must be carried out by the company but add nothing to the company's value proposition. These processes need to be automated in the most efficient way possible. They are often called "commodity processes" and are suitable for standard software package solutions or outsourcing to organisations that specialise in that area. Payroll is a good example of this. Many standard software packages are available in the market place. Alternatively, a computer bureau can be used to process the payroll on behalf of the organisation.

Low strategic importance, high process complexity and dynamics

This quadrant is for relatively complex processes that need to be done but do not add significant value to the company's products or services. They are not at the heart of the company's core competencies. Harmon suggests that these should be outsourced to organisations which have them as their core business.

High strategic importance, low process complexity and dynamics

These processes lie in the lower right quadrant of the model. They tend to be relatively straightforward processes which, nevertheless, have a significant role in the organisation's activities. They are central to what the business does. The aim is to automate these, if possible, to gain cost reduction and improve quality and efficiency.

High strategic importance, high process complexity and dynamics

Finally, in the top right hand quadrant are high-value, complex processes which often include human judgement and expertise and are often very difficult to automate. Harmon suggests that these might be the focus of major process redesign initiatives focusing on business process improvement through the improved performance of the people undertaking those processes.

In the context of 3C, the following recommendations are suggested.

(i)   Attendance at breakdowns

This appears to be of high strategic importance and, although some breakdowns are bound to be simple to fix, it requires the repairer to be knowledgeable, flexible and diplomatic. Consequently, it appears to be a candidate for the upper right quadrant of the process-strategy matrix. Hence it is suggested that the service should remain in-house and attention should be paid to improving the competency of the "service patrol engineers". Information technology should be harnessed to seek improvements in response time to breakdowns by improving the organisation and distribution of these engineers. Systems might also be developed to technically support engineers and to help them diagnose and fix roadside problems.

(ii)   Membership renewal

This should be a relatively straightforward process, so it sits in one of the two lower quadrants. It can be argued that it is a process that is core to the business and is not one (like payroll) which can be found across all businesses. It appears to be a candidate for the lower right quadrant. Hence it is a candidate for automation to gain efficiency. The organisation already has a bespoke system operated by in-house permanent employees. This seems an appropriate way of delivering this process. However, it might benefit from revisiting the way the bespoke system works. The scenario suggests that the current system sends out membership renewals on receipt of a confirmation from the member. The system might benefit from being built around a presumption of renewal, so that the member only contacts the organisation if he or she does not wish to renew.

(iii)   Vehicle insurance services

These appear to be a relatively complex process which is of little strategic importance to 3C. It appears to inhabit the top left hand quadrant of the matrix. Insurance is not only technically complex, it carries large risks and substantial regulatory requirements. It is likely that these regulatory requirements will undergo frequent changes. It would appear attractive to 3C to outsource this service to a specialist provider who would then badge it under 3C's name. This is relatively common practice and 3C's venture into insurance must have been very expensive. Outsourcing provides it with opportunities for providing a wider service with reduced in-house costs.

(iv)   Membership queries

Membership queries are of unpredictable complexity. They are also an important contact point between the company and their members. Failure to handle queries courteously and correctly could have important consequences for membership renewal. It is suggested that this is an upper right hand quadrant process – potentially complex and of high strategic importance to the company. Investment is required in people supported by innovative and speedy IT systems that allow the 3C staff to respond quickly and accurately to a wide range of questions. It is suggested that membership queries continue to remain in-house although the physical location of the call centre might reflect certain financial opportunities (e.g. low property rents and cheaper labour).

(v)   Vehicle history checks

Vehicle history checks appear to be of relatively low strategic importance to 3C. Automation should make such checks relatively straightforward, although the combination of accident damage, stolen vehicles, finance agreements and time when the vehicle was voluntarily taken off the road may make determining this history more complex then it first appears. Furthermore, the consequences of providing inaccurate or incomplete information may be quite severe. Someone who has unsuspectingly purchased a car which has been damaged and repaired might claim for damages against 3C when this was revealed. These damages might be extensive if someone died in the vehicle as a result of a botched repair. Consequently it is suggested that this is predominantly an upper left hand quadrant process which should be outsourced to an organisation which is already in this field.

The table below summarises the advice to the BAC:

Process	*Recommendation*
Attendance at repairs	Remains in-house. Improve competency of repair staff. Support them with IT systems.
Membership renewal	Remains in-house and revisit basis of automation.
Vehicle insurance	Outsource.
Membership queries	Remains in-house. Improve competency of call centre staff. Support them with IT systems.
Vehicle history	Outsource.

Tutorial note: *Clearly these are value judgements and credit would be given for coherently argued answers which do not match the examiner's conclusions.*

(b)   Advantages of outsourcing

In the question scenario the decision to outsource the purchase and maintenance of 3C vehicles is justified by its low strategic importance and its low to medium complexity.

Tutorial note: *However, this only makes it a candidate for outsourcing and so tangible and intangible benefits would have to be attached to this suggestion in a subsequent detailed analysis. This part of the question asks candidates to analyse the advantages of outsourcing the process of the purchase and maintenance of 3C vehicles.*

It is suggested that advantages would include:

Purchasing benefits from economies of scale

AutoDirect purchase thousands of cars and vans for their customers each year. They should be able to negotiate substantial discounts from manufacturers, some of which can be passed on to their customers.

Predictable costs

The vehicle lease payments with AutoDirect are monthly and they include full maintenance of the car, including tyres and exhausts. Hence 3C will have predictable costs for budgeting purposes. Previously, costs would have been variable and unpredictable, depending on the reliability of the vehicles.

1074

Reduced overhead costs – garage and purchasing

The overhead costs associated with the garage and the garage and purchasing employees have been lost (except for the one manager retained to manage the contract with AutoDirect). There may also be an opportunity for realising income from the sale of the garage site. It is described as being in a residential area with no room for expansion and severe parking congestion. It may be possible to sell the garage for residential development.

Higher vehicle availability

The central garage itself is a bottleneck. Vehicles have to be driven or transported to this garage from all parts of the country and left there while they are serviced or repaired. They then have to be driven back to their operational area. AutoDirect has repair and servicing centres throughout the country and so it will be possible for vehicles to be taken locally for services and repairs – thus reducing vehicle downtime.

Freeing cash to use for other investments – from purchase to lease

The policy of purchasing vehicles meant that a considerable amount of cash has been tied up in fast depreciating assets. Switching to leasing will release this cash for investment elsewhere in the company.

Access to expertise and legislation

It is likely that vehicles will become increasingly subject to legislation designed to reduce carbon emissions. This, together with the increasing technical complexity of vehicles, will mean that vehicles will become increasingly difficult to maintain without specialist monitoring and repair equipment. It is unlikely that 3C can maintain such a level of investment and so outsourcing to a specialist makes good sense. AutoDirect will have to monitor legislation, advise on its implications and implement its requirements for its large customer base.

Concentration on core business

Although this issue is not explicitly considered in the scenario it is something that impacts on all organisations. The management of the garage does not appear to be a core strategic requirement. It must consume some elements of senior management time. Outsourcing frees up that time so it can be used to focus on issues directly relevant to the customer and the business as a whole.

Answer 23 FLEXIPIPE

(a)   **Evaluation of decision to use a software package approach**

A critical evaluation of using the software package approach at Flexipipe could be structured around three factors:

(i)   The wisdom of using a package solution for a process where the company enjoys a *competitive edge* over its competitors.

(ii)   The difficulties of selecting an appropriate package in an environment where requirements are difficult to define and are still subject to change.

(iii)   The problem of successfully procuring a software package in an organisation which lacks both experience and a process for selecting and procuring a non-standard software application.

Tutorial note: *Other appropriate factors and relevant approaches would be given credit.*

(i)   Competitive edge

It is generally accepted that software package solutions cannot provide organisations with a competitive edge. By definition such packages are available to all companies in a sector or market and so any commercial advantages offered by the package are available to all organisations competing in that market.

It is recognised that the control of the production process at Flexipipe was very innovative. It provided the company with significant competitive edge over their competitors. For this reason, it seemed unlikely from the start that Flexipipe would find a package that fulfilled its exact requirements and that any selected package would constrain the production process. Indeed, this is what happened, with the new system unable to replicate the flexibility and efficiency of the existing one.

Initially, the company would have been advised to consider the location of the process on the Harmon process/strategy grid. The process is strategically important and relatively complex. Software package solutions should primarily be considered for reasonably straightforward commodity processes which have low strategic importance to the company, such as payroll and accounts. Thus, in the context of Flexipipe, a bespoke software solution would, from the outset, appear to have been more appropriate.

(ii)   Complexity and nature of requirements

It was recognised from the start that it was relatively difficult to specify all the requirements of the production process in advance because many decisions were intuitively taken by experienced managers and supervisors on the factory floor. It was often difficult for them to explain why they had taken certain effective decisions. It is very risky to select a software package against incomplete or unarticulated requirements. If significant requirements are missed or misunderstood then it is difficult to address the problems this might cause.

There are at least three potential approaches to addressing the problem of the software failing to fulfil requirements, but each of these has disadvantages:

(1)   Ask the software vendor to integrate these requirements into the next release of the package. However, even if the software vendor agrees, it may be a costly solution as well as allowing such innovations to become available to all users of the package.

(2)   Ask the software vendor to build a tailored version of the application to fulfil specific requirements. This is likely to be expensive (so reducing the cost advantages of buying a package) and cause long-term maintenance problems and costs as the tailored version has to be integrated with new releases of the standard software package.

(3)   Seek a manual "work-around" for the missing requirements. However, this may also be costly as well as reducing the business benefits which should have been obtained.

Whichever approach is taken, it is likely to either reduce the benefits or increase the costs of adopting a software package solution.

It was also recognised that requirements are likely to change in the long term. There is no guarantee that the software vendor will develop the package to fit newly emerging requirements and so the issues of tailoring and work-around will again have to be considered. Most package selection takes place against current requirements and so this approach is well-suited to circumstances where requirements rarely change and, if they do, they are specified by legislative bodies and the software vendors must make the changes to keep their product compliant. Payroll and integrated accounts applications are typical of this. Applications that are subject to long-term changes (such as the production process at Flexipipe) and do not require legislative compliance, are less appropriate to this approach.

(iii)   Absence of mature procurement process and management expertise

It was recognised from the outset that Flexipipe did not have an established process for software package selection and implementation. This was a very risky project in which to try and establish a process and select an appropriate package. Lack of procurement expertise in general has been a problem in the past for the company when a key supplier of raw materials for the pipes went out of business. This caused short-term production problems, although an alternative supplier had eventually been found. However, procurement still only employs two people full-time and they are relatively junior and overworked. The company appears to have a very immature procurement process.

The long-term commitment to an external supplier is very problematic in software supply, where moving formerly in-house applications to a new supplier can be technically difficult, expensive and disruptive. In general, there are significant risks associated with the long-term viability of software suppliers and the maintenance of software applications that are critical to the company. Companies go out of business, as in the case study scenario, and companies are sold. It is feasible that a software supplier might be bought by a competitor of Flexipipe, threatening long-term supply. These problems are largely absent in bespoke development, particularly if this development is undertaken in-house. The software program code belongs to the company (not the supplier) and its long-term development is under its control.

(b)   Evaluation of how a formal process for procuring package software would have helped

In the context of the Flexipipe project, here are some of the issues that could have been addressed by a formal software package evaluation process. It is important that candidates identify elements of the process relevant to the Flexipipe scenario. A generic evaluation process is insufficient.

The business case for all software procurement projects should be assessed to see if a package is an appropriate solution. In some instances a bespoke IT development may be better suited. As mentioned in part (a), the Harmon grid considers process complexity and strategic importance and it could have been used as a guide to assessing the appropriateness of the software package solution approach. If it had been used at Flexipipe then it seems likely that the software package approach would have been abandoned at an early stage of the project.

The requirements must be carefully and comprehensively specified before embarking on a procurement exercise. Difficulties with specifying requirements may again lead to a re-consideration of the bespoke approach. In the case study scenario, mention is made of the system failing to fulfil a number of functional requirements, such as monitoring process variance. The inference is that these requirements were either not specified or were incorrectly specified in advance and so were not part of the package assessment. Similarly, problems with "usability" may be due to the failure of defining specific usability requirements in advance and so these were not considered when the package was evaluated.

The tendering method has to be made more formal and competitive. A post-project review has shown that there were at least three other packages which should have been considered in the evaluation process. A more formal process would have had a mechanism for finding these potential suppliers. The openness of the tendering process would also have been assisted by advertising in trade magazines and internet tendering sites, which may have also brought forward other potential suppliers. This is an important step because it allows a transparency in the process, and avoids selecting a supplier purely on the recommendation of one internal employee: as in the case of Flexipipe. It would have avoided the situation of a package being selected solely on the basis of a visit to an exhibition.

Suppliers who submit tenders must be evaluated against criteria agreed in advance. Buying a software package leads to a long-term relationship between the supplier and the customer, so the latter must be comfortable with the supplier's credentials. In the context of Flexipipe this would involve setting standard measures and minimum values for liquidity, gearing and profitability. There also has to be some way of off-setting the supplier's suitability with the suitability of the product. That is, how a package with limited functionality from a well-established, financially sound supplier is evaluated against a more functional, usable package from a newly established company with high financial gearing and low turnover. The balance between such factors has to be established in advance, often using a high-level weighted matrix. In the context of the scenario, appropriate financial checks should have identified the high gearing and poor liquidity of the supplier that eventually led to its collapse.

A proper process also needs to be in place to evaluate the potential solution against the specified requirements. It is important to establish the "fit" between the requirements and the potential solution and to use this "fit" in the final selection. It has been stated elsewhere that it is unlikely that a package solution will exactly fulfil all requirements. However, if the "fit" is known and understood in advance then negotiation with users may lead to them dropping, modifying or finding workaround for these gaps. Perhaps some of the functional shortcomings identified by users might have been tolerated, if they had been known and understood in advance.

Finally, a planned implementation is an important part of the process. Perhaps the lack of usability of the software was down to the absence of training and the belief that users could "to pick up the software as they go along". This is a risky approach, even in circumstances even with experienced users and in a situation where the software product is a good fit with their requirements.

Answer 24 CHEMICAL TRANSPORT

Tutorial note: *Paul Harmon proposed a process-strategy matrix that considers the strategic importance of the process on one axis and the complexity of the process on the other. This leads to four quadrants for which Harmon suggests different generic process solutions. For example, for relatively simple processes of low strategic importance he suggests standard software package solutions or outsourcing. This answer considers the location of each of the three processes defined in the question together with potential solution options in the context of CT.*

(a)   **Analysis of process areas using Harmon's matrix**

Payroll is usually of relatively *low complexity and low strategic importance.* It is normally fulfilled by a commercial off-the-shelf software package. At CT the payroll requirements are relatively complex because of the combination of bonuses and deductions which have been developed and enhanced over the last few years. Consequently, payroll has been developed as a bespoke application by the in-house IT team. However, there is no evidence that the pay arrangements are effective. Drivers find them confusing and they certainly do not find them motivating. It could be suggested that CT should simplify its pay arrangements and adopt a commercial off-the-shelf package solution. Adopting such a solution would also address long-term costs and problems. Payroll is subject to continual and unpredictable legislative changes. With a standard package these changes are part of a fixed maintenance fee. Bespoke changes are unpredictable in both occurrence and duration and so are potentially time-consuming and expensive. Indeed, recent changes in legislation led to the IT team being fully occupied for three months, developing and testing the required modifications to the payroll system. There is also the chance that the IT team could make a mistake or miss something important in the legislation. IT savings could be recycled into the drivers' pay system. A simplified payment system could lead to drivers being offered better pay deals without costing the company any more overall. It could also help motivate the drivers more effectively, which the scenario indicates is not happening with the existing system.

The legal advice process is currently outsourced to a legal consultancy, although the cost of such advice is causing the company to consider appointing a full-time, employed expert. CT is operating in an environment that is continually subject to legislation. Chemical transport and handling is dangerous and appropriate legislation is inevitable. Drivers and driving hours and the maintenance of trucks and trailers are also likely to be subject to both national and international legislation. Legislation is time-consuming to monitor and the potential cost of non-compliance is very high. It could result in substantial damages or fines. CT recognises that the current legal experts deliver an excellent service. It seems unlikely that it will be easy to find a full-time expert with such a wide range of knowledge, so employment is risky and also likely to be relatively expensive. The person will be the sole expert and so, as well as the problems of verifying advice, it also seems likely that there will be problems in motivating and keeping such an employee in a job role where there is no onward career path. In Paul Harmon's terms, the legal advice process appears to be a *complex process with little strategic significance*. The advice for this type of process is to continue to outsource and maintain the service of the legal consultancy.

The extension of the website to allow the chemical wholesalers to place and track orders is strategically very important to CT. It recognises that failure to implement such functions will jeopardise future contracts. The chemical wholesalers may begin to look for an alternative distributor. CT probably recognises that such a feature might also help them sign up more wholesalers and so the extended website can be part of their business strategy. Whether the process is complex or not is a matter of judgement. There will be clear security issues and it will be important to partition the system so that competitors' details are kept securely and separately. It is also likely that requirements are not yet extensively defined and will change as the details of the wholesalers' requirements become clear. The company has an IT capability with some expertise in web-based systems. If a commercial off-the-shelf software solution is used to fulfil the payroll requirements, then this IT team is potentially freed up to work on the enhanced website system. Consequently it is suggested that this application is a *relatively complex process with strategic importance* and so is best developed in-house as a bespoke system.

(b) **Use of a CRM system at CT**

The provision of delivery placement and tracking is, at the moment, an important element of customer retention. However, in a wider sense the company's website has to be reviewed to see if it can be harnessed to acquire further customers, to enhance the service it offers (above and beyond placing and tracking deliveries) and also to assist in the long-term retention of customers. It must be recalled that the present website is only used for information purposes. It only contains information about the company: its structures, history, key contacts and case studies. However, it must also be recalled that CT only deals with a relatively small business market. In B2B applications there tends to be far fewer but larger buyers (Chaffey, 2007).

Customer acquisition

The scenario suggests that chemical wholesalers are CT's current customers. The site should be constructed with their interests and requirements in mind. Evidence suggests that CT has recognised expertise in the difficult and dangerous task of chemical distribution where there is a need for compliance with stringent and emerging legislation. The website needs to provide examples of this and also constant updates which tempt people to return to the site to view the latest information. CT does not have to reveal its complete expertise. However, regular, selected updates on new legislative requirements and new chemical distribution challenges may prompt return visits and so increasingly suggest to potential customers that this is a business avenue that is worth exploring. The case studies already on the website will strengthen the message of expertise and also demonstrate to potential customers that outsourcing to CT will have both business and financial benefits.

Testimonials from established customers will help support this message. It has to be recognised that it is a B2B website and that no contract or purchase will be entered into as a result of the website alone. It is about building up confidence and information that may lead to contact being made between CT and a potential customer. Overall, the website should look professional and business-like and appropriately discreet. Existing customers may not wish certain information to be given out and CT itself must not give too much valuable information to competitors about its pricing or its range of current customers.

It is also important that potential customers find the CT website when they are looking for information or for a potential haulier. Although it is less important than in a B2C website, it is still helpful if CT ensures that the website is optimised so that it appears high up in website searches. This is not easy to reliably achieve and so purchasing sponsored links can also be very valuable. The website address also has to be promoted in any offline marketing undertaken by the company. Again, it must be recalled that CT must have a relatively finite set of potential customers. These should be relatively easy to target with marketing information and sales calls that will include the website details.

CT may also benefit from collecting details about the people who are visiting its site. This may again be achieved through offering selected information only to visitors who leave their email address. So, although some technical information might be offered for free, other information (e.g. important changes in international legislation) might only be available to visitors who have provided their email details. These email details may just be used as part of an analysis (which companies are looking at us) or they might be used to target future promotional campaign.

Customer retention

Customer retention refers to marketing activities taken by an organisation to keep its existing customers. The scenario has already identified the placement and tracking of orders. Customers might be offered a service which helps them plan deliveries to help minimise distribution costs. This is potentially even more valuable if it can assist in distributing chemicals directly to the end customer, hence avoiding wholesaler storage costs. Payment for the delivery might also be organised through the website, with inducements made for fast on-line payment. Customer retention is improved by integrating the systems of the supplier and the customer. Not only does this provide a better and cheaper service, it also effectively makes it more difficult for the customer to move to an alternative supplier. Thus, as well as extending its web service, CT should consider establishing links to the front end of the process (ordering, planning) and to the back end (payment and reconciliation). Customers also value relevant management information. CT needs to identify what information it can offer its customers to help them run their company more effectively or keep down costs. For example, making an earlier delivery may enable the wholesaler to use the customer's storage facility rather than their own.

Tutorial note: *There is a lot of scope for variations on this answer and credit would be given as appropriate. However, answers must recognise that CT will require a B2B website and that purchase transactions are unlikely to take place on the strength of the website alone. The website will just be the potential start of a selling process.*

Answer 25 BRIDGE

(a) **Process for evaluating, selecting and implementing a software package**

Tutorial note: The structure of this answer is just one way which Bridge could have procured the software package in a structured way. Other answers with an appropriate approach would be given credit.

Stage One: Evaluation

This is concerned with establishing whether a commercial off-the-shelf software package would be an appropriate way of automating the CRM requirements. A framework such as the Harmon process – strategy matrix could be used. There is no evidence in the scenario that any alternative (outsourcing, bespoke software development) to the software package approach was considered. Generally, CRM applications are likely to be relatively complex and of medium strategic importance. Consequently, by chance, a software package approach does appear a reasonable response, although it would have been beneficial for that decision to stem from a proper evaluation, rather than the whim and the will of the new sales and marketing executive.

Stage Two: Business case

This stage would require the definition of a formal business case, including a financial evaluation of the proposed investment. This was avoided by negotiating the price down to below the capex threshold at Bridge. If this had not been done, then a business case would have been required. The failure to produce a business case has two consequences. First, it meant that no other likely costs associated with the software purchase were ever considered. These were either avoided (such as the training costs) or had to be funded out of the operational budget (the cost of data migration). Second, and more importantly, there was no attempt to establish what benefits the Custcare CRM package offered the organisation. These could have been financial benefits (so could be compared with costs using an appropriate investment appraisal technique) or they could have been intangible benefits (such as improved customer satisfaction). Both tangible and intangible benefits could have been subject to a benefits realisation review at the end of the project, to see whether the anticipated benefits had materialised. The failure to document the anticipated benefits in advance means that although the software is being used, there is an air of disappointment and deflation about the project outcome.

Stage Three: Requirements definition

This stage is concerned with defining the requirements which the software package is to be evaluated against. No formal requirements definition was performed at Bridge. Teri was enthusiastic about the product, based on her experience at her previous company. She felt that the requirements would be very similar at Bridge. In fact, she was proved correct, as far as the functional requirements were concerned. The sales and marketing staff appear to be quite happy with the features of the software and, indeed, it has provided valuable functionality which they did not anticipate. However, important non-functional and technical requirements were missed. These concerned the technical interface with the order processing system and the overall slow performance of the software. Performance and interface requirements should have been part of the requirements specification which the package was evaluated against. More thought could also have been given to supplier requirements: what Bridge would like from the supplying company. This would have prompted thoughts about support requirements and also the geographical location of the supplier. At the end of the interview Mick says, "I just wish we had chosen a product produced by a company here in Deeland". This could have been one of the evaluation criteria.

Stage 4: Evaluation of competing products

The need to compile and issue a formal Invitation to Tender (ITT) would have required Bridge to consider alternative products and suppliers. Even just following the capex requirements at Bridge would have forced the sales and marketing department to consider three competitive responses to their requirements. This was not done, no alternatives were considered. It may have been possible to find a solution which did fulfil the technical interface requirements and achieved the required performance. However, even if this were not possible, and Custcare remained the best solution, the formality of the ITT process would have allowed Teri to demonstrate that the package had been selected after proper consideration of alternatives. It would have introduced an element of due diligence and transparency which is missing from the project.

Stage 5: Contract negotiation

Once a potential solution is identified, a detailed investigation of the contract is required to remove or amend clauses which the customer is unhappy about. Contracts are usually framed in favour of the software supplier. It is at this stage that Bridge would have identified two issues which subsequently caused problems. First, the legal jurisdiction of the contract; this could have been changed, through negotiation, from Solland to Deeland. Second, the restriction on who can be employed as contract staff on Custcare projects. Again, this would probably have been removed after negotiation (or a preferential contract rate agreed). Contractual arrangements are very difficult to change retrospectively. They need to be reviewed before the purchase is completed. If insurmountable problems occur (e.g. a reluctance to vary a clause), then the customer can legitimately withdraw at this stage, citing the unacceptable risk the clause exposes them to.

Stage 6: Implementation

Effective training, appropriate documentation and successful data migration are central to the success of the project. Proper consideration of them also contributes to the business case (stage 2). Omitting training has been a false economy at Bridge, leading to too much use of an inadequate support agreement. Data migration had to be separately funded and turned out to be disproportionally expensive.

(b)   Advantages of adopting a software package approach

The Custcare solution did provide a quick solution to the CRM requirement at Bridge. *Speed of implementation* is a claimed advantage of commercial off-the-shelf software packages and this is valid in this scenario. It would be at least 18 months before the IT department could even start to look at the sales and marketing department's requirement. In contrast, the Custcare solution was up and running within three months.

The Custcare solution did provide comprehensive functionality. The sales and marketing department were impressed with the package. It did all the things they wanted it to do and it also gave them ideas and possibilities which they would never have thought of. Software packages have the advantage of incorporating *industry best practice* within a broad, comprehensive functionality. Custcare allows an organisation without a CRM, such as Bridge, to quickly get up to speed and to offer services as least as good as some of its competitors.

Despite the extra costs of data migration, the software package does appear to offer a relatively cheap solution. In general, software packages, where the cost of development and maintenance is shared amongst many customers, are *usually much cheaper* than bespoke alternatives. The Custcare solution has still cost less than $30,000. The internal IT department has quoted a price of $18,000 just for requirements analysis. Given that they still have to develop and test the solution, this suggests that the overall cost will be much greater than the money spent on the Custcare solution.

There have been no complaints about the robustness of the Custcare solution. The only difficulties concern its failure to meet certain requirements, and the problems of support and training. In general, software packages are of *better quality* than bespoke alternatives. The package has been extensively used by many users in a range of organisations and problems will have been progressively identified and solved. It is impossible to exhaustively test bespoke solutions, so they are often beset with robustness and reliability problems, particularly in the period just after implementation.

The two problems reported by Mick are relatively easy to solve. A piece of bespoke software could be developed as a bridge between the CRM and the order processing system. This *bridge* would import files from the CRM system in one format and then convert them into the format required by the order processing system, and vice versa. The performance of the software could be addressed by improving the specification of hardware at Bridge, or by scheduling jobs so that complex reports and queries are run when the system is not busy (e.g. overnight). These solutions are not ideal, but provide a reasonable way forward. Overall, the software package approach still seems a reasonable way forward.

Answer 26 VIVA ESPANA

(a) **Potential risks of the control weaknesses**

(1)   Holding of customer information

Holding customer information is necessary to service the needs of those customers. Customer data is also useful for marketing purposes in an e-commerce environment. However, organisations must comply with relevant laws relating to data protection (e.g. European Union directive 95/46/EC). Data protection legislation aims to protect the individual's privacy and prevent misuse of their data. VE needs to ensure that it is complying with relevant legislation, otherwise the company may face fines.

VE also has to ensure that the data it holds is stored securely. Customer data is not encrypted, so it could be argued that the company is not taking adequate care. Should data be stolen (e.g. by hackers) VE may be liable for damages from customers – particularly if credit card details are stolen and used fraudulently. VE may also be in breach of data protection legislation for inadequate security over personal data.

(2)   Lack of controls over access to materials

The lack of controls over customer passwords means the customers could be sharing passwords. One customer can order and pay for the products, but these can be downloaded multiple times, even simultaneously, by other people using the same password. This represents a potential loss of revenue for VE. Similarly, more than one person can participate in webinars using the same user name and password.

(3)   Hacking

Hacking means gaining unauthorised access to computer systems, typically through the internet or across internal networks. Hackers may be employees or external parties. The most obvious way to gain access is by guessing user names and passwords. Hackers can also access systems by exploiting vulnerabilities in the system, or by fooling employees into sharing their user names and passwords (e.g. by calling them and pretending to be from the IT department and asking them to confirm their user name and password).

Hackers could cause damage to VE in many ways. Commercially sensitive material such as course structures or materials could be stolen and passed on to competitors or made freely available on a "torrent" (with a resulting loss of revenue). As mentioned above credit card details could be stolen and used fraudulently, leading to customers taking legal action against VE for failing to protect the data adequately.

Many hackers perform the activity for fun rather than monetary gain and take pleasure from causing damage or disruption to computer systems. The costs to VE of this are likely to include disruption to activities (e.g. customers not being able to download materials or attend webinars) which may lead to a loss of goodwill as well as lost revenue.

(b) **Controls to mitigate the risks**

Customer data

A data protection compliance officer should be appointed who is responsible for ensuring that all customer data held is processed and secured in accordance with relevant data protection laws and regulations. Staff should also receive training so that they are aware of data protection rules.

Steps must be taken to secure customer data. Rafael has noted that customer data is not encrypted and clearly this should be remedied. A further control would be to keep customer data on a separate server so that fewer people have access to it.

Credit card information should not be saved. Once the payment has been received from the credit card company or agent the details should be deleted.

Controls over customers

Stricter policies should be put in place relating to passwords to prevent them being shared. Customers should only be able to log in from one device at a time, for example, and customers passwords should automatically expire after the end of the course.

Downloads of materials such as e-books should only be allowed once per password and a user name and password should only be accepted once for a particular webinar.

Regarding books it is difficult to stop customers buying materials and then photocopying them. An alternative would be to discontinue offering printed materials and allow "read only" on one or two electronic reader devices registered by the customer. Alternatively, if printing is to be allowed, this could be restricted to printing directly from the web without downloading materials. In this case the print facility could be programmed to include, on every page, the name of the person who printed it, the date of printing and a statement that only the individual is authorised to use the materials. Although this will not stop copying it should discourage it.

Hackers

Password policies must be put in place to make passwords harder to guess (e.g. a requirement to use upper and lower case letters and numeric characters). The strength of password should be shown as the customer is selecting it. The system should require users to change passwords regularly (e.g. every three months). If an incorrect password is entered three times for a particular user, that user should be blocked.

Firewalls can be used to prevent access to VE's internal systems from external networks. Alternatively, internal systems and networks should not be connected to the internet at all, except for those that are required for interaction with customers (e.g. the website and systems from which materials are downloaded).

Software updates should be applied regularly as these can fix identified vulnerabilities in systems. As this is a specialist area, it could be outsourced to organisations that are aware of vulnerabilities.

Tutorial note: *The question asked for **only two** controls for each of the areas of concern. This solution includes more than two for learning purposes, but you must follow the examiner's requirements in the examination.*

(c) **Methods to acquire new customers**

Customer acquisition means attracting more customers for the online training products of VE. This can come from using the website to attract potential customers or encouraging existing customers to move to online courses from the classroom courses. In the case of VE, the company would probably not wish to move customers from the classroom onto online courses, so focus should be on improving the visibility of the website.

Search engine marketing

Search engine marketing involves ensuring that when an individual searches the web for a Spanish language course (using a search engine such as Google or Bing), VE will be one of the first websites that will be listed. Search engine marketing relies on understanding the algorithms that the search engines use to identify websites when users enter a search. The use of key words such as "Spanish course" appearing many times on the website for example is a simple way that a search engine may select a website.

Pay per click adverts

Adverts and links to the website of VE could be placed on related websites (e.g. a website that discusses Spanish culture might be a good place to place an advert for VE). VE can then pay's the owners of the website when somebody clicks on the link (or offer a reciprocal link).

Online PR

Online PR involves using the internet in activities aimed at enhancing the reputation of an organisation. For example, press releases could be sent to journalists by e-mail focusing on particular activities organised by VE, or somebody could be asked to write a blog in which the activities of VE are mentioned.

Social networks

Social networks (e.g. Facebook and Twitter) are among the most visited websites on the internet. Companies such as VE can monitor discussions on these sites related to Spanish courses to find out, for example, what people are saying they need or expect. They can then respond by providing these. Having a Facebook page and a twitter account is likely to be important to VE so that the company can communicate with the wider potential market.

E-mail marketing

E-mails can be sent to potential customers advertising VE's courses. The difficulty here is in obtaining the e-mail addresses of interested people.

E-mail marketing also involves responding to incoming e-mails (e.g. enquiries from VE's website).

Offline campaigns

Traditional ways of advertising can also be used even for online businesses (e.g. TV advertising or advertising in magazines and newspapers). TV advertising may be expensive and is normally aimed at products that are likely to appeal to a wider audience, so may not be appropriate for VE, but magazines about further education or about Spain might be suitable places to place adverts.

Answer 27 THE MANAGEMENT PRESS

(a)   **Drivers and barriers to e-business adoption**

Drivers

- Cost reduction, specifically raw material costs (the cost of paper) and distribution costs to bookshops.

- Improved profit margin, perhaps achieved by removing the bookshop as an intermediary.

- Increased revenue, increasing sales (as well as profit margins) is an important objective.

- The desire to keep up-to-date (exemplified by the marketing director) and hence to avoid losing market share to businesses prepared to embrace e-business.

- Increased ecological concern about the use of timber for paper manufacture. The trees used to provide the timber are becoming increasingly scarce.

- People, in the shape of the marketing director and the graduate recruited to develop the website.

Barriers

- Concerns about the cost of developing the website, particularly when revenue and profits are decreasing. Marketing expenditure has been reduced and this is likely to continue.

- Concerns that it will destroy the relationship with bookshops and those sales will decrease overall as a result. Destroying existing channels is often a major barrier to change.

- Lack of technical ability within the company to develop and maintain the website and the impact this may have on its long-term viability.

- Concern about fraud and piracy. This may be within the context of the financial transactions of e-commerce. It may also reflect concerns about the pirating of books, leading to either cheap printed versions being produced and sold in local markets or to illegitimate copies being sold and distributed on the web.

- Other directors could be perceived as a barrier to the adoption of e-business.

(b)   **E-business and the marketing mix**

Product

At present, TMP offer conventional physical books. E-business may provide opportunities for either replacing or augmenting this product. For example:

- *Replacing* the book with an electronic alternative that customers can read directly from the screen, view through an e-book reader or print off at their own cost. This may allow the range of products to be increased, introducing books that would be uneconomic to produce conventionally.

- *Augmenting* the product by providing supplementary services and features. For example, many text books now have an associated website that includes further case studies, exercises, solutions, simulations etc. This may be particularly applicable to management texts where readers often require further information.

Using e-business to change the nature of the product should help reinforce two of the main drivers previously identified. E-business should help reduce raw material costs as well as helping the company meet environmental targets. Augmenting the product should help deliver a better quality product to customers.

E-business also offers opportunities for extending the product range, perhaps offering (through intermediaries) management training, financial advice and other related services.

Price

At present TMP largely sells through bookshops and so the TMP price has to reflect a profit margin for the bookshop. If TMP exploits e-business to develop a channel that eliminates bookshops, then it should be able to simultaneously discount the price of the book and yet still improve their profit margin. E-business may also be an opportunity to experiment with differential pricing. The scenario notes that overseas sales are low because of the relatively high sales price of books. TMP may be able to combine differential pricing (in local currencies) with electronic alternatives to find a product that is saleable in these markets.

TMP has to be aware of any price-comparison websites and be prepared to monitor costs on these sites and react accordingly. They also have to be aware of large established channels, such as Amazon. Such sites will expect keen pricing, but will also pay commissions on books sold through the site.

Finally, TMP might seek an alternative price strategy, based for example on subscribing to the site, rather than selling books. A "book" may become a continually updated web resource that customers pay to use on either a one-off or continuing basis. There is no need for them to actually own the book themselves. TMP therefore becomes a virtual library.

Direct pricing to customers also provides the opportunities for special offers, pre-publication prices and other deals. For example, special discount prices on related books can be offered to customers who have placed an order for a specific book.

Promotion

At present, promotion is restricted to a custom-built display case at bookshops and full-page display advertisements in magazines and journals. Such promotion reflects a conventional "push" approach to marketing that focuses on the product rather than the customers. If the website records the details of visitors, then the company can identify potential customers for its products and target them in mail-shots and on-line suggestions. For example, customers who have bought certain titles may have others suggested to them when they next visit the site. Many sites also make buying suggestions based on the behaviour of other customers, for example displaying "other titles which have been bought by customers who have bought this book".

E-business will require the company to consider both its online and offline promotion. TMP may be able to reduce its offline expenditure, cutting back on advertising. In its place it might spend elsewhere, particularly in making sure that it figures prominently in search engine listings. Links to other sites should also be considered, allowing promotion of TMP books on related sites. For example, internet sites providing management advice, information and glossaries may have a link to the TMP site. TMP pays commission to the site on sales made through such links. Banner advertising might also be considered on such sites. A similar approach might be used with academic websites where a TMP book is recommended reading for a course.

Place

Bookshops have limited reach, although they do provide the facility for the potential buyer to handle the book (see physical evidence). The display advertising has unpredictable reach. Circulation figures are usually provided by journals and magazines but this does not give any information on how many people actually read the advertisements in question. The scenario suggests that both bookshops and journals appear to have declining reach, based on statistics about their closure. The internet has global reach. The relatively small percentage of books currently sold outside Arcadia is attributed to the cost of those books. However, it may be that the rest of the world is simply unfamiliar with TMP's booklist, a shortcoming that will be addressed by the internet site

In wider e-business terms, a consideration of place will also lead to TMP considering whether it is economic to continue printing in Arcadia which is a high-cost economy. The printing works were established 50 years ago and it seems likely that cost-savings could be gained by printing and distributing the books in lower labour cost economies.

Physical evidence

One of the problems in buying books is the ability to look inside those books before purchase. Often titles are insufficient to make a purchasing decision. One of the advantages of the bookshop is that the potential buyer can physically inspect the goods, looking at the content in detail to ensure that it meets their needs. In contrast, physical evidence is not possible at all through display advertising in a journal.

On the website, it would be possible to allow the potential buyer to view the contents of the book in detail and (usually) one physical chapter. This so-called "look inside" facility allows them to base their buying decision on some (but not all) physical evidence. Further evidence can also be provided by unsolicited recommendations and reviews from other customers. Feedback, comments and rating systems are typical features on a website. These are rarely available through the bookshop. The bookshop employees have rarely read all the books they sell and, if they have read the book, are probably biased towards a sale. Sometimes, reviews have been placed in the book, often from a previous printing or edition. However, these are only the ones sanctioned by the publisher. Unsolicited references are one of the advantages of the website (as long as they are good!).

The problem of physical evidence can also be addressed by seeing the book as a website resource rather than a physical entity. If the reader pays for access, then very little expenditure is likely on a book that does not fulfil the reader's requirements and expectations.

Answer 28 CRONIN AUTO RETAIL

(a)   **Evaluation of application of principles in e-marketing**

Tutorial note: *This question uses four of the "6 Is" developed by McDonald and Wilson to explore the differences between traditional and e-marketing. Candidates' answers did not have to be strictly classified within each of the factors identified below as, in reality, suggestions will cross the boundaries of these factors.*

Interactivity concerns the development of a two-way relationship between the customer and the supplier. The traditional display advertising and mail-shots used by CAR are examples of "push media" where the marketing message is broadcast to current and potential customers. Their current website continues this approach, with the stock listing essentially representing a continually updated, but widely accessible, display advertisement. Supplementing mail-shots with e-mails could be immediately considered by CAR and would be a cheaper alternative to mail-shots. However, it still remains a "push technique" with little dialogue with the customer.

Tutorial note: *Here are three ideas that CAR could consider to improve the interactivity of its site. Other legitimate suggestions would also be given credit.*

(1)   Encouraging potential buyers on their website to ask questions about any car that they are interested in. Both questions and answers are published. This may provide someone with the vital information that clinches the sale. It also creates a great enthusiasm around the car. Buyers may move quickly so that they do not lose the opportunity to buy the car. On e-bay, customers are encouraged to "ask a question" of the seller and this often leads to long threads where the supplier and potential buyers interact.

(2)   Many buyers would like to test drive a car before they purchase it. CAR could provide the opportunity for customers to book a test drive over the Internet.

(3)   Once a purchase had been complete, CAR might encourage feedback which could be published on the website. In this instance, customers are actually providing information that is commercially useful to buyers. This may be in the form of testimonials, or in the form of more structured feedback that e-bay encourages. Suppliers who have 100% positive feedback backed up by testimonials from previous buyers are powerfully reinforcing their marketing message.

Intelligence is about identifying and understanding the needs of potential customers and how they wish to be communicated with. It is traditionally the area of market research and marketing research. Currently CAR does very little research. It relies on a database that only consists of people who have actually bought cars from the company. Collecting email addresses through promotions and interactivity initiatives (see above) provides a much greater pool of potential customers who can be kept up-to-date through email. It can also give CAR significant intelligence about the type of cars that they are interested in and at what price. At present, the buyers for CAR use their experience when buying cars at auction and there is some concern that they buy what they would like to drive, not what the customers want to drive. It would be useful to support this experience with quantitative information about the type of cars potential buyers are really interested in. This may lead to a change in buying policy.

Individualisation concerns the tailoring of marketing information to each individual, unlike traditional media where the same message tends to be sent to everyone. Personalisation is a key element in building an effective relationship with the customer. In the context of CAR, individuals who have shown interest in a certain model or type of car may be selectively emailed when a similar car becomes available. This approach may also be used for current customers. For example, someone who purchased a particular car two or three years ago might be e-mailed about an opportunity to upgrade to an updated model. For individualisation to be successful, sufficient details must be collected through the intelligence and interactive facets of the "6 Is".

Individualisation will also be key in offering relevant after-sales service. This may concern inviting customers to return their cars for servicing at the correct dates or offering services only appropriate to that type of car. For example, circulating details of air-conditioning renewal only to customers with air conditioned cars.

Independence of location concerns the geographical location of the company. Electronic media increases the geographical reach of a company. For many companies this gives opportunities to sell into international markets which had previously been inaccessible to them.

This facet of the new media is unlikely to be appropriate to CAR. Most sales are to customers who are within two hours' drive of the CAR premises. The commodity nature of the cars that CAR are selling means that similar cars will be available throughout the country, often from garages that offer local service and support. Independence of location would be more significant if CAR was selling collectors or classic cars where each car is relatively rare and people are prepared to travel long distances to view the car they are interested in. Furthermore, the long term lease on CAR's current premises makes it unlikely that they will be able to locate to a cheaper site and hence exploit the independence of location offered by the new media.

(b) **Principles of e-procurement**

Procurement is concerned with purchasing goods or services for the organisation. It is concerned with sourcing items at the right price, delivered at the right time, to the right quality, in the right quantity and from the right source. Many contemporary definitions of procurement also include the inbound logistics required to get the product from the supplier to the customer.

E-procurement looks at the opportunities presented by automating aspects of procurement to improve the performance of the five "rights" identified above.

Tutorial note: *There is a wide range of potential answers to this part of the question depending on the scope and focus of e-procurement selected by the candidate. Solutions may vary from the simple automation of part of the system, to re-thinking the way the company does business.*

Potential application at CAR

In the context of CAR, two distinct types of procurement can be identified:

(1)   Production-related procurement that is directly related to the core activities of the organisation. This relates to the purchase of cars for sale and the purchase of parts required for servicing or repairing vehicles.

(2)   Non-production procurement.

CAR has always purchased its vehicles through experienced buyers attending auctions. On average this attendance costs the company $500 per day, leading to the purchase (on average) of five cars. This purchasing cost of $100 per car represents 5% of the average profit margin on each car. This cost could be eliminated if cars were purchased through e-auctions, with bids made on-line. The risk here is that the cars bought were not of the right quality. CAR prides itself in the personal selection of its cars. However, it could be argued that cars which are less than two years old with a full service history are unlikely to have much wrong with them.

The parts needed for servicing and mechanical repairs are ordered from motor factors or manufacturers. A number of regular suppliers are retained, many in long-term relationships with CAR. This is known as systematic sourcing. Most of the problems here are caused by the need to pass requisitions for parts through a procurement manager. The first problem is the delay in the purchasing cycle. There is a backlog of requisitions that have to be reviewed, agreed and sourced by the procurement manager. This is particularly problematic when a customer's car is in the garage awaiting a part. The customer is likely to be frustrated and annoyed by the delay, whilst the car is occupying garage space that could have been profitably used for a fee-paying job. The second problem is the cost of the paperwork and the processing time of the procurement manager associated with the purchase.

The final problem is that purchases can only be made between 10.00 and 16.00 when the procurement manager is at work. Mechanics work 07.00 to 19.00 and are frustrated that they cannot make orders outside the times the procurement manager is at work. Giving the mechanics the systems and authorisation to order parts (up to a certain value limit) from specified suppliers over the Internet should deliver cost savings and speed up repairs and services. A direct ordering system should also reduce administrative errors and enhance customer goodwill. CAR might also use e-procurement to open up competitive bidding between potential suppliers; posting their requirements on their website and inviting competing bids. Parts could be sourced from a number of suppliers, taking advantage of the lowest prices for each part. This could be combined with just-in-time supply, reducing the cost of stock holding at CAR.

Non-production procurement is concerned with ordering things such as stationery, paper, ink toner and other office supplies. Christa Degnan *(quoted in Chaffney, E-Business and E-Commerce Management)* suggested that for "every dollar a company earns in revenue, 50 cents to 55 cents is spent on indirect goods and services – things like office supplies and computer equipment. That half dollar represents an opportunity. By driving costs out of the purchasing process, companies can increase profits without having to sell more goods". CAR is in this situation. It uses the same process for office supplies as it does for car parts. However, most office supplies are cheap, commodity products where sometimes the cost of ordering the product exceeds the value of the purchased product, particularly where a cumbersome purchasing process is in place. With little differentiation between products, it is the availability and cost of the product that become the most significant aspects in the procurement process. E-procurement should provide better information, identifying alternative suppliers and allowing spot sourcing of office products to fulfil immediate need.

Overall, e-procurement should reduce the administrative burden on the procurement manager, giving him or her the opportunity to concentrate on negotiating terms, agreements and product standardisation; more strategic tasks in the procurement process.

Answer 29 BA TIMES

(a)   **Use of interactivity, individualisation intelligence and independence of location**

Victor urgently needs to revisit his business model to look at the opportunities presented by new technology and new media. Revenues from his current business are falling due to reduced advertising spend and fewer subscribers. On the other hand, production, distribution and office costs are increasing. These problems are not unique to the *BA Times*. The sales of printed magazines and the profits of publishers are falling dramatically throughout Umboria.

Perhaps because of his conventional publishing background, Victor still perceives his core business as the publishing of a printed magazine. The *BA Times* does have a website, but it is designed to provide tempting tasters for the magazine, running extracts of stories that can only be read in full by people who subsequently buy a printed copy of the magazine. Thus the website is seen as a way of marketing the magazine and, in itself, provides far fewer services and information than the magazine. Emerging technology provides Victor with the opportunity to revisit this business model in the context of four of the "6Is" of e-marketing: individualisation, interactivity, intelligence and independence of location.

Individualisation

A survey of people who had not renewed their subscription revealed that some subscribers believe that the magazine includes too much information which is irrelevant to them. One respondent commented that, "I am studying the ABC syllabus and so in-depth articles on ICFC topics and examinations are not relevant to me. I quite enjoy reading the news parts, but not the in-depth analysis of examinations that I am not taking". One ABC candidate remarked that, "I have reached the final stage of my examinations. I do not want to read articles about the stages I have already passed. I reckon only about 15% of *BA Times* is relevant to me now".

A key feature of the new technology and media is the opportunity to *individualise* or tailor the product to meet specific requirements and for that tailoring to be driven and performed by the customer. So, for example, if all the resources are made available on a website, the customer only needs to access those resources that he or she wants. This can be achieved by him or her just ignoring menu options for other institutes or examinations or, more innovatively, by configuring the website so that it just reflects an individual's interest (*myBATImes*). Furthermore, through registering interests either directly on the website, or through linked social and business networking sites, the candidate can be kept informed of articles, news, comments and blogs relevant to their interests, institute and examination stage. A centralised website resource would allow Victor to expand the number of relevant resources available (which he is under pressure to do) without making his printed magazine any larger or more expensive. He can also supplement conventional text articles with webcasts and podcasts. If the candidate wants a hard copy of any article, then he or she can locate it and print it out, thus transferring printed costs to the subscriber. The website should be considered as a comprehensive knowledge centre where all relevant resources are stored.

Interactivity

A key characteristic of the internet is the opportunity it provides for interactivity. Traditional printed media (e.g. magazines) are predominantly *push media* where the message is broadcast from the company to the customer. There is limited interaction with the customer. Evidence of this is provided in the scenario, where, although there are readers' letters, the monthly gap between issues means that many topics just lose their currency, or are made irrelevant by changed circumstances. The only person who can immediately comment on topics raised in a reader's letter is the editor of the magazine. One of survey respondents commented on this. "Some of the readers' letters are really irritating or just plain wrong, but the editor seldom makes a comment! It really annoys me!" A key characteristic of the internet is *interactivity*. Issues raised on a website can be commented on immediately and threads developed. In general, the internet is a *pull media* where the customer initiates contact and is seeking information on a website.

Communities of interest are important features of the internet. The *BA Times* largely fails to exploit its unique position of being independent of the two large professional associations. It could provide writers with an opportunity for controversy and speculation, generating feedback which would unlikely to be acceptable to the official websites of the professional associations. The site itself can become a natural host to communities of interest, discussing and documenting topics relevant to that community and making resources available to new members. Feedback can also be provided on written articles, asking for clarification or providing extra information.

The interactivity of the website is also enhanced by the ability to continually update it. Reference has already been made to the time gap between issues. Significant events may take place the day after a print deadline. The website can be updated immediately to report on emerging issues and concerns. This should again increase the use of the website, ensuring that users see the *BA Times* as a valuable source of information.

Intelligence

The Internet can be used as a relatively low cost method of collecting information from and about customers. Online questionnaires can be used to help understand how users rate the website and to understand what products and services they are looking for. Website analytics can be used to identify which pages are looked at and what browsers and search terms are used to arrive at such pages. Both questionnaires and analytics will help Victor tailor the content to his potential customers.

By exploiting editorial independence and interactivity, the site can become the one-stop resource for all aspiring business analysts. If this becomes the case, then capturing information about visitors will allow Victor to build up a very significant resource which cannot only be used to improve the website but also (as long as permission is given) to provide intelligence to other companies which wish to exploit this market (e.g. learning providers and, indeed, the professional associations themselves).

Independence of location

Finally, a further clear benefit of contemporary technology is its ability to provide an organisation with independence of location. Although this answer has focused on the central role of a website resource, Victor could exploit opportunities for independence of location within the current printed magazine model. Production currently takes place in an expensive area of Umboria, a country where wage rates are also high. Production could be moved to a country where wages, equipment and operational costs are cheaper and then shipped to customers from there. Similarly, the Head Office could be moved to a cheaper area, offering the company potential savings on overhead costs.

(b) **Victor's concerns about effect of technology on his subscribers**

Victor himself is a potential barrier to the extensive use of new technology and media. His background is in printed magazines and this is a product that he feels comfortable with. He likes the physical, tactile feel of magazines and evidence suggests that his product is well liked and respected in the industry. But, increasing costs and changing reading habits mean that the future of the printed magazine industry looks bleak. However, even if Victor can overcome his preference for printed media, he has a further problem in understanding how new technology is going to turn round the fortunes of the *BA Times* and return it to profit.

A simple option is to *just employ new technology to reduce costs*. This might give him some breathing space in which to develop a future business strategy or plan his retirement. Alternatively, he could consider an option to embrace the new technology more extensively and re-position the printed *BA Times* as just one channel to his target market. It is possible that the introduction of a comprehensive web resource may lead to a further fall in the circulation of a printed copy version of the *BA Times*. However, this would have to be researched. Perhaps his readership contains people like himself who would still want to receive a physical copy of a magazine.

If a more radical shift to new technology and new media is to be justified, then Victor would have to be convinced of the possibility of generating income from at least three sources. These would offset a fall in income from the printed magazine and also address the issue of the financial viability of the company.

Increased advertising: The very breadth of the *BA Times* (news, articles, three associations, many examinations) probably makes display advertising only attractive to the larger learning providers which provide courses at all levels across all qualifications. Targeted advertising is much easier on the web and so the new resource may attract advertising from a wider range of learning providers. An extended product range (e.g. recruitment resources) made available on the website should also bring in new advertisers from different sectors. If Victor can establish the *BA Times* website as the premier one-stop resource for business analysts, then attracting significant advertising should be no problem.

Subscription services within the website: Many websites contain both free and subscription resources. High quality free services can be a taster for attracting customers to the resources which are only available for a subscription. This is an established approach in web-based services and is particularly relevant in a competitive environment like examinations.

Candidates may believe that investing relatively small amounts of money in extra services might give them an edge in preparing for examinations.

Income from selling intelligence: The facility of websites to capture information about visitors and their interests has already been discussed in part (a). This will be of potential use to other organisations and with the person's consent can be forwarded and sold.

Victor is also concerned about the reaction of advertisers to any proposal to adopt new technology within the *BA Times*. However, it is likely that Victor will receive a positive response from advertisers. At present, advertising revenue is falling. In general, there is a growing disenchantment with push marketing technologies, where advertisers cannot be sure that their message has reached the intended market. Advertising on a comprehensive website has many of the advantages that have already been discussed. Advertisements can be made specific and individualised, they can be quickly and easily updated, and the effectiveness of an advertisement or a campaign can be relatively easily analysed through the responses received from the website.

Finally, Victor is concerned about the effect on subscribers who cannot access a website or, like him, value a printed copy and wish to still receive one. At this stage, there is no reason why a smaller run of the printed version cannot be maintained by exploiting technology to reduce printing, distribution and office costs. Contribution to overheads will be reduced, but income from other sources (see above) should compensate for this. Some advertisers may also wish to continue advertising in the printed edition to supplement their web-based marketing.

The nature of the web resource also allows Victor to reconsider the range of products he has to offer. At present the magazine is focused on news and preparing candidates for examinations. Income is derived from learning providers advertising in the pages of the magazine. Victor might consider moving into related business areas that would appeal to his readership. From the feedback given, the most obvious candidate is probably recruitment. One of the respondents to the survey commented that, "I became a business analyst to get a job, not just to sit examinations and read about examining bodies". Victor might have lost focus here. For many candidates, taking examinations is a means to an end, not an end in itself, and job opportunities and careers do not seem to be considered in the *BA Times* at present. Articles about certain job roles and interview advice might be provided and a potential new income stream should open up for Victor from recruitment agencies placing advertisements for jobs which they have been contracted to fill.

Answer 30 ASW

(a)   **Alternative strategies to address slippage**

Deadline extension request

The case study scenario suggests that early delays in the project were caused by the absence of key CaetInsure staff and changes in user requirements in the re-insurance module. These delays meant that the full system specification was signed off three weeks later than initially agreed. Unfortunately, the delivery date of the whole project was not re-negotiated at this point as it was suggested that "time could be made up" during the programming stage. Furthermore, the marketing department of CaetInsure had already announced the launch of a new product to coincide with the implementation of the software and they did not want to change these dates. However, the project manager could now return to CaetInsure and inform them that it had not been possible to catch up with the proposed schedule and to remind them that the initial slippage had been caused by them. Although the deadline date is associated with a product launch it is unlikely that this is crucial. It is not a matter of life and death. It might be irksome to delay the launch by a few weeks, but it is unlikely that many people will notice or indeed care about it. There are many significant successful products which have been released long after their intended release date. In many ways it is an artificial deadline.

However, there are at least three problems associated with this suggestion:

(1)   The delay is now longer than the three weeks incurred at the specification stage. Consequently, the project manager will have to explain that there have been further delays to the project.

(2)   The project manager will have to be very confident about his revised delivery date. The project plan does not explicitly contain any time for programmers fixing faults found in system and acceptance testing and it seems very likely that faults will be found in this testing.

(3)   Some negotiation will have to take place on the late delivery penalty clause charges the sales account manager agreed in the initial contract. If some (or all) of these clauses are enacted then the profitability of the project will be significantly affected.

Functional reduction of the software

The scenario suggests that the re-insurance functionality has been a problem throughout the project. There may also be unresolved issues in other parts of the software. However, it must be remembered that the ASW product is a proven software solution, bespoke development is only concerned with customising the basic product to fulfil certain customer requirements. Therefore it is likely that there are large areas of the software that can be successfully delivered to the customer. The key issue here is whether this reduced functionality will fulfil the requirements associated with the proposed new product which CaetInsure intends to launch. If it does then the delivery of a partial solution does not have a significant business impact and the product launch can go ahead as planned. The project manager needs to discuss this with the customer as quickly as possible. He has to be sure that the reduced scope does indeed fulfil these requirements and, if it does, to focus testing, migration and document production on these parts of the software. He will also have to estimate the delivery time of the second phase of the software that fulfils the complete user requirement.

There are three elements of this suggestion that the project manager should bear in mind:

(1)   The impact of reduced scope on the penalty clauses of the contract. It would appear harsh to deliver a part solution but to still be fully penalised for not delivering the total solution. Consequently some contract renegotiation is necessary.

(2)   There will be an unexpected overhead associated with delivering a second phase which contains the full product. This is the overhead of *regression testing*, making sure that changes made to the product in the second release do not unintentionally affect the software solution that has already been delivered.

(3)   The specification of data migration programs will have to be reviewed to see if they need to be changed in the light of the reduced functionality. Any changes will affect data migration programs which are currently being written or tested.

Reduce or change testing parameters

A number of options might be considered around the testing of the software. One option is to considerably reduce system testing and hand over the software to acceptance testing ahead of the proposed schedule. The point has already been made that the software is essentially a package that has to be tailored for specific functions. Consequently, large areas of the software have been tested before, much of it by actual users out in the businesses that are using this solution. Programs for the CaetInsure version will have been unit tested by programmers before they have been released to system testers and so no area of the system is *untested*, although there will be areas that have not been *independently tested*. Another option is to reduce the scope of system testing, focusing it on testing functionality rather than usability (which will be one focus of acceptance testing) and performance (which can be difficult to perform effectively in a software house environment where the user's actual hardware configuration cannot be easily mimicked). A further option is to execute system and acceptance testing in parallel.

There are a number of issues with this approach which the project manager needs to consider, two are identified below.

(1)   The acceptance testers are likely to find significantly more faults than they would if full system testing had preceded acceptance testing. This can lead to a reduction in customer confidence which could jeopardise the whole project.

(2)   Faults identified by both system and user acceptance testers have to be carefully managed. Configuration management becomes a very significant issue and appropriate version control of the software is an essential overhead. Confidence is undermined by the constant releases of new versions of the software, some of which, due to poor configuration management, contain faults which have already been reported and fixed in earlier versions of the software.

Additional resource request

Finally the project manager may request further resources for the project. The current project plan is at a high level of detail. It does not show how many system testers are actually working on the system or how many technical authors are writing the documentation. It may be possible to add more resources and so reduce the elapsed time of the activity. Resources might also be asked to work smarter or work longer. For example, testing might be prioritised so that the most important areas of the software from the user's perspective are tested first. It may also be possible to automate certain areas of testing or to outsource it to specialist testing companies. Programmers might be asked to focus more on static testing (which is particularly effective at finding faults) and to work overtime to beat their deadlines.

However, the project manager must be aware that adding resources to a late running project often slows the project down as established members of the project team explain requirements, standards and procedures to any newcomers. A key factor here will be the precision of the requirements. If these are well specified then it should be possible to add testing staff reasonably effectively, or indeed to outsource testing to countries where it can be conducted relatively cheaply. It may also be possible to bring in technical authors and automated testing tools specialists who can speed up these activities. Programming is more of an issue. It will be very difficult to bring new programmers up to speed. However, it may be possible to transfer resources from other projects and to support the established programmers by providing appropriate hardware and software.

Finally, the addition of resources to the project will have an impact on project profitability. The project estimate will have assumed a certain commitment of resources. Adding resources will reduce the profit margin and indeed, in the extreme, may make the project itself unprofitable.

(b)   **Slippage solution recommendation and justification**

There is no correct answer for this part of the question. However, it is suggested that a combination of the above strategies would be appropriate. The deadline is not crucial in the wider scheme of things and there is no statutory requirement to deliver on time. However the deadline is significant to the customer and a failure to meet this deadline may cause internal problems and a "loss of face". This is particularly significant in this context because ASW is an external supplier. It might have been easier to negotiate an extended deadline if the software were being supplied by an internal IT department. Hence, it might be suggested that, in these circumstances, the deadline should not be extended for an initial release. However, it may be possible to negotiate the scope of this release, making sure that the key functions are in place and tested when the software is delivered. The customer might accept this reduction in scope as recognition of the delays caused earlier in the project when, due to the absence of key personnel, the full system specification was signed off three weeks late.

It could be argued that the current tasks of ASW, system testing and writing the user manual, could be shortened by adding further resources to the project. Effective testing will depend on the quality of the specifications but it may be possible to add more resources and back this up with reduced test coverage. The amount of testing performed is driven by risk. There has to be a balance between the cost and time of more testing and the consequences of failure. Although the insurance system appears to be mission-critical to CaetInsure, there is a robust current system that could be reverted to during the planned parallel running.

It would also appear that more resources could be added to writing the user manual. There is already slack between the scheduled completion of the user manual and its use in the training course.

ASW might also consider starting writing the data migration programs before week 22. It appears from the project plan that ASW are waiting for system testing to be complete before writing these programs. It may be possible to start beforehand, writing migration routines for the parts of the system that have already passed system testing.

The acceptance testing is outside the control of ASW. It is being performed by CaetInsure. However, again CaetInsure might consider reducing the time taken for acceptance testing by adding more resources to the task and by accepting a greater risk of failure during parallel running.

On balance, it might be suggested that further resources are quickly added to the project and that the test coverage is reduced. Hence the solution is largely concerned with adding resources and potentially reducing quality. If the customer is happy to slightly reduce the scope of the initial release to reflect past delays then this is a bonus. However, it is suggested that in this project the delivery date should remain fixed. Relaxing this is not an appropriate strategy in this instance.

Answer 31 MAHEM

(a) **Use of a project initiation document**

Meetings were held throughout the design and construction of the centre. These meetings focused on the building of the centre, monitoring progress and resolving minor issues that arose during construction. The successful completion of the centre on budget and ahead of schedule suggests that these meetings were effective. However, the absence of a wider **project initiation document** or **terms of reference** created problems that could have been resolved or better understood. An analysis of how a standard document could have helped address some of the issues that affected the construction and subsequent evaluation of the centre is given below.

There was confusion about the **objectives** of the project. The local authority is unable to recognise the distinction between *project objectives* and *business objectives*. The business objective of the project was to deliver payback in four years as required by the Private/Public investment policy. In contrast, the project objective was to build the centre by June 2018 for $600,000. By their very nature, the business objectives are not within the control of the project manager from the construction company responsible for building the centre. The achievement of the business objectives will involve much more than just delivering a building. They will concern marketing, sales and the successful operation of the centre. Evidence seems to suggest that the project manager was not (as the second project sponsor claimed) a failure. He delivered the building within budget and ahead of schedule.

The problem was the failure of the local authority to distinguish between the project objectives (constructing the building) and the wider business objectives which the building was to help satisfy. It appears that nobody was either aware of, or willing to take responsibility for these wider objectives. It is recommended that future projects should clearly distinguish between project and business objectives and assign responsibilities to each.

The **scope** of the project was well-defined by the standard architectural drawings agreed between the construction company and the project sponsor. The only significant problem concerned the quality of the internal painting. There is no way (post project) of reconciling this misunderstanding. The construction company felt that it had come to an arrangement about this with the initial sponsor, but no documentation could be found to irrevocably support this. The letter confirming the intended finish produced by the construction company was not counter-signed by the project sponsor. This is an important lesson for the construction company in future projects. Changes or clarifications to the specification must be counter-signed by both parties. This is also appropriate to the local authority's project management methods, continuing to demand that all changes must be counter-signed by both parties.

The **constraints** of the project were relatively well-defined in terms of time and cost, as these were defined in the original business case. However, tension was caused within the project when it became clear that certain labour and sourcing requirements of the Private/Public policy were not being adhered to. Specifically, these concerned the use of sub-contracted labour (not to be used without the commissioning agency's permission) and sourcing at least 80% of timber on the project from sustainable forests. The generic terms of the Private/Public investment policy were not made available to the construction company. It is suggested that the local authority should, in future, integrate such objectives explicitly into the project terms of reference.

The **authority** of the project is the sponsor responsible for making decisions about the project, providing resources, considering and agreeing changes. They should also promote the project within the local authority and accept the project once it has been completed. The original sponsor on the local authority was very supportive of the centre's design but their successor seemed unsure of her responsibilities and focused on obtaining concessions from the suppliers under the pretext of "value for money" rather than considering the wider issues, such as defining who had responsibility for delivering the business objectives. She also failed to promote the project to her fellow employees and tried to blame the builders for the failure. The role of the project sponsor should be formally defined within the local authority. Their responsibilities should be clear and failure to adhere to them should be addressed.

The **resources** available to the project were relatively well defined, although the lack of local authority staff able and willing to discuss disability access meant that the contractors had to use their own initiative in this area. Fortunately for them, they interpreted legal requirements correctly and the delivered centre was deemed to be compliant with legislation. However, this is a risky approach and is not recommended for the future. Local authority resources and support required by projects should be specifically defined in advance. If they are unavailable during the project then substitutes must be provided.

(b)   **Evaluation and analysis of proposed benefits**

This part of the question evaluates the four sets of benefits identified in the payback calculation. It requires the categorisation and critical evaluation of each benefit.

Ward and Daniel use the term **"observable benefits"** to describe the least explicit benefits such as increased staff morale in the case of the community centre. They suggest that such benefits should be assessed against clear criteria by someone who is qualified to make such an assessment. So, for example, current staff morale and motivation might be assessed in an independent survey and compared to results from a similar survey conducted once the centre has been built and occupied.

In the context of the centre it might seem reasonable to assume that improved staff morale and motivation will have a positive effect on the success of the centre. For example, it may lead to better customer service, which may, in turn, lead to customers returning more often or using more facilities whilst they are there. It may also lead to reduced staff turnover, so decreasing costs associated with recruitment, induction and training.

However, from a benefits perspective, two issues have to be specifically addressed:

(1)   The relatively significant estimated benefits attributed to improved staff morale in the original payback calculation must be questioned. In terms of increased benefits it is difficult to disentangle benefits due to this from other factors which might lead to increased customer use. In terms of reduced recruitment costs, there is little to suggest that staff turnover is high at the moment. 80% of the staff has been with the centre for over five years and there is an economic recession in the country, with unprecedented unemployment.

(2)   Perhaps more fundamentally, the whole basis of the benefit needs further consideration. It is unclear why moving to the new centre would necessarily improve staff morale and motivation in the first place. There may be some intellectual support for the view that a pleasant working environment contributes towards motivation, but, in the initial stages the centre is likely to have temporary teething problems leading to (at least in the short term) a more stressful work environment. Similarly, even if a survey found that morale and motivation had increased it would be hazardous to attribute this to the investment in the centre as it may be largely due to external factors affecting each individual.

A **measurable benefit** is one where an aspect of performance is currently being measured or could be measured. However, it is not possible to estimate with any certainty, in advance, how much performance will improve when the changes are completed. In the context of the centre, *increased income* seems a reasonable measurable benefit. It seems reasonable to expect that current income is measured and that similar measures may be collected in the future.

The estimates on the payback calculation need further scrutiny, particularly the large increases predicted for years three and four. It should be acknowledged that few benefits are instantaneous and that use will only increase as the reputation of the centre grows. However, this growth in customer use is not associated with any increased costs which would seem unlikely. Hence, the basis of these benefits requires further investigation.

A **quantifiable benefit** is one where there is sufficient evidence to forecast how much improvement or benefit should result from the proposed changes. In such circumstances the level of performance prior to the change is known and the improvement can be specifically attributed to the investment, rather than to other changes. Energy savings appears to fit into this category. Energy use could be established for the current building. The Private/Public investment policy requires buildings constructed under this arrangement to meet specified target energy levels. The construction methods and design of the building should reflect the need to meet this target. Thus there is a good basis for predicting energy savings, although, of course, the actual savings will not be known until after implementation.

Finally, a **financial benefit** is one where a financial value can be obtained by applying a cost, price or any other valid financial formula to a quantifiable benefit. Thus we might re-classify the quantifiable benefit of *energy savings* as a financial benefit, assuming that the new building meets the minimum level required by the initiative. There are still important assumptions here, and the real performance can only be assessed after the building has been used for a while. There is still an element of estimation, and indeed the new building may surpass the minimum levels assumed in the cost/benefit analysis. In contrast *rental savings* on the current properties are both definite and immediate and are correctly recorded in the payback calculation.

In summary, the benefits in the payback calculation should probably have been initially restricted to financial and quantifiable benefits. The other benefits are important and should have been documented in the business case, but it seems inappropriate to artificially quantify these benefits to satisfy the need to achieve a payback target. However, if the measurable benefits are included in the business case, their underlying assumptions and probability should be communicated to the decision-maker. Furthermore, efforts might also be made to better estimate the likely benefits, perhaps through looking at performance in similar centres, and using this as a benchmark to elevate the benefits to being, at least, quantifiable.

Answer 32 INSTITUTE OF INDEPENDENT ANALYSTS

(a)   **Evaluation of the financial case of the computer-based assessment project**

The table presented in the scenario suggests that the project is currently financially viable. It returns a net present value of $10,925. However, the basis of the discount rate selection could be questioned. Although there is little information in the scenario about this, it might be felt that it has been set artificially low to produce a positive NPV. Also, the duration of the investment appraisal is quite long (seven years). Three and five year appraisals are more common. So again, the basis of this could be questioned. Perhaps seven-year investment periods are common at the IIA, but this needs to be investigated and confirmed.

It would also be beneficial to perform a sensitivity analysis on the data. A relatively small change in the initial cost of the software makes the NPV negative.

Costs

Software costs

Although the software package has a fixed cost, the IIA wishes to make a number of significant bespoke amendments. The actual detail of these amendments is still under discussion. They are currently estimated at $25,000 and this cost is part of the year 1 payment. However, this estimate may change once the detail of the requirement is agreed. The IIA must keep bespoke requirements under review to ensure that costs do not rise substantially, invalidating the financial business case for the investment. The scenario also suggests that there are problems in defining the detail of the requirement and these may lead to project delays, meaning that benefits may not begin to accrue until year 3 (or beyond), which will seriously affect the financial viability of the project. The final delivered cost of the project will also determine the maintenance cost, as it is calculated at 10% of the final delivered software cost. So, an increase in the initial cost of the software will also have long-term implications which may again affect the overall viability of the project.

Question bank costs

External consultants are to be paid a fixed fee for each question they successfully deliver to the question bank. The current estimate is for the initial delivery of 2,000 questions (with payments spread over year 0 and year 1) and then the subsequent update and amendment of 100 questions per year. These costs are within the control of the IIA and so appear reasonably definite. However, it is unclear why a question bank cost of $50,000 would be incurred immediately (year 0) as question setters are only paid on the acceptance of their question. This demands further investigation. If it is incorrect and the costs are actually incurred in years 1 and 2, then the NPV of the project will be increased.

Security costs

This is a definite cost; a fixed price has been agreed with a security firm who have guaranteed it for the duration of the project.

Disruption costs

The IIA believes that implementing the new assessment system will lead to a temporary reduction in productivity and staff morale in the examinations department. They have estimated that this will cost them $15,000 in year 1 and 2 of the project. However, this is really an intangible cost and is impossible to accurately predict in advance.

Benefits

Reduced marker costs

The reduction in marker costs can be accurately predicted. Manual marking will not be required once the new assessment method is in place. In Ward and Daniel's terms this is a *financial benefit*, and it can be accurately predicted in advance. The only issue may be the timing of the benefits, given the current problems in specifying the bespoke system requirements.

Reduced administrative costs

The reduction in administrative costs is difficult to predict accurately in advance because the undefined bespoke software amendments will affect the administration of the assessment process. However, by simulating the new work process, it should be relatively easy to forecast how many administrative posts will be lost and at what cost. Thus, using Ward and Daniel's classification, this is either a *financial* (at best) or *quantifiable* (at worst) benefit. The IIA should revisit their cost saving estimates as soon as the bespoke element of the software is agreed.

Increased student numbers

The final benefit is extra income from increased student numbers attracted by the convenience of computer-based assessment. It is difficult to put a credible value on this in advance of the project. At best, using Ward and Daniel's classification, this is a *measurable* benefit. It concerns an aspect of performance which is currently being measured (student numbers), but it is not possible to estimate how much performance will improve when the computer-based assessment system has been implemented. It may be possible to get credible evidence from other professional bodies which have implemented computer-based assessment to support this, but there is no evidence that this has been done. It is the IIA's best guess.

Summary

There is a strong argument for taking disruption costs and increased student numbers out of the financial appraisal of the project. It is difficult to put credible values on these in advance of the project. The effect of doing this (for information) is shown below.

All figures in $000s				Year				
Costs	*0*	*1*	*2*	*3*	*4*	*5*	*6*	*7*
Initial software	200	200						
Software maintenance			40	40	40	40	40	40
Question bank	50	50	5	5	5	5	5	5
Security			20	20	20	20	20	20
Total costs	250	250	65	65	65	65	65	65
Income/Savings								
Marker fees	0	0	125	125	125	125	125	125
Admin saving	0	20	30	30	30	30	30	30
Total benefits	0	20	155	155	155	155	155	155
Benefits – costs	(250)	(230)	90	90	90	90	90	90
Discount factor	1	0.926	0.857	0.794	0.735	0.681	0.630	0.583
Present value	(250)	(212.98)	77.13	71.46	66.15	61.29	56.70	52.47
Net present value								(77.78)

The net present value is now less than zero, so there is no financial case for the project. However, this does not mean that the project should not go ahead. IIA management may feel that intangible benefits make the investment worthwhile and so the project may be progressed.

(b)   **Benefit owners, benefit maps and benefits realisation**

A *benefit owner* is someone who has responsibility for defining, agreeing and delivering a benefit defined in the business case. Without benefit owners, benefits are unlikely to happen. It is very unlikely that the project manager responsible for a change project (as alluded to by the IIA director) would be the benefit owner. Their responsibility is to deliver the project, not to operationally run the outcome of the project. This must be the responsibility of the business and so the benefit owner should be a person who has authority to make business decisions which help deliver the benefits. Many projects which have promised cost savings have not delivered them because no-one had responsibility for making those savings. It is very important that the IIA appoints a benefit owner for the administrative cost reductions. First, because the extent of those savings cannot be reliably estimated due to problems in requirements definition and, second, because someone has to actually make these staff cuts when the new system is in place to deliver the benefits promised in the initial business case.

A *benefits map* helps the benefit owner determine what has to be put in place to deliver the promised benefit. The map can also be used to show how the benefits relate to the objectives of the organisation. For example, increased student numbers may be part of improving the accessibility of the qualification. Benefits may require business changes and *enabling changes* which have to be put in place to deliver the benefit. For example, the eventual elimination of marker costs (a benefit) will only be achieved once a question bank has been defined (an identified cost). A process will have to be put in place to define how questions will be commissioned, how they will be evaluated and how they will be entered and maintained in the question bank. These business and enabling changes require tasks which will have to be estimated and scheduled in a project plan. They form the link between the IT enabler (the software solution) and actually delivering the benefit. The benefits map shows exactly what has to be done to actually deliver the promised benefit.

Benefits realisation is a post-implementation activity which actually compares the delivered benefits with the promised benefits (and costs) forecast in the business case. This is another key role for benefit owners. Also, because of the nature of the financial case (where benefits are delivered annually), it is useful if benefits realisation is a series of reviews. The primary objective is to establish which benefits have been delivered and which have not. Undelivered benefits are investigated and remedial action may be taken. Unanticipated benefits may have also emerged and these are also considered in the reviews. Lessons learnt are fed back into the *benefits management process*. It is often very difficult to disaggregate benefits as time passes. For example; an increase in student numbers may be due as much to the improvement of marketing, to the decline of competing institutes or to demographic change, as it is to computer-based assessment. However, benefits realisation remains worthwhile, if only to stress that someone has to have continuing responsibility for realising the promised benefits which justified the financial investment made by the organisation.

(c) **Business change lifecycle**

The business change lifecycle aims to ensure that proposed business changes are analysed adequately to ensure that they are aligned with the organisation's strategy, and that they are implemented effectively. The steps in the business change life cycle and how they might be carried out at IAA are as follows:

Alignment

The alignment stage is where it is recognised that business change is required to bring the business processes back in line with its strategy. This may be due to external changes leading to a change in strategy to avoid strategic drift. A senior member of staff – probably a board level member will be given responsibility for the change.

In the case of IIA, a need has been identified to change the assessment process from a conventional approach to a computer based approach. From the information provided, the main drivers appear to be the desire to provide instant results to candidates and the necessity of reducing the costs of marking examinations.

Definition

During this stage, a team is put together to perform the business case. In the case of IIA, the business case has already been performed and has been discussed in part (a) above.

Design

During the design stage, the change will be formulated. Benefit maps will be developed to determine what has to be put in place to deliver the benefits, as described in part (b).

The organisation may then determine whether it has the capabilities to deliver the proposed changes. In the case of the new online exam system, IIA will need the IT resources to develop and support the new system, and the resources and capabilities to develop the new question bank. It may be possible to outsource these; a decision has already been made to outsource the security of the system and external consultants will be used to write the questions for the question bank. However, the organisation will need to have internal staff with the capabilities to manage the developments.

Finally a course of action will be recommended. The recommendation at IIA has already been made; a software package has been identified, although this will require some additional customisation.

Implementation

The implementation stage begins once the changes proposed during the design stage have been approved. Budgets will be set for the project, based on the business case. The changes will then be implemented.

At IIA, the first task will be to specify in detail the changes required to the software, which will involve discussions with relevant users. Once this has occurred, the software will be customised and tested. It may be necessary to invest in additional hardware and the software will be loaded on to the new hardware. The question bank will also be developed.

Staff changes will have to be made as the new online system will require staff to perform different activities. In particular staff that administered the marking process may no longer be required now that the marking is performed automatically by the system; they will need to be redeployed. Staff will also require training in how to use the new system.

Realisation

This is the final stage of the business change life cycle and involves measuring the benefits that the business change has delivered and comparing these to the benefits promised in the business case. It is equivalent to the benefits realisation described in part (b) above.

Answer 33 8-HATS PROMOTIONS

(a)   **Evaluation of Barry's comments on investment appraisal approach used**

Tutorial note: *In the scenario, Barry commented on simple payback (and its supposed advantage over discounted cash flow), the selection of the discount rate, the role of the IRR, the importance of intangible benefits and the realisation of benefits. These five themes provide the structure for the answer set out below.*

Figure 1: Payback calculations for 8-Hats

Job One All figures in $000

C/F	0	−110	−60	−45	−5
	Year 0	*Year 1*	*Year 2*	*Year 3*	*Year 4*
Total costs	110	10	10	10	10
Total savings	0	60	25	50	70
Cumulative	−110	−60	−45	−5	55

Job Two All figures in $000

C/F	0	−90	−50	−35	−5
	Year 0	*Year 1*	*Year 2*	*Year 3*	*Year 4*
Total costs	90	20	20	10	10
Total savings	0	60	35	40	35
Cumulative	−90	−50	−35	−5	20

The calculations (Figure 1) show that Barry's assertion is not true, both jobs payback early in year 4. If payback (time to payback) had been used, Job One would probably still have been selected because it pays back more in Year 4 than Job 2.

Barry also seems to misunderstand the limitations of payback. It ignores all cash flows beyond the payback period, which in longer projects can be very significant. In this example, payback ignores the fact that Job 1 has a significantly higher net cash flow inflow on year 4 than Job 2.

Discount rate

Inflation is taken into account in setting the discount rate. However, interest forgone, the cost of capital (if money is being borrowed to fund the investment) and risk will also have an influence. Interest forgone is concerned with the opportunity cost of investing the money in a bank deposit account and earning interest. The cost of capital is concerned with the cost of borrowing money to fund investment. A risk premium would reflect the perceived risk associated with these two internal projects. The discount rate used will incorporate an allowance for risk which will determine the required rate of return or "hurdle rate" that a project must exceed for it to be viable. Information about risk-free interest rates during the period, the risk profile of the company and the company's cost of capital (using the Capital Asset Pricing Model) would also have been of relevance.

Even if there was an economic logic to changing the discount rate to 3% or 4% this would have no overall effect on the selection of the projects. In fact it is likely to have made Job 1 even more attractive than Job 2, as the cash flows in year 3 and 4 would have been discounted less. In fact, if a discount rate of 4%* is used then the gap in NPV between Jobs 1 and 2 increases.

Tutorial note: * *This calculation was not expected or required.*

Internal Rate of return (IRR)

The IRR is basically the discount rate that produces an NPV of zero for net project cash flows. If the selection is between two projects with the same scale of investment (which is the case here), then it has no effect on which project is selected. The project with the greatest NPV will usually produce the higher IRR. However, the IRR does become important when any project selected has to achieve a pre-specified company rate, or where projects with different scales of investment are being compared. This is not the case at 8-Hats.

Tangible and intangible benefits

The fundamental problem with investment appraisal generally is the reliability of cash flow estimates made for future cash inflows and outflows. For both jobs there seems to be an inclusion of specific monetary values for what appear to be intangible benefits – better information and improved staff morale. As Barry says, these are important, but it is very unlikely that either of these could be predicted with any certainty, particularly at the start of the project. Estimating for later time periods in the project is also very difficult and it is significant that these benefits increase as the project progresses. These intangible benefits amount to $110,000 for Job One and $50,000 for Job Two. If these intangible benefits are deducted from the analysis then, in fact, Job Two has a higher NPV than Job One. However, both are negative, suggesting that neither project should be attempted.

Benefits realisation

Finally, Barry has a fundamental misunderstanding of benefits realisation. The feasibility study is concerned with establishing the business case of a project and it should identify the project's benefits and costs. Benefits realisation is concerned with establishing whether the predicted benefits in the business case have been realised once the product or service delivered by the project has been in place for some time. It compares actual costs and benefits with those predicted in the business case. It cannot take place after the feasibility study of the project because at that point the project has not been completed and so any predicted benefits could not, at that stage, have been realised.

(b) **Matrix management structure**

8-Hats is currently structured in functional departments, with each function representing activities of the company that have either been acquired (e.g. travel) or organically developed. Each job is passed between functions, with each function focusing on optimising its part of the transaction. Thus the sales department concentrates on winning the job by fiercely reducing prices because the sales managers are rewarded on turnover, not profit. The events department focuses on providing the most rewarding client experience and the travel department on selling travel options with the best profit margin. The focus of the travel department can cause conflict with the sales and marketing department and the operations department has the problem of trying to profitably deliver an event at a price agreed by sales and marketing department but with the functionality promised by the events department. The finance department has responsibility for managing the cash flow of the job and the payment of invoices and collection of money owing. There have been occasions where a job has been jeopardised by the failure of the company to pay key suppliers on time.

The problems described above are typical of a functional structure and the "silo effect" caused by departments sub-optimising based on their own objectives and interests. The job, which is effectively being passed across the silos, suffers due to lack of co-ordination. Conflicts between two silos can often only be dealt with by managers who are above the silos. There is an example in the scenario where Barry has to intervene to arrange extra funding to pay supplier invoices when those suppliers threaten to boycott a folk music festival.

The matrix structure is an attempt to manage key elements of the company across the functional departments. This might be a product, project or a clearly defined client sector. In the context of 8-Hats it is jobs, which are effectively projects, and potentially, key accounts (e.g. Kuizan) that need to be managed across the functional silos.

Each job has the characteristics of a project. It has an established start, it runs for a few months, and then has a specified finish which is often the event itself (e.g. the folk festival or a Kuizan customer experience event). A multi-disciplinary project team drawn from all of the functional sections would allow continuity and focus on delivering a successful and profitable project. Because much of the company is project-based, a set of profitable projects should lead to a profitable company. Decisions within the project will, to some extent, reflect a consensus view of all concerned. The sales manager responsible for agreeing the deal would still be involved at event realisation and would also contribute to the management of cash flow through the complete project. This commitment to the project goal should lead to a more rewarding client experience. The need to keep clients satisfied is another potential element to the matrix, with account managers being appointed to key accounts with the responsibility of managing clients across both silos and projects.

The need for project teams to reflect a consensus view often means that decisions may take longer in a matrix structure and tension within the multi-disciplinary team may lead to a large amount of conflict. This conflict is more likely when cost and profit responsibilities are either unclear or counter-productive. At 8-Hats, the practice of rewarding sales managers on a turnover basis will have to be reviewed, otherwise there will be significant tension between the line (function) and the project.

It has also been claimed that job and task responsibilities are unclear in a matrix structure and so the company will have to address this. Johnson, Scholes and Whittington make the point that "one arm of the matrix has to lead in the sense that it dictates some key parameters within which the other arm must work". In the context of the case study scenario it seems reasonable to devolve profit responsibility and work allocation to the project, leaving the functions to provide technical support and (perhaps) appraisal and competence definition responsibilities. The line manager becomes primarily responsible for the person and the project manager for the project. Such a change would require key cultural changes at 8-Hats.

Answer 34 HOMEDELIVER

(a)   **Purpose of post-project, post implementation and benefits realisation reviews**

A post-project review takes place once the project has been completed. In fact, it can often be the last stage of the project, with the review culminating in the sign-off of the project and the formal dissolution of the project team. The focus of the post-project review is on the conduct of the project itself, not the product it has delivered. The aim is to identify and understand what went well and what went badly in the project and to feed *lessons learned* back into the project management standards with the aim of improving subsequent project management in the organisation.

A post-implementation review focuses on the product delivered by the project. It usually takes place a specified time after the product has been delivered. This allows the actual users of the product an opportunity to use and experience the product or service and to feedback their observations into a formal review. The post-implementation review will focus on the product's fitness for purpose. The review will not only discuss strategies for fixing or addressing identified faults, but it will also make recommendations on how to avoid these faults in the future. In this instance these *lessons learned* are fed back into the product production process.

A benefits realisation review also takes place after the product has been delivered. It is primarily concerned with revisiting the business case to see if the costs predicted at the initiation of the project were accurate and that the predicted benefits have actually accrued. In effect, it is a review of the initial cost/benefit analysis and any subsequent updates made to this analysis during the conduct of the project. It may be part of a post-implementation review, although the long-term nature of most benefits means that the post-implementation review is often held too soon to properly conduct benefits realisation. In fact, it can be argued that benefits realisation is actually a series of reviews where the predicted long-term costs and benefits of the business case are monitored. Again, one of the objectives is to identify *lessons learned* and in this case to feed these back into the benefits management process of the organisation.

(b)   **Post-project review**

The following issues that could have been raised at the post-project review are presented here with lessons learned that should be fed back into the project management process.

- The late allocation of HomeDeliver order administrators full-time to the project. Initially, employees were allocated part-time to the project. However this hampered project progress as these administrators also needed to undertake their normal operational duties. Consequently, the project began to significantly slip. Even though selected order administrators were added full-time to the project it was too late and the software was delivered two months behind schedule.

  Lessons learned: it is likely that deadlines will slip if appropriate employees are not allocated full-time to the project.

- The failure to consult catalogue supervisors and agents.
  There is evidence in the scenario that internal stakeholders were identified and consulted throughout the project. However, external stakeholders, such as the catalogue supervisors and agents, were not consulted at all. This meant that they had little understanding of the software prior to its implementation. It also meant that their requirements were not taken into consideration when developing the software. Hence the need to amend an order was not included in the software solution.

  Lessons learned: ensure that stakeholder analysis includes both external and internal stakeholders and make sure that external stakeholders are included in the requirements gathering process where appropriate.

- The scope of implementation, implementing all supervisors and agents immediately. In retrospect, implementing all supervisors (and their agents) was too ambitious and risky. It would have been wiser to establish a pilot project where only selected supervisors and agents used the new system. Experience from this pilot could have been used to modify the software and fix faults and omissions before rolling out to the rest of the organisation. The scope should have been defined in the project initiation document and this should have been risk assessed.

  Lessons learned: the risk assessment of the scope of projects is important and project managers should look to mitigate risk by reducing scope.

Post implementation review

The following issues which could have been raised at the post-implementation review are presented here with recommendations that should be fed back into the software development process.

- Faults and omissions in the computer software. The omission of the order amendment facility has already been considered. However, the failure of the software to work with a popular browser needs investigating. Testing should consider a range of browsers. The post-implementation review should also consider why these faults were not found before the software was released. A possible reason is that the software was tested by full-time employees of HomeDeliver in a controlled office environment. It was not acceptance tested by the part-time, home-based agents who were actually going to use the software. These people were likely to be less familiar with computer applications and were also likely to use a wide variety of hardware and software.

  Lessons learned: acceptance testing should be undertaken by real business users in the hardware and software environment they are actually working in. Testing across multiple browsers must be considered.

■ Faults in the documentation. The documentation supporting the implementation was both inappropriate and inappropriately distributed. Distributing the user manual as a PDF file raises at least two issues.

(1) Whether the email, and its attached file, had actually been received by the agent. A significant number of them claim that they did not receive the email.

(2) It seems unreasonable to expect self-employed agents to print out a large, colour manual at their own cost. A failure to print out and study the manual probably contributed to agents being unable to use the software to enter multiple orders for one household. Spelling and functionality faults in the manual undermine confidence in both the documentation and the software it supports.

Lessons learned: documentation must be carefully inspected before software release and its physical distribution should be carefully considered. Distributing documentation electronically may seem easy and cheap, but it may have important unanticipated consequences.

■ Training of employees. It was perceived that the software was easy to use and so no formal training was given to agents. However, this missed the opportunity to find early faults (e.g. not running under a certain browser). The inability of many agents to claim that the system could not support multiple orders from one household also suggests that the software was not as easy to use as its developers claimed.

Lessons learned: As well as imparting skills, training provides an opportunity to build rapport with users and to identify possible issues and faults with the software at an earlier stage.

(c) **The potential benefits to HomeDeliver of the new electronic ordering system might include:**

■ Staff savings from the reduction or elimination of order administrators at HomeDeliver. This benefit should be relatively easy to quantify.

■ Staff savings from reduced catalogue supervisor costs. In the new system, supervisors appear to have significantly less work and so each supervisor should be able to co-ordinate more agents. However, supervisors are currently rewarded on the basis of how many agents they administer. So savings could only be made if this contractual arrangement was changed.

■ Improved cash flow, because money is now sent daily rather than at the end of the week. Improved cash flow will reduce borrowing costs or increase investment income. This benefit should be relatively easy to quantify.

■ The system should lead to the customer receiving their goods more quickly. Orders are entered at the end of the day, not in the week after the order has been placed. This is a benefit for the customer, not HomeDeliver. However, it could be argued that improved customer service may lead to more customers and, because there is less elapsed time between order and delivery, to fewer cancelled orders. It would be relatively difficult to quantitatively predict both of these benefits in advance.

Answer 35 iTTRAIN

Tutorial note: *A number of different legitimate approaches could be used to answer this question. The structure used here is based on the student Accountant article "Business Strategy and Pricing". However, alternative frameworks would be acceptable as long as appropriate points are made.*

(a)   Pricing strategy

Mission and marketing objectives

Pricing is ultimately part of an organisation's strategy. It should reflect the organisation's self-perception and its feeling about its position in the market. Marco wants to position iTTrain as a quality provider to the business market. Does his suggested price of $750 per delegate reflect this? It could be argued that this is a reasonable price as long as other factors support it. He is not providing a "no frills" service to self-financed candidates, so his price can reflect this. His main benchmark is AQT, and he is suggesting a price which undercuts their list price ($900), and their discounted price ($810), so his company theoretically offers the same (or better) quality at a more competitive price.

Pricing objectives

In the short term, there can be a variety of pricing objectives. Sometimes, irrespective of long-term objectives, the need to survive and increase short-term cash flows will dictate price cuts. At present, Marco is not in this position. He wishes to establish iTTrain in the market place, and he is looking for short-term modest profitability. His price should reflect this.

Costing and financial analysis

Tutorial note: *The financial analysis may be undertaken in a variety of ways and appropriate credit would be given to alternatives. In the following analysis, Marco's suggested price of $750 per delegate is used as a basis of the analysis. Expected contribution is calculated by using the values from AQT.*

Figure 1 shows the contribution for class sizes of three to nine delegates on a course. iTTrain will not run courses with fewer than three delegates, and the training rooms at CityCentre have a maximum capacity of nine delegates.

The expected contribution per course has been calculated using the probabilities derived from courses at AQT. The delegate fee is $750.

Course length		3 days		All financial figures in $					
Probability	Delegates	Lecturer	Room	Manual*	Lunch	Total cost	Income	Contribution	Expected contribution
0·15	3	450	250	60	30	2,250	2,250	0	0
0·21	4	450	250	80	40	2,300	3,000	700	147
0·25	5	450	250	100	50	2,350	3,750	1,400	350
0·19	6	450	250	120	60	2,400	4,500	2,100	399
0·07	7	450	250	140	70	2,450	5,250	2,800	196
0·08	8	450	250	160	80	2,500	6,000	3,500	280
0·05	9	450	250	180	90	2,550	6,750	4,200	210

*Manual cost is per delegate per course   Total expected contribution   1,582

Figure 1: Contribution for class sizes of three to nine delegates

The expected contribution per course is $1,582.

Thus the breakeven on a course basis is $65,000 ÷ 1,582 = 41·09 courses.

The company plans to offer 40 courses per year. If the contribution per course is $1,582, then iTTrain will make a small operating loss ((40 × $1,582) – $65,000) = ($1,720)).

A consideration of the profitability at different delegate volume levels is also instructive, showing that an average attendance of six delegates per course is required to achieve operating profitability assuming that 40 courses a year actually do run. In other words, classes have to operate at a minimum of two-thirds capacity, on average, for the company to be profitable if only 40 courses actually run during the first year.

Number of delegates	Contribution	Fixed overheads	Operating profit/(loss)
	$	$	$
3	0	65,000	(65,000)
4	28,000	65,000	(37,000)
5	56,000	65,000	(9,000)
6	84,000	65,000	19,000
7	112,000	65,000	47,000
8	140,000	65,000	75,000
9	168,000	65,000	103,000

A number of options might be considered:

■ To increase the price towards their nearest competitor. For example, assuming the same attendance pattern as above, increasing the price towards that of their nearest competitor (AQT), at just under $800 per delegate, would maintain their competitive price advantage while potentially increasing the expected value, realising a modest profit. (Note that sensitivity analysis could be undertaken to verify this using the same method used to calculate the expected value based on a delegate price of $750.)

■ Decreasing costs: The lecturer and training room rates are standard rates. It may be possible to agree bulk booking discounts. A 5% discount on lecturing and room booking rates increases the expected contribution per course to $1,687·00 (assuming a course fee of $750). On 40 courses, this gives an expected income of $67,480, producing an operating profit $2,480, returning a modest operating margin of 3·68% (2,480 ÷ 67,840).

■ An exploration of other scenarios which combine increasing the price and decreasing the costs.

■ Revisiting overheads, although little information is given in the scenario about this. Marco might be prepared to take less income from the firm in its formative years.

The financial analysis suggests that the $750 delegate fee suggested by Marco appears to be too low to produce the modest profit he would like. It also has to be recalled that the analysis is based on statistical probabilities which are from a well-established training company. Marco has to consider the likelihood of a newly formed training company initially having the same attendance pattern as an established company such as AQT.

Importantly, he has also assumed that all 40 scheduled courses will run. This assumption has to be examined and the sensitivity of profitability to only a certain proportion of courses running has to be explored. Consideration might also be given to the likely proportion of under-subscribed courses at the price actually set. At first sight it appears that a course which does not attract enough delegates will not incur any cost, because all training provision costs are variable. However, there may be cancellation costs associated with the training venue and the freelance lecturer.

Competition

It appears that price is not the only determinant of consumer selection, otherwise the cheaper training providers would dominate the market. Consumers are clearly also affected by non-price factors such as quality of the training and the quality of the place (where the training is provided). Consequently, Marco can price the training at the price he has suggested because there is considerable evidence that consumers (particularly corporate buyers) are willing to pay that price (or more) to get a service which they are satisfied or delighted with.

Consumers

Suppliers have to keep in mind how much consumers are willing to pay. Evidence from AQT suggests that corporate customers (iTTrain's target market) are able to pay the price which Marco has suggested. In contrast, the cheaper "no frills" training providers appear to appeal to self-financed customers for whom price is an issue. The existence of training brokers as intermediaries in the supply chain does complicate the situation. If Marco wishes to offer them a margin as great as AQT, then he has to reduce his price (to training brokers) to $675 per delegate, which will obviously affect contribution.

Controls

The market is not subject to any legislative pricing controls.

Setting prices

As stated before, Marco wishes to set prices to show a short-term modest profit.

Strategic approaches (tactics or ploys)

A number of tactics or ploys can be used within the pricing strategy, for example: price skimming, penetration pricing, product-line pricing, etc. None of these appear to be particularly appropriate to iTTrain. However, many training companies (like airlines) provide "early-bird" (early booking) discounts in an attempt to quickly reach a critical mass. Early-bird payments also improve cash flow. iTTrain might also wish to consider "late booking" discounts, perhaps through training brokers, to provide extra contribution in courses which they are already committed to run.

Summary

Taking all factors into consideration, the suggested price of $750 per delegate appears to be broadly acceptable, except for its likely impact on the financial performance of the company as a whole, specifically the achievement of Marco's modest profit objective. He should consider raising the price to just under $800 per delegate, which gives him some margin of safety, particularly if costs can be reduced through bulk discounts. It also provides more leeway with the discounts he will have to give to training brokers. To some extent, Marco can experiment with the price level. It is the most flexible part of the marketing mix. In business nothing will remain constant. The economy, taste, innovation and competitor actions will change constantly, forcing prices to be continually reappraised. In reality most companies are price-takers, rather than price makers and Marco's pricing approach will have to reflect this.

(b) **Contribution of element of the marketing mix**

Physical evidence

The physical environment in which the service is offered is often central to the consumer's understanding of the service and to their satisfaction or enjoyment of the service. It must reflect customer expectations and the overall brand positioning. Marco has taken this into consideration in the selection of the CityCentre training centre as his course venue. As a result, delegates should experience a physical environment which reflects the quality of the teaching and course documentation. Marco also has the opportunity to give prospective buyers a feel for the physical environment by providing a virtual tour of the location on iTTrain's website. Physical evidence of good quality documentation and teaching can be provided through sample hand-outs and a sample teaching presentation. In the niche which Marco is trying to position iTTrain, physical evidence of the quality of the company is very important.

People

Most services require direct interaction between the consumer and the people who represent the service provider's organisation. In conventional terms, employee selection, training and motivation are significant considerations. Most successful businesses devote time and resources to managing their customer-facing staff. In the context of iTTrain, this is particularly significant. One of the most important people in the process, the lecturers, are not employees of iTTrain, they are self-employed contractors. Marco must ensure that lecturers are properly briefed, conduct themselves correctly and act in such a way that is consistent with the quality branding. Formal audits (observation of courses, feedback questionnaires) will be both a source of control and of marketing material (delegate testimonies). Marco also has to recognise that although he might make the initial sale, many subsequent sales may be down to the customer's enjoyment of the course and pass rates, and central to this will be the performance of the lecturers.

Process

The process which surrounds the service is often perceived, by the customer, as part of that service. There is a significant difference between purchasing a product and a service. The service is often consumed only once (course attendance) whilst a product (such as a computer) might be used many times. The service often requires direct interaction between the person ordering and consuming the service and the service provider (the lecturer). In contrast, the producer of a computer seldom meets the customer. Service is often abstract and transitory and this can accentuate the consumer's expectations and their reflections on the success of the experience. They often perceive that the ordering process, the ease of payment and the accuracy of joining instructions are part of the service and include them in their assessment. Thus Marco must ensure that all the processes which precede and follow the actual teaching process are effective and customer focused.

Answer 36 GREEN SOCKETT

(a) **Transformation of the finance function**

Current situation at Green Sockett

The finance department at Green Sockett is performing a very traditional finance role. Financial statements and management accounts are being prepared to assist the directors in decision making, customers are being invoiced, receivables are being collected and suppliers are being paid. Although these processes are critical, experience in many organisations is that finance departments can add more value than simply performing these particular roles, as discussed below.

Business partners

Many financial professionals like to think of themselves as business partners rather than simply "bean counters" or "score keepers". The traditional role of a CFO is to advise the board on areas relating to finance, such as raising additional finance and investment appraisal. Although these are important areas, finance directors also have commercial skills that could be used in general strategic decisions, not just financial decisions. In the case of Green Sockett, this would include providing advice at board meetings on areas such as acquisitions, pricing policy and marketing strategy. The modern CFO is an essential member of the management team, not simply the money man.

Identifying economies of scale

The existing management accounts of Green Sockett include a comparison of monthly costs and revenues against flexed budgets. These identify areas where costs are higher than expected. The traditional accountant might assume that having identified these variances it is up to the other managers to find ways to control them. The modern accountant, on the other hand, would be more proactive in identifying cost savings and economies of scale.

The finance department could review all business processes in the organisation and identify areas where efforts are being duplicated. It would then find ways to improve and standardise the business processes throughout Green Sockett. The procurement processes, for example, could be unified or standardised so that all procurement is performed centrally for all Green Sockett companies rather than individually.

More analysis of the numbers

The management accounts are fairly basic at the moment and use very traditional tools for analysing the performance of the business. The finance department could add more value by providing more relevant analysis of the numbers. In the biofuel division for example, where costs are high, financial analysis of the effectiveness of research on reducing costs could be performed to ensure that the benefits justify the costs.

It is recognised that in the modern business world, performance means more than simply numbers, and performance measurement should be expanded to include more non-financial performance indicators focussing on the drivers of success at Green Sockett.

The venture capitalists are likely to be interested in accurate forecasts of cash flows and the ability to provide them with a good return, as well as preparing the company for a flotation on the stock market. Such forecasts would require a more detailed understanding of the industry, which the finance department can provide.

Information systems

Developments in IT mean that more and more information is available to managers of a business. Although this can be beneficial, the amount of information can start to cause confusion. Managers may not be sure which are the best sources of information from among the many that are available. Different information systems within the organisation may duplicate data. The systems might not be producing the information that managers really need.

One of the skills that finance professionals have is managing and analysing information. The finance department can play a key role in development of new information systems by helping to identify and analyse the information requirements of managers and then helping to design systems that will provide it.

(b) **Use of budgets at Green Sockett**

At Green Sockett, budgets are flexed and compared against actual costs and revenues on a monthly basis. The overall aim of this is to ensure that costs are kept under control. If there are any large differences between actual costs and the flexed budget, these would be highlighted and management can take action in order to ensure that the variance is not repeated in future months.

Monthly budgets are more of a tactical (medium-term) plan than a strategic plan, so their use in strategic planning is tenuous. A budget should be consistent with a strategic plan and is a tool that should be used in implementing strategy. This may be important given the longer-term aim of floating the company on a stock market, since the company probably has longer term revenue, profit and cash flow targets. The budget shows the progress expected towards those plans from the current period.

Comparison of costs against the budget is useful in stable environments where the budget can be prepared with some degree of reliability. In less stable environments, it may be difficult to forecast costs reliably, meaning that it will be difficult to ascertain how much a variance is due to poor budgeting and how much is due to poor performance.

The solar plants and wind farms operate in fairly stable environments, with the big uncertainty being the weather, but variability in the weather would be taken account of in the flexing of the budget. Therefore the use of budgets would be more useful in these environments. The biofuel industry appears to be less stable due to developments in the production process, which may mean that budgets quickly become out of date and therefore less useful.

Flexing budgets is useful where costs are variable. In the case of the wind farm and solar plants, the majority of costs are probably fixed. The number of kilowatts of electricity generated relies on the amount of wind or sunlight. Total costs of running these plants would not vary much with the quantity of output, so the value of flexing the budget could be questioned here. In the biofuel plants however, there will be variable costs, so flexing the budgets would be useful.

Another weakness of budgets generally is that they focus exclusively on financial objectives. An organisation such as Green Sockett may have other objectives that it considers to be equally important such as the contribution that the organisation is making towards the development of alternative renewable sources of energy. These are not captured in budgets.

In conclusion, budgets can be considered to be a useful tool in helping to ensure that the financial strategies are achieved, but it should be recognised that they focus only on financial part of strategy. They are also less useful in uncertain environments such as the biofuel plant.

Answer 37 GIFT DESIGNS

(a) **Report on key issues relating to funding strategy**

Report

To: David Silvester
From: A Nanalyst
Subject: Funding strategy for Gift Designs

Clearly, you have identified a real business opportunity and face both business and financial risks in turning the opportunity into reality. One possible model you can use is that of the product life cycle which as a one-product firm is effectively the life cycle for the company. Linking business risk to financial risk is important – in the early stages of the business the business risk is high and the high death rate amongst new start-ups is well publicised and, consequently, there is a need to go for low financial risk. Funding the business is essentially deciding the balance between debt and equity finance, and equity offers the low risk that you should be looking for. As the firm grows and develops so the balance between debt and equity will change. A new business venture like this could in Boston Box terms be seen as a problem child with a non-existent market share but high growth potential. The business risks are very high and consequently the financial risks taken should be very low and avoid taking on large amounts of debt with a commitment to service the debt.

You need to take advantage of investors who are willing to accept the risks associated with a business start-up – venture capitalists and business angels accept the risks associated with putting equity capital in but may expect a significant share in the ownership of the business. This they will seek to realise once the business is successfully established. As the business moves into growth and then maturity so the business risks will reduce and access to debt finance becomes feasible and cost effective. In maturity the business should be able to generate significant retained earnings to finance further development. Dividend policy will also be affected by the stage in the life cycle that the business has reached.

(b) **Critical success factors as the business grows**

David even at this early stage needs to identify the critical success factors and related performance indicators that will show that the concept is turning into a business reality. Many of the success factors will be linked to customer needs and expectations and therefore where David's business must excel in order to outperform the competition. As an innovator one of the critical success factors will be the time taken to develop and launch the new vase. Being first-to-market will be critical for success. His ability to generate sales from demanding corporate customers will be a real indicator of that success.

David will need to ensure that he has adequate patent protection for the product and recognise that it will have a product life cycle. There look to be a number of alternative markets and the ability to customise the product may be a CSF. Greiner indicates the different stages a growing business goes through and the different problems associated with each stage. One of David's key problems will be to decide what type of business he wants to be. From the scenario it looks as if he is aiming to carry out most of the functions himself and there is a need to decide what he does and what he gets others to do for him. Indeed the skills he has may be as an innovator rather than as someone who carries out manufacture, distribution, etc. Gift Designs may develop most quickly as a firm that creates new products and then licences them to larger firms with the skills to penetrate the many market opportunities that are present. It is important for David to recognise that turning the product concept into a viable and growing business may result in a business and a business model very different to what he anticipated. Gift Designs needs to have the flexibility and agility to take advantage of the opportunities that will emerge over time.

Answer 38 ONEENERGY

(a)   **Financial review**

Overview

The judicious use of selected financial ratios should have indicated some cause for concern, leading to further investigation of the company and the industrial sector itself. It would have been very helpful to identify typical financial ratios in RiteSoftware's sector. However, in the absence of such information, comparison between the two years will provide some evaluation and a basis for further investigation.

However, before calculating and commenting on the ratios, there are a number of things directly discernible from the financial figures provided by the company.

- Goodwill is the most significant non-current asset. If the company is in the position that it needs further funding, then the extract suggests that there is little to secure this funding against. Most lenders prefer to lend against tangible assets (e.g. property). The value of goodwill has also increased substantially since 20Y1, suggesting an acquisition. It would be useful to investigate this further.

- Although trade receivables year on year have increased, in percentage terms, about the same as revenue, trade payables have increased significantly more. The efficiency ratios should cast more light on this; but it appears that the company may be using trade payables to finance cash flows. This hunch might be supported by the fact that the bank overdraft was actually reduced in 20Y2.

- Although sales revenue increased by 10% in the period, cost of sales grew by a greater percentage, leading to a reduction in profit. It seems reasonable to assume that labour costs largely contributed to this cost of sales increase. The percentage increase in staff was almost 30%, a significant proportion for a small company to integrate and profitably utilise.

- The extract from the accounts shows no retained profit, suggesting that this is being distributed to shareholders. This needs to be investigated.

Profitability

Two profitability ratios can be calculated from the extracted financial information. The ROCE (Return on Capital Employed) has almost halved. Although the actual profit remained the same, it was achieved with significantly higher borrowing.

The net profit margin has also almost halved. The absolute figures are also very low (less than 1% in 20Y2) and this needs further investigation to see if such a figure is viable, or representative of the industry sector.

Efficiency

The general observation about trade payables made above appears to be borne out by the ratios. The average receivables settlement remains the same, suggesting good credit management in an expanding business. However, average payable days have increased significantly and are now beyond the 30 days normal for this business.

Sales revenue per employee has dropped from $33,500 in 20Y1 to under $29,500 in 20Y2.

Liquidity

Liquidity (measured through both the current and acid test ratios) has declined slightly during this period. Also, the values are rather low (approximately 0.76:1) and so this too would need investigation. Perhaps liquidity is traditionally low in this industry sector.

Financial gearing

The two gearing ratios discernible from the extracted information both give cause for concern. The gearing ratio itself has jumped from 25% to above 43%. The interest cover ratio has dropped to 2 from 7.5. Again, the sector needs investigation.

Conclusion

The financial figures of RiteSoftware do suggest that everything was not well and that further investigation was necessary. The figures suggest rising debt, cash flow problems, lowering efficiency and very poor profitability. Further investigation might have revealed that RiteSoftware was typical of the industry. However, it might have also identified the problems that led to the company's eventual demise.

(b)   **Proper evaluation process of software supplier**

Tutorial note: *The lack of a formal evaluation of the financial figures of RiteSoftware is the subject of the first part of the question. However, the financial position is just part of the analysis required of the potential supplier. The question requires FOUR further ways in which OneEnergy failed to follow a proper evaluation procedure. In this model answer, the following four suggestions are provided. However, other appropriate suggestions made by the candidate will be given credit.*

Four suggestions OneEnergy could have followed in a proper evaluation procedure are:

(1)   A failure to investigate the supplier's organisational structure and ownership;
(2)   A failure to evaluate functional requirements;
(3)   A failure to evaluate non-functional requirements;
(4)   A failure to set proper evaluation criteria and follow a selection process.

Organisational structure and ownership

The evaluation should have included an investigation into the structure of RiteSoftware, its shareholders and directors. A simple inquiry at Companies House (for example) would have revealed that the managing director of RiteSoftware had the same surname as the HR director of OneEnergy. The HR director could then have been asked directly if he was related to the managing director of RiteSoftware. Of course, there may have been no impropriety intended, but the fact would have come to light and been considered in the evaluation. Many organisations will either not procure from companies where directors and senior managers have relatives or will ask for that information to be disclosed by the supplier in order that it can be weighted in the evaluation of alternative suppliers.

Functional requirements of the software

The evaluation process did not formally define the functional requirements of the required system. The scenario mentions that three months ago another set of amendments was requested from RiteSoftware to allow one of the divisions in OneEnergy to pay bonuses to lorry drivers in a certain way. This functional requirement should have been defined in advance in the process and it would have then been compared with the functions offered by the package. The gap between requirement and package could then be evaluated in advance. This allows two things.

(1)   The match of functionality and package will form part of the evaluation. It is not expected that every function requirement will be completely fulfilled but the degree of compromise has to be assessed in some way.

(2)   An understanding of the gap allows the compromise to be managed in advance. For example, in the context of the pay for lorry drivers it might have been possible to change the pay structure in such a way that rewarded the drivers but avoided the expense of commissioning and maintaining software amendments.

Non-functional requirements of the software

Many software packages do actually offer most of the functionality that the users require. However, how they deliver that functionality is very important and usability can be a great differentiator between competing packages. In the scenario, it seems clear that non-functional requirements such as user-friendliness have not been considered properly in the evaluation. If they had been then it would be unlikely that users would have problems understanding some of the terminology and structure of the software. Problems leading to comments such as "it just does not work like we do" should have been identified in advance.

Understanding user competencies and expectations would allow the gap between users' ability and the requirements of the package to be properly assessed. This measure would be part of the evaluation. Again, if the package is selected, the gap can be planned for in advance so that the extra training costs, alluded to in the scenario, are budgeted for at the outset.

Evaluation criteria and process

Finally, the scenario suggests that the board decided to purchase the RitePay software package without evaluating alternative solutions. It was felt that payroll rules and processes were relatively standard and so there was no need to look further than a package recommended by the HR director. Certainly, the discovery that the HR director is related to the managing director of RiteSoftware now puts his impartiality in doubt. Furthermore, subsequent requested amendments to the functionality of the package suggest that OneEnergy's payroll rules were not as standard as expected. However, the real problem with choosing one solution without evaluating alternatives is that there is no auditable evidence about how the supplier and the product were selected. At best this looks amateurish; at worst it might cause concern to the non-executive member of the board and its internal auditors. The scenario suggests that the company does have a policy on competitive procurement. Avoiding it raises the chance of impropriety, reduces the opportunity of negotiating a good deal and should attract the attention of non-executive directors and other significant stakeholders.

Answer 39 DESPARD

(a)   Calculations for the current year

(i)   Contribution per unit $50 × (75 ÷ 25) = $150

			$000
(ii)	Total contribution	(5,000 × $150)	750
	Less Total fixed costs	(5,000 × $70)	(350)
	Total profit		400

(b)   **Calculations for next year**

		$/unit
Selling price	50 × (100 ÷ 25) × 1.08	216
Less Variable cost	(50 × 1.12)	(56)
Contribution		160

		$000
Total fixed costs	(5,000 × $70) × 1.12	392
Target/required profit [as per (a)(ii)]		400
Required contribution for next year		792

Number of units required = (792,000 ÷ 160) = 4,950 units.

(c)   **Semi-variable cost**

A mixed or semi-variable cost is one that is partly fixed and partly variable in behaviour. An example would be power costs (e.g. gas or electricity) which consist of a fixed charge irrespective of the number of units of power consumed and a variable charge based on the number of units of power consumed.

For cost-volume-profit analysis the fixed and variable elements need to be separately identified by using, for example, the high low method or linear regression. Each would then be considered along with the other variable and other fixed costs in the analysis.

Answer 40 WORLD ENGINES

(a)   **Decision tree and evaluation of its implications and shortcomings**

Decision tree for the information in the scenario

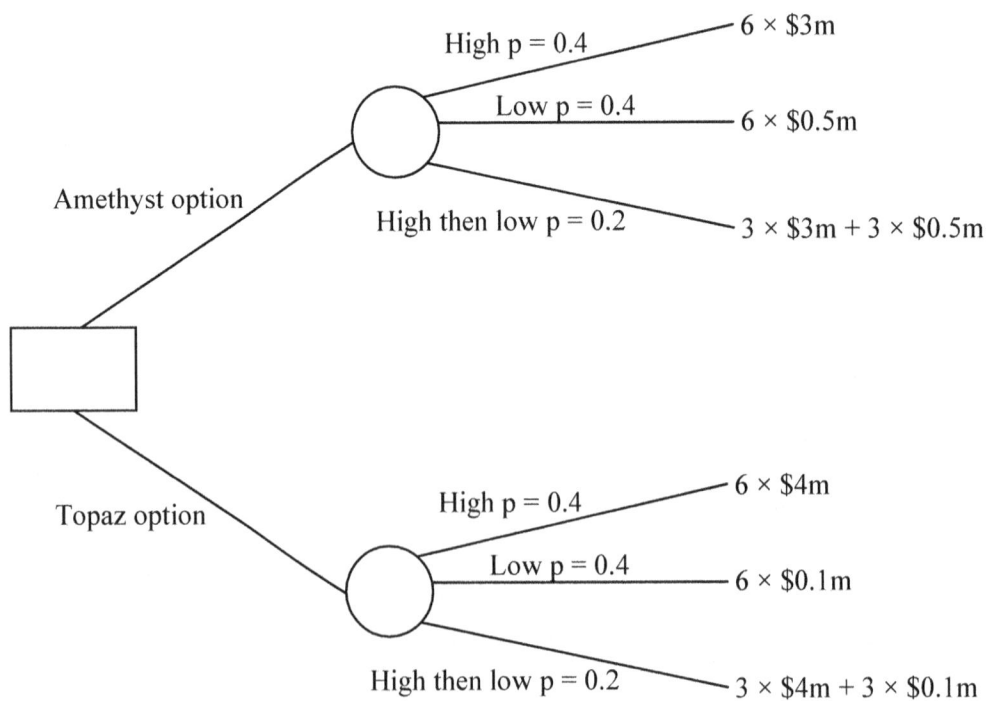

Expected value of Amethyst

($18m × 0·4) + ($3m × 0·4) + ($10·5m × 0·2) = $10·5m MINUS cost of $7m = $3·5m

Expected value of Topaz

($24m × 0·4) + ($0·6m × 0·4) + ($12·3m × 0·2) = $12·3 MINUS cost of $8m = $4·3m

The analysis suggests that the Topaz option should be chosen.

This decision tree is based on the information available at this point in time. The probabilities set in the workshop are subjective and are not based on an analysis of past statistical data. As the divisional director recalls in the scenario, "it was relatively hard to get everyone to agree and debate at the workshop became a little heated". The sensitivity of the outcome to slight alterations in probability assessments should be undertaken. It is also unlikely that the predicted returns will be completely accurate. The basis of these estimates is not given, but a further sensitivity analysis, this time focusing on returns, would be valuable. The predicted annual return of Topaz ($4 million per annum) under conditions of high demand needs particular attention. This value (and its associated probability) contributes about 78% of the total expected value of this option. If the annual returns are overestimated by 10% (say $3·6 million per annum not $4·0 million), then this ceases to be the best option.

Software prices may also be negotiable, and changes in prices and structure may also need to be experimented with. The decision tree will have been just one input into the procurement decision.

(b)   Other factors to consider in deciding which option to select

As highlighted in part (a), the decision tree is only one input to the procurement decision. The scenario states that the returns used in the decision tree analysis were based on tangible benefits. The business case for each option would also have to state *intangible benefits* offered by each option. For example, the Topaz option offers a more contemporary user interface and this may provide intangible benefits associated with a better user experience. Intangible benefits need to be identified and listed for each option.

Importantly, the risk associated with each option will also have to be considered and documented. An element of this is reflected in the scenario. Amethyst, a well-established supplier, is perceived as a less risky option than the relatively newly formed, smaller Topaz. The relative supplier risk is not reflected in the decision tree. This risk, and other risks identified for each option, must be documented in the business case.

It may also be necessary to assess the relative impact on the organisation of each option. The options appear to differ in their functional scope and power and these differences might have disproportionate effects on the degree of change necessary within the organisation to accommodate the solution and the effect that each option has on organisational processes and the people with responsibility for those processes.

Finally, an effective selection process should allocate appropriate weight to features associated with the supplier of the solution. This is not just financial robustness, but also factors such as the availability of support, the presence and effectiveness of a user group, process certification etc. Similarly, the product needs to be assessed for functional fitness and for overall product characteristics (e.g. usability, flexibility and its overall design philosophy). We are told that Topaz is modular and up-to-date and this may be in its favour, but it will not be reflected in the decision tree analysis.

(c)   **Avoidance or mitigation of risks**

The risk assessment for Topaz has documented concerns about the long-term viability and stability of the supplier. Current financial analysis reveals a profitable, liquid and lowly geared company. However, the company is relatively young and it has a very small turnover compared to WE. It also has to be recognised that WE intends to enter a long-term relationship with this supplier. Hence the continuing success and viability of Topaz is important to WE. A *risk avoidance strategy* would be to avoid purchasing from small, newly-established companies. Hence Topaz would not be considered.

Should this risk actually take place, and Topaz goes out of business, then its impact may be mitigated by the following:

- The software used in the product is perceived to be innovative, modular and up-to-date. WE should ensure that this software is lodged in an *escrow* agreement. In such an agreement the source code is stored with an independent third party. If Topaz goes out of business, then their customers (including WE) have access to the software source code which should allow them, or their appointed agents, to maintain and support it.

- WE should also consider establishing in-house expertise in the programming language used by the Topaz product. This could have two objectives:

    (1)   As a basis for developing a long-term in-house software application that could be used to replace the software elements of the product offered by Topaz. The team could also be used to develop other significant applications required by the company. The software is contemporary and powerful and so other applications within WE should not be difficult to find.

    (2)   To provide a basis for enacting the escrow agreement if Topaz goes out of business. Access to the source code is particularly appropriate if an in-house team is able to pick up the software, maintain it and develop it.

- WE is a very significant company, with considerable assets. It should be relatively easy for it to maintain funds which could be used for purchasing Topaz should it run into difficulties. Many large companies take this approach as it secures software supply and potentially severs the supply, in this case, of the software to competitors.

WE need to maintain a contingency plan for moving to an alternative supplier or an in-house team. This contingency plan could be linked to monitoring the financial performance of Topaz. Many financial organisations offer a continuous monitoring facility to ensure that suppliers are not just evaluated at the point of purchase, but throughout the subsequent business relationship. This is particularly important when the supplier's application is business-critical to the customer and any interruption in supply would have significant implications.

The key lessons learned from the fatal air crash should result in WE developing risk avoidance or mitigation actions to make sure that such catastrophic events do not happen again, or, if they do happen, that they have less impact on the organisation. Potential actions include:

1.   Not permitting teams to travel together – the complete evaluation team was in the aircraft. Many organisations insist that key employees do not travel together to conferences and meetings.

2.   Looking for safer transport alternatives – the fatal journey was on a small commuter plane travelling a distance which might have been undertaken by car or train. The riskiness of different ways of travelling needs to be considered. Small commuter airlines and aircraft may have less stringent safety procedures than larger, mainstream airlines. Again, this would have to be investigated.

3.   Eliminating unnecessary travel – was the journey necessary? Encouraging employees to work from the home or the office reduces the risk of travel accidents by avoiding travel in the first place. The company might not only consider electronic meetings as a way of cutting costs, but also as a way of reducing the chance of fatal travel accidents.

4.   Finally, ensuring that all documentation is up-to-date and self-explanatory, so that it can be picked up easily by other employees of the organisation, hence avoiding the situation described in the scenario where the divisional director has to piece together fragments of documentation left by the unfortunate team.

Answer 41 ATD

(a)   Explanation of data and evaluation of techniques used

ATD has been reliant on intuitive estimating, with the sales manager predicting sales from his experience. The company is now evaluating more formal techniques of estimating and a business analyst has produced initial spreadsheets using linear regression and time series analysis. The business analyst has now left the company, leaving his work unexplained.

Figure 1 is a least square analysis of the sales data, defining the equation of a straight line that "best" fits the data by minimising the squares of deviations of actual values from the mean. In least squares analysis, one set of data is defined as the independent variable (x – in this case, time) and the other set of data, sales, is defined as y – the dependent variable. From the data presented in Figure 1 the line of best fit is:

$y = 125 \cdot 022 + 1 \cdot 84x$

This equation can be used to predict a value for the next quarter (2017 quarter 3):

$y = 125 \cdot 022 + 1 \cdot 84(15)$
$y = 152 \cdot 62$

The positive value of b suggests that the overall sales trend is upwards.

The correlation coefficient "r" shows the strength of the statistical relationship between the two variables. In Figure 1 the value of r is $0 \cdot 253$, which suggests that the two variables are weakly connected. The coefficient of determination (r2) shows that $6 \cdot 4\%$ of the variation in sales (y) is due to the passage of time (x). Low coefficients of correlation (and determination) are usual when data is widely scattered around the mean and/or are related in a non-linear fashion. Both these factors might be applicable here, particularly due to the pattern caused by large seasonal variations.

At ATD, linear regression appears to be of little practical use. The predicted value for 2017 quarter 3 appears too low (it is lower than all actual quarter 3 figures to date and much lower than the previous quarter 3 figure of 169). The technique might be more useful if the annual data was plotted (hence eliminating the seasonal variation) or to identify alternative variables which better explained the seasonal variation and to calculate a correlation coefficient between these and the sales data.

Time series analysis uses a moving average to define a trend. In Figure 2, the moving average has been calculated on a quarterly basis, which seems appropriate as this is how the data has been presented. The trend line is calculated from the average of the first two quarters (e.g. quarters 1–4 and quarters 2–5) to allow the trend to be centralised against an actual sales value. The difference between the actual values and the trend line is also averaged to produce a seasonal variation. Any difference left between the actual sales value and the seasonally adjusted trend is defined as a residual variation. Figure 2 also shows the seasonally adjusted trend values.

Forecasting future values is achieved by extrapolating the trend line and then adding or subtracting the seasonal variation. There is no agreed way of extrapolating the trend. A scatter graph could be drawn and a trend line drawn by hand. Alternatively, a least square regression of the trend values could be performed to define a line of best fit. Using a "best guess" approach, a trend value of 149 might be hypothesised for quarter 1 of 2017, giving a predicted value of 134·3 (149 – 14·7), just below the actual recorded value of 137. Predicted values would also be calculated for subsequent quarters. For example, based on a (hand drawn) trend value of 151, the predicted value for quarter 3 of 2017 would be 173·55 (151 + 22·55), which subjectively seems much more realistic than the 152·55 suggested by the least squares analysis.

The moving average method also explicitly defines the significant seasonal variations for this product and so reflects these in the predicted values, meaning that production capacity, inventory levels and resource purchase requirements are sensitive to the fluctuating demand. The high residual variation in 2015 quarter 4 probably needs some investigation. It is possible that demand is falling faster than might be expected and this will have important consequences for estimated sales figures.

One of the problems of both techniques is that forecasts are based on past data. Sudden changes in the market will not be immediately reflected in the forecasts. Thus there may still be a role for the sales manager to use his experience, intuition and judgement to amend the forecasts produced by the statistical analysis.

Finally, of the two approaches presented here, time series analysis seems the most appropriate technique for sales forecasting at ATD.

(b) **Introduction of a formal budgeting process**

A budget is essentially a short-term business plan. It is usually expressed in financial terms and it serves as a mechanism for converting the long-term plan and objectives of the company into an actionable blueprint for the near future, usually the next year. Most businesses have sales ambitions and it is the achievement of these that drive many budgets. At ATD, like in many organisations, the ability to sell sufficient products is the main problem. Setting and achieving sales targets, both in terms of volume and price, is a preoccupation, and in most organisations it is the limiting factor that the budgetary system is based around. In such circumstances, the sales budget is the first budget to be prepared as it determines the overall business activity for the forthcoming period. It is the level of sales that determines inventory requirements, production capacity, raw material purchases, etc. At ATD, the sales forecast not only determines the level of activity but also the pattern of that activity, with seasonal variations that will have to be taken into account in other activities. Such seasonal variations might reveal other limiting factors, such as production capacity or inventory storage space and these would have to be investigated and policies determined.

Budgets should allow proper, realistic targets to be set not only for sales but also for functions where there is clear accountability (e.g. production management and inventory management). Targets need to be rigorous and achievable. They also need to be connected to clear organisational demarcation where targets are under the control of a manager who has responsibility for that target. Thus budgeting should improve forecasting through requiring a rigorous and collectively responsible process. Flexing the budget would allow the performance of parts of the organisation to be assessed in the context of missed sales targets. For example, an analysis might reveal that the production manager has reduced target raw material costs even though lower sales volumes mean that overall revenue targets have not been met. At present, the production manager is frustrated because he feels that he is working "tirelessly to keep costs down, but my only reward is that I cannot replace one of my best purchasing administrators who left last month". However, we only have his assertion about his ability to keep costs down. With a flexed budget, the business can actually see if he has effectively controlled costs. Flexed budgets and their associated variances provide an important insight into how different functions or departments (and their managers) are actually performing.

There is also significant evidence to suggest that departmental managers will be motivated if they are required to strive to achieve targets that they themselves have helped set, fostering a sense of ownership and commitment. This would help address the managers' feelings of powerlessness and the sense that they are undervalued. Their morale should improve as they see their experience and opinions valued. Benefits should also accrue for the organisation as a whole. As knowledge from different departments is pooled, understanding, target setting and co-ordination should be improved due to the number of different departments involved in budget setting.

Because budgets include planning, feedback and control elements, they offer important insights into how an organisation should react to failed sales targets. The response of the CEO has been to take general measures which appear, on the face of it, to offer immediate savings, but have an unpredictable effect. Such indiscriminate measures as a ban on business travel, cancelled marketing initiatives and a complete freeze on recruitment may be legitimate responses, but without a budget, it is not really possible to assess their effectiveness. A proper variance analysis might suggest better reactions, and indeed if reduced sales targets are compensated for in some way by reduced raw material and labour costs, then the overall performance might not warrant, in the short term, such an extreme response. The organisation needs to respond to variances and exercise proper controls, revising plans (and budgets) if necessary. The suggested measures may be counter-productive. For example, banning business travel might prevent the production manager from travelling to a supplier where he would be able to negotiate reduced material costs. Cancelled marketing initiatives might further affect the capability of the organisation to meet sales targets and a complete freeze of recruitment may affect the organisation's effectiveness and its capacity to deliver products on time and to the required quality.

Thus a formal budgeting process would allow ATD to address three particular areas of concern. The ability of the organisation to make realistic forecasts, the poor morale of departmental managers and the appropriateness of the organisation's response to its failure to hit predicted sales targets.

Answer 42 RICK HEIN

(a)   **Application of product life cycle model**

The product life cycle model suggests that a product passes through six stages: introduction, development, growth, shakeout, maturity and decline. The first Rock Bottom phase appears to coincide with the introduction, development and growth periods of the products offered by the company. These highly specified, high quality products were new to the country and were quickly adopted by a certain consumer segment (see below). The life cycle concept also applies to services, and the innovative way in which Rock Bottom sold and marketed the products distinguished the company from potential competitors. Not only were these competitors still selling inferior and older products but their retail methods looked outdated compared with Rock Bottom's bright, specialist shops. Rock Bottom's entry into the market-place also exploited two important changes in the external environment:

(1)   The technological advance of the Japanese consumer electronics industry.
(2)   The growing economic power of young people, who wished to spend their increasing disposable income on products that allowed them to enjoy popular music.

Early entrants into an industry gain experience of that industry sooner than others. This may not only be translated into cost advantages but also into customer loyalty that helps them through subsequent stages of the product's life cycle. Rock Bottom enjoyed the advantages of a first mover in this industry.

Hein's leadership style appears to have been consistent with contemporary society and more than acceptable to his young target market. As an entrepreneur, his charismatic leadership was concerned with building a vision for the organisation and then energising people to achieve it. The latter he achieved through appointing branch managers who reflected, to some degree, his own style and approach. His willingness to delegate considerable responsibility to these leaders, and to reward them well, was also relatively innovative. The shops were also staffed by young people who understood the capabilities of the products they were selling. It was an early recognition that intangible resources of skills and knowledge were important to the organisation.

In summary, in the first phase Rock Bottom's organisation and Hein's leadership style appear to have been aligned with contemporary society, the customer base, employees and Rock Bottom's position in the product/service life cycle.

The second phase of the Rock Bottom story appears to reflect the shakeout and maturity phases of the product life cycle. The entry of competitors into the market is a feature of the growth stage. However, it is in the shakeout stage that the market becomes saturated with competitors. The Rock Bottom product and service approach is easily imitated. Hein initially reacted to these new challenges by a growing maturity, recognising that outrageous behaviour might deter the banks from lending to him. However, the need to raise money to fund expansion and a latent need to realise (and enjoy) his investment led to the company being floated on the country's stock exchange. This, eventually, created two problems.

(1)   The need for the company to provide acceptable returns to shareholders. This would have been a new challenge for Hein. He would have to not only maintain dividends to external shareholders, but he would also have to monitor and improve the publicly quoted share price. In an attempt to establish an organisation that could deliver such value, changes were made in the organisational structure and style. Most of the phase 1 entrepreneur-style managers left. This may have been inevitable anyway as Rock Bottom would have had problems continuing with such high individual reward packages in a maturing market. However, the new public limited organisation also demanded managers who were more transactional leaders, focusing on designing systems and controlling performance. This style of management was alien to Rick's approach.

(2)   The need for the organisation to become more transparent. The publishing of Hein's financial details was embarrassing, particularly as his income fuelled a life-style that was becoming less acceptable to society. What had once appeared innovative and amusing now looked like an indulgence. The challenge now was for Hein to change his leadership style to suit the new situation. However, he ultimately failed to do this. Like many leaders who have risen to their position through entrepreneurial ability and a dominant spirit, the concept of serving stakeholders rather than ordering them around proved too difficult to grasp. The sensible thing would have been to leave Rock Bottom and start afresh. However, like many entrepreneurs he was emotionally attached to the company and so he persuaded a group of private equity financiers to help him buy it back. Combining the roles of Chairman and Chief Executive Officer (CEO) is also controversial and likely to attract criticism concerning corporate governance.

In summary, in the second phase of Hein's leadership he failed to change his approach to reflect changing social values, a maturing product/service market-place and the need to serve new and important stakeholders in the organisation. He clearly saw the public limited company as a "shackle" on his ambition and its obligations an infringement of his personal privacy.

It can be argued that Hein took Rock Bottom back into private ownership just as the product life cycle moved into its decline stage. The product life cycle is a timely reminder that any product or service has a finite life. Forty years earlier, as a young man, Hein was in touch with the technological and social changes that created a demand for his product and service. However, he had now lost touch with the forces shaping the external environment. Products have now moved on. Music is increasingly delivered through downloaded files that are then played through computers (for home use) or MP3s (for portable use). Even where consumers use traditional electronic equipment, the reliability of this equipment means that it is seldom replaced. The delivery method, through specialised shops, which once seemed so innovative is now widely imitated and increasingly, due to the Internet, less cost-effective. Consumers of these products are knowledgeable buyers and are only willing to purchase, after careful cost and delivery comparisons, through the Internet.

Hence, Hein is in a situation where he faces more competition to supply products which are used and replaced less frequently, using a sales channel that is increasingly uncompetitive. Consequently, Hein's attempt to re-vitalise the shops by using the approach he adopted in phase 1 of the company was always doomed to failure. This failure was also guaranteed by the continued presence of the managers appointed in phase 2 of the company. These were managers used to tight controls and targets set by centralised management.

To suddenly be let loose was not what they wanted and Hein appears to have reacted to their inability to act entrepreneurially with anger and abuse. Hein's final acts of reinvention concerned the return to a hedonistic, conspicuous life style that he had enjoyed in the early days of the company. He probably felt that this was possible now that he did not have the reporting requirements of the public limited company. However, he had failed to recognise significant changes in society. He celebrated the freeing of "Rock Bottom from its shackles" by throwing a large celebration party. Celebrities were flown in from all over the world to attend. It seems inevitable that the cost and carbon footprint of such an event would now attract criticism.

Finally, in summary, Hein's approach and leadership style in phase 3 became increasingly out of step with society's expectations, customers' requirements and employees' expectations. However, unlike phase 2, Hein was now free of the responsibilities and controls of professional management in a public limited company. This led him to conspicuous activities that further devalued the brand, meaning that its demise was inevitable.

(b) **Franchising**

At the end of the first phase Hein still had managers who were entrepreneurial in their outlook. It might have been attractive for them to become franchisees, particularly as this might be a way of protecting their income through the more challenging stages of the product and service life cycle that lay ahead. However, by the time Hein came to look at franchising again (phase 3) the managers were unlikely to be of the type that would take up the challenge of running a franchise. These were managers used to meeting targets in the context of centrally determined policies and budgets in a public limited company. Hein would have to make these employees redundant (at significant cost) and with no certainty that he could find franchisees to replace them.

At the end of phase 1, Rock Bottom was a strong brand, associated with youth and innovation. First movers often retain customer loyalty even when their products and approach have been imitated by new aggressive entrants to the market. A strong brand is essential for a successful franchise as it is a significant part of what the franchisee is buying. However, by the time Hein came to look at franchising again in phase 3, the brand was devalued by his behaviour and incongruent with customer expectations and sales channels. For example, it had no Internet sales channel. If Hein had developed Rock Bottom as a franchise it would have given him the opportunity to focus on building the brand, rather than financing the expansion of the business through the issue of shares.

At the end of phase 1, Rock Bottom was still a financially successful company. If it had been franchised at this point, then Hein could have realised some of his investment (through franchise fees) and used some of this to reward himself, and the rest of the money could have been used to consolidate the brand. Much of the future financial risk would have been passed to the franchisees. There would have been no need to take Rock Bottom public and so suffer the scrutiny associated with a public limited company. However, by the time Hein came to look at franchising again in phase 3, most of the shops were trading at a loss. He saw franchising as a way of disposing of the company in what he hoped was a sufficiently well-structured way. In effect, it was to minimise losses. It seems highly unlikely that franchisees would have been attracted by investing in something that was actually making a loss. Even if they were, it is unlikely that the franchise fees (and hence the money immediately realised) would be very high.

REVISION QUESTION BANK – BUSINESS ANALYSIS (P3)

Answer 43 ACADEMIC RECYCLING COMPANY

(a)   Leadership styles of Sully Truin

Prior to attending the course, Sully Truin appeared to have, in McGregor's terms, many elements of a Theory X manager about him. He felt that it was necessary to closely control and direct staff in order to get them to do what was needed. He perceived that, in general, employees wished to avoid responsibility and so wanted to be closely directed and controlled. This belief was reflected in work design in the company where employees were increasingly restricted to relatively simple repetitive tasks, for which he had defined well-established procedures. While he was attending the course, Sully still had relatively trivial control issues referred to him and he was exasperated by his employees' inability to take actions to resolve these issues. His initial diagnosis of this reluctance was that this was due to their personal inadequacies rather than the result of the work situation that he had created. In terms of the Tannenbaum and Schmidt model, Sully originally displayed a manager-centred leadership, whereby he made a decision and then announced it. Finally, in terms of the Blake and Mouton managerial grid, Sully's style is primarily that of authority/obedience. His main concern is task completion, with a leadership style which dictates what should be done and how it should be done.

The course questioned Sully's tough-minded management approach, promoting a more democratic style where leadership responsibilities are shared with subordinates, who are also involved in the planning of tasks, not just their execution. The course essentially suggested that Sully changed his style of leadership, moving to the right on the Tannenbaum and Schmidt model and towards a stereotypical Theory Y manager. The course was run by a company who promoted the benefits of a democratic style of management.

However, contingency or situational theorists have argued that there is no one "best leadership style" and that style has to be contingent, at least, on the nature of the work to be done and the needs of the people doing that work. Within the context of the case study scenario, the choice of leadership style probably depends on three factors:

(1)   *The characteristics of the leader.* As already discussed, Sully tends towards a Theory X style. However, his willingness to change style as a result of the course might suggest that his approach may be due to a lack of confidence in his subordinates rather than the reflection of deeply held values about leadership.

(2)   *The characteristics of those led.* It could be argued that Sully's style has necessarily led to him employing people who are comfortable with his style, and demand a work environment which is routine, well-specified and tightly controlled. When Sully changes his style after the course, they are unable to contribute effectively and are left confused and anxious. It is their suggestion that Sully returns to his old style of leadership.

(3)   *The situation itself, the nature of the task.* In the case study scenario, the task has been increasingly constrained, so that it can be closely defined and controlled by Sully. It is relatively simple but decisions on problems have to be taken quickly. This is why they are referred to Sully. He is good at making an instant decision and has the authority to back it up. When subordinates were asked to take responsibility for these decisions, they felt that they did not have sufficient authority or experience and so they consulted their colleagues, which took time, before arriving at a decision.

Contingency or situational theorists would probably be critical of a training course that appeared to encourage a management style that would be unlikely to be appropriate for all situations. Even the most democratic of managers has to adopt an authoritarian style at some point to get certain things done or problems resolved.

From a contingency perspective, it could be argued that before going on the course, ARC had a relatively good fit between leadership, subordinates and the task. Sully Truin was relatively well-liked, he was trusted by his employees to make decisions, and his power was high. As owner of the company he has the power to reward and punish employees. The tasks required of employees were clearly laid down and were well defined.

Reversion to Sully's old style of management might make employees feel more comfortable but it does not solve the fundamental problems. The company is still over-reliant on Sully and, as well as causing him personal health problems, this also severely restricts the company's ability to expand. The company could look more closely at the definition of the task and the competencies required of employees. The speed of change may have also been an important factor in the failure of Sully's new democratic approach. His sudden conversion from Theory X to Theory Y manager was too much, too soon and left employees anxious and confused.

Tutorial note: *This part may be answered in a number of ways. However, the main focus of the answer should be on Sully Truin's leadership style both before and after the management training course and the effect these styles have on his employees. Credit would also be given for commenting on the speed of change and its consequences, as well as the principles of a training company offering a course which promotes a particular style as the "best approach to leadership". The model answer includes reference to underpinning theories that are assumed knowledge from F1 "The Accountant in Business".*

(b)   Principles of job enrichment and its application in the contracts office

In general, business systems have five types of business activity: planning, enabling, doing, monitoring and control. In the scenario, employees are primarily responsible for doing and monitoring. However, the control activity, taking action when the monitoring shows that some action is required, is undertaken by Sully Truin. This manifested itself in the emails and phone calls he received whilst he was on the management training course.

The term job enrichment refers to a number of different processes including job rotation, enlarging and aggregating tasks. However, the term has become specifically used to refer to a policy of vertical task amalgamation. It is roughly analogous to merging the swim-lanes of a current business process model. An enriched job often contains responsibility for planning the job and for taking control actions when they are required.

There are five core characteristics of enriched jobs.

(1)   *Skill variety:* The job requires the use of a range of skills and talents.

(2)   *Task identity:* (sometimes called closure): the job includes all the tasks needed to complete an identifiable product or process.

(3)   *Task significance:* the degree to which the job has an impact on other people's lives or work.

(4)   *Autonomy:* employees have a degree of freedom, independence and discretion in scheduling and organising the work.

(5)   *Feedback:* the degree to which employees possess information of the actual results of their performance.

In the context of these characteristics, giving employees responsibility for responding to problems (a controlling activity) was a first step towards job enrichment, particularly as it would lead to task closure (completing the solution of an operational problem) and emphasise the task significance (the impact of the decision on the field crews).

However, Sully's sudden change of style caused two problems.

(1)   It exposed gaps in the knowledge and skills of the employees. These might be addressed through coaching from Sully.

(2)   It identified that the employees were happier following well-established routines and were quite content to be led. Asking them to take responsibility for decision-making led to anxiety and procrastination, culminating in their request for Sully to return to his old style of leadership. The strength of the employee's need for growth in the job is an important moderator.

Such moderators explain why jobs which have considerable potential to motivate will not automatically generate a high level of motivation and satisfaction for all employees. Evidence suggests that the employees at ARC are naturally content within their job. People who have found the job too restrictive have left the company.

If Sully pursues his ideas for job enrichment, then he will have to carefully assess his current staff to see which, if any, are willing to pursue this wider role. Evidence suggests that "employees with low growth needs are less likely to experience a positive outcome when their job is enriched" (Bratton and Gold). Consequently, Sully may have to bring new people in from outside if he wants to pursue his job enrichment policy.

His assessment of the skills, competencies and desires of his employees has to be even more comprehensive if he wishes to extend jobs to include planning and enabling tasks. However, such an extension would allow them to assist him finding and establishing contracts, helping grow the company.

DECEMBER 2014

Answer 1 ROAM GROUP CO

(a)   **Independent report**

   (i)   *Introduction*

The Roam Group currently consists of three operating companies: Stuart Roam Road Transport, Stuart Roam Warehousing and Stuart Roam Rail. Roam Group Co (The Roam Group) is a corporate holding company which facilitates the acquisition of operating companies in the Group. This first part of the report evaluates the performance and contribution of each of the three current operating companies and assesses their relative significance in The Roam Group's future business strategy. The portfolio analysis references two significant models: the Boston Box (or BCG matrix), suggested by the Boston Consulting Group, which uses a classification based upon a company's market growth and market share, and the parenting matrix of the Ashridge Portfolio Display which focuses on the fit between the company and its parent.

Stuart Roam Road Transport

Stuart Roam Road Transport (SRRT) is a central part of The Roam Group. Not only does it reflect the original business purpose of the Group, but it is also a fundamental part of its current business strategy, linking customers to rail, warehouse and, potentially, airports. It is also the largest revenue generating part of the Group, contributing 57·4% of the Group's revenues in 2016 and 54·8% of its operating profit. The company has extensive experience in road freight and it is now the dominant company in this business sector. There is also a clear emotional attachment to the industry, with the managing director taking time out once a month to return to everyday trucking. It has an outstanding brand image, promoted partly through significant non-corporate initiatives (the New-Roamantics), which give it free high-profile promotion. The brand image is supported by a clever catch phrase painted on every truck and by the ownership of a modern, reliable, efficient fleet of trucks. In terms of the Ashridge portfolio model, partly because of the historical development of the group, SRRT is definitely a heartland business.

The road freight market has experienced relatively little growth over the last four years (2·5% growth). SRRT has increased its market share over this time (from 25% to 28%), with a 15% increase in revenues. In Boston Box terms it is a cash cow, although fairly low margins reduce the amount of money it can produce for investment in itself or in other companies in the Group. These relatively low operating profits appear to be typical for the industry sector, with SRRT consistently performing slightly better than industry averages.

Stuart Roam Warehousing

Stuart Roam Warehousing operates a number of efficient, automated warehouses around the country. The physical size of these warehouses provides another opportunity for promoting the brand image and colours of The Roam Group. There is clear synergy with the road transport operation. Indeed, the Group probably had little hesitation in entering this sector of the market. Powerful external forces (including the growth of outsourcing, the growth of internet shopping and retailers requiring an integrated logistics solution) meant that the business case would have been overwhelming.

As a whole, the sector is expanding. The market has grown from revenues of $2,850m to $3,200m dollars in four years – a growth of 12·3%. Stuart Roam Warehousing has experienced a 26% growth in this time period, although their market share is still less than 10% (9·8%). Operating margins are slightly higher than the road transport sector and the ROCE is also higher. Stuart Roam Warehousing contributes over 40% (40·5%) of the operating profit of the whole Group. In the Boston Box analysis, there is a practical problem in defining what is meant by "high", so the company is either a question mark or a star depending on the assessment of its market share. However it is classified, it needs further nurturing and investment. In the context of the Ashridge portfolio model, the company appears to be a heartland business. The Group has a good feel for the business and there seems to be a good fit between the business opportunities and the characteristics and capabilities of the Group as a whole. Overall, its financial performance is largely in line with industry averages.

Stuart Roam Rail

The rail freight market appears to be expanding rapidly. There is a 26% rise in industry revenue between 2012 and 2016. Perhaps this reflects the increasing cost of road transport, increasing road congestion and fears about the environmental impact of road transport. However, Stuart Roam Rail is a very small player in this market. It has failed to match growth (only 6·6% growth over this period) and its market share has fallen (from 4·2% to 3·6%). Its financial performance is relatively poor, reporting lower operating margins and ROCE than the industry averages. Importantly, the acquisition of FDRC by the Group does not seem to have made a positive impact. In fact, despite an increase in revenues, overall financial performance appears to be worse. In 2013 (the last year the company traded as FDRC), the company reported an operating profit of 4·95% (4·75% in 2016) and a ROCE of 3·85% (3·5% in 2016). This decline in performance is important to bear in mind when considering the possible acquisition of Godiva airport.

In Boston Box terms, Stuart Roam Rail is definitely a question mark (problem child, wildcat). The Group needs to investigate why the company is failing to grab an increasing market share of a rapidly expanding industry. There are at least three possibilities contained within the scenario:

(1)   The company is small and will find it difficult to match the economies of scale enjoyed by the two large rail freight companies. This probably contributes to high operating costs.

(2)   The company has no expertise in the bulk freight contracts (coal, iron ore, oil) which dominate the Meeland economy. This will make it difficult to take these contracts from the current incumbents.

(3)   It is unclear whether the transport of consumer food and drink is really suitable for rail transport. The company is distributing to supermarkets, many of which are unlikely to be directly accessible to the rail network. Road transport is a much more flexible alternative.

There are also cultural problems within The Roam Group. The company is used to dealing with a transport method where the medium (roads) is free and drivers are relatively unskilled. In the rail network the transport medium (rails) is charged on a usage basis by a monopoly supplier. Train drivers have to undergo extensive training and are constrained in their route selection. Road and rail are both methods of transport, but they have quite different characteristics. In the context of the Ashridge portfolio model, this cultural problem might suggest that the company is a value trap business. It is typical of a company which initially appears attractive because there appears to be opportunities for the parent to add value.

Value trap businesses should only be included in the strategy if they can be moved into the heartland. This will probably only be possible if new skills, competencies or resources are gained by The Roam Group.

However, on the upside, the company has developed an innovative mini-container system for transferring goods from road to rail and for storage in the warehouse. Also, the supermarkets, aware of the demands of the green consumer, are attracted to rail alternatives and perhaps see this as the primary way of distributing in the future, particularly if loads can be quickly transferred onto road vehicles for the last part of the journey from the railhead to supermarket.

Conclusion

In summary, SRRT and Stuart Roam Warehousing are both heartland businesses. However, the similarities between rail transport and distribution and road transport and distribution may have been misjudged. The rail company is potentially a value trap business and the Group will have to reconsider how to move it into the heartland. In Boston Box terms, it is also a problem child (question mark, wildcat) and so their strategy for moving it into the heartland must also address the underlying reasons why market share is falling in a rapidly expanding business sector.

(ii)   Introduction

This section of the report considers the proposed acquisition of Godiva airport in the context of its suitability, acceptability and feasibility.

Suitability

The suitability of a strategy addresses the circumstances in which the organisation is operating – its strategic position. Here we have to ask the question, does the acquisition of Godiva airport by The Roam Group make sense? It does appear to be appropriate at a very superficial level – provided by Sir John Watt in his press release. Road, rail and air are all means of transport with different strengths and weaknesses. However, analysis has already revealed (part (i)) that the similarities between road and rail are much less than might be expected. This is particularly true from a customer perspective. Supermarkets tend to have many individual sites, convenient for road transport but not for rail. There are still doubts whether rail can be used as a significant way of distributing consumer food and drink from the warehouse to the supermarket. The integrated mini-containers represent a possible solution, but the cost of unloading and loading at the rail terminal might make their extensive use unlikely on cost grounds. Even if the mini-container system can be extended to aircraft, airports are relatively few and far between, making distance to supermarket sites even more of an issue. Furthermore, air freighting consumer goods is unlikely to deliver the economies of scale associated with rail freight, or to appeal to the eco-sensibilities of the supermarkets.

However, this broad consideration of the complementary nature of transport alternatives hides another, more fundamental issue. The Roam Group is considering buying an airport, not an airline. This is roughly analogous to buying a station (or set of stations) for Stuart Roam Rail or a portfolio of toll roads for Stuart Roam Road Transport. Sir John Watt's statement does appear to imply the purchase, use or formation of an airline sometime in the future, but that is all. The Roam Group has no experience in running airports and although they intend to offer the opportunity to "no-frills" airlines to offer scheduled passenger services from the airport, there is no evidence that any airline is currently interested in this option. Indeed, the relatively sparsely populated hinterland of the airport makes it difficult to imagine that there would be much demand for such services. If "no-frills" airlines were to fly out of Godiva, it seems likely that they would have done so by now.

Acceptability

The acceptability of the strategy is concerned with expected outcomes in terms of return, risk and shareholder reaction. Returns are the benefits which stakeholders would expect to get from the strategy, both in financial and non-financial terms.

The financial performance of the airport can only be assessed from the snapshot of its 2016 performance. It would have been useful to have been given access to data for previous years. However, the industry average performance figures given by the aviation industry consultant can give some measure of the airport's relative performance. Unsurprisingly, the primary asset of the company is the airport site itself which is valued at $6m.

Trading profitability appears quite reasonable. The gross profit margin is 28·2% and an operating profit margin 15·4% (compared to a 17·5% industry average). Indeed, the operating profit compares favourably with the companies currently in The Roam Group. It is much better than, for example, Stuart Roam Rail. However, it has taken significant investment to generate these returns and the Return on Capital Employed (ROCE) is much lower than the industry average. Even if the ROCE calculation excludes interest costs in its calculation (as in Atrill and McLaney), it is still only 2·2%, a very low return. In contrast, liquidity is relatively good (a current ratio of 2·5 – average 2·25), although there appears to be a disproportionally high inventory value. When this is excluded, the acid test ratio is only 1·125, compared to an industry average of 1·5. Gearing is higher than the industry average (59·1% compared to 40%). Finally, in a country where the normal payment period is 30 days, the airport is achieving this for receivables, but is paying in over 60 days (62·6 days). This needs to be investigated further. It might be due to administrative incompetence or to cash flow constraints, with suppliers providing free credit.

Overall, the financial situation is mixed. The airport is trading quite reasonably, but its performance is affected by long-term debts which contribute to a high gearing and a low ROCE. The acid test ratio is of some concern, particularly as customers are paying on time, but payments to suppliers are over twice the accepted payment norm in Meeland.

Risk concerns the probability and consequences of the failure of the acquisition. From the perspective of the resources of the Group, the cost of the acquisition is relatively small and any operating losses could easily be absorbed. A failed acquisition would not be catastrophic for the Group. However, the case has already been made for further investment in Stuart Roam Rail and Stuart Roam Warehousing (two potential problem children) and these may be partially starved of funds due to money being invested in the airport. Managers and employees in other companies may become demotivated by investment in, what might appear to them, an ego-driven vanity project.

The shareholders might also be ambivalent towards the purchase. The Roam family still own the majority of the shares. Their hearts appear to be in road freight, and an investment in an airport might be a step too far.

Feasibility

Finally, feasibility is concerned with whether an organisation has the resources and competencies to deliver a strategy. The issue of financial resources has been considered in the previous section. However, a consideration of competencies is particularly relevant here.

There seems little doubt that the company has significant competencies in road transport and it has been able to adapt these to warehousing. However, these competencies have not proved useful in the rail transport industry. Indeed, since the acquisition of FDRC, the performance of the company has deteriorated. This makes it doubtful that The Roam Group will be able to turn round the performance of an airport – an organisation which is not directly involved in transport. The appropriate competencies are just not in place.

Conclusion

It is the final point about competencies which reinforces the view that the purchase of Godiva airport is an inappropriate strategy and a poor investment for the Group. The company can clearly afford the purchase price of the airport, and absorb any subsequent operating losses, but this will be at the cost of reducing shareholder value and reduced investment and performance in other companies in the Group. Money and management focus would be much better spent on improving the market share of Stuart Roam Warehousing and the overall performance of Stuart Roam Rail. From a suitability perspective, the acquisition does not make sense because it does not appear to address the requirements of customers. It is surprising that someone as experienced as Sir John Watt is advocating this acquisition.

However, one final point must be raised. Perhaps the acquisition is not about airport and "no-frills" airlines; or indeed, about air freight at all. In a country where land for warehousing is getting scarcer and more expensive, Godiva airport offers 450 hectares of land. At commercial warehousing costs, this would cost $9m to buy. At the offer price of $7m, The Roam Group is getting a discount of about 22% on normal land values. Perhaps land is at the heart of the purchase, particularly as the airport site is next to a motorway and a town where SRRT has three depots and warehouses. The declared strategy might not be the real motive. Getting cheaper land for warehouse development might be the real reason for this acquisition, and from that perspective, it makes a lot more sense, particularly if it frees up existing Roam sites within the town which can be sold for housing or office development.

(b)   **Route to competitive advantage**

Johnson, Scholes and Whittington identify four ways of sustaining a price-based strategy: to accept reduced margins, to win a price war, to reduce costs or to focus on specific segments of the market. Elements of all of these might be discerned from the case study scenario. Indeed, the company's focus on consumer food and drink for supermarkets is a continuing example of the last of these strategies. However, this model answer focuses on possibilities offered by reduced margins and a price war.

An organisation pursuing elements of a low price strategy may be prepared to accept a reduced margin, either because it can sell more volume than its competitors or because it can cross-subsidise that business from other business units in the portfolio. The Roam Group can pursue both these options within the context of Stuart Roam Road Transport. It is a dominant player in the road transport market place (generating high volume and revenue) and it is generating good returns in the warehousing business which could be used to cross-subsidise the transport section. It is generally accepted that margins are relatively low in road transport, so reducing operational margins still further might force rivals to exit the business. Market growth is relatively static (2·5% over the last five years), so continued growth requires SRRT to take market share from its rivals. A price war might also achieve this aim. The company is financially sound and evidence suggests that it has greater financial resources than many of its competitors. If it chose to, SRRT should be able to initiate, sustain and win a price war with short or medium-term losses in contribution driving competitors out of the market.

With respect to differentiation, Johnson, Scholes and Whittington offer three ways of sustaining differentiation: creating difficulty of imitation, pursuing imperfect mobility and the re-investment of margin. Two of these are considered here. Imperfect mobility of resources or competencies can be achieved in a number of ways. Two approaches might be applicable at SRRT. It can attempt to increase the difficulty and cost to the customer of switching its supplier. The integration of road transport, warehousing and rail transport using the mini-containers developed by the company might be a key feature here. Nobody can match this flexibility at present (particularly with the eco-friendliness of rail travel which is especially attractive to supermarkets).

It may be possible to imitate it, but it will require considerable investment. However, what is virtually impossible to imitate is the contribution of the New-Roamantics. This is not a carefully crafted management initiative but a group which has spontaneously developed through a shared interest in the Stuart Roam trucks. It is a unique way of promoting the brand. It is unlikely that customers will buy solely because of it, but it does ensure that Stuart Roam is always in their consciousness and there is a certain aspect of fame by association. Subtly encouraging and rewarding this club will maintain an important differentiator between the Stuart Roam Road Transport company and its rivals.

Answer 2 STELLA ELECTRONICS

(a) **Evaluation of current process**

Issues

- There are too many handoffs in the current process, particularly given the need to connect to each section by telephone. It seems likely that bottlenecks will form around these handoffs.

- The role of the supervisor is particularly redundant from the perspective of Stella Electronics (SE). Enquiries for other companies should not be part of their process and, from their perspective, the supervisor adds no value.

- The payment or service contract reference number and the password are requested relatively late in the process. The need to have these available could have been flagged earlier in the process, perhaps at first contact with the supervisor.

- On average, 153 people per day (600 calls × 0·85 × 30%) do not know their reference number. This means that SE is billed $153 per day for calls which are not resolved. It also wastes the end customer's time and money and is a potential source of complaint and dissatisfaction.

- On average, 18 people (17·85) per day ((600 – 90 – 153) × 5%) do not know their password. This means that SE is billed $18 per day for calls which are not resolved. It also wastes the end customer's time and money and is, again, a potential source of dissatisfaction and complaint.

- Although the split of staff across the sections seems reasonable at first sight (six people in technical support for 60% of queries, three people in Stella support for 25% refunds, and one person in the contracts section for 15% of queries), this masks two problems:

  (1) The contracts section is disproportionately understaffed (it should have 1·5 staff); and

  (2) More importantly, 100% of the calls have to pass though the three people in Stella support. This must be a bottleneck, and is likely to be the main reason for the poor service experienced by the end customer.

Potential improvements

Tutorial note: *There is a range of potential improvements that might be suggested. Some ideas are presented below, but other legitimate answers would be given credit.*

- A dedicated phone number could be given to SE customers to eradicate the need for a TCG supervisor.

- Different phone numbers could be given to SE customers for the three different types of query. Thus there will be a dedicated refund line, a dedicated contracts line and a dedicated technical support line.

- Staffing levels could be changed to reflect the frequency of calls. For example, an extra person could be provided in the contracts section, although this does not address the support bottleneck.

- The role of routing calls could be performed by an automated telephone system. For example, option 1 could be refunds, option 2 for technical queries and option 3 for service contracts. This would also provide a mechanism for handling other types of queries (option 4), which could be the responsibility of the supervisor if his or her role is retained.

- Customers requesting refunds or requiring technical support could be informed earlier in the process of the need to have their contract reference number and password ready. This could be given in the automated reply (see point above) to the initial phone call or menu choice selected or it could be requested by the supervisor, if this role is retained. The need for this could also be prominently displayed on their company's website.

- Multi-skilling staff so that they could effectively handle any part of the process would reduce handoffs. It may be difficult to include technical support in a multi-skilled role, but it certainly seems feasible to merge the refund and service contract roles. Reducing the number of swim lanes is an effective way of improving a business process.

(b)   **Outsourcing**

The financial case for outsourcing still remains very strong. At present, the cost to SE is $600 per day for a service provided by 10 people, giving a 24 hour service. SE has calculated that it will cost $50 to employ a person with similar competencies in Arborium for an eight hour shift. This produces a 24 hour cost of $150. If SE continues to employ 10 staff, then the total cost will be $1,500 per day. There would also be capital costs of re-establishing the infrastructure to provide the support service, including telephones, office furniture and training costs. There will also be operational costs (e.g. electricity and office rent and property charges).

So a like-to-like switch back to an in-house support unit seems impossible to justify on cost grounds. However, SE could consider alternative ways of dealing with calls. Technical queries could be addressed by improving support documentation (reducing the demand for queries) and by publishing frequently asked questions (FAQs) on its website. Email support could also be offered. The processing of refunds and the handling of service contracts could be provided by an online process. This seems particularly suited to refund processing. Contracts, which appears to require a dialogue between the customer and SE, seems less of a candidate for this. Improvements in query handling might also allow SE to reduce the number of people working in the centre to a level where the cost of the service would be roughly the same as the outsourced equivalent.

The cultural context of outsourcing needs consideration. Outsourcing, and particularly offshoring, appears to have a negative impact on customers who, as well as having difficulty in understanding the call centre staff based in different countries, increasingly view offshoring as a way of exporting employment. As the number of people out of work in Arborium continues to grow, so the pressure increases on companies to bring work back in-house. SE might be able to make some marketing or public relations capital out of bringing support back in-house and into the country.

Service is a primary activity on the value chain. It is a key point where customers interact with an organisation and form their opinions about it. At present, many customers have a negative view of SE informed by their contact with the TCG call centre. Queries take too long to process and there are problems in understanding the call centre staff. SE needs to consider whether it is wise to outsource such a customer-focused activity. Perhaps the support activities (information technology, procurement) of the value chain are better candidates for outsourcing.

However, it also has to be recognised that support is not a core activity of SE. It is primarily an electronics retailer. It might be reasonable to conclude that a company such as TCG, dedicated to providing call centre support, should give a better service, leaving SE time to focus on its core competencies and activity.

In the short term, it would seem sensible to introduce improvements at the TCG call centre. The service is already relatively cheap and could be made cheaper by reducing the number of calls (through improved documentation and website support) and by reducing the number of calls which are not resolved. In the longer term, SE might wish to re-consider the wisdom of outsourcing a customer-facing service and they may, on ethical grounds, wish to invest in jobs in the country where most of their customers are. Publicising this socially responsible decision might also boost sales.

Answer 3 TKP

(a) Principles of effective risk management

The first stages of risk management are the identification, descriptions and assessment of the risk. This assessment is primarily concerned with the *likelihood* of them occurring and the *severity* of impact on the organisation or project should they occur. Sometimes the likelihood is a subjective probability, the opinions of experienced managers or experts in the field. On other occasions, there is some statistical evidence on which to base the assessment. For example, in project 1, TKP identified that 20 IT software companies with annual revenues between $3m and $10m went out of business last year. This represented 10% of the total number of software companies reporting such revenues. Its report to the client suggested that there was a 10% chance of the current preferred supplier (who had a turnover of $5m) ceasing business and this would have a significant short-term support implication. This compared to a business failure rate of 1% for software companies with an annual revenue exceeding $100m. The client felt that the probability of supplier failure was too high, so eventually bought a software solution from a much larger, well-known, software supplier. In this case, the likelihood of the risk led the client to changing its procurement decision. The risk itself does not go away, large companies also fail, but the probability of the risk occurring is reduced.

The *avoidance (or prevention) of a risk* is a legitimate risk response. In project 1, the client could avoid the risk "failure of the supplier" by commissioning an in-house bespoke solution. Similarly, TKP itself avoids the risks associated with trading in different cultures, by restricting its projects to clients based in Zeeland.

There are three further responses to risks:

(1)   *Risk mitigation (or risk contingency) actions* are what the organisation will do to counter the risk, should the risk take place. Mitigation actions are designed to lessen the impact on the organisation of the risk occurring. In project 2, TKP recommends that the producers of the iProjector should establish an escrow agreement with the company which produces the chip which enhances the quality of the projected image. It was agreed that design details of this chip should be lodged with a third party who would make them available to the producers of the iProjector should the company which owned the enhanced image technology cease trading.

This is a mitigation approach to the risk "failure of the supplier". The supplier is relatively high risk (less than three years of trading, inexperienced management team), and the product (the iProjector) is completely dependent upon the supply of the image enhancing chip. The failure of the business supplying the chips would have significant impact on iProjector production. If the escrow agreement had to be enacted, then it would take the producers of the iProjector some time to establish alternative production. Consequently (and TKP have suggested this), it might be prudent to hold significant stocks of the chips to ensure continued production. In such circumstances, the need to mitigate risk is more important than implementing contemporary just-in-time supply practices. In some instances a mitigation action can be put in place immediately. In other instances risk mitigation actions are only enacted should the risk occur. The risk has been recognised and the organisation has a rehearsed or planned response. For example, in project 1, TKP has identified "poor quality of current data" as a risk associated with the migration of data from the current systems to the proposed software package solution. It has established a strategy for data cleansing if that risk actually materialises. Importantly, the client knows in advance how to respond to a risk. It avoids making a hasty, ill-thought out response to an unforeseen event.

(2)   *Risk transfer actions* are concerned with transferring the risk and the assessment and consequences of that risk to another party. This can be done in a number of ways. TKP itself has liability insurance which potentially protects the company from the financial consequences of being sued by clients for giving poor advice. TKP has identified this as a risk, but is unlikely to be able to assess either the probability of that risk occurring or establishing meaningful mitigation measures to minimise the effect of that risk. Consequently, the responsibility for both of these is transferred to an insurance company. They establish the risk, through a series of questions, and compute a premium which reflects the risk and the compensation maximum which will have to be paid if that risk occurs. TKP pays the insurance premiums. TKP itself also transfers risks in project 2. It is unsure about how to establish patents and so it refers the client to another company. Transferring avoids the risk associated with "establishing the patent incorrectly" and the financial consequences of this.

(3)   Risk may be identified but just accepted as part of doing business. *Risk acceptance* is particularly appropriate when the probability of the risk is low or the impact of that risk is relatively insignificant. Risks may also be accepted when there are no realistic mitigation or transfer actions. In project 2, the producers of the iProjector are concerned that there is "a risk that a major telephone producer will launch a product with features and functionality similar to ours". This is a risk, but there is little that can be done about it. Risks of competition are often best accepted.

The discussion above is primarily concerned with deciding what action to take for each risk. Once these actions are agreed, then a plan may be required to put them into place. For example, establishing an escrow agreement will require certain activities to be done.

Risks must also be monitored. For example, in project 2, the risk of supplier failure can be monitored through a company checking agency. Many of these companies offer a continuous monitoring service which evaluates financial results, share prices and other significant business movements. Reports are produced, highlighting factors which may be of particular concern. Risks will also disappear once certain stages of the project have been completed and, similarly, new ones will appear, often due to changes in the business environment. Many organisations use a risk register or risk log to document and monitor risks and such logs often specify a risk owner, a person responsible for adequate management of the risk.

(b) **Principle of the triple constraint**

Every project is constrained in some way by its scope, time and cost (the "triple constraint"). Scope concerns what has to be delivered by the project, time is when the project should deliver by, and cost is concerned with how much can be spent on achieving the deliverable (the budget). Quality is also an important feature of projects. Some authors include quality in their triple constraint (instead of scope), others add it as a further constraint (quadruple constraint), whilst others believe that quality considerations are inherent in setting the scope, time and cost goals of a project. How a particular project is managed depends greatly on the pressures in the triple constraint.

Project 1

The reluctance of the company to re-visit the business case means that the budget (or cost) of the solution is fixed. The implementation date might be desirable, but it does not seem to be business critical. It is an internal system and so any delays in implementation will not affect customers. It will also be a relatively seamless transition for most employees in the company. They already record the time record details which the new system will collect and so all they will see is a changed user interface. Only the direct users of the output (account managers and the project office) will be affected by any delay. The scope of the software package is also pre-defined. If it fails to meet requirements, then the users will have to adjust their expectations or business methods. There is no money to finance customisation or add-on systems, so in this sense the scope of the solution is also fixed. The quality of the software, in terms of its reliability and robustness, should also be good, as it is a popular software solution used in many large companies.

Project 2

The launch date is fixed. It has been heavily publicised, the venue is booked and over 400 attendees are expected, including newspaper journalists. Thus the time of the project is fixed. However, although orders will be taken at the launch, the product is not expected to ship until a month after launch. Thus the scope of the product shown at the launch date might be restricted and inherent quality problems might not yet be solved. Any defects can be explained away (this is a pre-production model) or, more effectively, they may be avoided by ensuring that the product is demonstrated to attendees, not used by them. The project manager must ensure that key functionality of the product is available on launch date (e.g. producing an image of a certain quality), but other functionality, not central to the presentation (e.g. promised support for all image file formats) could be delayed until after the presentation. The company should make extra funds available to ensure that the launch date is successful.

Answer 4 NOBLE PETS

(a)   **Strengths and weaknesses of the Milton plant**

There are five primary activities in the value chain: inbound logistics, operations, outbound logistics, sales and marketing and service:

Inbound logistics are activities associated with receiving and storing the inputs to the production process. In terms of the costs identified in the scenario, inbound logistics are concerned with raw foodstuff costs, the costs of cans and the transport costs (goods inward). In two of these areas (raw foodstuff costs and can costs) Noble Pets appears to be competitive. However, goods inward costs are higher than any of its competitors. The fact that raw foodstuff costs and can costs are competitive makes it seem unlikely that the high goods inward costs are due to procurement failings. What seems more likely is that the location of the factory makes transport costs higher.

Travelling on relatively minor rural roads and negotiating the congested town centre and the growing suburbs of Milton will affect the fuel economy of the trucks which make deliveries to the plant. This will place Noble Pets at a disadvantage compared with competitors who may be located adjacent to major motorways. There is also some reputational damage caused by complaints from local residents kept awake by the trucks.

Operations are concerned with the production activities associated with turning inputs into their final form, outputs. Production at Noble Pets involves the processing of the raw materials, canning and labelling. In the context of the scenario, these are represented by production costs and direct labour costs. Direct labour costs are roughly in line with its competitors. However, production costs are higher. This is probably associated with the ageing technology of the plant itself. Although it was innovative when it was installed 40 years ago, technology changes have meant that there are more reliable and efficient alternatives available. The physical site is also constrained by housing developments which were built subsequent to the plant. Thus the original plant could not be expanded to obtain any further economies of scale.

Outbound logistics are the activities involved with distributing the product to the customer, in this instance the wholesalers and supermarkets. This area is represented by transport costs (goods outward) included in the table given in the scenario. Like inward logistics, these transport costs are higher than Noble Pets' competitors. This is again partly due to the nature of the roads which lead to the factory and to the congestion in Milton. It also seems very likely that most of the company's customers have relocated to locations which have good road links. Wholesaler and supermarket distribution centres are relatively flexible and footloose and most locate to easily accessible locations. A further problem with outbound logistics is the size of the trucks which can be used to carry the final product. The larger 44 tonne vehicles are banned from Milton town centre, so the company has to continue using the less cost-effective 36 tonne trucks. Again, it is likely that its competitors will be benefiting from the lower unit transport costs offered by the larger trucks.

Sales and marketing is concerned with the activities which make the buyer aware of the product (marketing) and also provide a means by which the buyer can purchase the product (sales). No details of the costs of sales and marketing are provided in the table. However, marketing is an acknowledged strength of the firm and has allowed the company to command a premium price for its products. The term "noble" itself has positive connotations and appeals to the buyers' sense of duty to feed their pets with what appears to be a superior product. This is significant, because the firm is targeting the buyers of a product who are, in this case, not the consumers of that product. In fact, the consumers' feedback is probably restricted to the pet's reluctance to eat the food. So advertising campaigns which stress the need for people to give their pets the best and that the best is provided by Noble Pets are very effective.

Interestingly, the trend to move from moist foods to dry foods (discussed in part (b)) has been driven by buyers wanting more convenient foods rather than the preferences of the pets themselves.

Service activities are designed to support or enhance the product. Normally, these include services such as installation, repair, training and part supply. In the context of Noble Pets, this can be perceived as the factual information sheets and website designed to promote responsible and appropriate pet ownership. Although the advice is product neutral, its association with Noble Pets enhances the reputation of the company and makes it more likely that consumers will buy its products. The apparently unbiased advice which Noble Pets gives to the community is again an acknowledged strength of the company.

Summary

Noble Pets is a company trapped by its location and its technology. These have led to high transport costs and uncompetitive production costs. It may be possible to address the latter by installing new equipment which is more efficient and reliable, but the business case for replacing all the moist food production facilities depends on future trends in the relative popularity of dry and moist foods. However, it is difficult to see how the company can reduce its transport costs if it remains at the current site. Perhaps it has to continue relying on strong branding and praiseworthy service to allow it to charge a premium price for a product to buyers who are unaware that its content is really very much the same as its competitors' cheaper alternatives.

(b)   **Pet food industry**

(i)   Analysis of trends

It is immediately clear from Table Two that the sales of moist pet foods are decreasing and the sales of dry pet foods are increasing. The decline in moist foods was particularly severe in the period 2010–2013. Since then, the downward curve has flattened out. The rate of increase for dry food sales has decreased in the last few years, but it is still showing healthy year-on-year growth. This change in pattern is due to the buyers of product requiring something which does not smell and can be left for longer in the pet's bowl.

The total sales of pet foods are worth closer examination:

| Year | Moist food | | Dry food | | Total |
| | Production | Percentage | Production | Percentage | Production |
	(000s tonnes)		*(000s tonnes)*		*(000s tonnes)*
2010	370	55·9%	292	44·1%	662
2011	350	53·3%	307	46·7%	657
2012	331	50·8%	321	49·2%	652
2013	325	49·7%	329	50·3%	654
2014	315	48·0%	341	52·0%	656
2015	310	46·9%	351	53·1%	661
2016	310	46·3%	359	53·7%	669

This shows that, overall, pet food sales declined from 2010 to 2014 and only in 2016 rose above the 2010 level (and even then, by only just over 1%). Thus Noble Pets has been competing in, at best, a stagnant market dominated by four companies. The only way that any of these companies can grow is to take market share from each other and hence (in Porter's terms) competitive rivalry is high, compounded by low switching costs from one brand to another. It is probably these strains within the industry which has prompted Noble Pets management to ask the Milton plant to review its value chain.

The Milton plant has also suffered from a change in buying tastes. In 2010, moist pet foods accounted for 55·9%. In 2016, this figure had reduced to 46·3%. Although Noble Pets' share of this market remains the same (30%), this is a reduction in real terms of 18,000 tonnes of production (from 111,000 to 93,000 tonnes).

(ii)   Moist pet food – demand forecast

The regression analysis for moist food sales suggests the following line of best fit.

$y = a + bx$
$y = 369·5714 - 9·86x$

The negative value of b shows that the slope of the curve is downwards. Substituting values for 2017 (8), 2018 (9) and 2019 (10) into this equation gives the following (rounded) forecasts.

2017: 291   2018: 281   2019: 271

These values do appear to be too low, given the flattening out of demand in 2014, 2015 and 2016. The line of best fit is influenced by the rapid decline in the first four years of the analysis. Thus these forecasts appear too pessimistic when extrapolating the linear line of best fit.

The correlation coefficient r is negative (–0·94432), which is what would be expected given the production decline. The coefficient of determination of 0·89174 (r^2), suggests that 89% of the variation can be explained by the passage of time or, more sensibly, by some factor or factors which have changed over this time (e.g. buyer behaviour). However, the correlation coefficient measures the strength of the linear relationship, and there does appear to be some obvious curve in the original data values.

Although the market for moist food has declined rapidly in the last few years, this decline appears to have been arrested. However, the steepness of this decline, in the early years of the analysis, has meant that the line of best fit produces estimates which appear too pessimistic. A free-hand extension of the curve joining the actual data points is likely to give estimates of over 300,000 tonnes for the next three years. This will have to be taken into account when deciding any further investment in the Milton plant. If Noble Pets retains its 30% share of the market, it still has a demand for 90,000 tonnes of moist pet foods. The other two factories producing moist pet food are relatively small, producing 40,000 tonnes between them. Thus a detailed financial analysis can reasonably be based on a demand of at least 50,000 tonnes in the period 2017–2019, even if the other plants work at full capacity.

Professional Level – Essentials Module

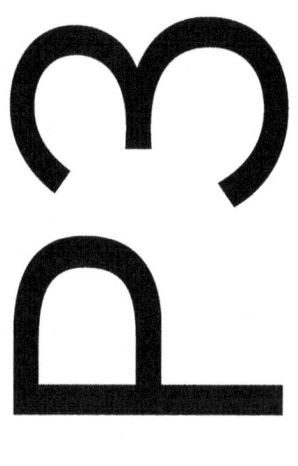

Business Analysis

Monday 8 June 2015

Time allowed

Reading and planning: 15 minutes
Writing: 3 hours

This paper is divided into two sections:

Section A – This ONE question is compulsory and MUST be attempted

Section B – TWO questions ONLY to be attempted

Do NOT open this paper until instructed by the supervisor.

During reading and planning time only the question paper may be annotated. You must NOT write in your answer booklet until instructed by the supervisor.

This question paper must not be removed from the examination hall.

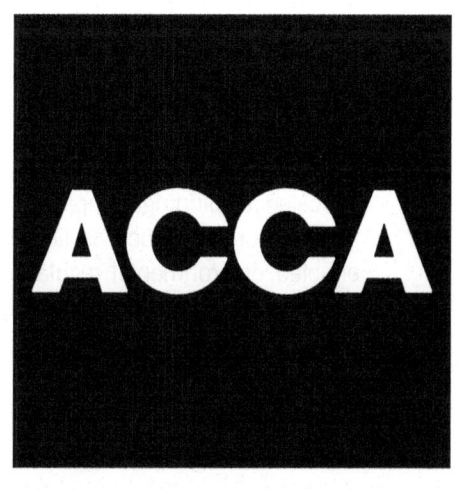

The Association of Chartered Certified Accountants

Section A – This ONE question is compulsory and MUST be attempted

1 Introduction

2Tel is one of the largest mobile network operators in the world. It has grown mainly through significant acquisitions and it has extensive experience in buying companies and integrating them into the group. 2Tel continually invests substantial funds in research into network technologies. Like all global mobile network operators, it is constantly looking for technical opportunities for making its networks quicker, more reliable and, if possible, cheaper to install and maintain.

A business opportunity has arisen in The Federated States (TFS) where network operator licences are about to be renewed. 2Tel is currently evaluating this opportunity and is considering either bidding directly for a licence (as 2Tel) or acquiring a current licensee and bidding through this company. 2Tel is interested in entering the highly regulated mobile network market in TFS, even though most of its acquisitions to date have been in countries where there is little or no government regulation of the mobile network operators.

The Federated States (TFS)

The Federated States is a densely populated country with a population of 70 million people. The country has experienced five years of economic decline, characterised by high unemployment, falling incomes, and rising personal and government debt. Crime rates are also increasing. A year ago, a new government was elected with a mandate to tackle the economic problems of the country. Its priority has been to reduce the national debt and to help achieve this aim, it has introduced higher taxes and cut welfare benefits. The removal of these welfare benefits provoked civil disturbance and rioting, where shops were looted and burnt and mass demonstrations, usually ending in violence, were held in the streets of major cities.

TFS is an increasingly socially fragmented country with vocal minority groups representing a wide range of pressure groups and communities. It has a comprehensive and complex legal system, presided over by senior judges who were largely appointed by the previous government. The current government has suggested that many recent judgements made by these judges are politically-motivated and are designed to hold back the government's reforms. The employment laws of TFS make it relatively expensive to employ people (there are minimum wages laws) and also difficult to dismiss them (employment protection laws). Legal proceedings are often time-consuming and expensive.

A report into the riots and demonstrations highlighted the role mobile phones and social networks played in co-ordinating attacks on shops and people. The report acknowledged that such communication devices had long been a widely used tool in organised crime in TFS, but that it had now also become a significant factor in organising mass disobedience. In an effort to prosecute offenders, the government asked mobile phone network operators to give it information about text messages and the timing and duration of phone calls which possible offenders had sent and received during the period of the riots. The information provided was used as supporting evidence in court, and helped convict a number of people.

The releasing of this information to the government has proved controversial. The network operators have been criticised by civil liberties organisations which believe that this is personal, confidential information and, under the terms of the Data Protection Act of TFS, should not have been released without the person's consent. On the other hand, the government has praised the network operators for their good citizenship and believes that the data provided is exempt from the Act as the Act allows data to be exempt if it is used 'for the detection and prevention of crime'. An influential newspaper, whilst recognising the contribution of the networks to the successful prosecution of offenders, felt that 'instead of helping catch offenders, the networks, by making their services unavailable might have prevented the offences in the first place'. One of the current network licensees, Z-Tel, is being sued for damages by people who claim that their confidential information has been illegally released to the government. The case has yet to be presented to a court, but lawyers for both sides are confident of success.

Licensing arrangements in TFS

Communication network licences are granted to mobile network operators for an eight-year period. Licences are allocated to bidding companies on the basis that the companies meet a certain number of criteria. This includes financial criteria, such as liquidity and gearing, and environmental criteria. Successive governments of TFS have enacted environmental regulations and set environmental targets (such as carbon emissions and recycling rates) which all companies operating in TFS have to achieve.

Beyond these minimum criteria, the licences are allocated to the highest bidders, the companies which offer the most money for a licence. There are four current licensees and these were the four highest bidders in 2009, the last time that the licences were granted. During the licence period, no new network operators can enter the market. All four licensees are of a similar size, although their profitability varies (see Table one). The government is keen to ensure that no one network provider dominates the market.

Table one: Comparative data (2014) for the four licensees

All figures in $m	Z-Tel	T-Me	Tello	Co-nekt
Revenue	750	700	725	740
Gross profit	350	300	325	325
Net profit	125	80	100	125

The licences are due for renewal in three years' time. At present, the rules for licence granting are exactly the same as for the previous licence allocation – four licences given to the four applicants who fulfil the minimum criteria and make the four highest bids. However, some government ministers are unhappy about this and are lobbying for a change which favours bids from current licensees. The government has already stated that any of the current licensees which fail to be reallocated a licence will be paid a $100m exit fee to help the losing company adjust to the loss of its licence. This will be paid for by the company which is replacing them, and is in addition to the contract fee paid by the successful bidder to the government. Some government ministers feel this bias towards current licensees should go further. One government minister recently suggested that 'the help provided to us during the recent riots should be acknowledged in some way'. There has also been a suggestion that there should be more than four licensees. This would increase competition and would also raise more money for national debt repayments. However, except for introducing an exit fee, the government has not yet officially stated any changes to the rules on licence allocation.

The network operators are monitored by a regulator, Ofnet, appointed by the government. In general, Ofnet has been supportive of the four current mobile network operators and it has openly praised their attitude and service on a number of occasions. Ofnet's primary focus is on pricing, service availability and service transfer. All prices are agreed in a series of meetings between the regulator and the licensees. As a result, the prices set by the four operators are very similar and are slightly less than the operators would like them to be. The companies, therefore, have to compete on branding, service support and network quality. In many geographical locations, one of the networks often provides a better signal quality and network speed, and indeed poor signal coverage is the most often cited reason for customers changing service operators. It is already possible for subscribers to move to a different service provider, but Ofnet believes, that this should be made even easier, and so is bringing in regulations to enable this. Licensees who do not comply with these regulations will be fined. The licensees are unconvinced of the demand for moving provider. One commented 'most subscribers move due to poor network service, and they can already do this!'

Mobile devices in TFS

Despite the economic decline of the last five years, mobile devices are seen as essential to most people within TFS. The demand for mobile devices and the networks which support them has increased dramatically in the last five years. Furthermore, mobile devices are particularly prized by the young, who see having the latest up-to-date technology as an important status symbol. Consequently, the manufacturers of mobile devices continually update the features and functionality of their devices. This has had an important effect on the mobile networks. Demand for services has increased not only due to an increase in calls, messages and web browsing but also due to the increasing demand which improved services place on network availability, bandwidth and speed. Thus the network operators have to continually upgrade the technologies and configurations which support their service networks. Most people in TFS rent their phones as part of a contract with the network provider. The minimum contract period is for one year, although many people tie themselves in for longer periods to take advantage of lower prices. Most people upgrade their phones when they renew their contract, to ensure that they have the device with the latest features. Old phones are returned by customers to their network provider, who, in turn, sends them back to the original manufacturer. The environmentally-friendly disposal of these mobile phones is a continual problem for the mobile phone manufacturers.

Research into the tendering process

2Tel has commissioned research from Professor Tan of Midshire University, an acknowledged expert in probabilistic decision making, into the TFS bidding process. Here are some of his conclusions. He has determined probabilities using a bid price of $550m and the probabilities are based on four licences being available.

(1) If the bidding rules are not changed before the next licence allocation, then every bidder has a 0·4 probability of being granted a licence if their bid is for $550m.

(2) If the bidding rules are changed before the next licence allocation to favour current licence holders, then a current licence holder has a 0·6 probability of being granted a licence if they bid $550m for the licence. A new bidder has only a 0·2 chance of being allocated a licence if they bid $550m for the licence. These probabilities are based on research in other countries where bidding is biased towards the current licence holders.

(3) It will cost current licence holders $10m to prepare a bid for a licence. New bidders, because of their unfamiliarity with the bid process, will incur a cost of $20m to prepare their bid.

2Tel is particularly interested in acquiring T-Me, the smallest of the current licensees. Their research suggests that they can implement efficiency gains which will generate $100m net profit per annum for the final two years of the current contract. This compares with T-Me's current net profit levels of $80m per year. Further efficiency gains and increased usage will lead to $120m net profit per year for the eight years of the contract, should the offer for T-Me be successful. An initial approach to T-Me has suggested that an offer of $400m for T-Me would be accepted.

The same net profitability for the contract (eight years at $120m per annum) is also expected if 2Tel decides not to acquire T-Me and is successful in a direct bid for a licence.

Before entering any market (or industry), 2Tel commissions an independent briefing paper from a business analyst which considers both the external environment of that market or industry (the wider macro-environment which the market or industry works within) and the competitive environment of the market or industry itself (the market or industry the proposed company will work within). These briefing papers conclude with a brief summary of the opportunities and threats posed by the environment. These briefing papers are used by the board of 2Tel as part of its evaluation of whether a market is attractive to enter. In this case, whether it should attempt to enter the TFS mobile operator industry, and if it does attempt to enter, whether it should enter directly or through acquiring a current operator.

Required:

(a) Write the briefing paper required by 2Tel. The briefing paper should:

    (i)   Analyse the macro-environmental factors affecting the TFS mobile operator industry;   (14 marks)

    (ii) Analyse competition within the TFS mobile operator industry;   (8 marks)

    (iii) Conclude with a summary of the opportunities and threats identified in the analysis.   (4 marks)

    Professional marks are available in part (a) for the structure, coherence, style and clarity of the briefing paper.

    (4 marks)

(b) 2Tel also requires an evaluation of the relative advantages of bidding for a licence, either through acquiring T-Me, or through bidding directly. The evaluation should analyse four specific scenarios (acquire and not gain licence; acquire and gain licence; bid directly and gain licence; bid directly and not gain licence). The analysis of each scenario should include the financial implications of each scenario. The evaluation should conclude with your recommendation on the preferred entry strategy.

    Required:

    Produce the evaluation of each scenario as required by 2Tel.

    Note: Construction of a decision tree is not required and ignore the time value of money in your evaluation.

    (20 marks)

(50 marks)

2   Yvern is large region in the country of Gaulle. It is ethnically and culturally distinct from the rest of the country and it has aspirations for independence. The desire for this independence is reflected by consumers in Yvern preferring to buy products which have been produced in the region.

Yvern Trinkets Regional (YTR) is a manufacturer of giftware products aimed at the Yvern market. Its products are bought primarily by residents of Yvern and visitors to the Yvern region. It is the third largest company of its type in the region, and the 50th largest producer of giftware in Gaulle. Its marketing message stresses the regional identity of the company and its employment of local skills and labour. It currently manufactures four products, designated here as products A, B, C and D. The company does not sub-contract or outsource any element of production and it has never done so. Data concerning products A, B, C and D are given in Table one.

	A	B	C	D
Monthly production (in units)	2,000	5,500	4,000	3,000
Direct materials cost ($ per unit)	3	5	2	4
Direct labour cost ($ per unit)	9	6	9	6
Variable production overheads ($ per unit)	2	3	1	2

Table one: Production and marginal cost data for the YTR product range

YTR recently appointed a new managing director, born outside the region. He has been tasked with improving the profitability of the company.

After a short period of consultation, the new managing director produced a proposal for the board. Here is an extract of his proposal.

'First of all, we need to be clear about our generic strategy. Strategists have suggested that we have four alternatives. I have reproduced them in this slide (shown here as Table two).

Cost Leadership	Differentiation
Cost Focus	Differentiation Focus

Table two: Generic strategies

My vision for YTR is that we should pursue a **cost leadership** strategy. I have already established that our products can be produced by an established company in the distant country of Tinglia at the following prices (see Table three). These costs include the delivery of products to our warehouse here in Yvern.

	A	B	C	D
Buy-in price ($ per unit)	11·5	16·5	12·5	13·5

Table three: Contract prices per unit from the external supplier in Tinglia

Our financial director of YTR has also estimated that we have company-wide fixed overheads of $75,000 per month. He assures me that $16,000 per month of these is directly attributable to the production of products A, B, C and D, evenly split across the four products, each having $4,000 of fixed overheads. So, we could save overheads of $16,000 per month by outsourcing all of our products to the Tinglia supplier.

I realise that this leaves us with $59,000 per month fixed overheads, but I will be looking for savings there also. The information technology of YTR is outdated and inefficient. Productivity benefits will follow from harnessing the power of modern technology.

However, returning to my main concern: production costs. My view is that increased profitability can only be achieved if we take advantage of the cheaper production costs now available to us. All four products can be produced more cheaply by the supplier in Tinglia. So, this strategy of outsourcing is the one we should pursue to achieve our cost leadership strategy.'

Required:

(a) Evaluate the claim that 'all four products can be produced more cheaply by the supplier in Tinglia' and discuss the issues raised by outsourcing the production of YTR's products to Tinglia. (15 marks)

(b) Examine the relevance of each of the four generic strategies shown in Table two to the competitive environment in which YTR operates and evaluate the choice of a cost leadership strategy by YTR's managing director. (10 marks)

(25 marks)

3 The town of Brighttown in Euraria has a mayor (elected every five years by the people in the town) who is responsible for, amongst other things, the transport policy of the town.

A year ago, the mayor (acting as project sponsor) instigated a 'traffic lite' project to reduce traffic congestion at traffic lights in the town. Rather than relying on fixed timings, he suggested that a system should be implemented which made the traffic lights sensitive to traffic flow. So, if a queue built up, then the lights would automatically change to green (go). The mayor suggested that this would have a number of benefits. Firstly, it would reduce harmful emissions at the areas near traffic lights and, secondly, it would improve the journey times for all vehicles, leading to drivers 'being less stressed'. He also cited evidence from cities overseas where predictable journey times had been attractive to flexible companies who could set themselves up anywhere in the country. He felt that the new system would attract such companies to the town.

The Eurarian government has a transport regulation agency called OfRoad. Part of OfRoad's responsibilities is to monitor transport investments and it was originally critical of the Brighttown 'traffic lite' project because the project's benefits were intangible and lacked credibility. The business case did not include a quantitative cost/benefit analysis. OfRoad has itself published a benefits management process which classifies benefits in the following way.

Financial: A financial benefit can be confidently allocated in advance of the project. Thus if the investment will save $90,000 per year in staff costs then this is a financial benefit.

Quantifiable: A quantifiable benefit is a benefit where there is sufficient credible evidence to suggest, in advance, how much benefit will result from the project. This benefit may be financial or non-financial. For example, energy savings from a new building might be credibly predicted in advance. However, the exact amount of savings cannot be accurately forecast.

Measurable benefit: A measurable benefit is a benefit which can only be confidently assessed post-implementation, and so cannot be reliably predicted in advance. Increase in sales from a particular initiative is an example of a measurable benefit. Measurable benefits may either be financial or non-financial.

Observable benefit: An observable benefit is a benefit which a specific individual or group will decide, using agreed criteria, has been realised or not. Such benefits are usually non-financial. Improved staff morale might be an example of an observable benefit.

One month ago, the mayoral elections saw the election of a new mayor with a completely distinct transport policy with different objectives. She wishes to address traffic congestion by attracting commuters away from their cars and onto public transport. Part of her policy is a traffic light system which gives priority to buses. The town council owns the buses which operate in the town and they have invested heavily in buses which are comfortable and have significantly lower emissions than the conventional cars used by most people in the town. The new mayor wishes to improve the frequency, punctuality and convenience of these buses, so that they tempt people away from using their cars. This will require more buses and more bus crews, a requirement which the mayor presents as 'being good for the unemployment rate in this town'. It will also help the bus service meet the punctuality service level which it published three years ago, but has never yet met. 'A reduction in cars and an increase in buses will help us meet our target', the mayor claims.

The mayor has also suggested a number of initiatives to discourage people from taking their cars into the town. She intends to sell two car parks for housing land (raising $325,000) and this will reduce car park capacity from 1,000 to 800 car spaces per day. She also intends to raise the daily parking fee from $3 to $4. Car park occupancy currently stands at 95% (it is difficult to achieve 100% for technical reasons) and the same occupancy rate is expected when the car park capacity is reduced.

The new mayor believes that her policy signals the fact that Brighttown is serious about its green credentials. 'This', she says, 'will attract green consumers to come and live in our town and green companies to set up here. These companies and consumers will bring great benefit to our community.' To emphasise this, she has set up a Go Green team to encourage green initiatives in the town.

The 'traffic lite' project to tackle congestion proposed by the former mayor is still in the development stage. The new mayor believes that this project can be modified to deliver her vision and still be ready on the date promised by her predecessor.

Required:

(a) A 'terms of reference' (project initiation document, project charter) was developed for the 'traffic lite' project to reduce traffic congestion.

Discuss what changes will have to be made to this 'terms of reference' (project initiation document, project charter) to reflect the new mayor's vision of the project. (5 marks)

(b) The new mayor wishes to re-define the business case for the project, using the benefits categorisation suggested by OfRoad.

Identify costs and benefits for the revised project, classifying each benefit using the guidance provided by OfRoad. (14 marks)

(c) Stakeholder management is the prime responsibility of the project manager.

Discuss the appropriate management of each of the following three stakeholders identified in the revised (modified) project.

(i) The new mayor;
(ii) OfRoad;
(iii) A private motorist in Brighttown who uses his vehicle to commute to his job in the town. (6 marks)

(25 marks)

4 TMZ is a music company based in the developed country of Artazia. It was founded in 1963 when it started to sign emerging rock and roll artists to its record label. TMZ offers a contract in which the artists receive royalties based on the sales of their music. As part of this contract, TMZ record the music, distribute it and promote it. Most of the contracts are for a defined number of songs or records. For example, in 1980, TMZ contracted the heavy metal band, Vortex31, to produce ten albums, to be delivered over seven years. Extracted financial data for the period 1965–2000 is given in Table one. During these years TMZ successfully signed bands offering different and emerging types of music (pop, punk, garage, grunge, patio) and also successfully altered the physical media of distribution, from vinyl records to tape cassette and subsequently to compact disc (CD).

All figures in $million	1965	1970	1980	1990	2000
Revenue	10	70	120	150	170
Gross profit	4	30	45	50	50
Net profit	3	22	30	30	25

Table one: Revenue and profit information: TMZ (1965–2000)

The company remained profitable in this period, despite musicians taking longer to produce albums and senior management adopting a relaxed and indulgent approach to their creative artists.

In 1999, the first file sharing company was formed in Artazia, allowing people to easily share their music files with each other. During the next decade, numerous file sharing and digital downloading companies were launched. As early as 2003, the possible implications of this growth in file sharing and digital downloading were highlighted by a number of employees in TMZ. However, senior management at TMZ were dismissive of this threat, suggesting that the contracts with their artists were 'watertight'. Table two shows revenue and profit information for 2003–2007.

All figures in $million	2003	2004	2005	2006	2007
Revenue	165	150	130	100	80
Gross profit	45	30	10	0	(10)
Net profit	20	5	(15)	(20)	(30)

Table two: revenue and profit information: TMZ (2003–2007)

Senior management at TMZ believed that this decline in performance was due to them providing the 'wrong music, promoted to the wrong people at the wrong price'. During this period the company signed new artists, increased advertising and cut prices. However, this did not halt its decline.

Losses were also made in 2008 and 2009 and the company was only kept afloat by fresh injections of shareholder capital. During these years, the company took legal action against what they considered illegal downloading and file sharing. It won a number of small cases but its actions angered many music fans, who felt that music labels had been greedy in the past. It also upset some of its artists who now benefited from the opportunity the internet gave them to sell music directly to their fans.

In 2009, a new CEO was appointed from outside the music industry. In 2010 he announced a new strategy. TMZ was no longer interested in contracting new artists to the label. Instead it would focus on deriving profit from its established artists and music catalogue. He came to licensing agreements with some large digital downloading operators and stores, allowing them to access or sell the music of established artists. However, he continued litigation against others. He also began to generate revenue from licensing the music for use in computer games, television advertisements and personalised ringtones.

In 2011 the company reported a gross profit for the first time since 2005. In 2013 and 2014 it recorded a small net profit. The CEO stated that TMZ was now a 'slimmer, fitter company. We are a learning organisation, developing the resilience needed to trade successfully in the ever-changing digital music age'. However, he warned that TMZ, like others in the industry, would continue to pursue actions against the illegal downloading of music. 'There is a generation where many people consider music and all creative content should be free. However, we see signs that this assumption is becoming less widely held. The next generation is questioning it. Like many others, we continue to seek ways of distributing music which is fair to both the consumer and the artist. We are constantly monitoring trends and patterns in consumer behaviour. We will not get caught out like we were ten years ago. We won't be fooled again!'

Required:

(a) Analyse the performance of TMZ from 1965 to the present. Include in your analysis reference to the principles and any evidence of strategic drift. (15 marks)

(b) The current CEO claims that TMZ is a learning organisation. Discuss the principles of a learning organisation and its implications for TMZ. (5 marks)

(c) Knowledge management is closely related to the concept of the learning organisation. Explain knowledge management and its relevance to TMZ. (5 marks)

(25 marks)

End of Question Paper

1   (a)   (i)   Introduction

2Tel is one of the largest network operators in the world. It is aware that licences for providing mobile networks in The Federated States (TFS), a densely populated country with 70 million people, are due for renewal in three years' time. It is currently evaluating whether it wishes to bid for one of these licences, either in its own right, or through the prior acquisition of one of the current licensees.

It has commissioned this briefing paper into the business environment which the current licensees operate in. This briefing paper begins with an analysis of the wider macro-environment of the industry, using a PESTEL analysis. The paper then considers the competitive forces within the industry using aspects of Porter's five forces framework.

The briefing paper concludes with, as requested, a summary of the opportunities and threats which 2Tel should consider before it decides to enter this market.

Political perspective

Licences are granted by the government for eight years and so it may, at first sight, appear that licence allocation is an important political factor in the mobile network industry. However, the previous government effectively de-politicised the awarding of licences by defining selection rules based on certain minimum criteria (for example, financial and environmental criteria) and the size of the bid. The licences are awarded to the four highest bidders who fulfil the minimum criteria. So, the current performance of licensees is not currently taken into account in the bidding process. This has implications for 2Tel. From a political perspective, there is no particular benefit to be gained by bidding as a current licensee. The praise of Ofnet and the gratitude of the government for the network operators' phone and message information used to convict offenders in the recent riots count for nothing in the selection process. At present, under the current rules, 2Tel has as much chance of winning a licence in its own right. Indeed, this is reflected in Professor Tan's research and his suggested bid success probabilities.

However, it has to be recognised that the selection criteria are politically decided and so there is a possibility that the current government will change the selection rules before the licences come up for renewal. Issues with the current scheme have already been recognised and it has been agreed that companies who fail to retain their licence will be paid an exit fee of $100m. This will mean, for example, if 2Tel wins one of the licences in its own right then it will have to compensate the company which has lost the licence. Thus there will be a $100m fee for new entrants, which is additional to the bid for the licence. Furthermore, a possible change in selection rules raises at least two issues. Firstly, the government could change the rules so that incumbent licensees were favoured (as long as they have performed effectively) and so there would be a benefit to be gained from acquiring a current licensee. Again, this has been recognised in Professor Tan's research and his allocation of bid success probabilities. There appears to be some support for this change of rules within the government. One government minister has suggested that 'the help provided to us (by the network operators) during the recent riots, should be acknowledged in some way'. Secondly, in an attempt to raise more money to address the national debt, the government could decide that more than four companies should be licensed in the future, increasing competition in the sector and raising more income for the government. This might affect the profitability of the existing licensees.

A very significant political issue is the presence of a regulator (Ofnet) in the sector, who particularly focuses on pricing, service availability and service transfer. The prices of all the four licensees are negotiated with the Ofnet regulator and, consequently, the prices of all four networks are very similar. Ofnet also requires the four licensees to have arrangements in place which allow customers to easily transfer from one network to another. Ofnet has generally praised the performance of all four licensees, except in this last area. It has suggested that it is still too difficult for customers to move network provider, and it intends to bring in regulations which make it easier. Fines will be imposed on networks which do not follow these regulations. The powerful role of the regulator is of particular significance to 2Tel. 2Tel has traditionally operated in countries where there is little or no government regulation of network operators. In these markets prices can be largely determined by the company itself, free from external influence.

Technology of mobile networks

Two aspects of technology are important to licensees operating in TFS. Firstly, innovations in mobile telephone technology are very important to the network licensee because, as well as encouraging the use of the network, new products also tend to make greater demands on those networks, in terms of speed and bandwidth. Thus there is need for continual investment in the network. Secondly, this investment includes a need to continually review the technology and configurations available for constructing and supporting the network itself. There is a need to invest in new technologies and technical configurations which offer greater speed, reliability and, if possible, lower costs. However, it has to be recognised that both of these technology factors are not unique to TFS, and are likely to be even more significant in markets which 2Tel is already competing in.

Sociocultural and economic considerations

The possession of a state-of-the-art mobile device remains an important status symbol in TFS. Having the latest features and applications is important to people and so devices are regularly upgraded, hence having features which place significant demands on the network, as discussed in the previous section of this report.

The role of the mobile phone network in assisting organised crime and civil disobedience has posed dilemmas for the network operators. On the one hand, they have been praised for their good citizenship in passing relevant information to the police. However, on the other hand, they have been criticised by civil liberties bodies for making this information available. An influential newspaper, whilst recognising the contribution of the networks to apprehending offenders, also criticised them for not withdrawing the networks at the height of the riots. 'Instead of helping catch offenders, the networks, by making their services unavailable, might have prevented the offences in the first place.' 2Tel has to be aware that TFS is an increasingly socially fragmented country with vocal minority groups representing a wide range of pressure groups and communities.

One of the licensees is currently subject to legal action where people are suing the company for releasing information to the government. The company, and the information it holds, is subject to the Data Protection Act, which exempts information held to prevent or aid the detection of crime, but lawyers for both the company and the offenders are confident of success when the case comes to court.

The election of the current government was prompted by a belief that its policies would address the five years of economic decline presided over by the previous government. In general, the population is suffering from high unemployment, static incomes and, more recently, increased taxes and removal of benefits (this measure provoked the riots already discussed) imposed by the austerity government. However, these economic problems do not appear to have any discernible effect on the use of mobile devices. During this five-year period of decline, the use of the mobile networks has increased significantly. This may, of course, be partly as a result of the regulator, who can reasonably be assumed to exerting a pressure to keep prices low. However, it must also be some reflection of the importance which the population as a whole places on mobile phones and being able to make mobile calls. It is seen as a necessity, rather than a luxury.

Legal and environmental issues

Reference has already been made to the Data Protection Act (sociocultural) and regulation from Ofnet (political). TFS has many laws which are enacted within a complex and expensive legal system. Employees are expensive to employ and are difficult to dismiss. Furthermore, legal outcomes are difficult to forecast due to the unpredictable conduct of judges.

Like all companies operating in TFS, the network operators are expected to comply with environmental regulations. However, environmental issues are more an issue for the mobile phone manufacturers and the environmentally-friendly disposal of these mobile phones is an ongoing problem for the manufacturers, but this is not a problem for the network operators.

(ii) Importantly, from a Porter's five forces perspective, there is no threat of new entrants into the industry during the licence period. However, at the end of the licence period, anyone who meets the bidding criteria can potentially be allocated a licence and enter the market place. So, the licences are an effective barrier to entry during the licence period. At bidding time, it is access to capital which forms the largest barrier to entry, as the success of the bid (at present) is largely determined by the size of the bid. This access to capital is particularly significant to potential new entrants as they will potentially be required to pay a $100m entry premium.

Again, from a five forces perspective, the policy of Ofnet to make network transfer relatively easy theoretically increases the bargaining power of customers, and this should exert a downward pressure on prices. Customers are tied into annual contracts, but it should become increasingly easy for them to transfer supplier with no switching costs. At present, evidence suggests that few customers do actually change operators. This may be because of the difficulty of switching (which is the view of the regulator) or it may be because no great price advantage can be gained by switching provider. Evidence suggests that most move due to poor service or poor reception in their geographical area. The fact that mobile charges are so similar between the four rival companies (mainly due to the regulator) means that there is little incentive to move on price grounds.

Porter's five forces framework has competitive rivalry at its centre. When considering competitive rivalry within the industry, there are certain factors which should contribute to vigorous competition; for example, low switching costs and undifferentiated products. However, competition is limited to four similar size companies competing in a growing market place which is subject to price regulation. Competition on price grounds is very difficult because of the activities of the regulator, who is keen to satisfy the government's wish for no supplier to dominate the market. Thus competitive rivalry is restrained and, to some extent, controlled and competition is based largely on coverage, service, and brand image. It is likely that if one supplier did begin to dominate the market, then the regulator would impose rules to re-balance competition.

At present, it is difficult to envisage any threat of substitute products to the mobile networks. Even the threat of 'doing without' seems unlikely, given people's increased dependence on the mobile phone.

(iii) The conclusion of this briefing paper is, as requested, a summary of the opportunities and threats associated with this market.

Opportunities

The relatively imminent re-licensing of mobile networks provides a significant business opportunity. This business is then largely protected (within constraints imposed by the regulator) for eight years. The licences provide an effective barrier to entry.

Despite the economic decline of the country, sociocultural trends suggest a buoyant demand for network services. As mobile products become more sophisticated, it seems reasonable that this demand will continue to increase for the foreseeable future. There appears to be very little threat of substitutes to the mobile network and people are reluctant to 'do without'.

The current licensees acknowledge that technology has to be continually updated. 2Tel is an acknowledged technology leader with expertise in markets which are, at least, as demanding.

Threats

There is a concern that the government will change the licensing bidding criteria, to favour incumbent licensees, before the next granting of licences. This would be a threat to 2Tel's chance of entering the market in its own right.

The market is highly regulated and pricing has to be agreed with a regulator. 2Tel is inexperienced in working in such an environment and it may be seen as a threat to 2Tel's independence and also to its long-term profitability.

The legal framework in TFS is burdensome and legal outcomes are, to some extent, unpredictable. Threats of legal action and the effects of social disruption may lead to 2Tel to conclude that TFS is not a particularly attractive market to enter. There are threats associated with political interference, public criticism, legal action and legal compensation.

(b) Scenarios

Developing scenarios is particularly appropriate where there is a high level of uncertainty and so it is impossible to build a single view of how environmental influences might affect an organisation's strategy. The case study scenario is dominated by two very significant environmental factors. The first is the bidding rules for the mobile technology licences. These rules are decided by government and current rules do not favour the current licensees. However, there is evidence that the government is moving its position on this and it has already introduced one measure which will help current licences, the payment of a $100m exit fee to licensees who fail to get their licence renewed, to be funded by an extra entry fee by the successful licensees. The other factor is the price which competing companies are willing to pay for the licences.

2Tel wishes to evaluate the two options of bidding for a licence. The first option is to acquire T-Me, one of the current licensees. The second option is to bid directly for a licence. It wishes to consider four scenarios.

(1) Acquire T-Me and then failing to gain a licence.
(2) Acquire T-Me and then gaining a licence.
(3) Bidding directly for a licence as 2Tel and failing to gain a licence.
(4) Bidding directly for a licence as 2Tel and gaining a licence.

Buying T-Me

Buying T-Me offers a number of advantages:

(1) If bidding rules are changed to favour current licensees, then 2Tel (through T-Me) has a better chance of being granted a license. Research by Professor Tan shows that in countries where current licensees are favoured, then a current licencee has a 0·6 probability of being granted a licence, compared with probability of 0·2 for new bidders.

(2) T-Me has experience of the bidding process in TFS. It has been suggested that the cost of putting the bid together (bid cost), will be half that of a new inexperienced bidder.

(3) T-Me is experienced in working in the TFS culture and with the people of TFS. It is a country which is heavily regulated and T-Me has worked effectively with the industry's regulator (Ofnet) over the period of this licence. 2Tel does not have experience of operating in a heavily regulated environment. Its main networks are in countries where regulation is weak or non-existent.

(4) There are short-term opportunities for improving the financial performance of T-Me. 2Tel has suggested that it can raise net profit to $100m per year in the final two years of the contract. This appears to be a very reasonable target. The figures in Table One suggest that T-Me's net profit margin is currently 11·42%, the lowest of the four competing companies. A net profit of $100m (on current revenue) would bring the net profit margin up to 14·29%, still below the average industry performance of 14·7%.

2Tel has been informed that they may be able to acquire T-Me for $400m. Their research (conducted by Professor Tan) suggests that the next eight-year contract can be won for $550m and that a net profit of $120m can be driven out of the company for the next eight years. Here is an analysis for the two scenarios which require the purchase of T-Me. All figures are in $million.

Buy T-Me and fail	Outflows	Inflows
Purchase of T-Me	400	
Bid cost	10	
Net profit (2 years)		200
Exit income		100
Total	410	300
Net gain (loss)		(110)

Buy T-Me and gain	Outflows	Inflows
Purchase of T-Me	400	
Bid cost	10	
Contract fee	550	
Profit (2 years)		200
Profit (new contract)		960
Exit income (Note 1)		100
Total	960	1,260
Net gain (loss)		300

(Note 1) Assumes exit at the end of the licence period and that this exit income is still at current levels.

Bidding directly for a licence

Bidding directly for a licence has a number of advantages:

(1)   If bidding rules are not changed, then 2Tel has the same probability of successfully gaining a licence as T-Me.

(2)   One of T-Me's competitors is currently in a legal dispute concerning the disclosure of information to the government. If they lose this court case (and many anti-government judgements are being made at present), then successful claims may be made against the other network operators. Bidding directly for a licence avoids any potential legal costs associated with contesting claims and compensating potential claimants.

(3)   It avoids the cost of purchasing T-Me. There are likely to be significant costs associated with performing due diligence on T-Me and negotiating and finalising the acquisition.

(4)   It avoids having to impose organisational change at T-Me in an attempt to drive out short-term improvements in net profit. 2Tel has estimated that it can increase net profit to $100m per annum. It does appear to have a successful acquisition record, but it also has to be recognised that there is significant evidence to suggest that planned performance improvements in acquired companies are often not realised, particularly in the short term.

Here is an analysis of the direct bidding scenarios.

Bid and win	Outflows	Inflows
Bid cost	20	
Contract fee	550	
Exit fee (payable to losers)	100	
Profit (new contract)		960
Exit costs (Note 1)		100
Total	670	1,060
Net gain (loss)		390
Bid and lose	20	
Net gain (loss)		(20)

(Note 1) Assumes exit at the end of the licence period and that this exit income is still at current levels.

Analysis

From the perspective of risk aversion, the bidding directly for licences appears the best option. Potential losses are minimised ($20m, compared to $110m) and potential returns maximised ($390m compared to $300m). If expected values are used which represent the current bidding rules, then this conclusion remains valid.

Scenario	Net gain (loss)	Probability	Expected value
Buy and lose	(110)	0·6	(66)
Buy and win	300	0·4	120
Bid and win	390	0·4	156
Bid and lose	(20)	0·6	(12)

The buying option has a net expected gain of $54, compared to a net expected gain for the bid option of $144m.

However, if the bidding rules are changed to favour the incumbent, then the buy option has a greater expected return ($136m compared to $62m).

Scenario	Net gain (loss)	Probability	Expected value
Buy and lose	(110)	0·4	(44)
Buy and win	300	0·6	180
Bid and win	390	0·2	78
Bid and lose	(20)	0·8	(16)

However, a number of issues have to be raised.

(1) The statistical probability values for the changed bidding rules are based on research conducted in other countries where bidding is biased towards the current licence holders. These may not be appropriate for TFS. They could be too high or too low.

(2) Expected values are really more appropriate for a series of decisions, where, over time, the return will tend towards the expected value. The actual values will occur (subject to forecast errors) – not the expected ones.

(3) The bid price of $550m is itself an estimate and the probabilities of bid success only relate to this bid price. The analysis might suggest that a higher bid is made, which should have a higher probability of success. For example, a direct bid of $750m from 2Tel would still lead to a net profit of $190m for the contract – a return of over 20%.

(4) No probabilities have been attached to the chance of the government changing the selection rules before the next licences are allocated.

2Tel might also like to take a second look at the buy and lose option. The unattractiveness of this scenario is largely due to the proposed purchase price of T-Me. It may be possible to reduce or restructure this price, or both. For example, the company could offer $290m now, and $110m on successful gaining of the next contract. However, the possible compensation claims are problematic. They are difficult to predict and at this stage, it would seem unlikely that they can be insured against (risk transfer).

Conclusion

Under the current licence allocation arrangements, the agreed price for T-Me is too high, given the risks involved. So, the recommendation is to bid directly for the licence. However, if the purchase price for T-Me could be re-negotiated or re-structured, then there are advantages of acquiring T-Me and using this as a vehicle for the bid.

However, if the bidding rules change to favour the incumbent licensees, then purchasing T-Me becomes the preferred approach from a financial perspective. However, the spectre of possible compensation payments remains and these might be powerful enough to still persuade the board of 2Tel that a direct bid, unencumbered by the past, might still be preferable, even though the chance of winning the licence might be reduced.

2 (a) Here is a monthly analysis of the data given in the scenario.

Product	A	B	C	D	Total
Production (units)	2,000	5,500	4,000	3,000	
Unit marginal costs					
Direct materials	3	5	2	4	
Direct labour	9	6	9	6	
Variable production overheads	2	3	1	2	
Variable cost per unit	14	14	12	12	
Total monthly variable cost	28,000	77,000	48,000	36,000	
Fixed monthly overheads	4,000	4,000	4,000	4,000	
Total in-house monthly cost	32,000	81,000	52,000	40,000	205,000
Buying costs per unit	11·5	16·5	12·5	13·5	
Total monthly buy in cost	23,000	90,750	50,000	40,500	204,250

The data suggest that only products A and C can be sourced more cheaply through outsourcing. Products B and D can be produced more cheaply in-house.

If products A and C are sub-contracted, the company would then have spare capacity. There is no evidence from the scenario that there is any demand for further production for B and D. More research has to be conducted to see if, in fact, production capacity is a limiting factor at the company and can be effectively utilised to produce more of B and D. If this is the case, then there would be a powerful argument for outsourcing A and C.

The reaction of the company's workforce also has to be taken into consideration. If production of B and D cannot be expanded to take up the spare capacity, then redundancies may be required and so strike action may take place as a result of an industrial dispute. Evidence also suggests that products A and C require more labour intensive processes. So even if spare capacity is used up, demand for labour would reduce. There are also likely to be costs associated with redundancies which do not appear to have been taken into consideration.

The company has no experience in managing an outsourced supplier and ensuring that supplied products are of the required quality. Contractual terms will have to be established for specifying the terms of supply and for specifying service level agreements and penalties for failing to supply. Quality acceptance criteria will have to be established and a process set up for formally accepting the products produced by the outsourcer. This management of the outsource supplier will require one-off and continuing costs which do not appear to have been factored into the proposal.

The company has always advertised itself as producing locally in the region. It is part of their marketing campaign and an attraction to local customers. Sourcing the products through geographically remote outsourcers invalidates the marketing message and may also lead to adverse customer reaction. The company needs to understand the reasons why customers buy its products in the first place before it makes such a decision.

The justification for outsourcing product C is purely made on the saving of fixed costs attributable to its manufacture. The variable production cost of C is actually less than the buy-in cost ($48,000 compared with $50,000), but the addition of the fixed overhead makes the outsourcing option cheaper. There are two issues here: the reliability of this estimate of fixed costs and the likelihood that these savings can be delivered by management when the production of the product is outsourced. It seems unlikely that all four products will have exactly the same direct effect on fixed costs; it looks more like an arbitrary figure. Furthermore, on many occasions, fixed costs savings do not actually materialise. Management fails to deliver.

Finally, the outsourcing prices offered may depend upon outsourcing the whole of production to Tinglia. If this is the case, then the outsourcing option is very slightly cheaper ($204,250 compared with $205,000) but this again depends upon the reliability of the fixed overhead data and the ability of management to save these fixed costs once production is outsourced. The cost of shutting the production capacity in Yvern and employee redundancy costs also have to be taken into consideration.

Summary

The decision to make or buy certain products should not be taken on cost savings alone. The company has considerable experience of making the products and the location they are produced in appears to be important to both the company (from its marketing message) and its customers. In contrast, the company has no experience in outsourcing and managing outsourced providers. In addition, the new managing director's assertion that 'all four products can be produced more cheaply by the supplier in Tinglia' is ambiguous. If he means that the products can be made more cheaply in Tinglia *if all four products are outsourced*, then he is just about correct, although data on overhead costs would have to be reconsidered and other costs associated with outsourcing investigated. However, if he means that all products can *individually* be produced more cheaply in Tinglia, then he is clearly incorrect. Products B and D can be produced more cheaply in-house. However, partial outsourcing may lead to spare labour and machine capacity issues in the factory in Yvern.

(b) The managing director states that he wishes to follow a generic strategy of *cost leadership*. However, it seems likely that he has misunderstood the term or that he is knowingly using it as a euphemism for cost reduction. His slide missed out important information.

	Strategic advantage	
Target	**Low cost**	**Unique**
All customers	Cost Leadership	Differentiation
Market segment	Cost Focus	Differentiation Focus

A generic strategy of cost leadership means being the lowest cost producer *in the industry as a whole*.

It seems unlikely that the company can pursue such a strategy. It has larger rivals (who will be able to obtain better economies of scale) both within the region and within the country as a whole. There is no evidence of technical advantage, and indeed the managing director has commented on outdated information technology. There is no suggestion, either, of other factors which would allow the company to achieve cost leadership, such as having favourable access to sources of supply, or raw materials or labour.

A differentiation strategy assumes that competitive advantage can be gained, in the industry as a whole, through particular characteristics of a company's product. Companies which pursue such a strategy worry less about costs and seek, instead, to be perceived in the industry as unique. For example, the product may be innovative or superior in some way. Again, this does not appear to apply to YTR, in the context of the industry.

Both cost leadership and differentiation require superior performance, which does not appear to be a characteristic of YTR.

A focused or niche strategy takes place when a firm concentrates its attention on one or more market segments or niches. In doing so it could aim to be a cost leader for a particular segment. This is the cost focus strategy identified in the managing director's slide. This is often associated with an environment where 'broader scope' companies exhibit an element of over-performance, offering a particular segment much more than it wants, at a price which reflects this. This may be a possible strategy for YTR if their products are largely indistinguishable from other producers in Yvern. However, outsourcing production does not appear to be the right way of pursuing this strategy.

Alternatively, a company might pursue differentiation for a particular segment; a differentiation focus strategy. This strategy seeks to provide a perceived high quality product to a selected market segment or niche. Such products may be heavily branded and sold at a substantial price premium. There is evidence to suggest that YTR has a strong brand and meets a demand for regional, locally produced products.

A better strategy for YTR is focus, where it can serve a particular niche where it can largely insulate itself from the competition. Porter suggests that a company must pursue one of these strategies. Both cost leadership and differentiation require superior performance and some form of focus strategy is easier, as it is simpler to dominate a niche market.

3 (a) Objectives and scope

From the perspective of the 'traffic lite' project, the change in mayor has led to an immediate change in the objectives driving the project. This illustrates how public sector projects are susceptible to sudden external environmental changes outside their control. The project initially proposed to reduce traffic congestion by making traffic lights sensitive to traffic flow. It was suggested that this would improve journey times for all vehicles using the roads of Brighttown. However, the incoming mayor now wishes to reduce traffic congestion by attracting car users onto public transport. Consequently she wants to develop a traffic light system which will give priority to buses. This should ensure that buses run on time. The project is no longer concerned with reducing journey times for all users. Indeed, congestion for private cars may get worse and this could further encourage car users to switch to public transport.

An important first step would be to confirm that the new mayor wishes to be the **project sponsor** for the project, because the project has lost its sponsor, the former mayor. The **project scope** also needs to be reviewed. The initial project was essentially a self-contained technical project aimed at producing a system which reduced queuing traffic. The revised proposal has much wider political scope and is concerned with discouraging car use and improving public bus services. Thus there are also proposals to increase car parking charges, to reduce the number of car park spaces (by selling off certain car parks for housing development) and to increase the frequency, quality and punctuality of buses. The project scope appears to have been widened considerably, although this will have to be confirmed with the new project sponsor.

Only once the scope of the revised project been agreed can revised **project objectives** be agreed and a new **project plan** developed, allocating the resources available to the project to the tasks required to complete the project. It is at this stage that the project manager will be able to work out if the proposed delivery date (a **project constraint**) is still manageable. If it is not, then some kind of agreement will have to be forged with the project sponsor. This may be to reduce the scope of the project, add more resources, or some combination of the two.

(b) Cost benefit

The re-defined project will have much more tangible effects than its predecessor and these could be classified using the standard approach suggested in the scenario. Benefits would include:

- One-off financial benefit from selling certain car parks – this appears to be a predictable *financial benefit* of $325,000 which can be confidently included in a cost/benefit analysis.

- Increased income from public bus use – this appears to be a *measurable benefit*, in that it is an aspect of performance which can be measured (for example, bus fares collected per day), but it is not possible to estimate how much income will actually increase until the project is completed.

- Increased income from car parks – this appears to be a *quantifiable benefit* if the assumption is made that usage of the car parks will stay at 95%. There may indeed be sufficient confidence to define it as a *financial benefit*. Car park places will be reduced from 1,000 to 800, but the increase in fees will compensate for this reduction in capacity. Current expected daily income is 1,000 x $3 x 0·95 = $2,850. Future expected income will be 800 x $4 x 0·95 = $3,040.

- Improved punctuality of buses – this will again be a *measurable benefit*. It will be defined in terms of a Service Level promised to the residents of Brighttown. Improved punctuality might also help tempt a number of vehicle users to use public transport instead.

- Reduced emissions – buses are more energy efficient and emit less carbon dioxide than the conventional vehicles used by most of the inhabitants of Brighttown. This benefit should again be *measurable* (but non-financial) and should benefit the whole of the town, not just areas around traffic lights.

- Improved perception of the town – the incoming mayor believes that her policy will help attract green consumers and green companies to the town. Difficulties in classifying what is meant by these terms makes this likely to be an *observable benefit*, where a group, such as the Go Green team, established by the council itself can decide (based on their judgement) whether the benefit has been realised or not.

The costs of implementing the project will also have to be re-assessed. These costs will now include:

- The cost of purchasing more buses to meet the increased demand and frequency of service.

- The operational costs of running more buses, including salary costs of more bus drivers.

- Costs associated with the disposal of car parks.

- Costs associated with slowing down drivers (both economic and emotional).

The technical implementation requirements of the project will also change and this is almost certain to have cost implications because a solution will have to be developed which allows buses to be prioritised. A feasibility study will have to be commissioned to examine whether such a solution is technically feasible and, if it is, the costs of the solution will have to be estimated and entered into the cost-benefit analysis.

(c) A stakeholder grid (Mendelow) provides a framework for understanding how project team members should communicate with each stakeholder or stakeholder group. The grid itself has two axes. One axis is concerned with the power or influence of the stakeholder in this particular project. The other axis is concerned with the stakeholder's interest in the project.

The incoming mayor: High power and high interest. The mayor is a key player in the project and should be carefully and actively managed throughout. The mayor is currently enthusiastic about the project and this enthusiasm has to be sustained. As the likely project sponsor, it will be the mayor's responsibility to promote the project internally and to make resources available to it. It will also be up to her to ensure that the promised business benefits are actually delivered. However, she is also the person who can cancel the project at any time.

OfRoad – a government agency: OfRoad were critical of the previous mayor's justification for the project. They felt that the business case was solely based on intangible benefits and lacked credibility. It is likely that they will be more supportive of the revised proposals for two reasons. Firstly, the proposal uses the classification of benefits which it has suggested. Secondly, the proposal includes tangible benefits which can confidently be included in a cost-benefit analysis. OfRoad is likely to have high power (because it can intervene in local transport decisions) but relatively low interest in this particular project as the town appears to be following its guidelines. An appropriate management strategy would be to keep watch and monitor the situation, making sure that nothing happens on the project which would cause the agency to take a sudden interest in it.

The private motorist of Brighttown: Most of these motorists will have a high interest in the project, because it impacts them directly; but, individually, they have very little power. Their chance to influence policy has just passed, and mayoral elections are not due for another five years. The suggested stakeholder management approach here is to keep them informed. However, their response will have to be monitored. If they organise themselves and band together as a group, they might be able to stage disruptive actions which might raise their power and have an impact on the project. This makes the point that stakeholder management is a continual process, as stakeholders may take up different positions in the grid as they organise themselves or as the project progresses.

4 (a) There is considerable evidence to suggest that *strategic drift* particularly affects organisations which have experienced a long period of relative continuity during which strategy has either remained unchanged or changed incrementally to react to relatively minor changes in the external environment or industry. This appears to be the case at TMZ. It had enjoyed 35 years of success and growth based on contracting musical artists to its record label and recording and distributing their songs and music through an appropriate physical media. Table one shows that revenues increased continuously in the period 1965–2000. Profit margins fell during the period, reflecting problems in cost control as established musical acts took longer to produce albums and senior staff of TMZ adopted a more relaxed and indulgent approach to their artists. However, even at the end of the period, TMZ remained a profitable company.

Table one: gross and net profit margin – 1965–2000

	1965	1970	1980	1990	2000
Revenue ($million)	10	70	120	150	170
Gross profit margin	40·00%	42·86%	37·50%	33·33%	29·41%
Net profit margin	30·00%	31·43%	25·00%	20·00%	14·71%

During this period, the company had reacted positively to significant changes in its environment. Sociocultural changes, represented by musical fashion and technology changes (from vinyl, through tape cassette to compact disc (CD)) had been successfully surmounted. However, such success can often lead to complacency, with the organisation continuing to pursue a strategy which progressively fails to address the changing strategic position of the organisation and this failure leads to deterioration in organisational performance. This is known as *strategic drift*.

Evidence for this strategic drift starts to emerge in 2003, four years after the launch of the first file sharing company. People within TMZ warned about the possible implications of digital downloading of music. However, senior management at TMZ had rejected this warning and believed that the drop in revenue was due to 'the wrong music, promoted to the wrong people at the wrong price'. They adopted a policy of signing new artists, increasing advertising spend and cutting CD prices. In the policy, 2003–2007, revenues dropped significantly and the company made significant losses (see table two).

$million	2003	2004	2005	2006	2007
Revenue	165	150	130	100	80
Gross profit	45	30	10	0	(10)
Net profit	20	5	(15)	(20)	(30)
Gross profit margin	27·27%	20·00%	7·69%	0·00%	(12·50%)
Net profit margin	12·12%	3·33%	(11·54%)	(20·00%)	(37·50%)

Table two: gross and net profit margin – 2003–2007

Johnson, Scholes and Whittington suggest that it is important to realise why strategic drift occurs. They suggest that managers, faced with the complexities of steering an organisation, tend to look for solutions based on the *current ways of doing and seeing things*, grounded in the *existing organisational culture*. So, for example, when revenues from compact discs (CDs) started to decline, the senior managers at TMZ instigated relatively conventional responses to falling sales (increased advertising, reduced prices) and also adopted approaches which had worked before (signing new artists). These may have worked if the environmental change had not been so significant. However, what they failed to realise was that the way people were consuming music was fundamentally changing.

The realisation of performance problems is often followed by a period of flux where no clear direction is pursued. When conventional strategies failed, TMZ resorted to litigation, suing the companies who downloaded music to consumers. In effect, TMZ was attempting to preserve the status quo, trying to ensure that the market remained the same as the one they had operated in so successfully for 40 years. However, not only did this not arrest the decline of the company, it also led to problems with both performers and music fans. In 2010, with the very existence of the company threatened, management was able to define a strategy which worked with the digital download and music-sharing community, to establish a completely different business model based on licensing and ring tones.

This illustrates that a period of flux may itself be followed by *transformational change*, in which there is a fundamental change in strategic direction. TMZ re-defined its business model in 2010. It was fortunate that it had enough stakeholder investment to see it through a difficult period. In many organisations transformational change takes place too late and the organisation fails.

Johnson, Scholes and Whittington suggest that the challenge for managers is to stand apart from their own experience and organisational culture so that they are able to recognise the emerging strategic issues which they face. They also suggest that a second challenge relates to the management of strategic change. New strategies might require actions outside the scope of the existing culture. Thus people within the organisation are required to substantially change their core assumptions and their ways of doing things. The senior management at TMZ were warned about the possible effect of digital downloading, but they were unable to change their basic assumptions about how the music industry worked.

(b) The learning organisation

The point has already been made that strategic drift will take place when changes in an organisation's environment take place at a greater rate than the rate of strategic change within the organisation itself. In such circumstances, the organisation begins to be increasingly misaligned with the environment it is operating in. The challenge is to try to ensure that misalignment does not occur in the first place, but if it does, to tackle it quickly.

The likelihood of strategic drift suggests that the strategy development process in an organisation needs to encourage people to have the capacity and willingness to challenge and change their core assumptions and 'ways of doing things'. This is one of the commonly claimed principles of a 'learning organisation'.

Traditionally, organisations have been organised and structured around order and control. They were built for stability and continuity, rather than change. However, influential writers have increasingly claimed that this is unsuitable for the dynamic conditions of trading in the 21st century. They have suggested that modern society and all of its institutions are in a continuous process of transformation and to react to this we all must become adept at learning. 'We must become able not only to transform our institutions, in response to changing situations and requirements; we must invent and develop institutions which are 'learning systems', that is to say, systems capable of bringing about their own continuing transformation.' (Donald Schon)

The learning organisation is an 'ideal' towards which organisations should evolve in order to respond to contemporary pressures. It is characterised by a view that both collective and individual learning is key to organisational success. A learning organisation is one which is capable of continual regeneration based on the knowledge, experience and skills of individuals working in an organisational culture which encourages mutual questioning and challenge. It emphasises the potential capability of an organisation to regenerate from within.

Advocates of the learning organisation suggest that the collective knowledge of all the individuals within an organisation greatly exceeds what the organisation 'knows' in its formal documentation, filing and information systems. They suggest that it is the responsibility of management to encourage processes which reveal the knowledge of individuals and encourage the sharing of this knowledge. Hence the learning organisation is closely connected with the principles of knowledge management, the other strand in the CEO's policy statement. As a result of free-flowing knowledge, individuals within an organisation become more sensitive to the changes happening around them and this helps them contribute to identifying opportunities and threats in the external environment and also to them developing strategies to tackle these threats or to exploit the opportunities.

In such an approach managers play a less directive and a more facilitative role. It is easy to see the attraction of this to TMZ where the impact of digital downloading was already being discussed in 2003, but was dismissed by complacent senior management. In contrast, in a learning organisation, ideas which do not fit in with current norms are not dismissed or ignored, but acted upon. Questioning and challenging the 'taken-for-granted' is essential if an organisation is to avoid strategic drift. It helps build a resilient organisation which does not take success for granted and reinvents itself using internal capabilities to build a new business model. A new business model was eventually adopted by TMZ, but only when it was close to extinction and radical change was needed to ensure survival.

(c) Knowledge management

Johnson, Scholes and Whittington define organisational knowledge as the 'collective and shared experience accumulated through systems, routines and activities of sharing across an organisation'. Managing organisational knowledge is important because as organisations get larger, it becomes more difficult to share what people know. The organisation increasingly does not 'know what it knows' and so it makes unnecessary mistakes, duplicates activity and misses opportunities as a result of this. Furthermore, it is also increasingly likely that organisations, particularly in countries such as Artazia, will have to achieve competitive advantage through accumulated experience (their knowledge), rather than through conventional assets such as physical resources. Fearghal McHugh writing in the *Student Accountant* (issue 07/2010) suggested that 'having knowledge can be regarded as more important than possessing the other means of production – land, building, labour and capital – because all the other sources are readily available in an advanced global society'.

Knowledge management itself has been facilitated by the increasing functionality of computerised information systems. In this context an important distinction is made between data, information and knowledge. Knowledge is primarily associated with the discovery of trends or patterns of behaviour. Discovering such patterns would have helped TMZ realise that consumers were moving away from purchasing physical music media to downloading its digital equivalent. In the market which TMZ currently finds itself in, discovering patterns and trends remains extremely important as consumer behaviour is still unpredictable and is affected by new technologies, emerging legislation and changes in values.

Conventional knowledge management systems are often based around an intranet application where all explicit knowledge about processes, procedures, standards, products, customers and policies are stored. Such repositories are convenient places to locate explicit organisational knowledge and they have practical benefits, such as eliminating the costs of storage, printing and distribution. Data warehouses can store vast amounts of information and provide the basis of reports, comparisons and responses to queries posed at different levels of summation. Data mining software may be used to discover previously unknown relationships between data and these can be used to guide decision-making and predict future behaviour.

However, although technology has provided many opportunities to analyse the formal data captured by an organisation, the social aspects of knowledge sharing remain important. Employees need opportunities to develop, discuss and share information which they feel would be mutually beneficial. Not only might this require physical facilities (coffee areas, restrooms, social and sports clubs), it also requires a culture of trust in the organisation supported by a leadership approach which values learning and an organisational structure which supports communication and information sharing. Thus there is a clear link between knowledge management and the principles of the learning organisation. Social networks can also be used to support this facet of knowledge sharing and indeed might be the natural preference of the younger employees of the organisation. It is in the social aspects of knowledge sharing that many employees reveal their tacit knowledge (knowledge which they do not know they know, as opposed to explicit knowledge) which can be vital for the effective performance of a particular task.

Professional Level – Essentials Module

Business Analysis

September/December 2015

Time allowed

Reading and planning: 15 minutes
Writing: 3 hours

This question paper is divided into two sections:

Section A – This ONE question is compulsory and MUST be attempted

Section B – TWO questions ONLY to be attempted

Do NOT open this question paper until instructed by the supervisor.

During reading and planning time only the question paper may be annotated. You must NOT write in your answer booklet until instructed by the supervisor.

This question paper must not be removed from the examination hall.

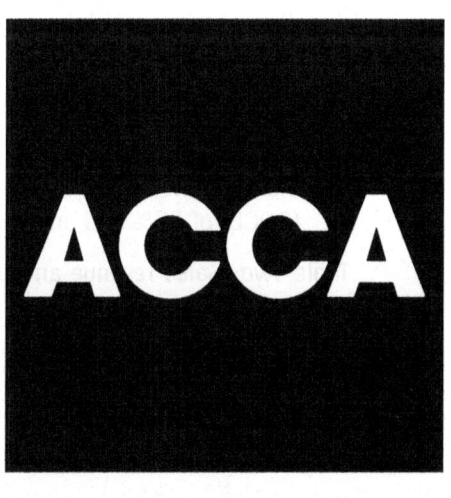

The Association of Chartered Certified Accountants

Section A – This ONE question is compulsory and MUST be attempted

1 Introduction

A business architecture training market has developed in the last two decades in the continent of Eastaria to train business analysts in this important subject area. QTSBA and Aspire to Knowledge (A2K) are both specialist providers of business architecture training and compete in this market. QTSBA is part of the Quality Training Synergies (QTS) Group and it is the market leader in this niche market. QTS Group is currently considering the possible acquisition of A2K with the intention to merge it with QTSBA after acquisition.

QTS Group

QTS Group is a significant, publicly quoted, training and education provider in Eastaria. QTS Group controls a number of independent trading companies which serve niche training markets across Eastaria. Every day, companies across QTS Group deliver more than a thousand courses. To help establish a common delegate experience, QTS Group insists on a standard, centrally defined approach to training in an attempt to ensure that courses are delivered in a consistent way. Revenue and net profit for the group is shown in Table One.

	2009	2010	2011	2012	2013	2014
Revenue ($m)	600	605	610	710	800	875
Net profit ($m)	70	65	70	85	100	110

Table One: Revenue and net profit for QTS Group (2009–2014)

Much of the recent growth of QTS Group has been achieved through acquiring niche information technology training companies. QTS Group has a good reputation for managing such companies post acquisition. In the three companies acquired in the last two years, profitability (as measured by the ROCE and the net profit margin) has increased in all three companies post acquisition. QTS Group believes that it has core competencies in acquisition and strategic change implementation, and that these core competencies are demonstrated by the improved performance of these recently acquired companies.

However, shareholders of QTS Group remain concerned about the group's current high level of retained earnings. They perceive that recent acquisitions by QTS Group have delivered value to shareholders because there has been an increase in both the dividend payout ratio and in earnings per share. A vociferous minority of shareholders are lobbying the board to continue this policy of acquisitions, using the retained profit of the group to drive further growth, particularly in terms of revenue and profit. In acknowledgment of this, the QTS Group board has announced an 'acquisition fund' of $30m to further acquire companies and finance post-acquisition change. A2K is the first of a number of companies which QTS Group is looking to evaluate for possible acquisition.

Business strategy is decided at group level and then implemented by the individual companies. There is a formal reporting system from these companies to the group.

Although growth in the business architecture training market has slowed, QTS Group is committed to remaining in this market. It forecasts future world-wide growth in this market and it intends to look for opportunities outside of Eastaria in the future. Revenues and other relevant information from the business architecture training market in Eastaria are shown in Table Two.

	2009	2010	2011	2012	2013	2014
A2K revenue ($m)	12·0	14·0	16·0	17·0	17·0	16·5
QTSBA revenue ($m)	39·0	40·0	42·0	45·0	46·0	48·0
Total market revenue ($m)	175·0	190·0	196·0	200·0	202·0	202·0

Other information:

(1) QTSBA is the market leader in this market sector
(2) The second largest training provider, CompTrain, recorded revenue of $31·31m in 2014
(3) Independent research shows that companies operating in this market have an average return on capital employed (ROCE) of 25% and an average net profit margin of 10%

Table Two: Sales revenue and other relevant information in the business architecture training market in Eastaria (2009–2014)

QTSBA

In 2011, QTSBA appointed an experienced senior management team to improve the company's performance in the business architecture training market. To attract capable managers, QTSBA offered remuneration packages which were linked directly to achieving sales revenue performance targets.

It is acknowledged within QTS Group that QTSBA has strong sales and marketing competencies and it has recently won two major government business architecture training contracts. However, it is having difficulties finding experienced trainers and it needs to quickly recruit these trainers as a number of training programmes it has successfully bid for are about to commence. It is also acknowledged in QTSBA that the sales and marketing department of QTSBA has spare capacity, 'we could sell more if we had more to sell' is a common complaint of the sales and marketing team.

QTSBA has attempted to produce e-learning products in the past. However, the project to develop these products was unsuccessful. A team of software developers was recruited and an e-learning development platform selected. However, the company found it difficult to control the programmers' work. As one senior manager commented, 'we are training course providers, not a software house.' It transpired that the purchased e-learning platform was slow and inflexible and the learning solutions produced by the team were not what customers wanted. After two years, the project was abandoned, the programming team disbanded and the investment written off.

Aspire to Knowledge (A2K)

A2K was established in 1986 by Lee Wan and Kim Cross. In 2002, up and coming business architecture guru Kath Goff joined the company. These three people are still the primary shareholders of the company. Lee owns 25% of the shares, Kim owns 35% of the shares and Kath owns 35% of the shares. The current marketing director and sales director of the company each own 2·5% of the shares. Lee and Kim are now retired and the board consists of Kath Goff (as chief executive officer – CEO), the marketing director and the sales director.

A2K's organisational structure is shown in Figure One. This chart only shows full-time business architecture trainers. The company also employs a number of sub-contracted trainers who are self-employed and who undertake training for A2K on an ad hoc basis.

Figure One: A2K's organisational structure – 2014

Kath Goff is an intelligent, charismatic individual with an in-depth knowledge of the business architecture training market. Although strategy is nominally the responsibility of the board, in practice the strategy reflects her vision. Indeed, she makes most of the significant decisions in the company. The marketing director has attempted to question her judgement in the past and has put forward alternative strategies. However, these have been quickly dismissed by Kath, claiming that he 'just doesn't understand the business architecture market'. Kath has also issued a number of public rebukes to other members of staff and employees who have found her direct approach unacceptable have quickly resigned and moved to other companies.

The early success of A2K was largely based on Lee and Kim's distinctive and innovative approach to training. The company soon became known as a company which did things slightly differently, with courses which were both challenging and humorous. To try and maintain this spirit, Kath still arranges regular company events, trying to recreate what she now considers to be the golden age of business architecture training. Indeed, Lee and Kim are always invited back to the annual 'celebration event' where Kath, Lee and Kim sit together all evening recounting tales from the old days. The current full-time trainers find such events tiresome and demotivating. They feel that customers now expect more professional, standard courses and that delegates' expectations have changed and are now more exacting. The full-time trainers employed by A2K are continually rated as 'excellent' by customers. However, these trainers are frustrated by their lack of input into company strategy and training decisions, as well as by the continued presence of Lee and Kim at company events. They find it hard to reconcile exciting tales of the past with the increasingly aging, fragile men sitting next to the CEO.

A2K has a small, but experienced e-learning software development team. A number of e-learning products have been produced over the last few years and are available for immediate purchase on the company's website. Sales are relatively strong and the unit profit margin, like all e-learning products, is significant as there is virtually no variable cost in delivering an e-learning course to a customer. However, the e-learning team is demotivated. It is concerned at the company's apparent lack of commitment to e-learning (as against conventional face-to-face training) and the young head of e-learning, Ash Tag, is particularly angry at the company's reluctance to give him (and hence e-learning) a place on the board.

A2K was particularly successful in 2010, 2011 and 2012 when it successfully competed against QTSBA for a number of major business architecture training contracts (see Table Three).

Although A2K has traded relatively successfully since its inception, the CEO has been increasingly concerned that costs are not properly under control. She has evidence that costs per training day have risen whilst revenue per training day has fallen, due to increased competition in the business architecture training market. This has led the CEO to become increasingly involved in the day-to-day operations of the company, particularly in monitoring the financial situation, because she has little confidence in her finance staff.

All figures in $m	2009	2010	2011	2012	2013	2014
Share capital	3·00	3·00	3·00	3·00	3·00	3·00
Other reserves	0·40	0·40	0·40	0·40	0·40	0·40
Retained earnings	0·80	0·90	0·80	0·80	0·70	0·60
Revenue	12·00	14·00	16·00	17·00	17·00	16·50
Net profit	1·75	1·65	1·65	1·60	1·45	1·40

Table Three: A2K – Figures extracted from financial statements: 2009 to 2014

Preparing for acquisition of A2K

The board of QTS Group is now preparing to approach A2K with an acquisition offer. Representatives of QTS Group have already met informally and independently with Lee and Kim (who both indicated their willingness to sell at the right price) and with the board of A2K (the CEO, sales director and marketing director). The latter meeting was quite strained, but the impression was formed that the acquisition would be considered favourably if the CEO, sales director and marketing director were employed, post-acquisition, in an autonomous company within QTS Group. This was put on the agenda, but no promises were made. Privately, the QTS Group board are sceptical whether these three senior managers could work in a more formal organisation or indeed, whether they are needed at all. They have no plans to make A2K an autonomous company within the group and indeed their intention is to merge the company with QTSBA.

Required:

The managing director of QTS Group has approached you as a business analyst and asked you to produce a briefing paper which addresses a number of key issues:

(a) Identify and discuss the benefits and advantages to QTS Group and QTSBA of acquiring A2K. The managing director stresses that he just wants the benefits and advantages considered. He wants you to focus on the positive factors which would emerge from this acquisition. (19 marks)

(b) QTS Group policy mandates that a strategic change evaluation should be undertaken before any possible acquisition is made. This looks at strategic change in terms of time, preservation, diversity, capability and readiness. These are five selected elements from the Balogun and Hope-Hailey model which considers the contextual features of strategic change.

Evaluate the strategic change required at A2K if the company is acquired and subsequently integrated with QTSBA. This evaluation should use the contextual features of time, preservation, diversity, capability and readiness. (15 marks)

(c) Finally, the managing director is interested in the organisational culture of A2K. He is concerned that it 'is just such a different company to us'. So, the final part of your briefing paper is to explain the principles of organisational culture and the concept and application of the 'cultural web' and Mintzberg's organisational configurations.

Explain the concepts of organisational culture, the cultural web and organisational configurations in the context of the possible acquisition of A2K and its post-acquisition integration with QTSBA. (12 marks)

Professional marks are available in question 1 for the tone, clarity, vocabulary and approach of your answer.

(4 marks)

(50 marks)

Section B – TWO questions ONLY to be attempted

2   Introduction

The Institute of Certified Operations Managers (ICOM) has a professional scheme of examinations, available to its student members, which leads to certified operations manager status when completed and supported by an acceptable portfolio of practical experience. ICOM also supports full members (those who have achieved certification, or have completed examinations and are in the process of gaining relevant experience) by offering a range of member services, including professional development courses. Similar services are offered by their close rival, the Operational Management Institute (OMI).

ICOM has experienced a decline in both full membership and student membership in the last five years, despite there being an increased demand for operations managers in organisations. In contrast, OMI has published data showing that it has increased student membership by 27% and full membership by 12% in the same time period. The revenue and profitability of ICOM, a company limited by guarantee, have also declined over the last five years.

There are opposing views within ICOM about the reason for the decline. Some directors, including John Turvey, believe that the absence of a formal strategic plan, identifying critical areas for success, has meant a lack of direction and focus. However, another member of the senior management team has suggested that the main reason for ICOM's problems is the inefficiency of the student recruitment process. He feels that the company needs to understand how other organisations (such as OMI) do this and to put changes in place to improve the process at ICOM.

Strategic planning

To support his viewpoint, John Turvey was asked to write a strategic plan to address how to regain lost membership and to grow market share, to compete with OMI. A mission statement, critical success factors (CSFs) and key performance indicators (KPIs) were to be included within the plan. As he had not completed a strategic plan before, John has asked for your views on the draft plan, part of which is shown below, which he intends to share with senior management.

Mission statement

I suggest that we replace our current mission statement 'Simply the best in operations management' with a more focused statement which states that 'Our mission is to satisfy the needs of our members, to inspire our student members and to motivate our staff to provide the best possible service'.

CSFs

These are the things we are going to focus on in the long term to help us to achieve growth and fulfil our mission statement. Altogether I have identified 35 critical success factors. The full list is available on our staff intranet, but the most important ones are shown below:

1.   To satisfy our members
2.   To grow membership by 5% year on year for the next five years
3.   To maximise profits within acceptable risk
4.   To ensure that the syllabus is in line with the current operations management environment

KPIs

Here are the KPIs which we should measure to help us assess the CSFs listed above:

1.   95% of members rate us as excellent in an externally administered customer satisfaction survey
2.   To implement a vigorous marketing campaign
3.   Return on capital employed (ROCE) and margin of safety
4.   To recruit an examinations manager to rewrite the syllabus

We should also adopt an integrated reporting approach so that stakeholders understand our mission, our strategy and all aspects of our business performance.

Required:

(a) Critically evaluate the mission statement, critical success factors and key performance indicators suggested by John Turvey. (15 marks)

(b) Discuss how benchmarking could be used at ICOM, identifying any limitations in its application. (5 marks)

(c) Discuss the role of integrated reporting in relation to communicating strategy and business performance at ICOM. (5 marks)

(25 marks)

3   Introduction

Mantis & Gear (M&G) was formed over 50 years ago to manufacture branded electrical and electronic goods for other companies. These goods are made to the specification required by these companies, whose own brand logos are attached to the products during the production process. M&G currently manufactures hundreds of products, although some are very similar in specification, with slight differences due to the requirements of each customer. M&G does not sell its own products to individual domestic consumers. Sales teams therefore focus on high volume sales to large companies.

The electrical and electronic goods market is increasingly competitive, with overseas companies entering the market. M&G's customers have responded to this by demanding lower prices and better quality products from M&G. As the electrical and electronic goods market is technologically innovative, there is also a requirement to continually develop new products or enhance existing ones.

The sales manager, James Slater, has revealed his sales team figures for the year 2014 and is excited to announce that the team has exceeded sales volume targets. However, his enthusiasm is not shared by the business controller, Furzana Khan, who has written a report to the chief executive officer (CEO) suggesting that there are fundamental performance problems in the company. An extract of her report is given below:

Business performance

'In a period of increased competition and growing product ranges, we are failing to keep control of the profitability of our business. Table 1 presents a summary of our performance for 2014, showing problems with our pricing and/or our cost control. This has affected profitability.

	Budget units	Actual units
Sales volume	243,000	270,000
	Budget $'000s	Actual $'000s
Sales revenue	36,450	36,450
Direct materials	(15,795)	(18,630)
Direct labour	(3,402)	(4,725)
Fixed overheads	(8,250)	(11,450)
Operating profit	9,003	1,645

Table 1 – Budgeted versus actual performance for 2014

I recommend that we move from our traditional absorption costing system to that of activity based costing (ABC) in order to better understand our costs and to introduce an appropriate strategy to turn around our business performance. Specifically, we should ensure that we incorporate both product and customer costing into our ABC analysis to determine our profitable and unprofitable products and customers.'

James Slater has seen the report and has angrily confronted Furzana. 'We are in a period of increased competition and have successfully managed to grow our sales in difficult times. We even managed to fulfil some special orders with very short lead times. We should be celebrating these successes, not treating them as poor performance. We should expect some fall in profitability as our customers are able to shop around, so we have to make our products and our prices more attractive to them. The new costing system that you are proposing will just be a paper exercise for you to criticise the efforts of the sales and production teams. I will do everything I can to stop the introduction of this costing system.'

(a) It is clear that the business controller and the sales manager have different opinions about the current performance of the company.

Required:

Analyse the data shown in Table 1, suggesting possible reasons why performance may not be as positive as that portrayed by the sales manager. (15 marks)

(b) The sales manager, James Slater, described activity based costing as 'a paper exercise for you to criticise the efforts of the sales and production teams'.

Required:

Briefly explain the principles of activity based costing and the reasons for its development. Evaluate whether it may be beneficial to M&G, making reference to any benefits and limitations of activity based costing and any problems associated with its implementation. (10 marks)

(25 marks)

4   Introduction

Cooper University is situated in the country of Mowria, which has over 300 universities. University tuition fees have increased in the last few years and students are expecting a better level of service as a consequence of this. Results of student satisfaction surveys are published by the Mowrian government, and can greatly influence the students' choice of university.

At Cooper University, students are assessed in two ways: by examinations and coursework. Both types of assessment contribute towards the degree classification awarded to students. In a recent, internally commissioned, student experience report, Cooper University received some negative feedback from students on the coursework organisation, submission and feedback process. Consequently, the university is keen to rectify problems in this process.

Details of the coursework organisation, submission and feedback process are described in the next section and summarised in Figure One.

Coursework organisation, submission and feedback process

At the start of a new semester, an administrator distributes term dates and coursework guidance to lecturers. There are many different subjects within a course and each subject is managed by a different lecturer. The guidance includes a stipulation that coursework should be marked and returned to students within two teaching weeks of the submitted coursework being collected from the course administration office by the lecturer. Lecturers write their own coursework requirements and set their own deadlines, informing the head of department so that a consolidated course schedule can be produced.

Coursework requirements are uploaded by lecturers onto a virtual learning environment (VLE) system, which is accessed by students. Lecturers release these requirements at the beginning of the course, in accordance with the administrative guidelines. Students download the requirements and then complete and submit their work.

Students are required to submit two copies of their completed coursework: a hard copy to the administration office and a soft copy uploaded into the VLE system. The VLE system produces an automatic receipt showing the date and time coursework was submitted, as proof of the upload. An administrator periodically sorts the submitted hard copies by subject, ready for lecturers to collect. Lecturers collect the coursework when they have some free time in their schedule for marking.

Once collected, lecturers mark the coursework and type their feedback into a new word processed document, and then upload that document against the student profile on the VLE. The VLE issues an automatic email to students informing them that feedback is available. The lecturer also collates total marks onto a spreadsheet and emails this to the administrators. The administrators input these marks manually into a computerised administration system and then send a report to the head of department, who records the marks against the individual student's assessment profile.

Figure One – Coursework organisation, submission and feedback process

10

Student feedback

The following extracts from the student experience report are representative of the feedback received from students:

'I received one mark from the VLE system, but when my end-of-year results were released the mark was different'

'My feedback was on a separate document so I found it difficult to relate to the coursework submitted'

'I accidentally submitted an unfinished piece of coursework to the administration office but submitted the correct one to the system. The lecturer marked the unfinished piece'

'It takes weeks to receive my marks, by which time I've forgotten what the coursework was about. When I asked the lecturer she said she had marked it within the time allowed'

'We always have about four pieces of coursework to submit at the same time, and then weeks where nothing is required. I wish the university would manage our programme better'

'The lecturer said he did not receive the hard copy of my coursework but I know I handed it in. This was counted as a non-submission'

'There were errors in the initial coursework requirements, which were subsequently significantly changed. I had already started the assignment so this time was wasted'

'I completed and submitted my coursework early in order to manage my workload better, but then the lecturer gave an additional lecture to help us with our coursework. This contained very useful information, which we had not previously covered. I was not allowed to resubmit my work and so suffered from being efficient'

'My lecturer wasn't very supportive when I had personal problems.'

'My course didn't seem well coordinated. Some topics were repeated and others failed to cover the syllabus, making it difficult to move up from one year to the next'

With increases in student tuition fees and therefore student expectations, the role of university lecturers is changing. They are expected to play a more proactive role in the development of students and in monitoring students' well-being. There is a need for lecturers to assist in the development of new courses and subjects and to work closely with each other to ensure that the link between subjects is rational and appropriate.

Currently, there is an extensive guidance document for lecturers, mapping out the way in which all activities should be carried out within their role; the coursework organisation, submission and feedback process is just one of many process maps. There is a high turnover of lecturing staff, some of whom have stated that they are getting little job satisfaction from what should be a rewarding and challenging job.

Required:

(a) **Identify, and explain, four problems in the current coursework organisation, submission and feedback process and suggest appropriate solutions to address each of these problems.**   (16 marks)

(b) **Changes in organisational processes often require the redesign of jobs.**

   Discuss how the jobs of lecturers at Cooper University could be redesigned, using relevant approaches to job design, so that they better meet the needs of their students and the university.   (9 marks)

(25 marks)

End of Question Paper

1 (a) Introduction

Revenues in QTS Group have grown significantly in the last five years, from $610m in 2011 to $875m in 2014. Most of this growth has been achieved through the acquisition of smaller training companies operating in a number of niche markets.

QTS Group is now considering the acquisition of A2K, a training company specialising in business architecture training. One of its companies, QTSBA, is already a market leader in this training sector, with 23·76% market share, compared with the next largest supplier, CompTrain, which has 15·5% of the market. A2K is solely focused on the business architecture training market and currently has a market share of 8·17%.

This briefing paper identifies the benefits and advantages to QTS Group and QTSBA of proceeding with the acquisition of A2K.

Further growth through acquisition

A major reason for growing through acquisition is the speed it offers, both in increasing revenue and in entering new markets and/or offering new products. Further growth is particularly attractive to three sets of stakeholders at QTS Group or QTSBA:

- The sales department of QTSBA: who have customers with impending training needs which need to be successfully fulfilled. Finding experienced trainers is an issue. A2K has an experienced training team which would be immediately available, together with an established pool of sub-contractors.

- The shareholders of QTS Group: who have expressed their desire for the retained profit of QTS Group to be better employed in producing revenue, profit and company growth.

- The senior management team at QTSBA: who are on salary remuneration packages which are directly linked to achieving sales revenue performance targets.

Acquiring a new product, entering a new market

As previously stated, acquisition also allows an organisation to quickly enter a new market and/or acquire a new product. In some circumstances it is the only way of entering an emerging market because internal development is too slow or too expensive. Indeed, this is the situation at QTSBA, where the acquisition of the A2K e-learning team will allow QTSBA to:

- Acquire new, established products which they can offer to the market, immediately generating revenue with a significant unit profit margin.

- Acquire e-learning development expertise which can be used to successfully develop new products. QTSBA has already had a failed project where its own uncontrolled software developers used inappropriate software to develop e-learning solutions which were not attractive to customers. A2K has a successful track record in e-learning development and product sales. Acquisition allows the immediate possession of these competencies.

- E-learning may be a key part in extending business architecture training to areas beyond the continent of Eastaria. It might also be possible to use the e-learning team to develop products for other companies in the group.

Establish a dominant position in the business architecture training market

QTS Group has made a management decision to remain and compete in the business architecture training market. However, it acknowledges that the market growth for business architecture training is slowing, although it is expecting future growth, particularly outside Eastaria. Table A illustrates market growth and market share in the business architecture training market, 2009–2014.

Revenue	2009	2010	2011	2012	2013	2014
A2K revenue ($m)	12	14	16	17	17	16·5
Year on year growth		16·67%	14·29%	6·25%	0·00%	–2·94%
QTS revenue ($m)	39	40	42	45	46	48
Year on year growth		2·56%	5·00%	7·14%	2·22%	4·35%
Total market revenue ($m)	175	190	196	200	202	202
Year on year growth		8·57%	3·16%	2·04%	1·00%	0·00%
Market share						
A2K	6·86%	7·37%	8·16%	8·50%	8·42%	8·17%
QTSBA	22·29%	21·05%	21·43%	22·50%	22·77%	23·76%

Table A: Market growth and market share in the business architecture training market 2009–2014

Table A illustrates that the market grew by 8·57% in 2010. However, since then, growth has slowed and by 2014, there was no market growth at all. A2K's growth outstripped the market in 2010, 2011 and 2012, during which it successfully won a number of contracts which QTSBA also bid for. However, since 2012 its growth and market share has declined. It seems likely that the company's performance has peaked and that it is now finding it difficult to compete successfully in an increasingly competitive market place. In contrast, after its poor performance in 2010, QTSBA's growth has continually outstripped the market, suggesting that it is successfully anticipating and serving the needs of the market. In BCG terms, QTSBA looks like a cash cow for QTS Group.

Taking a competitor out of a stagnant market place, and at the same time increasing market share to 31·93% has two advantages to QTSBA. First, it reduces the competition in the market, easing competitive rivalry and downward pressure on prices, and second, it means that QTSBA will become twice the size of its nearest competitor, with the operational advantages and brand visibility which this will bring.

Acquiring A2K appears to be a suitable option for QTS Group because it allows QTSBA to increase its market share in a relatively stagnant market place, and (through e-learning) provides opportunities for product and market development.

Exploiting core competencies

The acquisition of A2K will give QTS Group the opportunity to further exploit its core competencies in acquisition and change implementation. The financial performance of the three training companies which QTS Group has acquired in the past two years has improved after acquisition. The return on capital employed (ROCE) and the operating profit of all three companies have increased post acquisition.

There will be also be opportunities for cost efficiencies, associated with economies of scale (for example, in producing course material) and with sharing centralised services. For example, QTSBA already has well-established and successful sales and marketing departments which should be able to easily absorb the work of the current A2K team. There appears little need to retain A2K's marketing and sales directors and all their team, bringing immediate cost savings (after redundancy costs) to QTSBA.

Assessing feasibility is concerned with whether the company has the resources and competencies to deliver the promised strategy. There does not seem any issue here. Although no price for A2K has yet been agreed, it is unlikely to make too much of a dent in the $30m of retained earnings which QTS Group has earmarked to fund acquisition and post-acquisition change. As stated already, there is evidence to suggest that it has both the resources and competencies to deliver this strategy.

Benefits to shareholders

The acceptability of an acquisition is concerned with the performance outcomes of a strategy. This can be looked at in terms of return, risk and stakeholder reactions. Returns are the benefits which shareholders are likely to receive from the strategy. A number of shareholders have already campaigned for the retained profit in QTS Group to be invested in further acquisitions. They are clearly encouraged by the fact that recent acquisitions have apparently led to increased shareholder value, both in the dividend payout ratio and in earnings per share.

In terms of acceptability, risk is concerned with the probability of the failure of a particular strategy and the impact or consequences of this failure.

Table B summarises the financial performance of A2K. Although there are some concerns about its performance, the company is still trading profitably and has relatively large retained earnings. The risk of an inappropriate acquisition seems very low.

	2009	2010	2011	2012	2013	2014
Share capital ($m)	3·00	3·00	3·00	3·00	3·00	3·00
Other reserves ($m)	0·40	0·40	0·40	0·40	0·40	0·40
Retained earnings ($m)	0·80	0·90	0·80	0·80	0·70	0·60
Revenue ($m)	12·00	14·00	16·00	17·00	17·00	16·50
Net profit ($m)	1·75	1·65	1·65	1·60	1·45	1·40
ROCE	41·67%	38·37%	39·29%	38·10%	35·37%	35·00%
Net profit margin	14·58%	11·79%	10·31%	9·41%	8·53%	8·48%

Table B: Financial performance of A2K, 2010–2015

The ROCE is a fundamental measure of business performance, considering the net profit generated by the long-term capital invested in the business. The ROCE for A2K has declined from 41·67% in 2009 to 35·00% in 2014, but still remains relatively high (the industry sector average is 25%) probably reflecting the relatively low initial investment made by the founders of the company. The company also has fairly substantial retained earnings ($600,000).

The net profit margin is often regarded as the most appropriate measure of operational performance. Just like the ROCE, the net profit margin has declined from a high of 14·58% in 2009 to 8·48% in 2014. This is below the industry sector average of 10·00%. This supports Kath's view that the costs of the company have not been properly controlled in the last few years and that there is a fall in delivery efficiency. However, it seems likely that cost savings and increased sales post acquisition, will quickly return A2K to profitability which is at, or above, the sector average.

Overall, QTS Group shareholders are likely to support a proposed acquisition of A2K. It is a low risk option which fulfils their demand for further investment and the company's past record suggests that the acquisition will quickly contribute to higher shareholder returns. QTS Group is arguably, in corporate parenting terms, a synergy manager, enhancing value across a number of business units. In this instance it is potentially acquiring a company whose market is very well known to the current managers of a company already in the group.

(b) This part of the briefing paper briefly explains five contextual factors in strategic change and explores how these are likely to apply to the situation at A2K, should the acquisition go ahead.

Time: this is concerned with how quickly change is needed. A business facing rapid declines in revenue and profitability may have to be turned around very quickly. This is not the case here. Revenue growth at A2K has slowed, but the company is still profitable, although not as profitable at it used to be. QTS Group has a large 'acquisitions fund' to spend on acquisitions and post-acquisition change in companies which it purchases. Consequently, the pace of change could be quite leisurely, perhaps implemented in an incremental process. However, the problem with this could be the attitude of the three senior managers (the CEO, the sales director and the marketing director) if they remain within the merged company. The point has already been made that there is no apparent need to retain the sales and marketing director. It seems unlikely that the senior managers at A2K will either survive or embrace the kind of change envisaged by QTS Group and so changes to these key positions might have to be made very quickly, followed by reassuring customers that it is 'business as usual'.

Preservation: considers the organisational resources and characteristics which need to be maintained. These are key competencies which must not be lost if QTS Group is to improve (or at least maintain) the performance of A2K. At A2K, the key resources to preserve appear to be the full-time business architecture trainers and the e-learning team. The trainers are perceived as excellent (by customers) and the e-learning team has developed effective and innovative e-learning solutions. In contrast, QTSBA already has established sales and marketing departments and so these do need to be preserved.

Diversity: reflects on the diversity of experience, views and opinions within an organisation. It is concerned with the homogeneity of staff groups within the organisation and how they see the world. It is argued that change is hampered by a lack of diversity because everyone in the organisation sees the world in a similar way. This is likely to be an issue at A2K; although some of the trainers may have some diversity of experience, the views and opinions within the organisation are set and controlled by the CEO. Anyone with different views has left or has had their views publicly rejected. There is little diversity to build upon and so change is unlikely to be welcome or understood. QTS Group has to be aware of this. Change will have to be promoted by managers brought into A2K.

Capability: concerns experience of managing change in an organisation. As far as A2K is concerned, there is little capability in implementing change, and indeed relatively little experience of change. Thus managers employed by A2K are unlikely to have the capability to implement the changes which QTS Group will require. In contrast, QTS Group has experience of post-acquisition change in a number of companies and it is, the company believes, one of its core competencies. It will have to introduce managers into A2K charged with implementing the changes it requires. These managers will have to be appointed at a senior level, probably to replace the current board members of A2K.

Readiness: examines the readiness for change of the workforce. It seems clear that both the trainers and the e-learning team are ready for change. The trainers are disillusioned by their lack of input into business policy and training decisions and the e-learning team is angry at the lack of commitment to e-learning (as against conventional face-to-face training) and the reluctance to give e-learning a voice on the board. So, both of the key resources which have to be preserved are ready and open for change. This is a positive factor for QTS Group. It is likely that there will be pockets of resistance (sales, marketing) but it seems increasingly unlikely that these will be preserved in their current state. The current board is also unlikely to embrace change (and indeed might actively oppose it) and so the importance of acting quickly to replace this team is again reinforced.

(c) This final part of this briefing paper explores the importance of organisational culture and briefly explains the concept and application of the cultural web and organisational configuration in the context of the proposed acquisition of A2K.

Organisations vary in their personality and atmosphere. They have different ways of doing things, different attitudes towards customers and staff, different levels of freedom and responsibility. These things help define its organisational culture. When one organisation wishes to acquire or merge with another, it helps if it has an understanding of the culture of the organisation it is considering acquiring. Understanding that culture will help in diagnosis, perhaps identifying that current problems in the company being acquired are due to cultural issues, and in transition, as the company is moved to the culture which the acquiring company believes it should exhibit.

Johnson, Scholes and Whittington conceive organisational culture as consisting of four layers: values, beliefs, behaviours and paradigm, a set of taken for granted assumptions. The *cultural web* is a way of exploring two of these layers, the behaviours and the paradigm. Behaviours are explored in terms of the stories, symbols, power structures, organisational structures, control systems, rituals and routines, which all surround the central paradigm.

In the context of A2K, the *stories* told at social gatherings suggest that the CEO looks back with enthusiasm at a simpler, golden age with the two founding directors as heroes delivering training courses with a whimsy and a humour missing from the standardised events which are now delivered by the full-time training staff. The *ritual* of inviting these two founding directors to the annual 'celebration event' further excludes the current full-time staff, as the CEO sits next to these two former directors, and stories are retold all evening. Not only do the full-time trainers feel excluded, they also find it hard to reconcile these stories with the two bald, aging, fragile men sitting next to the CEO. QTSBA can exploit this aspect of culture by ensuring that such events are more focused in the future and that the people telling these stories are removed or not invited.

Power at A2K is invested in the leadership (the CEO) and this power structure is reinforced by an *organisational structure* which is very flat. The main power holders (the CEO, and to a lesser extent the marketing director and the sales director) are potential blockages to the changes which QTS Group is likely to propose. This understanding again reinforces the need to remove these people as part of the acquisition process.

Organisations are usually structured in some way to deliver the products and services they offer. Within this structure there are formal and informal organisational processes which take place within internal and external relationships which the organisation has established. Structure, processes and relationships work together. They have to be appropriate for the situation of the organisation and they have to match each other. This matching means that organisations tend towards a limited set of standard configurations. Henry Mintzberg has suggested six stereotypical configurations.

A2K appears to be a *simple* or *entrepreneurial* configuration. The organisational structure is simple and there is little middle management. Indeed, two-thirds of the staff report directly to the CEO. The CEO provides strong charismatic leadership and has a tendency to be autocratic. Unwelcome suggestions made by the marketing director have been summarily dismissed in the past. The strategy of the organisation reflects the vision of the CEO. However, the expansion of the company has meant that the CEO has become increasingly concerned with operational issues and problems and has lost sight of the strategy. This has been exacerbated by the need for her to spend more time monitoring the financial situation of the company. Indeed, Mintzberg identified this issue as a potential problem in an entrepreneurial organisation. The CEO becomes so enmeshed in operational problems that they lose sight of strategy.

In contrast, QTS Group displays elements of a *machine bureaucracy* with a centralised bureaucratic management, formal procedures and a functional organisational structure. Due to its size and client expectations, it needs to deliver its products in a standard, controlled, consistent way. It is a large, mature organisation and such organisations often tend towards a machine configuration. QTS Group has to be aware of the implications of bringing such a culture to A2K. There may be a concern that it will introduce a configuration where there is inconsistency between the structure, process and relationships. However, as noted before, they are likely to find allies in the full-time trainers and the e-learning staff who might adapt well to a more formal structure based on meritocracy, not autocracy.

The cultural analysis of A2K again suggests that although the CEO, sales director and marketing director wish to remain in their posts after the takeover, it is unlikely that they will be able to adapt to a transition to a different culture. This is yet another reason for recommending that these three managers are excluded from the post-acquisition company. Consequently, agreeing an appropriate severance arrangement with the current A2K board is likely to be an important part of the acquisition negotiation.

2 (a) A mission statement defines the overriding direction and purpose of an organisation. Some organisations also have vision statements stating what the company aspires to. However, for the purpose of this answer, vision and mission are perceived as the same thing.

Most organisations have settled into an approach where a short snappy statement is supported by a much deeper description of what the organisation is about, its stakeholders and how it wishes to interact with those stakeholders.

The current mission statement of ICOM 'Simply the best in operations management' is a slogan and says nothing about who it is the best for. John Turvey's suggested replacement is much more specific, identifying the external stakeholders it is serving (members and student members) and, importantly, valuing the internal stakeholders (the staff) who will service and inspire the external stakeholders. This more specific statement should allow the organisation to tie the mission statement in with critical success factors. However, it could retain the current mission statement as a broad statement, using John Turvey's suggested replacement as a supplementary description of what the organisation is about.

Critical success factors (CSFs) are the things which the organisation must be good at to succeed. They are the few key areas where things must go right for the business to flourish. Some writers take a more limiting view. Johnson, Scholes and Whittington believe that CSFs are the product features which are particularly valued by a group of customers and, therefore, where the organisation must excel to outperform its competition.

John Turvey has identified 35 CSFs, which seems more than a few key areas and may lead to a lack of focus on the truly critical areas. He may need to reduce these in order to ensure success in a few key areas.

To satisfy our members seems a reasonable CSF, as it aligns directly with the mission statement.

To achieve a growth in membership by 5% year on year for the next five years is not necessarily something which the members themselves will value, unless it brings added benefits to them. Furthermore, CSFs should not have specific time-bound targets associated with them.

The need to maximise profits within acceptable risk is not acknowledged in the mission statement, but it is a given of most commercial organisations.

To ensure that the syllabus reflects the current operations environment is also aligned to the mission statement's desire to inspire student members

However, it is noticeable that there are no CSFs mentioned which are associated with staff and their motivation, despite the inclusion of this commitment in the mission statement.

Key performance indicators (KPIs) are the measurements used to monitor the achievement of the CSFs. They suggest how a CSF should be measured, but they do not include the measurement itself.

The only correctly expressed KPI is the third one (ROCE and the margin of safety). The ROCE will provide an indication of the efficient use of capital in generating profit. The risk taken is measured by the margin of safety which shows how far the current income would have to fall to result in a breakeven situation. Notice that neither the ROCE nor the margin of safety are given specific values. These specific values will be given in performance objectives which relate to defined timeframes. This allows the KPI to remain the same, but the performance objective can change.

The first suggested KPI can be improved by omitting the 95% target. At present, it is a mix between a KPI and a performance objective. An appropriate KPI would be 'the percentage of members rating us as excellent in an externally administered customer satisfaction survey'.

KPIs should be quantifiable, such that they can be compared to a standard or target, or an alternative performance, such as a prior year, or a competitor. There is no real quantifiable comparator for the other two suggested KPIs. For example, the KPI 'recruit an examinations manager to rewrite the syllabus' will either happen, or it will not. This KPI, and the KPI to implement a vigorous marketing campaign are really just actions, not KPIs.

Again, there is no key performance indicator associated with internal staff and their motivation.

(b) Benchmarking is where one organisation compares its performance in a specific area to another organisation, the benchmark, to identify how much room there is for improvement. It then attempts to implement improved practices to narrow the gap between its own performance and the performance of the benchmark. In the context of the scenario, benchmarks might be used to improve the student recruitment process. Improving this process should help the company achieve CSFs and KPIs associated with student membership. For example, increasing the number of students registering with ICOM.

There are two main approaches to benchmarking which are relevant here:

- Competitive benchmarking within the same industry. In this case ICOM would benchmark itself against OMI. However, it may be that competitor information is not available or that competitors use different measurement techniques, providing an invalid comparison. Concerning student recruitment, comparative information is available. However, there is likely to be an absence of supporting information. ICOM cannot be sure how OMI has actually achieved a growth of 27% in student members. ICOM can benchmark its growth against OMI, but it has no insight into how OMI is achieving this growth, so it does not know what it needs to put in place to improve its student recruitment performance. The use of a percentage as a benchmark also needs comment. OMI's increase might be based on a much lower starting level and the percentage increase might not be a usable benchmark for ICOM.

- External functional benchmarking where a particular function (such as student recruitment) is compared with that function in the organisation which performs it best, regardless of what industry the company is in. Non-competing organisations are more likely to share data than competitors. For example, an accountancy institute might be prepared to share membership recruitment information with ICOM. However, given that the comparator will be in a different industry, the competitive situation might be quite different and this reduces the usefulness of the comparison. For example, competitors might act differently and rules for student membership may be dissimilar. However, with external functional benchmarking it is more likely that the comparator will not only share results, but also the process which has achieved these results. This will give important information to ICOM about what it needs to put in place to improve its performance.

(c) 'An integrated report is a concise communication about how an organisation's strategy, governance, performance and prospects lead to the creation of value over the short, medium and long term' (IIRC draft framework, April 2013).

Financial reports have long been part of business culture. The content, structure and rules for constructing these reports are still important. For most organisations, growth and profitability are still significant goals and this is reflected in the CSFs and KPIs of ICOM. Here, profitability will be measured by the ROCE and the ROCE will either be explicitly stated in the company's financial report or can be calculated from the provided financial data.

However, the development of approaches such as the balanced business scorecard has prompted companies to set performance measures in non-financial areas, such as customer satisfaction and process efficiency. However, within the normal financial reporting framework, there is no place for the company to report its progress (or lack of it) in these important non-financial areas.

The integrated report provides the opportunity for the organisation to restate its mission and how its strategy addresses this mission. Central to this will be a discussion of the CSFs and the KPIs which have been identified to measure business performance. KPIs will have associated performance objectives which can be reported in the integrated report.

Thus, the report not only restates the KPI and its associated performance objective, it also reports on whether that performance objective has been met and, if it has not, discusses reasons for failure and the actions which are being taken to ensure that this objective is met in the next reporting period. For example, it is in the integrated report where ICOM will report on its efforts to meet certain customer satisfaction targets and student recruitment targets. If it fails to meet these targets, then it will explain how this failure is being addressed.

However, an integrated report should be more than a summary of information from other communications; it should explicitly connect the information to communicate how value is created. Thus current and potential stakeholders should have better information about the future value of the organisation in which they are interested. Through a restatement of the mission statement, stakeholders will also have the direction and purpose of the organisation emphasised and re-affirmed.

3 **(a)** The sales manager is correct in that the sales volume has outperformed budgeted sales volume by 27,000 units, or 11·1% over budget. This is a positive sign in a situation where there is increased competition and more demanding customers.

However, profitability is much lower than budgeted at 4·5% rather than the 24·7% budgeted, or the 27% expected if the budget was flexed to represent actual sales volume. This could have a serious impact on the future sustainability of the business. The flexed budget can be analysed to determine where performance has been worse than expected. Differences between expected and actual performance can then be investigated. The flexed budget and variances are as follows:

	Budget units	Actual units	Flexed budget	Variance to flexed
Sales volume	243,000	270,000	270,000	
	Budget $'000s	Actual $'000s		$'000s
Sales revenue	36,450	36,450	40,500	4,050 Adverse
Direct materials	15,795	18,630	17,550	1,080 Adverse
Direct labour	3,402	4,725	3,780	945 Adverse
Overheads	8,250	11,450	8,250	3,200 Adverse
Operating profit	9,003	1,645	10,920	

From the above, it can be seen that all calculated variances are adverse when considered against the flexed budget. Although the actual sales revenue is the same as budgeted, this is from a much higher sales volume. The average selling price per unit was budgeted at $150, but the average actual selling price per unit was $135, a decrease of 10%. It may be that this was reduced in order for the sales team to hit targets, especially if their commission is based on sales volume rather than revenue. Alternatively, it could be that the price was necessarily reduced in order to cope with increased competition.

Direct materials should have cost $17·55m for the actual units produced. However, they cost $18·63m, an adverse materials variance of $1·08m. This may either be due to the price or quality of materials used, but further information would be required to determine which. It is possible that price may be an important factor, as the sales manager mentioned fulfilling orders with a short lead time. This may have meant that higher prices were paid if materials were sourced at short notice, or not using economic order techniques. Furthermore, it was stated that customers wanted 'more attractive' products, which may have led to more advanced component parts, thus increasing costs. In addition, the industry is a dynamic industry with rapidly developing technology; the cost of new technology may be higher than the standard costs budgeted for. This is one of the difficulties of using standard costing in an environment where products are frequently enhanced or new products developed.

Direct labour has also shown an adverse variance of $945,000. This may be due to either the rate paid, or the hours worked on products. If orders were satisfied at short notice, this may have required overtime, which could affect the labour rate variance causing it to be higher due to enhanced overtime payments. In addition, special and customer-specific orders may require longer than standard hours as they may not yet have benefitted from the learning curve effect associated with standard, repeat orders.

Fixed overheads show a $3·2m adverse variance, which is 39% higher than budgeted. This is clearly a major problem and suggests that either the standard absorption rate of overheads is incorrect, or that overheads have not been controlled throughout the year. The focus on meeting increased orders may have distracted management attention from overhead control, thus leading to inefficiencies related to these costs. Overheads include those indirect elements of cost which are not specifically attributed to a product, such as cleaning materials, machine maintenance, supervisor salaries and factory rent and rates, heating and lighting. By treating them as fixed overheads, the suggestion is that they should not change with a variation in activity volumes. It is vital that the company analyses the overhead spend urgently, as this has had a major impact on profitability.

Overall, M&G should have made a budgeted profit of $10·92m on the actual sales, but instead made a profit of $1·645m, a difference of $9·275m.

One of the problems of using a standard costing system is that standard costs are based on historical information, and in a changing environment these are unlikely to remain accurate for long. It may be that the standards used in the budget are simply no longer realistic, and these need analysing before the blame is placed upon any particular department within the organisation. The suggestion of activity based costing could certainly assist with this in terms of understanding the overheads, although it will have no impact on the labour or material standards used; these would need separate analysis.

(b) Activity based costing attempts to discover what drives costs to be incurred. Cost pools are established which include all of the costs caused by one cost driver. These cost pools are then absorbed into products based on the driver activity related to each product. For example, M&G may recognise the cost driver 'machine set ups' which would occur every time the manufacturing line is set up to produce a different product or model. Following the initial recognition of costs, drivers and activities, overhead costs can then be allocated to products or customers accordingly.

Activity based costing was developed to improve the accuracy of costing in an environment where methods of production were becoming more automated and less labour intensive. The introduction of greater product ranges also demanded enhanced costing methods in order to both understand how costs were driven (and hence determine how to successfully reduce costs) and also to enhance product pricing in an increasingly competitive environment. For M&G, given the falling profitability and the increasing competition, it is important that the company determines how to reduce costs and become competitive on price without affecting profitability.

Although activity based costing should prove to be beneficial in the long term, the initial implementation of the method is a time-consuming and complex task which requires the identification of numerous activities and their cost drivers. In reality, these may number in their hundreds or even thousands. Given the volume of products in M&G's portfolio, this is likely to be an especially complex task. In addition, as new products and methods are introduced, the analysis of activities and drivers needs to be updated. The introduction of activity based costing may take up to a year and will require the participation of managers and staff in all departments. Given the growth of the company, it may be that departmental managers are feeling under pressure of enhanced activity volume and may not give sufficient thought to the identification of activities and their drivers, which would make the results irrelevant.

Additionally, some managers may be resistant to the idea of change. The pressure of work mentioned above may contribute to resistance. The impact of the change on their roles would also be a contributory factor. The sales manager, specifically, feels that performance is good and may see the introduction of new costing and pricing methods as something which will make it more difficult for him to hit targets. His participation is important as he will need to determine the cost drivers relevant to sales activities. This participation is essential to determine the profitability of customers, a key feature of activity based costing, and this itself may lead to resistance as he may see it as a route to losing some of his more 'lucrative' contracts.

The majority of M&G's customers are repeat business customers and, even if activity based costing were to be successfully introduced, they may not accept changes in pricing. For example, analysis might suggest that a product incurs greater costs than expected and so its price is increased as a result. The customer for this product may refuse to pay this price and so seek an alternative supplier for the product. This may, however, be beneficial to M&G to focus on more profitable customers or products, providing market share does not fall substantially.

Despite the limitations, in a period of increasing overheads (M&G's overheads are 39% greater than budgeted) and falling profitability, the use of activity based costing to determine cost behaviour can lead to increased efficiency as cost drivers are recognised and a focus placed on reducing the main cost drivers. Therefore the implementation of this method could bring future cost advantages to M&G, and help to regain the previous levels of profitability.

Tutorial note: *Although this solution suggests that ABC would be beneficial to M&G, the opposite viewpoint would be equally acceptable if supported by reasoned justification.*

4   (a)   Tutorial note: *There are more than four problem areas to discuss. Candidates are only expected to discuss four.*

The current process has a number of problems which may be causing the student comments in the student experience report.

– **Timing of coursework deadlines**

The course appears to be badly coordinated in that similar deadlines are set for different subjects. This causes periods of high activity for students, followed by periods of low activity. It would be preferable if the workload was evened out over the duration of the programme. This would address one of the student comments:

'We always have about four pieces of coursework to submit at the same time, and then weeks where nothing is required. I wish the university would manage our programme better'

A solution would be to coordinate this at the start of the course. The head of department could play a more proactive role and communicate with the lecturers after coursework deadlines have been submitted, to organise a more balanced schedule across all subjects.

– **Timing of the coursework requirements publication**

The lecturer releases the coursework requirements on the VLE at the beginning of the course, and so requirements are available before the work has been covered in class. This means that students may complete the work without having all of the relevant information to help them. As one student commented:

'I completed and submitted my coursework early in order to manage my workload better, but then the lecturer gave an additional lecture to help us with our coursework. This contained very useful information, which we had not previously covered. I was not allowed to resubmit my work and so suffered from being efficient'

A solution may be to issue a timed release on the VLE, which will release the coursework details as soon as the lectures relating to that topic are complete. This could also assist with students feeling that too many pieces of coursework need completing simultaneously, as it will stagger their release.

– **Release of marks**

It appears there are three different records of student marks, and all are input manually, which could lead to errors. The student who commented that their end of year results gave a different mark would be rightly concerned that the incorrect mark had been allocated to their degree classification.

'I received one mark from the VLE system, but when my end-of-year results were released the mark was different'

As a solution, the data should be input only once, by the lecturer marking the work, and a summary of the marks should be available for download by the head of department and the administrator, should they still need to do this. The VLE system could also be linked to other systems within the university, automatically feeding marks directly into these systems, so avoiding input errors.

– **Accuracy of coursework requirements**

It appears that there are problems with the accuracy of coursework requirements, and that adjustments have been made after they have been published. As one student commented, this meant that time was wasted on work which was not necessary.

'There were errors in the initial coursework requirements, which were subsequently significantly changed. I had already started the assignment so this time was wasted'

An additional step could be added into the process, whereby another lecturer proof reads the requirements and checks them for accuracy, relevance and validity. Although this would add time to the overall process, it does not appear that time is an issue at the start of the process.

– **Marking and feedback activities**

The guideline relating to the timing of marking is a little vague, *'within two teaching weeks of the submitted coursework being collected from the course administration office by the lecturer'*, and allows the lecturer to delay collection of the scripts in order to delay the marking. This could be one of the reasons why students complain about the time taken to mark their coursework.

'It takes weeks to receive my marks, by which time I've forgotten what the coursework was about'

Additionally, there appears to be no communication to the lecturer when coursework is ready to mark. The VLE or the administration office should inform the lecturer that scripts are available.

It would appear that the lecturer marks the hard copy and types their feedback onto a new word processed document which is then uploaded on to the VLE. This appears to lead to the feedback being difficult to understand, as the feedback is on a separate document. As one student commented:

'My feedback was on a separate document so I found it difficult to relate to the coursework submitted'

There are a number of possible solutions to these problems. The hard copy seems to be redundant if the VLE system is used for feedback. One possibility is to drop the hard copy submission to the administrator so that the student makes just a single submission on the VLE. The system could send an automated email to the lecturer once a submission has been made, or the lecturer could periodically log on to the system to view submissions.

The VLE system could be upgraded to allow online marking, with the online annotation of scripts, and automatic addition of marks awarded. This would align the feedback to the coursework and would ensure that the lecturer marks the correct, up-to-date version of the work submitted. This should help eradicate the following problems.

'The lecturer said he did not receive the hard copy of my coursework but I know I handed it in. This was counted as a non-submission'

'I accidentally submitted an unfinished piece of coursework to the administration office but submitted the correct one to the system. The lecturer marked the unfinished piece'

The university guideline should be amended to suggest that marking should be completed within a set number of weeks of the coursework submission date, not the date that the lecturer collects the scripts from the administration office.

It may be possible for the administrator to be removed entirely from the process; guidelines could be issued by the head of department, and it has already been suggested that marks could be automatically fed into the administrative systems, eliminating the need for manual input.

– **System deficiencies**

The system does not appear to allow for the re-submission of completed coursework. This means that if an upload does not occur correctly, or the student uploads the wrong document, they may be assessed unfairly.

'I completed and submitted my coursework early in order to manage my workload better... I was not allowed to resubmit my work and so suffered from being efficient'

It should be possible to submit coursework more than once, with a new receipt given each time, until the final submission deadline. To ensure that the correct file is uploaded, there should be an additional process whereby the system opens the uploaded file and asks the student to verify that it is the correct, up-to-date version.

(b) Any changes in processes, in this case driven by customer (student) expectations, can lead to changes in job design. Both the changing process and the changing requirements of the student will lead to a number of new responsibilities and capabilities required of different staff.

There are a number of different approaches to job design, including scientific management, job enrichment, Japanese management and re-engineering. The current approach seems to be quite close to that of scientific management, but the suggestion of 'one best way' associated with this approach may be less relevant in the changing environment.

Re-engineering requires a fundamental rethink in how processes are carried out and often leads to the automation of roles. Whilst some automation may be required in this instance, it is unlikely at this stage that lecturers will be completely replaced by technology.

The Japanese model focuses on lean methods and minimisation of waste. Whilst still relevant to service industries, it is more commonly used in a manufacturing environment and is less common in an academic environment. However, some elements may be introduced here, such as a reduction in overlap of taught subjects, but is unlikely to have a major influence on changing the current job design of lecturers.

Job enrichment would seem to be a more appropriate approach to job design in this scenario, given lecturer concerns and the need to move away from the current scientific management model. This should satisfy the needs of the lecturer, the student and the university. Elements of job enrichment may arise as a result of process changes discussed in the first part of this answer.

For example, the suggested process change creates a requirement for the head of department to become more engaged with the lecturers, who would need to work with them to coordinate the assessments to meet the needs of the students. This may enrich their role as they become more involved in planning and decision-making. From the feedback, it would suggest that this coordination would also need to extend to the course content to ensure a lack of repetition and a rational continuation of studies. In addition to providing job enrichment to the lecturers, this would address the following student's concern:

'My course didn't seem well coordinated. Some topics were repeated and others failed to cover the syllabus, making it difficult to move up from one year to the next'

Lecturers, who traditionally appear to work alone, will be required to cooperate with each other, and play a much closer role in the development and well-being of students. This means that they will need to develop social and pastoral skills. They are used to working to strict guidelines and processes and it is likely that this will need to change to meet the individual requirements of students.

It would seem that job enrichment would assist in retaining lecturers, who do not seem to be stimulated by their roles. Job enrichment would allow them to be challenged as it brings in some responsibility for planning and control. Perhaps an opportunity to manage a subject, as part of the programme team, may allow for some planning and control activities in addition to planning of coursework. The analysis of student performance and feedback and lecturer involvement in determining improvements would also enrich their roles.

Job rotation, with lecturers teaching different subjects each year, may make jobs more challenging, but this in turn should make the job more interesting as it does not become routine.

Hackman and Oldham suggest that job enrichment involves five key characteristics, one of which is task identity, or the inclusion of all tasks needed to complete a process. So, if lecturers were to be responsible for the entire outcome of a subject, from the creation of the syllabus content, the writing and marking of coursework, the planning of lessons and the analysis of results, this would suggest an enriched role. Another of the five suggested characteristics is autonomy, whereby the lecturers should have discretion in the organisation of their work. A removal or reduction in the strict guidelines would help in achieving this.

Job redesign should also exploit the use of technology, even if not using it to fully re-engineer processes, and this needs to be considered in the university. Even though a VLE system exists, it is not fully utilised and manual processes still dominate.

University lecturers are knowledge workers and therefore the organisation should carefully consider how they treat them. Knowledge is a vital asset to universities and should be acquired, managed and exploited to make the most of it. The turnover of lecturers means that knowledge is being lost to the university and this needs to be controlled. If the university were to introduce activities which further develop the knowledge of lecturers, such as research seminars and attendance at conferences, this may stimulate learning and creativity and encourage lecturers to remain and to stay motivated.

In order to ensure that job redesign fully meet the needs of the university and the students, the new roles should be carefully analysed. This can be done through the use of a competency framework. The university should list all the competences required as an institute and further narrow these down to departmental and individual competences. This framework can then be used to assess any further staff development requirements.

'My lecturer wasn't very supportive when I had personal problems'

It may be that the lecturer appeared unsupportive to the student quoted in the feedback because they simply did not know how to react to that student. A competency framework for lecturers may include the addition of a section on pastoral care. The university may choose to run internal courses to ensure that staff has the acquired necessary competences in this area. There may be an existing requirement for communication skills, but this may be emphasised in relation to internal communication within the course team. Meetings may be scheduled to enable this.

The competency framework may assist in succession planning, which seems essential in a university hoping to improve its student experience, but subject to a high turnover of lecturing staff.

Professional Level – Essentials Module

Business Analysis

March/June 2016 – Sample Questions

Paper P3

Think Ahead

The Association of Chartered Certified Accountants

Section A – This ONE question is compulsory and MUST be attempted

1 Introduction

QTP Co produces timber framed windows for builders' merchants, property builders and property maintenance companies. It does not sell windows directly to the general public. Members of the general public (and small building companies) can buy QTP windows through the builders' merchants supplied by QTP. These builders' merchants supply a wide range of products for property maintenance and improvement. They are usually located in large warehouse premises on the outskirts of towns and cities.

There are three primary raw materials (or components) for the windows which QTP makes.

- Timber (wood) which it orders from timber suppliers. Worldwide demand for timber is increasing and timber prices are relatively high and supply of some of the specialist timber which QTP requires is often in short supply.
- Glass which it orders from specialist glass manufacturers.
- Fittings, such as bolts, latches, handles, etc which it sources from a number of small specialist producers.

QTP has a number of departments. This scenario considers just five of these departments and each of these departments is exactly aligned with activities of the value chain. They are:

- Inbound logistics and procurement
- Production
- Outbound logistics
- Marketing and sales
- Service

Production takes place on one dedicated production line where one machine (and supporting labour) undertakes all the tasks concerned with converting the components into the finished windows. There are no plans to buy a second machine or open up a second production line. Production takes place from 08.00 to 17.00 (nine hours). Although employees take breaks, these are organised so that the production line is always staffed. It is not possible, because of technical and environmental constraints, to extend the working day or organise a night shift. The company is effectively restricted to a nine-hour working day. Setting up and setting down of the machine has to take place within this nine-hour day.

Outbound logistics has a small fleet of vehicles which are used to deliver finished windows to the customer. Effective scheduling of this fleet is currently a problem and vehicle maintenance is becoming more expensive as the vehicles get older.

Standard and bespoke windows

The company offers both standard windows and bespoke windows.

Standard windows are made to a specification decided by QTP and they are produced to inventory. These windows are advertised in the company's catalogue and on its website. Customer orders for these windows are supplied from inventory and next day delivery is promised. The production of these windows is based on sales forecasts made by the marketing and sales department. These forecasts are used by the inbound logistics and procurement department to place orders for the raw materials for the windows. Because relatively large orders for components are placed in advance, QTP usually obtains significant discounts on published component prices.

Bespoke windows are produced to a specification required by the customer, usually resulting from consultation and negotiation between the marketing and sales department and the customer. They are made to exactly fit the customer's needs, in terms of timber type and quality, glass specification, window size and types of fitting. The marketing and sales department provides the customer with a proposed delivery date. A copy of the order, and the proposed delivery date, is also given to the production department, so that they can schedule the making of the windows and to inbound logistics and procurement so that they can order specific components for the windows.

At present, there is often a conflict between the production of standard and bespoke windows. It is essential that QTP achieves the promised delivery date for bespoke orders. To achieve this, it is often necessary for scheduled runs of standard windows to be postponed so that bespoke windows can be produced. This leads to less efficient use of the machine and labour (due to set up and set down time) and also to components for standard windows being held in inventory for longer than planned. Furthermore, component prices for bespoke orders are usually higher, reflecting smaller volumes and the need to fulfil tight deadlines. Bespoke window production and delivery to customers usually takes place as quickly as possible, to ensure that promised deadlines are met and inventory storage of finished windows minimised.

In the past, it was possible for bespoke orders to use common components bought in for standard windows. However, this led to continual disruption of the production of standard windows and now components for standard and bespoke orders are kept quite separate and are stored in different areas of the warehouse.

In general, the marketing and sales department prefers to make bespoke sales, rather than sales of the standard windows. They believe that bespoke windows provide exactly what the customer wants and this distinguishes QTP from its competitors who are more focused on selling standard windows. Unlike these competitors, the marketing and sales department at QTP contains staff who are experienced in window design and applications and customers value this. There is evidence that some important customers purchase their standard windows from QTP even though they could buy similar windows cheaper elsewhere, because they value QTP's flexibility in supplying them with bespoke windows. The marketing and sales director claims that, 'we have sales people who really understand windows and what customers want and need. We are not trying to sell them windows off-the-shelf, just because we have them in inventory.'

Furthermore marketing and sales staff claim that bespoke windows deliver higher revenue and higher profit to QTP than standard windows. However, this is challenged by the production manager who would prefer production to be focused on standard windows. Sales staff are currently rewarded on the basis of average revenue per window. At present, approximately 30% of QTP's sales volume is for bespoke windows, but this share is increasing annually.

Table One shows selected data for the production of standard and bespoke windows.

	Standard window	Bespoke window
Revenue and costs per window ($)		
Average revenue	85	110
Average inventory (storage) cost	15	5
Average raw material cost	20	40
Average transport cost (Note 1)	15	10
Average labour cost ($)	12	15
Average machine cost ($)	8	10
Production data		
Average number of windows produced per hour	12	10
Wastage rate for windows produced	2%	5%
Average set up time (Note 2)	10 minutes	15 minutes
Average set down time (Note 3)	20 minutes	45 minutes
Average production run (Note 4)	4 hours	2 hours
Other data		
Number of customer complaints per thousand windows	2	10

Table One: Selected QTP data: standard window and bespoke window production

Note (1) Transport costs concern distribution costs of finished goods to customers. Costs of inbound components are borne by the supplier.

Note (2) Time taken to set up the machine for a single production run of windows to one specification.

Note (3) Time taken to set down the machine (resetting parameters, cleaning, etc) from a single production run of windows to one specification.

Note (4) Time of a single production run of windows to one specification.

Important: The machine is restricted to a nine-hour working day. Set up time and set down time must be within this nine-hour working day.

Management concerns

Senior management at QTP is exploring the possibility of moving the company to solely standard window production OR solely bespoke window production. They are also investigating issues in the five departments which are aligned to the activities of the value chain. They previously employed a business analyst who provided them with an analysis of the service department at QTP, documented in Appendix 1. Management has engaged you as her successor and they now require similar analyses for the remaining four departments.

Appendix 1: Analysis of service department in the value chain

Figure One: The service department at QTP: current analysis

Service

Service is concerned with activities which enhance or maintain the value of the window. This includes installation, repair, training, supply of parts and window adjustment. At QTP, service is primarily concerned with window replacement (repair).

Replacement of standard windows is usually required as a result of window deterioration. Evidence suggests that this is sometimes associated with windows or window components being held in inventory at QTP for too long and suffering some minor damage or imperfection, which has subsequently worsened. However, there is also evidence that some problems are a result of incorrect fitting. Standard window replacements are provided to the customer, usually for next day delivery. These are provided free-of-charge if the problem is due to faulty manufacture.

Problems with bespoke windows are usually associated with initial fitting and failure to meet specification. The window may be slightly too large, or the timber slightly the wrong colour. Because such windows are made to order, replacement can take some time, although the company attempts to 'rush through' such replacements, placing emergency component orders and interrupting scheduled production.

Figure Two: The service department at QTP: potential role after switch to standard windows production only OR bespoke windows production only

Switching completely to standard windows production

If production is switched completely to standard windows, then service will be primarily concerned with the replacement of defective windows. Better inventory management should lead to fewer problems with components and finished windows as both will remain in inventory for less time. Consideration could also be given to providing training on installation, so potentially reducing the number of defective windows caused by poor installation. This might involve formal certification for qualified installers. This should be attractive to customers, as it will reduce their wastage rates. QTP might also consider providing a guaranteed installation service itself. This might be particularly attractive to property builders who find it uneconomic to employ full-time window installers.

Switching completely to bespoke windows production

If production is switched completely to bespoke windows, then service will be primarily concerned with rectifying problems which arise as a result of the window failing to meet specification. Improved specification methods, using better computer aided design (CAD) software should reduce the need for service. The concept of providing a window installation service is particularly attractive for bespoke windows as slight failures in fit might be remedied on site, rather than returned to the factory. This eliminates delay and the cost of transporting the windows to and from the factory. Failures in appearance (such as timber colour) could be avoided by a pre-installation visit where a sample of the bespoke window (one window) could be confirmed with the customer.

Required:

QTP management would like you to prepare a briefing paper which:

(a) Analyses the current issues in the remaining four departments under consideration (inbound logistics and procurement, production, outbound logistics, marketing and sales), with appropriate reference to each department's role in the value chain. Appendix 1 Figure One is representative of the approach required.

(20 marks)

(b) Evaluates the financial case for EITHER producing and selling standard windows only OR producing and selling bespoke windows only. The evaluation should include both options and could include any comments you have on the limitation of the data given in Table One. However, you should assume that the data given in this table accurately reflects the current situation.

(12 marks)

(c) Analyses how the company could restructure elements of each of the remaining four departments (and hence the value chain) in the future for EITHER a switch to only standard windows production OR a switch to only bespoke windows production. Appendix 1 Figure Two is representative of the approach required and it clearly shows that you should include BOTH options in your analysis.

(14 marks)

Professional marks will be awarded in question 1 for the structure, tone, coherence and clarity of your briefing paper.

(4 marks)

(50 marks)

2 Shop Reviewers Online (SRO) was founded in 2010 by Amy Needham. She felt that many customers buying from online stores were misled by advertising and that too often, purchased products turned out to be unreliable, faulty or failed to meet the customers' expectations. Amy believed that the online retail industry was increasingly acting unethically, caring only for profits at the expense of the needs and expectations of customers.

Consequently, she set up SRO to 'provide an unbiased review of online stores to ensure the customer has all available information'. The company offers reviews of current online stores and provides direct links for customers to shop at the stores featured on its site. The reviews include price comparisons, provided by SRO, as well as general reviews provided by registered users of the site. The company has two main revenue streams. The first is advertising revenue from online stores who place advertisements on the SRO site. The second revenue stream is commission from sales by online stores to customers who have clicked on the sponsored links provided on the SRO website. This commission is only paid by stores who have entered into such a commission arrangement with SRO.

SRO relies upon its website being available online 24 hours a day, 7 days a week. For this reason it has backup servers running concurrently with the main servers on which data is processed and stored. The servers are directly linked so that any update to the main servers automatically occurs on the backup. The servers are all housed in the same computer centre in the company head office. The computer centre has enhanced its security by implementing a fingerprint recognition system for controlling access to the site. However, as the majority of staff at headquarters are IT personnel, and often temporary staff are hired to cover absentees, the fingerprint recognition system is not comprehensive and, to save time, is often bypassed. Similarly, to save time needed to set up new permanent staff with passwords to access the company's systems, a general 'administrator' user has been created, with the password 'password'. Many temporary staff access the system in this way.

SRO has an intelligent software application which constantly searches the internet for product price changes, uploading these into the reviews of the online store in question. Sometimes, however, there have been problems. Usually this is when the application has not recognised an outdated page and has replaced the correct latest price with an old price found on the outdated page. Furthermore, this intelligent software application needs permanent continual access to the internet, and SRO has identified a problem with its firewall which has prevented the software application from sometimes updating the internal systems. For this reason, it has removed the firewall protection to help ensure that the correct up-to-date prices of all online stores are shown on the website.

SRO rarely generates other elements of reviews (such as product experience), leaving this to registered users of the site. However, it will, occasionally, submit its own review to help boost a store which pays a higher commission rate than its competitors. SRO is always honest in its reviews, but the more reviews a store has, the higher up the search list it appears, when a customer searches for a specific product.

Registered users can submit as many reviews as they wish. Unregistered users may also submit reviews, which will be published under the name 'anonymous', but these reviewers will be unable to comment on the reviews of others. SRO checks reviews for appropriate content, but does not contact the store to verify the accuracy of the review.

SRO is about to undertake an audit of the adequacy of its general and application IT controls. In addition, SRO is currently undertaking an internal ethical governance audit, which has identified two main areas of concern:

(1) **Commercial conflicts of interest**

As mentioned earlier, SRO's business objective is to 'provide an unbiased review of online stores to ensure the customer has all available information'. However, the audit has revealed that both SRO's revenue streams may cause an ethical dilemma with regards to this objective.

(2) **Company offices**

SRO has little need for traditional offices, as it does not have a direct customer-facing role. It mainly requires IT technicians to support its automated services. The company has carried out research which suggests that the IT skills it requires could be sourced at a much lower rate overseas. It is considering relocation to one such country. This country has low rates of corporation tax and cheaper labour costs. However, the country itself is poorly regulated and does not have legislation concerning the quality of information systems or the security of data contained within them, particularly relating to personal data. The culture of the country is such that accepting unauthorised payments for services is also not unusual. Whilst SRO does not condone this in its code of conduct, it is aware that such issues exist in the country under consideration.

Required:

(a) Evaluate the adequacy of the general and application controls in place within SRO, with respect to its information technology and information systems. Suggest any improvements you consider to be necessary.

(15 marks)

(b) Assess the corporate governance and ethical dilemmas identified by SRO in its possible relocation to the foreign country and discuss the implications of these on organisational mission, purpose and strategy.

(10 marks)

(25 marks)

3 The Holiday Company (HC) currently offers travel agency services by giving travel advice and making travel bookings for customers who physically visit the offices located in most major towns in the country. However, it is progressively reducing this part of the business while simultaneously trying to achieve a greater proportion of its revenue online.

To help meet this objective, HC is in the process of forming a new business unit to market and sell luxury holidays. The holiday product range marketed by this new business unit will be named Inspirations. It is intended that Inspirations will provide a high quality, bespoke holiday service for discerning clients. HC has decided that this new business unit will have its own mission statement of 'delivering a high quality service for discerning travellers'. The new managing director of Inspirations has stated that it has an objective of achieving annual revenue of $100m by 2018. This would be approximately 25% of the total forecast revenue for HC that year, but it is expected to represent only about 5% of the total number of holidays sold by HC. The type of holidays offered by Inspirations is already provided by some of HC's competitors.

Dilip Kharel, the new director of marketing of Inspirations, has stated that the internet should be increasingly used as the main source of marketing and selling the holidays, as 'the days are almost gone when families visit a 'high street' travel agency to plan their holiday; it's all done now from the comfort of the home'. He believes that potential customers of Inspirations will not want to visit high street travel agencies.

HC currently makes extensive use of traditional marketing techniques, sending out travel brochures containing all of its holidays to potential customers. However, as Dilip has recognised, 'the problem is that we don't even know if our customers bother opening these, or if they put them directly into the dustbin.' These brochures are often produced months in advance, and may advertise holidays which are no longer available. Customers will not discover this until they visit one of the travel agents. The company currently does make some use of targeted emails, but it has been accused of sending spam mail in the past and mass mailing a weekly email of all current holiday offers to everyone registered on its database.

Dilip is keen to embrace the opportunities offered by electronic marketing and believes that Inspirations can benefit greatly by exploiting the principles of intelligence, individualisation, interactivity, integration and independence of location which are central to electronic marketing.

Inspirations will offer holidays in a wide variety of locations, including the Caribbean, Africa and Asia, and plan to offer 'themed' trips, such as gourmet food holidays and heritage trips. Different countries may have different requirements for visiting tourists, such as visa regulations. Inspirations does not own hotels or aircraft and therefore the majority of holidays offered will be provided by third-party suppliers, such as hotel and airline companies. This means that Inspirations can lack control over some elements such as passenger taxes. Inspirations will have representatives on site in all resorts to meet guests at airports and to address any issues they have with the holiday. However, the hotels and excursions will not be solely or exclusively offered to Inspirations guests. For example, there will be other guests at a hotel who have not booked through Inspirations.

Dilip is concerned about this. He feels that the company needs to be able to differentiate itself, either in the overall holiday experience itself or in the marketing of it, so that customers are more likely to book such holidays through Inspirations, rather than through a competitor, or indeed through booking with the hotel directly. He also recognises the importance of adopting an appropriate pricing strategy which meets the needs of the organisation (HC and Inspirations) and customers alike.

Required:

(a) Evaluate how the principles of intelligence, individualisation, interactivity, integration and independence of location could be exploited when marketing the new range of holidays to be offered by Inspirations.

(15 marks)

Dilip Kharel recognises the importance of a pricing strategy which supports the overall corporate and business strategies of the organisation.

Required:

(b) Describe a strategic approach to establishing prices in the context of Inspirations. You should recognise both economic and non-economic factors in your approach. (10 marks)

(25 marks)

4 The country of Westoria has a well-respected public health service funded primarily through general taxation. The Westoria Public Health Authority (WPHA) is responsible for delivering this health service through a network of hospitals in Westoria.

WPHA is under increasing pressure to demonstrate to taxpayers that it is using public finances wisely and so it wishes to accurately monitor and control health service expenditure. However, it is proving difficult to confidently track the budgeted and actual finances of individual hospitals, as each is operating its own form of budgeting and cash management. Consequently, WPHA has decided to introduce a single computer-based system which will allow all hospitals to enter and manage financial information in a standard way. This system will be part of an authority-wide enterprise resource planning system (ERPS) which will allow WPHA to monitor and control the finances of the entire authority. Currently, the input and consolidation of WPHA information is a time-consuming process, importing data from individual hospitals into a series of spreadsheets to provide total figures for the authority as a whole.

At a recent WPHA board meeting, the head of the authority suggested that the scope of the ERPS should be widened to incorporate other elements of operational and management information. She pointed out that some previous commercial off-the-shelf (COTS) software solutions which the authority selected and implemented had not worked well. She gave two specific examples:

– The payroll system does not support payment increments for non-standard working, such as overtime rates. To allow this, payroll staff currently have to change the employee's standard hourly rate for the time period in question and then change it back again. This is time-consuming and payment errors have been made when payroll staff have forgotten to change the rate back again.

– The human resource management system does not support the temporary transfer of staff between hospital departments. To compensate for this, human resource staff have to action a permanent move for a short time period and then action a reverse move at the end of that period.

She therefore felt that the introduction of the ERPS would be an opportunity to address outstanding problems and to improve and standardise the systems in use.

The board agreed the ERPS should, as a minimum, also include payroll and human resource management modules within the overall product. However, given budget limitations, the board decided that a commercial off-the-shelf ERPS solution should be selected and implemented. They all agreed that this would be a cheaper solution than a bespoke system and would be well suited to their needs, as it should fulfil the standard requirements they envisaged. Furthermore, it had always been the policy of WPHA not to employ internal IT system developers. Currently, the IT support team consists of one operational member of staff at each hospital and a central team of ten staff who assist in addressing major IT problems encountered at any of the hospitals. The IT support team has also produced ways to bypass issues with previously implemented COTS package solutions.

This lack of internal IT resource, and the recognition that previous COTS implementations had been less successful than predicted, has prompted WPHA to seek the advice of an external software systems consultant.

The consultant has suggested that the evaluation and implementation of the ERPS package should follow a four-stage process:

– Evaluate whether a COTS solution is an appropriate approach
– Define the requirements for the new software
– Evaluate competing packages
– Implement the selected package

However, the head of the authority believes that the external consultant is being over-cautious in his advice and approach and that the first two stages are not needed. In her words: 'We know that a COTS solution is the right approach for us as we have little alternative, so why spend time doing the first step? We also know that we've been pretty poor at defining what we want in the past; so why not recognise our deficiencies and go straight to stage three and look at competing packages to see which products provide the best features?'

The HR director, who has experienced the problems of the human resource and payroll systems at first hand, disagrees. He feels that the consultant's four-stage process is insufficient. He believes that, 'it is important that we consider all four elements of the POPIT (four view) model, which provides four key areas to be considered when a process is to change. These four key areas are people, organisation, processes and information technology. Only the last of these will be considered in the consultant's four-stage process. If we ignore the remaining three areas we are in danger of another failed software project, which is likely to further upset taxpayers and, perhaps, threaten the future of the authority itself.'

Required:

(a) The external consultant suggested a four-stage process for the evaluation and implementation of the proposed commercial off-the-shelf ERPS package.

Discuss the four-stage process for the evaluation and implementation of a software package, and the significance of each stage in the context of the previous and proposed COTS solutions at WPHA.

(16 marks)

(b) The HR director has suggested that all elements of the POPIT model should be considered.

Explain, in the context of WPHA, the need for considering the people, the organisation and the processes involved when carrying out a business change project.

(9 marks)

(25 marks)

End of Question Paper

1 (a) Inbound logistics and procurement

Inbound logistics is concerned with activities associated with receiving, storing and disseminating inputs to the production process. It encompasses materials handling, warehousing, inventory control, vehicle scheduling and returns to suppliers. It is responsible for bringing raw materials into the organisation and storing it ready for use. Standard window and bespoke window production pose different problems for the department.

In standard window production components tend to be bought in bulk and stored on-site waiting production. This incurs storage costs and there may also be costs associated with wastage and obsolescence. These costs are exacerbated by the problem of mixing standard and bespoke window production. The scenario suggests that bespoke production often displaces standard production, for example, in order to accommodate a customer's increasingly urgent request. This means that components bought in to fulfil a planned standard production run can be left in storage for longer than was anticipated. However, standard window production does facilitate the bulk buying of components and so raw materials should be cheaper.

In bespoke production, there should be fewer storage costs, as the components are moved quickly through to production to fulfil a customer's order. However, because component lead times are lengthier, buyers often pay more for the windows to secure quick supply and to reflect the lower order quantities normally associated with a specific bespoke order.

AT QTP, raw material costs are significantly higher for bespoke windows than for standard windows and this reflects the premium prices expected to be paid for low-volume urgent supplies. However, storage costs (part of which will be storage of raw materials) are much lower, suggesting that the order quickly moves through the QTP factory. However, the number of complaints raised by bespoke window customers perhaps suggests that for many, the order does not move quickly enough.

For both standard and bespoke production, the supply of timber is a problem. Prices are rising and there is an increasing shortage of specialist timber. However, from the perspective of QTP, inbound transport is not a problem. This is provided by the suppliers.

Production (Operations)

Production is concerned with the activities required to transform inputs into the final product. In this case it is the production line process of QTP, transforming timber, glass and fittings into standard and bespoke windows. As well as assembly, production also considers packaging and equipment maintenance.

In most organisations, production is most effective when producing long runs of standard products to inventory, minimising set up time and set down time (and associated costs). The production of well-understood standard products reduces the need for quality control and also minimises wastage. In contrast, bespoke production is usually associated with relatively short runs (reflecting individual customer order quantities) and higher set up and set down time (and costs). Specialised bespoke set ups have to be carefully quality-controlled and wastage rates (because of the unfamiliarity with the task) tend to be higher.

These general observations appear to be supported by the data at QTP. Set up and set down times for bespoke windows are much longer, meaning that the production line is idle for twice as long. The average production run is also shorter and wastage rates are higher. The number of customer complaints (per thousand units) is also higher. Some of these complaints are likely to be about the quality of the delivered window. Bespoke units have to be exactly to the specification of the customer, whilst standard units are to the specification of QTP. It is the responsibility of the customer to ensure that these standard units are fit for purpose.

The production manager's enthusiasm for standard windows is understandable. It maximises production efficiency, at the same time minimising wastage and complaints.

Outbound logistics

Outbound logistics is concerned with the activities associated with collecting, storing and physically distributing the product to buyers. It encompasses finished goods warehousing, material handling, delivery vehicle operation and order processing. Again, different issues are raised by standard window and bespoke window production.

Standard production leads to higher storage costs as windows are stored waiting to be sold to potential customers. The storage of these finished windows may lead to wastage, as windows are made unsellable due to storage conditions: damp, extremes of temperature, fire, flood. Pilfering from employees and obsolescence, as demand dries up for a standard window, may also affect stored windows.

Once sold, customers expect almost immediate delivery of stored windows, making it difficult to plan the routes of the delivery fleet in advance, particularly as that fleet also has to deal with the urgent delivery of bespoke orders. The effective use and maintenance of its own fleet of vehicles is a clear problem for QTP.

In contrast, delivery for bespoke windows produced to order can be planned well in advance and the customer given a specific delivery date. In general, the windows are delivered as soon as they are manufactured and so storage costs are lower. This is reflected in the QTP data where storage costs of bespoke windows are one third those of standard windows. Transport costs are also lower, reflecting the relative ease of planning the efficient delivery of bespoke orders.

Marketing and sales

These are activities associated with inducing the customers to purchase a product and then facilitating that purchase. It includes advertising, promotion, quotations and pricing.

15

At QTP, marketing and sales is rewarded on the basis of revenue per window sold. The data suggests that the average revenue per window is higher for a bespoke window than it is for a standard one. Consequently, there is an incentive to steer customers towards bespoke windows rather than standard ones.

Marketing and sales also argues that the bespoke approach means that customers always receive exactly the windows they want, rather than ordering standard windows which do not fit their exact needs. This pre-sales customer design service is perceived as an important strength of QTP and it is what distinguishes the company from its competitors. The marketing and sales director claims that 'we have sales people who really understand the windows and what customers want and need. We are not trying to sell them windows off the shelf, just because we have them' in inventory. Fulfilling exact requirements is an important part of building the customer relationship. It is claimed that some important customers purchase standard windows from QTP even when they could be sourced cheaper elsewhere, because of QTP's past flexibility in developing bespoke windows for them. Thus there are important cross-selling opportunities between standard and bespoke windows.

However, the bespoke approach causes both internal and external tensions. Pressure from customers leads to the marketing and sales department putting pressure (in turn) on inbound logistics and procurement to secure the quick delivery of the required components. As noted already, this leads to high raw material costs. Once the raw material has arrived, pressure is put on production to expedite the order and postpone planned standard production runs. This leads to machine and labour inefficiency. Marketing and sales contend that bespoke orders are still more profitable than orders fulfilled from inventory, but the production manager disputes this.

The bespoke approach probably also demands the active management of customers. It is possible that the customer is constantly enquiring about the status of their order, and delivery on the planned date is essential if the customer is to achieve its own deadlines and profits.

(b) **Tutorial note:** *The analysis of standard window production might use the current pattern of machine utilisation or it might use a pattern where the production run is uninterrupted. Credit will be given for either and for both.*

Financial analysis

Standard windows:

Machine utilisation (average day)

Set up	Production	Set down	Set up	Production	Set down
10 minutes	4 hours	20 minutes	10 minutes	4 hours	20 minutes

Effective machine time per day: 8 hours

Number of units produced: 8 x 12 (8 hours, 12 units per hour) 96 units

Average window wastage per day (96 x 2%): 1·92

Sellable production per day: 94·08 units

Revenue: 94·08 x $85 = **$7,996·80**

Cost of production/window

	$
Storage cost	15
Raw material	20
Transport cost	15
Labour cost	12
Machine cost	8
Total	70

Production cost: 94·08 x $70 = **$6,585·60**

Daily contribution: $7,996·80 – $6,585·60 = **$1,411·20**

Bespoke windows:

Set up	Production	Set down	Set up	Production	Set down	Set up	Production	Set down
15 minutes	2 hours	45 minutes	15 minutes	2 hours	45 minutes	15 minutes	2 hours	45 minutes

Effective machine time per day: 6 hours

Number of units produced: 6 x 10 (6 hours, 10 units per hour) 60 units

Average window wastage per day (60 x 5%): 3

Sellable production per day: 57 units

Revenue: 57 x 110 = **$6,270**

Cost of production/window

	$
Storage cost	5
Raw material	40
Transport cost	10
Labour cost	15
Machine cost	10
Total	80

Production cost: 57 x $80 = **$4,560·00**

Daily contribution: $6,270·00 – $4,560·00 = **$1,710·00**

So, on this basis, bespoke production produces less revenue per day, but is more profitable.

Given the window mix at the moment, the expected daily contribution would be:

$1,411 x 0·7 + $1,710 x 0·3 = 987·70 + 513·00 = **$1,500·70**

The data is based on a mixed standard/bespoke production cycle where planned production runs are often cancelled or interrupted by bespoke production requirements. Thus the pattern of use in a production facility dedicated solely to standard windows should be different. For example, in a fully standard window production environment it should be possible to increase effective machine time to 8 hours 30 minutes (1 set up, production, 1 set down). This would lead to a production run of 102 units (8·5 hours x 12). Given a 2% wastage rate, this would lead to an average daily production of 99·96 units, producing a revenue of 99·96 x $85 = $8,496·60. Cost of production would be 99·96 x $70 = $6,997·20.

Thus contribution would be $8,496·60 – $6,997·20 = $1,499·40, still below the daily contribution of the bespoke alternative. However, this assumes that all other costs would remain the same in a fully standard configuration.

The data provided only concerns direct costs. There is no consideration of overheads. It may be possible that a production line dedicated to standard window development may allow for a reduction in marketing and sales staff and service employees as the windows need less negotiation and support. In contrast, a production line dedicated to bespoke windows may lead to fewer warehousing and distribution staff. Revenues will also be less, so there may be an opportunity to lose staff from general administrative functions.

(c) **Switching completely to standard windows production**

Inbound logistics: It should be possible to reduce the storage costs of components, as they should be stored for shorter periods as production is now based on a planned cycle, uninterrupted by bespoke work. Less time in storage should also reduce wastage and obsolescence.

There may also be opportunities for exploiting just in time (JIT) supply principles, moving storage costs to the supplier and so reducing inbound storage costs at QTP even further. The company might also consider backward integration, looking to acquire timber production facilities so helping secure the supply chain and also, potentially, reducing raw material costs.

Production (Operations): Production efficiencies should be gained from being able to plan production in advance. If set up and set down times remain the same (and this seems a reasonable assumption), then production can be increased to 102 units per day, before wastage. The calculation for this is shown in part (b) of this solution.

Outbound logistics: Planned production should lead to a better utilisation of the distribution fleet. However, this is an area where QTP might consider outsourcing to a specialist logistics company who can exploit economies of scale which are not achievable with a small fleet of vehicles. It can be argued that distribution is not a core competence of the company and would benefit from outsourcing.

Marketing and sales: There are opportunities for head count reduction in marketing and sales as sales switch to standard windows with specifications available in catalogues and on the internet. The focus is now on promotion and order taking, not the negotiation of individual orders. In standard window production, sales forecasting is paramount. This is an acknowledged weakness of the current marketing and sales team and this would have to be addressed.

Overall: In this approach, QTP is an order-obtaining organisation, obtaining orders from customers for goods which it has already produced. Standard window production to inventory should lead to a more efficient window production. However, it may also lead to the loss of customers who value the company's ability to deliver a mixture of standard and bespoke windows. There is evidence to suggest that such customers currently place orders for standard windows even though they could be sourced more cheaply elsewhere. QTP might lose these customers in the future.

Focusing on standard production may also mean that QTP is focusing on a commodity-type market where there will be continual downward pressure on prices.

Switching completely to bespoke production

Inbound logistics: Because orders are definite, component storage costs should be relatively low, but components cannot be ordered in advance and bulk discounts negotiated. Thus in this case there seems an even stronger case for backward integration. Securing supply is even more vital in bespoke production where supplying the customer at the promised time is paramount. It is also acknowledged that raw material costs are currently high for bespoke windows and so owning the means of timber supply should help reduce this cost.

Production (Operations): Production is driven by definite orders from customers, not 'made to inventory' production runs based on forecasts. Freeing up capacity should allow the quicker production and delivery of bespoke orders. Production planning is now primarily concerned with scheduling definite orders to meet the agreed delivery date.

Outbound logistics: Inventory holding costs should be relatively low as deliveries can be planned around customer order dates. Because these are well known in advance, then a delivery schedule can be planned, although this is likely to be sub-optimal, based around the need to deliver to certain locations on certain dates, rather than planning an optimal route around standard delivery locations. Overall, fewer units will be produced and so it might be possible to reduce the size (and hence cost) of the delivery fleet. The certainty of deliveries might also make this a strong candidate for outsourcing. This could deliver significant cost savings.

Marketing and sales: Moving to bespoke production plays to the strengths of the current marketing and sales department. These could be perceived as core competencies which the company needs to exploit. Furthermore, because they are rewarded on average revenue per window, this will also appeal to the department from a reward perspective. The need to acquire new customers may make other elements of the marketing mix, such as promotion, increasingly important.

Overall: In this approach, QTP is an order-receiving organisation, producing windows for orders it has received. This is the preferred approach of the current marketing and sales team. Bespoke production will still allow QTP to fulfil standard windows (they will just be produced as bespoke items) and so customers' needs will be fulfilled, although they may have to pay higher prices than before for such windows. QTP will be positioning itself as a niche provider, able to charge a premium for a specialised service. So, its market positioning will be quite different.

2 (a) SRO has recognised the importance of the need for functioning systems at all times, and so have ensured that a backup is available. This is key, as any loss of functionality will affect its ability to operate, given that the entire operations are carried out online. However, there are some problems with its general controls, which could severely disrupt business.

General controls

These are controls which relate to the computer environment and, hence, could affect any or all applications in use. These may be policies with regards to the treatment of hardware or procurement, for example, or could be specific security procedures which are in place. SRO appears to recognise the need for general controls by having a separate computer centre, with secure access, a firewall and a password system to protect against unauthorised access. However, despite this recognition, there are a number of areas where the general controls are inadequate.

The computer centre is not secured despite the capability to do so. The reason given is not sufficient to risk security controls for. Although the 'majority of staff' at headquarters are IT support personnel, there are still some staff who should not have access to the computer centre. Indeed, not all IT staff need access to the main servers. Temporary staff should not fulfil roles which are strategically important and so, to risk the entire operations by providing them with unrestricted access, SRO is not showing adequate control. Similarly, the use of a general user id and simple password means that they have access not just to the hardware, but to the entire system too. The user id and password would be simple to guess should anyone be attempting to hack into the system. SRO must immediately revert to the fingerprint access system, and must ensure that all staff are aware of the importance of preventing unauthorised access. The 'administrator' user should be removed immediately, and only those with administrator rights should be afforded them in conjunction with their unique user id. Temporary staff should be issued with unique user ids so that SRO can ascertain who has carried out any transactions on the system. In addition, users should be reminded of the necessity of changing passwords regularly and not writing them down anywhere. This could be enforced in training and by the provision of a procedures document.

The firewall has been turned off to allow the intelligent software to upload its finding onto SRO's system. Unfortunately, turning off the firewall not only allows this to happen, it also opens the systems to the threat of hackers. The firewall should be immediately re-installed. If it is finding difficulties with the application, it may be that there is a security risk with that. This should be thoroughly investigated and corrected.

SRO has taken precautions to have a backup system in place as contingency against disasters. However, the system should be in a remote location, rather than in the same location as the main servers. If there were a fire, for example, both the main servers and the backup servers would be affected. Similarly, by having a direct link between the servers, any data corruption or unauthorised access would affect both the servers and their backups. There should be a slight time delay in the connection to prevent this from happening, so immediately a problem is detected the link could be terminated, allowing the backup to be unaffected.

The controls mentioned above would affect all systems. There are some controls which affect only specific applications used by the organisation. These are known as application controls and help ensure that transactions are authorised, and are completely and accurately recorded, processed and reported.

Application controls

There are some issues with the application controls on the review system, which form a threat to the accuracy and reliability of the information provided on the system.

The intelligent software itself appears to provide out-of-date information and there is, currently, no way of assessing whether this is the case. A verification check may be necessary to ascertain the date of the initial posting of information and whether this is earlier or later than the date of information already held.

The reviews posted by users may, or may not, be a fair representation of the service offered. SRO does not verify that the information is correct, nor do they verify whether the users are who they claim to be. Indeed, the ability for users to post anonymously means that they could post whatever they like. There is a possibility that the users may be employed by the stores being reviewed, and giving positive reviews in order to benefit from them. Alternatively, they may be posting negative reviews about their competitors, again compromising the reliability and independence of the reviews. If this were happening, and were to be discovered, it could threaten the entire existence of SRO. It may be that a control needs to be included whereby reviewers can only submit a review if there has been an actual transaction with the store. Similarly, the stores should have the opportunity to respond to a review, made simpler if there is a transaction identifier available.

Overall, it appears that, despite having many of the tools in place, SRO is not using them adequately. Procedures should be clearly defined and adhered to in order to protect from such risks.

(b) There are two areas of concern identified by SRO:

Commercial conflicts of interest

SRO's business objective is to 'provide an unbiased review of online stores to ensure the customer has all available information'. So, to meet this objective they should focus on both the terms 'unbiased' and 'all available information'. The fact that SRO provides some reviews itself, which, although honest, seek to show certain stores in a positive light, goes against this objective.

The dilemma for SRO is that the online stores themselves provide both sets of revenue streams for SRO. It is in SRO's interest that the reviews are accurate, otherwise they will lose its users who rely on SRO for an honest and truthful review. Should they use another comparison site, or shop around themselves, SRO will no longer gain commission or advertising revenue. However, if the reviews are negative, it is also unlikely that the store in question will advertise in future on SRO's site and commission sales will also fall, as users of SRO's site will not follow links towards a store with negative reviews.

SRO either needs to change its business objective to remove the terms 'unbiased' and 'all available information', or they need to consider how to do this whilst maintaining their revenue streams. Ideally, the provision of honest reviews should encourage the stores to provide a good service at all times and then this would no longer be an issue.

Relocating company operations

SRO is considering moving its operations to an overseas country with tax and cost benefits. Whilst this may seem to be an attractive option from a financial perspective, there are other elements which should be considered.

The dilemma is that the benefits obtained financially may be counteracted by operational problems. The country they are considering relocating to is poorly regulated and does not have legislative controls with regards to the quality of information systems or security of data contained within them, even for personal data. This could lead to the risk of loss of personal data of the registered users, which could cause great reputational damage, should it occur. SRO has already recognised some control issues with its systems and it is likely that these would be worsened in a poorly regulated country.

It is mentioned that the country's culture is such that accepting unauthorised payments is considered acceptable, even if it is not publicly acknowledged. SRO would have the dilemma of whether to behave within the culture of the country, even though such business behaviour may be seen as illegal or considered unethical in its home nation, or whether to take a stance against it, and thus put themselves at a competitive disadvantage. The latter would be in line with their current code of conduct, but it may be difficult to convince locally sourced staff of this.

Given that Amy created the company quite recently, in 2010, with the aim of overcoming the unethical behaviour she perceived to exist in the online retail industry, it would appear that both of the dilemmas considered above would risk the entire paradigm of the company, its reason for existence.

3 **(a)** Dilip is justified in his decision to attempt to exploit the principles of electronic marketing, as companies can benefit greatly from this approach. The five principles referred to in the question requirement may be exploited as follows:

(i) **Intelligence**

The internet can be used as a low cost option of gathering intelligence about customers and potential customers. The website could use cookies to track the customers' mouse clicks, and see what has been of interest to them, and at what point they leave an area of the site. For example, do they get as far as looking at availability of a holiday and then leave the site when the price is displayed, or do they move on to another area on reading details about the hotel being offered? This can help to determine new product lines and other elements of the marketing mix.

If customers register on the site, then the company can also track their individual preferences over time, and this can help to exploit individualisation. As Dilip says, the company currently has no idea whether customers even read their brochure. The use of e-marketing will allow analysis of who visited which part of the site, how long they stayed there, whether they went on to get more information and how many times they re-visit the same page.

(ii) **Individualisation**

The current approach of sending the same marketing, covering all holidays, to every client is not appropriate for the luxury, bespoke service which Inspirations wishes to offer.

Inspirations should ensure it makes use of the features of promotion which offer individualisation, given that they are offering a bespoke service, which is, by its nature, individual. This is only possible if the company also exploits the use of intelligence, as previously mentioned. For example, if a customer has shown interest in gourmet food holidays, information relating to these can be shown on the home page. It may then offer a personalised home page when that customer visits again, with specific suggestions for them.

Customers should be able to save information on holidays which they are interested in and return to these. Inspirations could send emails if there is anything similar which may be of interest to those customers. Or, if a customer has booked a specific holiday in the past, such as a river cruise, the company may send them an email in the future with similar holidays.

(iii) Interactivity

This principle works on the idea of a 'pull' marketing approach, whereby the customers are driving the marketing and selling process, rather than the company 'pushing' its holidays at them. Given that the company wishes to sell bespoke holidays, this element is crucial.

The interactivity should begin with the use of search engines, such that when a potential customer types 'luxury holidays' or 'bespoke holidays', for example, Inspirations is one of the first to appear in the search results. Once on the website, the customer should be able to search from easy menus, such as 'destination' or 'holiday type'. The customer should then be shown a range of options, and further action on their part may lead them to further details regarding the holiday being viewed. In this way, the customer will only view holidays and further information which is of interest to them.

Further interactivity may be provided in the form of a two-way dialogue with a holiday adviser, through an online chat function. This could work well with HC's new business unit if the adviser is knowledgeable and able to offer enhanced services, such as managing the overall booking. This could be a valued differentiator for Inspirations: offering a personalised service, as if in-store, without the customer having to be inconvenienced by visiting the store.

(iv) Integration

Holiday companies could make great use of integration, which is about sharing knowledge and marketing activity between different parts of the company. For example, if customers switch to Inspirations holidays, having previously been a customer of HC, this information could be shared such that there is already some knowledge of the customers' preferences.

Inspirations could also integrate the different elements of the holiday experience and the databases of different companies supplying the services. For example, it may be possible for the customer to book hotels, flights, car hire and excursions. Inspirations could integrate the information, such that once a customer has booked a holiday, marketing information could be sent for the elements which have not been included. Once a holiday has been booked, the website may offer suggestions for upgrades and further options. If, for example, a holiday is booked at a particular destination, then trips available at that destination may be marketed. Depending upon the holiday purpose, different add-ons could be offered. For example, the gourmet trips for food lovers could forward details of excursions to food production facilities, with booking offers if combined with an existing holiday.

(v) Independence of location

Independence of location allows the possibility of selling into global markets. Provided Inspirations has access to flights departing from different countries, there is nothing to stop it operating as a global travel provider. It is intending to make more use of online sales, with the internet being the main source of marketing this new business, therefore high street branches are not necessary in this instance.

In order to exploit the global market, Inspirations must ensure that it offers the ability to view holiday prices, and pay, in foreign currencies. It should also ensure that it considers the current trends of holiday destinations for different markets worldwide.

(b) There are a number of influences which must be considered when determining a pricing strategy which will deliver the business and corporate objectives of an organisation.

Mission and objectives

Clearly, the objectives which are to be achieved should form a key element when determining the pricing strategy. HC's new business unit has the mission of 'delivering a high quality service for discerning travellers', and aims to 'achieve revenue of $100m by 2018'. If the business unit is aiming for high quality, then its pricing strategy should be in line with this, in order that customer perception is in line with what the company hopes to deliver. This may lead to a premium pricing strategy for Inspirations to maintain the suggestion of a difference between the standard holidays offered and the new range of holidays. Prices should be higher to reflect the quality offered. HC must also consider the desired revenue, 25% of total company revenue but only 5% of volume; this suggests that the pricing must be set at a higher level than current offerings in order to achieve this. Price is a key element in differentiating its product.

Whilst organisations may use discounting as an aid to getting market share, a clear objective of HC, the use of discounting, in this market segment, would contradict the desired message of premium quality.

Cost

If a price fails to take cost into consideration, then the organisation may not be profitable and difficulties may arise in the long term. Although organisations have been known to sell products as a loss leader in order to attract other purchases, it does not seem as if this would be an appropriate strategy for Inspirations. It must cover its costs when deciding its prices.

The premium holidays offered will make use of the best hotels, with high ratings and quality features, and intend to use premium airlines and seat options only. These will be costly to the company and should be incorporated into the price. Inspirations could choose to price each individual option on a 'cost plus margin' basis, or simply ensure that the overall cost is covered when deciding the final price using some other basis.

Competition

There are a number of competitors already operating in the luxury holiday market, and Inspirations must consider what it is charging for equivalent services. Given the transparency of information available over the internet, customers will easily be able to compare holidays and prices. Inspirations does not own the hotels it intends to use for the holidays offered, and will not have exclusive use of them. Therefore, the price should either match those offered by similar competitors, or they should differentiate in some way and therefore be able to charge a justifiably higher price.

Customers

Customers will have a limit regarding what they are prepared to pay for a particular offering. Inspirations must ensure that its pricing is within that limit for its target customer group. Given that these are luxury holidays, Inspirations are targeting higher income customers. Whilst price competition may not be the main focus for these customers, they will still want perceived value for money. This will determine the upper price they are prepared to pay.

Controls

There are a number of external influences affecting the travel industry. Although it is often the airline or the hotel company which is subjected to these influences, such as local passenger taxes and visa requirements, the holiday company must consider these when determining its pricing strategy. For example, should these be incorporated into the price of the holiday or shown separately? Also, can the airline or hotel companies impose controls on the holiday company, such as a legal requirement not to discount their prices in any way?

Overall, therefore, Inspirations should consider a combination of the above influences to ensure that it sets a price which delivers a profitable product which meets the corporate objectives.

4 **(a)** The head of the authority has not fully learned from the prior mistakes of WHPA's software projects. Had the four-stage process been followed, the authority might not have implemented systems which did not fulfil their needs, and caused operational difficulties.

The content of each of the stages, and their significance to this project and to WHPA, may be summarised as follows:

Stage one – Evaluate whether a COTS solution is an appropriate approach

The business case for the system should be assessed to determine whether a COTS solution is appropriate, or whether a bespoke system would be better suited to the needs of the organisation. The head of the authority seems fairly clear that a COTS would be most appropriate, although the decision appears to be mainly on cost grounds. It is likely that this would be important, given that the majority of funding is from taxation, but it should not be the only deciding factor. Complexity of a process often has an impact on whether a COTS package is appropriate, as does the availability of suitable packages. It does not seem in this scenario that the process to be automated is particularly complex and it also seems relatively routine in nature. This would need to be verified, but if it were true, then the COTS approach is probably the more appropriate.

If this stage were omitted, it is possible that the authority would make the wrong choices on the basis of cost alone. This could make the entire project a waste of time and funding as it may lead to another failure.

Stage two – Define the requirements for the new software

It is quite clear from the scenario that WHPA has suffered in the past from a failure to define requirements correctly. Hence, this is not a good reason for omitting this step entirely. The head of the authority suggests they 'go straight to stage three and look at competing packages to see which provides the best features', but it would be impossible to ascertain which was most suited if the requirements had not been defined. Indeed, if they omit this step, then it is likely that this system will also require workarounds as the previous systems have done.

Requirements defined within this step will encompass various functional and non-functional requirements. Functional requirements should include the operational processes which must be possible using this system, such as the ability to adjust payroll for one-off events. It is important to consider potential future requirements, such that the system will continue to be valuable into the future.

Non-functional requirements may include requirements from the supplier, such as support mechanisms. It would appear that WHPA is limited in its IT support provision, so this may be considered an important requirement.

There may also be technical requirements. It is likely that the authority will not wish to spend more than necessary and therefore it could be essential that the software is able to operate on the existing hardware.

Stage three – Evaluate competing packages

Given the responsibility towards the public in providing a value for money service, it is important that WHPA gets the best package in terms of meeting their needs within budgetary constraints. By evaluating competing packages, rather than simply considering one, the value for money should be greater as the best package will be selected.

The evaluation process could follow a 'tender' approach, whereby suppliers bid to supply the software required, giving feedback to them on which requirements are met (or not) and to what extent. The process should certainly be formalised, and this could help to provide accountability to the public that the best system has been selected. The tenders should be evaluated against the requirements given at stage two, in addition to any other criteria, such as implementation deadlines, overall budget, etc. The comparison may use a weighted ranking basis to ensure the decision is not based on a single factor, but gives the best option overall. Without this, a public organisation may be tempted to simply choose the cheapest option, given their budgetary limitations.

Stage four – Implement the selected package

There should be a planned implementation which includes testing, training, installation and data transfer. This is a key part of the process which connects strongly with the overall reliability of the system. A system which is not tested adequately by users (in addition to the software developers) may not meet the needs of the organisation, or may be found to be lacking user-friendliness. A failure to train staff could lead to resistance and problems in data transfer could invalidate the entire output of the software.

(b) The HR director is concerned that the focus is simply on the information technology rather than the people, processes and organisational structure. The POPIT model recognises the equal importance of each when enhancing a business process. This has been developed to take a more holistic view of process change, considering those elements which could affect the success of the project.

Processes seem to be a key area which should be considered. One process which is particularly important is the level of IT support available within the organisation. Organisations with poor IT support in place are likely to need to address this, as part of process improvement. WHPA has been subjected to system workarounds, having to 'fiddle' data to achieve the desired output in the payroll and HRM systems, for example. This is probably due to the very limited IT support available.

Manual processes should be identified to determine whether there is scope to eliminate these. It would appear that this has already been done to an extent by considering the need for an ERPS to assist in organisation-wide reporting, currently a labour-intensive process. WHPA should take the opportunity to see whether there are other such processes which could be eliminated. Given the few processes described, none of which seem to run efficiently, it is likely that there may be others.

The organisation aspect of the POPIT model considers elements of structure, management configuration and support and roles and responsibilities, for example. The board seems to support this change in the organisation, but it is likely to also impact upon the management in the individual hospitals. It needs to be considered whether the management in the separate areas of the organisation will support this change. If not, it could have an impact on the success of the change project. The board may need to convince them that the new system will make life easier for all, rather than be introduced to 'spy' on their budgeting and management control systems.

Roles and responsibilities should also be considered, specifically within the change process itself. Who will be involved in the change project and how will it affect their day-to-day roles? They will need to be given clear guidance of what is expected as well as the resources needed. For example, it seems that the head of the authority is keen to keep costs low; those involved would need to be assured that the project would be given sufficient resources to succeed.

People can be a key reason for failure of a project. If there is resistance, then it may impede the progress of the project, impact upon the end result, or even halt a project completely. Staff morale and motivation should be taken into consideration and the authority should ensure that any possible negative impact is mitigated. It may be that reward systems need to be introduced which align with the new process and ultimately the goals of the authority.

The skills also need to be considered. It would appear that the authority does not currently run a high level of information systems. Therefore, personnel may not be in possession of adequate skills for the new system. This is itself can be a cause for resistance. Training should be considered as part of the change process.

Although IT skills may not be fully present, the staff should be skilled in their individual area of work. For this reason, they should be encouraged to participate in the design of the new system. Had this happened in the past, the systems might have been designed to fully meet departmental needs, rather than finding workarounds.

Overall, therefore, the HR director is right to consider the other elements of the POPIT model, as to do so should positively affect the outcome of this project.

1 **(a)** 1 mark for each appropriate point within each department up to a maximum of 5 marks. Four departments are under consideration giving a total maximum of 20 marks.

(b) Up to a maximum of 12 marks.

For both standard and bespoke windows (4 marks each) – as below:

– Effective machine time per day (1 mark)
– Number of units produced per day (0·5 marks)
– Wastage per day (1 mark)
– Revenue (0·5 marks)
– Production cost (0·5 marks)
– Daily contribution (0·5 marks)

Recognition that this is based on current pattern (1 mark)
No consideration of overheads (up to 2 marks)
Sensitivity analysis (up to 2 marks)

(c) 1 mark for each aspect of the value chain/department up to a maximum of 4 marks per department up to a maximum of 14 marks.

Professional marks are given for the structure, tone, coherence and clarity of your briefing paper (4 marks).

2 **(a)** Up to 1 mark for each appropriate point up to a maximum of 15 marks.

(b) Up to 1 mark for each appropriate point up to a maximum of 10 marks.

3 **(a)** Up to 3 marks per heading discussed, up to a maximum of 15 marks.

(b) Up to 2 marks per heading discussed, up to a maximum of 10 marks.

4 **(a)** Up to 4 marks per heading. Up to a maximum of 16 marks overall.

(b) Up to 3 marks per heading. Up to a maximum of 9 marks overall.

Professional Level – Essentials Module

Business Analysis

September/December 2016 – Sample Questions

Time allowed: 3 hours 15 minutes

This question paper is divided into two sections:

Section A – This ONE question is compulsory and MUST be attempted

Section B – TWO questions ONLY to be attempted

Do NOT open this question paper until instructed by the supervisor.

This question paper must not be removed from the examination hall.

Think Ahead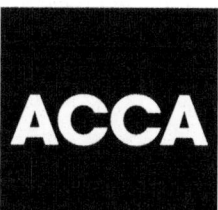

The Association of
Chartered Certified
Accountants

1 Introduction

Man Lal relaxed in business class as the aircraft skimmed across the Uril Mountains. Generally he considered himself a contented man. He had successfully built his company, Ling, to be the largest light bulb manufacturing company in the world, with global revenues of $750m. From its factories in Lindisztan it supplied a worldwide market for LED (light emitting diodes) light bulbs. Lal congratulated himself on the fact that he had quickly spotted the potential of LED light bulbs and had entered large-scale production whilst his rivals were still focusing their production on candescent and halogen bulbs. The world now realised that LED light bulbs provided a cheaper, more energy efficient, greener solution than all of its alternatives. To that end, many countries had passed legislation requiring domestic and business consumers to replace candescent light bulbs with greener equivalents. In fact, he was on his way right now to Skod, a country which had passed efficient lighting legislation which, from 2017, banned the use of candescent bulbs in commercial premises and outlawed their production and importation after that date. Domestic consumers were expected to replace their candescent bulbs with newer technology as their bulbs failed. Man Lal confidently expected that LED would be, for many, the newer technology of choice.

The visit to Skod was of great significance to Man Lal because it was here that he did his business studies degree at Skodmore University. Indeed, he was due to give a lecture to the staff and students of the university the following day and he felt great personal pride in returning to describe the extent of his success and the fulfilment of his personal ambitions. He was also planning to visit a company called Flick which Ling was considering acquiring. This would be a new growth method for Ling. Up to now its worldwide expansion had been achieved by establishing wholly owned distribution companies in each targeted country. All production had remained in Lindisztan. However, for various reasons, Ling was now considering entering the Skod market by acquiring one of its light bulb producers, Flick.

In fact, remembering this brought a slight frown across Man Lal's face. To help fund his global expansion, he had sold 49% of Ling to institutional investors. These institutional investors required growth and high dividends and he was having difficulty meeting their demands. There was now very little growth in the domestic Lindisztan market and the distribution approach used to expand into foreign countries was taking a long time to mature. The investors were demanding quicker growth and acquisitions appeared to promise this. Despite paying high dividends over the last few years, the company still had significant retained profits and this was another issue for the institutional shareholders. They felt that this money should be used to promote growth and have agreed to a $400m acquisition fund. So, thought Man Lal, what better place to start those acquisitions than Skod, the place where I studied as a poor overseas student so many years ago. However, he had to admit to himself, he was still much happier with organic growth through setting up his own distribution companies. Ling had made a few acquisitions in Lindisztan, but had never bought a foreign company and he was worried about the risk of failure.

Turbulence buffeted the aircraft as it made its final descent into the capital of Skod. To distract himself, Man Lal picked up the latest copy of *Lighting Tomorrow*, the research magazine of the light bulb industry. He skim read an article on tubular daylight lighting which promised to reduce the need for electric lighting by introducing more daylight into a building. Effective daylighting (it said) is achieved through the strategic placement of skylights and windows, as well as lighting controls which monitor available daylight and respond as needed to decrease or increase electric lighting. Perhaps I need to look into this, thought Man Lal.

At the airport, Man Lal took a taxi to his hotel. He could not help but notice that Skod was not as neat and tidy as it used to be. A lot of shops and buildings had been closed down and there was graffiti across many buildings and bridges. 'Skod for Skodders', said one, 'Skod jobs for Skod people', said another. Man Lal remembered now that the Skod nationalist movement had become increasingly popular. He mentioned this to the taxi driver. 'Yes', he said, 'Most people are fed up with Skod being pushed around by the International Financing Consortium (IFC), we want prosperity and jobs for people who grew up here.'

Slightly unnerved, Man Lal, checked in at the hotel. He switched on the television. He watched with interest as Niklas Perch, the newly elected nationalist leader of the Skod government, outlined his plans for the future.

'We are committed to a return to prosperity', he said. 'To achieve this we have to make some short-term adjustments which may be unpopular with our trading partners. We are currently considering the imposition of import taxes as a way of protecting our home industry. We wish to create a protected commercial environment here in Skod in which our companies can prosper.

'We must also ask our citizens to continue with their energy saving measures. As you know, the government has agreed that all street lighting will be turned off from 2300 hours to 0500 hours. I have also decreed that all government offices must proactively embrace energy saving lighting and heating. In the same way, I expect our citizens to look at ways of saving money and energy.

'The government also recognises that the country continues to be in a recession, and that disposable income is falling for all people. However, I cannot condone the recent demonstrations against, and boycott of, foreign goods and food products. We must rebuild our country peacefully and legally. I would ask all citizens to support me in this.'

Just then, the air conditioning failed and the television went off. Another energy failure in Skod. There were three further failures that night. The hotel manager apologised to Man Lal in the morning. 'I am sorry', he said 'but despite higher energy prices, this is an increasing feature of life in Skod.'

Skod electric light bulb industry

All electric light bulbs are largely made out of glass and metal and this is likely to remain the same in the foreseeable future. In Skod, 90% of glass is produced by three companies. However, for all of these three companies, light bulb manufacturers are unimportant customers. Most glass manufacture goes to the construction industry, light bulb manufacturers take less than 0·5% of the country's glass production. Metal manufacture in Skod is dominated by one company, OmniMetal. Most metal is sold to the automobile industry. Light bulb manufacturers take less than 0·1% of OmniMetal's production. However, the quality of glass and metal required by the light bulb manufacturers is quite standard, so switching between suppliers is, in theory, relatively easy. Light bulb manufacture takes place in factories which require substantial initial investment and have no obvious alternative use.

In Skod, light bulbs are low cost commodity products which are replaced infrequently by domestic consumers. Commercial consumers change their light bulbs a little more often and some businesses have recently switched all their bulbs to LED to save energy, reduce costs in the long term and to reflect their aspirations as 'green businesses'. There is very little brand awareness in the light bulb market and all the light bulbs have to fit the standard sockets used in the country.

Electric light bulb manufacture in Skod is dominated by the five companies listed in Table One. Two years ago a large American light bulb manufacturer, Krysal, attempted to enter the market. The five dominant companies in the industry reacted to this by cutting prices, running marketing campaigns which emphasised the benefits to the country of home-based production and lobbying supermarket groups to not stock products produced by the new entrant. Krysal withdrew from the market after six months. When not focused on fighting new entrants, the five main competitors are regularly involved in price cutting, disruption of competitors' distribution channels and aggressive marketing.

Company	Revenue (2015)	Revenue (2010)
Voltface	$85m	$80m
LiteWorld	$80m	$80m
Flick	$70m	$65m
ABC	$65m	$60m
L2L	$60m	$60m
Other companies	$140m	$145m
Total	$500m	$490m

Table One: Skod-based light bulb manufacturers

The products produced by the Skod light bulb industry are largely sold through supermarket groups (50%), household product superstores (30%) and large electrical chains (10%). The rest of the production is sold through small shops, except for a tiny percentage of production (less than 1%) which is sold directly to large organisations, such as government departments. However, light bulbs do not constitute a large sales item for any of these distribution channels. In fact, in a recent report, light bulb sales were one of the products which contributed less than 0·1% of a major supermarket's revenue.

The light bulb companies in Skod have largely focused on candescent (60% of production) and halogen (30% of production) technologies. Man Lal intends to fund the updating of the production facilities at Flick to allow the production of LED lights, alongside the continued production of candescent and halogen light bulbs. He wants to achieve this before domestic competitors in Skod gear up their own LED light bulb production. He believes that Ling's competencies in LED manufacture will give Flick a head start. Initial discussions with Flick suggest that the company is open to acquisition and a bid price has been agreed which is acceptable to both parties. Financial information for Flick and the Skod light bulb industry as a whole is shown in Appendix One.

[P.T.O.

Appendix One: Financial information for Flick and the Skod light bulb industry

Extract from financial statements

All figures in $millions

	Flick 2015	Skod industry totals 2015
Assets		
Non-current assets		
Property, plant, equipment	190	1,635
Goodwill	10	100
Total non-current assets	200	1,735
Current assets		
Inventory	45	200
Trade receivables	20	250
Cash and cash equivalents	35	115
Total current assets	100	565
Total assets	300	2,300
Equity and liabilities		
Share capital	150	1,000
Retained earnings	50	340
Non-current liabilities		
Long-term borrowings	70	750
Current liabilities		
Trade payables	29	200
Current tax payable	1	10
Total current liabilities	30	210
Total liabilities	100	960
Total equity and liabilities	300	2,300
Revenue	70·0	500·0
Cost of sales	(55·0)	(350·0)
Gross profit	15·0	150·0
Administrative expenses	(4·0)	(30·0)
Profit before tax and interest	11·0	120·0
Finance cost	(2·5)	(50·0)
Profit before tax	8·5	70·0
Tax expense	(1·0)	(12·0)
Profit for the period	7·5	58·0

Note: The Industry total column is for the Skod light bulb industry as a whole (including Flick).

Required:

(a) Analyse the macro-environmental factors affecting the Skod light bulb industry using a PESTEL framework. Your analysis should reflect the fact that Ling might enter this industry directly by setting up a distribution company for its products or through the acquisition of Flick. (7 marks)

(b) Assess the attractiveness of the Skod light bulb industry using Porter's Five Forces framework. (13 marks)

(c) Ling is considering entering the Skod light bulb industry by acquiring Flick.

Evaluate the potential acquisition of Flick by Ling from the perspectives of suitability and acceptability.
(18 marks)

(d) The finance director of Ling is concerned that Ling has no expertise in acquiring foreign companies and he is advocating a strategic partnership with Flick instead.

Discuss the appropriateness of such an approach to facilitating Ling's proposed entry into the Skod light bulb market. (8 marks)

Professional marks are available in question 1 for the structure, coherence, style and clarity of your answer.
(4 marks)

(50 marks)

Section B – TWO questions ONLY to be attempted

2 Webfilms was originally a film rental organisation, offering DVD rentals which were sent to customers and returned using parcel couriers. Webfilms enrolled members who paid a monthly fee and could rent as many films as they liked, receiving their next choice as soon as a previous film was returned. However, Webfilms found this model was not as successful as it had hoped. It struggled to gain a large customer base and high courier fees made it difficult for the company to make a reasonable profit.

The company underwent a radical strategic change and remodelled itself as an internet television network screening films and drama series. This service is now available in over 25 countries worldwide. All programmes are original and so have not been previously shown on any television channel in any country. The programmes are all produced by a creative team at Webfilms, headed by Paolo Butterfield, and all are only available in English. Members pay a monthly subscription charge and have access to unlimited viewing. Webfilms relies entirely on member subscriptions for funding as, to enhance the customer experience, its programmes do not carry advertising. Webfilms considers itself to be a focused differentiator, offering only programmes which it feels will attract a younger audience (the teens and twenties).

Until recently, Webfilms had no close competitors in this form of internet television. Indeed, it was the main substitute for traditional television channels, causing a downturn in that industry. However, its success has been noted and this has led to the emergence of a number of competitors in different countries. These competitors have recognised and capitalised on any perceived weakness of Webfilms. So, for example, some of them include programmes which are not in English and others also include popular programmes which have also been shown on other television channels. This means that customers need to only subscribe to one television service.

The CEO of Webfilms, who previously transformed the organisation from a postal to internet-based service, has recognised that strategic change is required in order for Webfilms to continue competing effectively in a dynamic market environment. Her proposal to the board included the following key points:

- The creation of a wider range of new programmes, including documentaries and current affairs programmes
- The inclusion of popular programmes which were created for one country's viewers being shown in other countries
- Broadening the types of programmes so that the company can appeal to all age ranges
- Introduction of on-screen advertisements to create another revenue stream
- Translation of the most popular programmes into languages other than English
- The introduction of new services including broadband provision and online gaming
- A focus on efficiency, using the existing customer base to expand and to gain economies of scale, before any new competitors can gain a large market share
- The drive for efficiency should not be at the cost of quality, allowing the company to operate a hybrid strategy

The CEO is keen to pursue a boundary-less organisational model. Three options are presented in her proposal:

Hollow – where *non-core processes* are outsourced to external providers.
Modular – a hollow organisation which outsources some elements of the *production process*.
Virtual – an organisation with no formal geographical structure, but operates through a series of linked IT systems, partnerships and collaborative agreements.

She further stated that it would be imperative to set **all** the new key points of the strategy in place as soon as possible, to be implemented on a pre-announced date, with a large marketing campaign to support it.

At a meeting with the creative director, Paolo Butterfield expressed concerns about many of the changes being suggested: 'This is an effective demotion for me and my team. Customers pay their monthly fees because they love what we do, and yet you want to change it. Why are we following the crowd, when our existing business model is successful?' The CEO responded, 'There is no demotion. You will still be responsible for the creative element, just not producing all the programmes. This will allow you to take a much more strategic view of what we show, where and in what language. Argue as much as you like, but this is going to happen, it's up to you whether you want to be involved in deciding how such change will take place.'

The meeting ended with some disharmony and a further meeting was arranged to determine which form of boundary-less working would be the most appropriate for Webfilms.

Required:

(a) Balogun and Hope Hailey developed a change model which examines the contextual features which can influence the success or failure of strategic change.

Assess how five of the internal contextual features defined in Balogun and Hope Hailey's model (time, scope, readiness, preservation and power) would influence the likely success or failure of the strategic change proposed by the CEO for Webfilms. (16 marks)

(b) **Discuss how the different models of boundary-less working (hollow, modular and virtual) might be used to deliver parts of the CEO's future strategy for Webfilms.** (9 marks)

(25 marks)

3 Retail World (RW) is a major international retail chain, selling groceries, clothing, electronic items, toiletries and homeware items. It has grown rapidly across a number of different countries, offering a broad product range to suit a wide range of customer segments. Growth has been through the expansion of existing stores, in addition to the opening of new stores.

The new finance director, whose background is in a non-retail environment, is keen to understand the sales trends of the organisation, as well as the industry, in order to help develop a strategy which can take advantage of these trends in the future. A business analyst has provided summarised internal sales data for this purpose. The company's IT systems are fully integrated and associated controls are rigorous, allowing the data to be manipulated in many ways. The analyst has provided time series analysis (Figure 1) and regression analysis (Figures 2 and 3). He wanted to explore the possibility of identifying different causal relationships, carrying out least squares regression analysis linking sales to both time (Figure 2) and number of stores in operation (Figure 3).

The number of stores has grown annually and the analyst believes that this is a better indicator of the expected future revenue than simply the passage of time. The average number of stores expected to be in operation in 2017 is 3,700 rising to 4,000 in 2018.

Figure 1 – Time series analysis

Year/quarter	Sales ($m)	Trend (T)	Deviation	Svar (1)	Res	Sadj (2)
2013 2	88					116·25
2013 3	110					121·38
2013 4	134	121·38	12·63	14·60	–1·98	119·40
2014 1	150	122·50	27·50	25·02	2·48	124·98
2014 2	95	123·25	–28·25	–28·25	0·00	123·25
2014 3	112	123·75	–11·75	–11·38	–0·38	123·38
2014 4	138	124·38	13·63	14·60	–0·98	123·40
2015 1	150	126·00	24·00	25·02	–1·02	124·98
2015 2	100	128·63	–28·63	–28·25	–0·38	128·25
2015 3	120	131·38	–11·38	–11·38	0·00	131·38
2015 4	151	134·00	17·00	14·60	2·40	136·40
2016 1	159	136·00	23·00	25·02	–2·02	133·98
2016 2	112					140·25
2016 3	124					135·38

Notes:

(1) Svar is the expected seasonal variation, calculated by averaging the variations of each quarter.
(2) Sadj is the sales total, adjusted for average seasonal variation.

Figure 2 – Least squares regression analysis (time)

An extract of the values used in the calculation of this is shown below. This illustrates the basis of the regression analysis. **All values** were used in the calculation of the least squares regression formula.

Year/quarter	quarter (x)	revenue (y)
2016 1	12	159
2016 2	13	112
2016 3	14	124

The least squares regression formula derived from **all data** was found to be:

$$Y = 110.93 + 1.81x \qquad r = 0.33$$

Figure 3 – Least squares regression analysis (number of stores)

The values used in the calculation of this are shown below:

Year	stores (x)	average quarterly sales (y)
2013	2,400	111
2014	2,750	124
2015	3,200	130
2016	3,512	132

The least squares regression formula derived from this data was found to be:

$Y = 69.50 + 0.02x$ $\quad\quad\quad\quad$ $r = 0.94$

The finance director was interested to receive the analysis, saying, 'We can use this to estimate what our revenues might be in the future, both quarterly and annually.' However, he also stated that it was not quite as useful as he would have hoped for, commenting, 'I have been hearing a lot about big data at industry meetings I have attended. I think we should investigate the ways in which we could use this, and the benefits we might hope to obtain from it.'

Required:

(a) **Analyse the data given above in the time series analysis and least squares regression analysis (Figures 1, 2 and 3) and evaluate the appropriateness of each technique in forecasting future sales and developing strategic plans.** (15 marks)

(b) **Discuss how three 'Vs' of big data (volume, velocity and variety) could be used to enhance strategic development within RW.** (10 marks)

(25 marks)

4 Introduction

Maratec is a bespoke furniture company, making unique pieces of furniture to clients' specifications. The products are manufactured using a combination of highly technical machinery and skilled craftsmen. Maratec's current clients are wealthy individuals who want a custom-built piece of furniture for their own homes. The company has one showroom where samples of bespoke pieces of furniture are displayed. These sample pieces are not for sale.

The company wishes to implement a planned growth strategy. To enable this, the company has increased its manufacturing capacity with the aim of selling to corporate clients such as hotels. Producing a greater number of bespoke pieces for the same client would deliver some economies of scale. The production manager claims this strategy would reduce set up times and increase procurement discounts, as raw materials would be bought in bulk.

Procurement

High quality materials are used in bespoke furniture manufacture and Maratec uses a specialist procurement company to source specific materials, such as high quality pieces of oak wood of given dimensions. This is an expensive method of procurement and can also delay production, as Maratec cannot confirm an order with the procurement company until a design is agreed with a client. As order to delivery time is already high, Maratec is keen to reduce this procurement time.

The production manager has suggested the implementation of e-procurement, to support planned business growth. He is considering moving to e-procurement, but is keen to ensure that such a move will not lead to a lower quality of raw materials. If e-procurement is adopted, the company will recruit a full-time procurement manager and cancel its agreement with the specialist procurement company.

Marketing

Until now, Maratec has relied predominantly on word-of-mouth marketing. Most new clients have commissioned pieces of furniture after seeing a bespoke piece in an existing client's home. High quality brochures are produced annually and are available on request. They are also placed on display at exhibitions and in the showroom. A new marketing manager has been recruited and has been tasked with analysing whether e-marketing could enhance the current marketing mix. The marketing manager has also identified the following issues:

Visualisation of the product – Because the products are bespoke, it is difficult for a client to visualise what the finished product will look like. This can sometimes lead to a failure to make a sale, as the customer is not sure what they are getting.

Pricing – As materials are not sourced until a design is agreed, it is difficult to provide accurate up-front prices. Maratec currently uses cost plus pricing, but the marketing manager understands that this may deter some clients.

Showroom – There is only one showroom and it is not considered worthwhile opening more as more pieces of furniture would have to be created especially to furnish it. Therefore it is not possible for many potential clients to see the quality of the furniture.

After-sale support

As there is no guaranteed delivery time for the products, Maratec provides production progress updates to their clients on request. When the client phones or emails, the production team photograph the work-in-progress and send the pictures to the client. The client can also visit the manufacturing plant to check on progress, but this requires prior arrangement due to legal health and safety requirements.

Maratec intends to remain a producer of bespoke furniture items. It does not wish to produce standard products or produce to inventory. The only non-commissioned pieces of furniture it produces are for display in the showroom.

Required:

(a) **Evaluate the use of e-marketing at Maratec to enhance each of following five elements of the marketing mix: price, promotion, place, processes and physical evidence.**   (15 marks)

(b) **Describe the principles of e-procurement and explain the benefits and risks to Maratec.**   (10 marks)

(25 marks)

End of Question Paper

Answers

1 (a) A PESTEL analysis identifies the main drivers in the external environment which are largely outside the control of the company. The relevance of these factors may depend upon whether Ling decides to enter the light bulb market directly or to enter it by acquiring a Skod-based company. In some instances the driver affects the industry wherever it is based.

Political

The government is considering the imposition of import taxes. This would be a threat if Ling decides to enter the market place using the distribution company approach and keep manufacturing in Lindisztan. However, it presents an opportunity if Ling decides to acquire Flick and continue to run it as a Skod-based company.

Economic

Although the country of Skod is in recession and consumer disposable income is falling, it seems unlikely that such a low cost commodity product will be greatly affected. This is an industry which is unlikely to be touched by changes in economic prosperity. The only minor issue may be the effect of switching off street lights. This may lengthen the life span of the bulb. However, overall, this is likely to have very little effect on total light bulb demand.

Sociocultural

There is a growing nationalist movement in Skod who are keen to keep jobs within the country. There have been instances, in other industries, where imported goods have been boycotted. It seems unlikely that a backlash against foreign goods would affect such an unglamorous product as a light bulb. However, it is possible, and any potential consumer backlash can be avoided by buying a Skod-based company and manufacturing light bulbs in the country.

Technical

Ling has so far benefitted from technological innovations which has put it ahead of competitors who have focused on candescent and halogen bulbs. However, other lighting initiatives, such as the tubular daylighting devices discussed in the *Lighting Tomorrow* article need to be continually monitored. This monitoring is required whether Ling enters the Skod market directly, or acquires a company such as Flick.

Legal

The 'efficient lighting' legislation due to become law in Skod in 2017 is an opportunity for Ling to enter the market with its innovative LED products. This is an opportunity whether the company enters the market directly or buys a home-based company such as Flick.

Environmental

Businesses and consumers in Skod are increasingly aware of energy issues. This is partly due to increasing energy prices as well as more frequent breaks in the electricity supply (such as the power cuts which affected Lal's hotel). The LED bulbs offered by Ling are greener and more efficient than candescent and halogen bulbs, which are still widely made in the home industry. In the case of businesses, many are quickly moving to LED light bulbs to reduce running costs and boost their environmental credentials. The environmental attractions of its products is important to Ling but again this is independent of whether they are made by a home-based company or one based abroad.

   (b) **Bargaining power of buyers**

In this scenario, the buyers of the industry's products are large supermarket groups, household product superstores and large electrical chains. These buyers, particularly the supermarket groups, purchase a large volume of the industry's products (90%) and so, on the face of it, they can demand favourable prices. However, the products the buyer purchases from the industry represents a relatively insignificant fraction of the buyer's costs or purchases. A recent report suggested that light bulb sales contributed less than 0·1% of a supermarket's revenue. Light bulbs are much less important to supermarket groups than food and drink. When the product sold by the industry is a small fraction of the buyers' total costs, then buyers are less price sensitive. They are more likely to bargain with food suppliers than light bulb suppliers.

Buyers' bargaining power in the light bulb industry is strengthened by the product being undifferentiated, with low customer switching costs. However, the buyers are extremely unlikely to move backwards in the supply chain to manufacture their own light bulbs and so this potentially limits their bargaining power. Again, their focus is likely to be elsewhere.

Some of the factors which concern the buyer also relate to the consumer (end customer) as well. To the end customer, light bulbs are undifferentiated and there are no switching costs. Light bulbs are an insignificant fraction of their total spend and so they are unlikely to shop around to get the lowest price.

Bargaining power of suppliers

A supplier group is more powerful if it is dominated by a few companies and is more concentrated than the industry it sells to. This appears to be the case in Skod, where 90% of glass production is accounted for by three companies and metal production is largely concentrated in the hands of one very large company, OmniMetal. The customers (such as Flick) are large but they are more fragmented than the suppliers. Furthermore, the supplier group is, by and large, not obliged to contend with other substitute products for sale to the industry. Light bulbs are largely made of glass and metal and it seems unlikely that this will change in the near future. This lack of substitutes increases the power of the supplier.

The industry is not an important customer of the supplier group. Most glass is sold to the construction industry. Most metal is sold to the automobile industry. The light bulb manufacturers use less than 0·5% of the country's glass production and less than 0·1% of its metal production. This lack of importance increases the supplier group's power, because suppliers' fortunes are not closely tied to the industry and they will not need to protect it through reasonable pricing. Another factor increasing suppliers' power is that the products (glass and metal) are a vital part of the buyers' (customers) light bulb business. On the other hand, the supplier group's products are largely undifferentiated and switching costs between suppliers appears to be reasonably low. Finally, it seems unlikely that the supplier group poses a credible threat of forward integration into light bulb manufacture and this will be a factor which reduces supplier bargaining power.

Threat of new entrants

Ling is considering entering this market and so the barriers to entry and the potential reaction of current suppliers is important to consider here. The main barriers to entry appear to be:

Economies of scale: The five large dominant companies in the industry should be enjoying economies of scale which force any potential new entrant to come into the market with large scale production, which carries with it a high risk of failure. This is not an issue for Ling who also currently enjoys economies of scale in its manufacture. However, it will deter many other entrants.

Capital requirements: The manufacture of light bulbs requires new entrants to invest large financial resources into production plants. Although capital may be available, the risk associated with large-scale entry may lead to high premiums on borrowed capital.

Access to distribution channels: This may be very significant, as the distribution channels are very specific (supermarket groups, large home products superstores and major electrical chains). The new entrant will have to persuade these channels to accept its products, perhaps through offering price discounts. It seems unlikely that the new entrant can create a completely new channel. Selling directly to the consumer seems unlikely in this industry where individual purchases are both infrequent and low value.

The reaction to new entrants of existing firms in the industry is likely to be relatively forceful as they have a history of vigorous retaliation to prospective entrants. The upsurge of nationalism in the country will also give them a powerful card to play in this retaliation.

Threat of substitute products

Substitute products are products which can perform the same function as the product of the industry under consideration. It is hard to envisage any potential substitute for light bulbs except for candles which, in the long term, are likely to be much more expensive. Another possible substitute is to do without. This is the approach taken by government policy on street lighting. It is turned off from 2300 hrs to 0500 hrs. However, it seems unlikely that many consumers will prefer to sit in the dark instead of using a relatively cheap lighting product. In the short term, the threat of substitute products seems very low. However, in the long term, the tubular daylight lighting initiative described in *Lighting Tomorrow* is a possible substitute product as it aims to reduce the need for electric lighting.

Competitive rivalry in the industry

Equally balanced competitors. When an industry is dominated by a few firms and these firms are relatively well balanced in terms of size, it creates potential instability because they may be prone to fight each other. This appears the case in Skod where five fairly similar sized firms produce 72% (2015) of the light bulbs sold in the country and wage short-term price cutting wars, disrupt competitors' supply lines and react aggressively to potential new entrants.

Slow industry growth. Despite the switch to new technologies, there is little market growth. From 2010 to 2015 the market only grew by just over 2%. In such a situation, the only way a firm can increase market share is to take it from one of its competitors. Consequently, slow industry growth increases competitive rivalry.

Lack of differentiation or switching costs. Competitive rivalry is increased where the product is perceived as a commodity. In such circumstances the buyer's decision is largely based on price and service and pressures for intense price and service competition result. Light bulbs are definitely a commodity product in Skod.

High exit barriers. Exit costs are high because of the investment required in plant and the fact that light bulb factories cannot easily be adapted for other uses. When exit costs are high, companies hang on in the industry often resorting to extreme tactics which weaken the profitability of the industry as a whole.

(c) One of the elements of **suitability** is a consideration of how well the strategy fits with future trends and changes in the environment. This environment has already been considered in the PESTEL and five forces analysis. Acquiring Flick is particularly appropriate in the context of the government's threat to impose taxes on imported goods. The increasingly nationalistic Skod population can also be acknowledged if the acquisition is carefully handled. Ling can stress that it is investing in Flick to secure its future and to create jobs for the people of Skod. The impending efficient lighting legislation also provides an opportunity for Ling, but this is irrespective of whether the company enters the market directly or acquires Flick. However, it is better placed to quickly meet this demand through acquisition. Direct entry is generally a slower approach to growth, as Man Lal has acknowledged.

Entering the market through acquisition also means that it can use the effective distribution channels which are already in place. There is no guarantee that the established distribution channels would welcome a new entrant into the market and indeed they may demand price reductions in exchange for distribution access. Acquisition also means that no new capacity is brought to the market. Ling can then focus on increasing market share in a competitive, relatively slow-growing market. Entering directly is likely to prompt a hostile reaction from competitors currently in the market. Acquiring Flick might also invoke a hostile reaction, but it is likely to be more muted because it does not immediately alter the balance of power in the market.

However, in the longer term, the worldwide size of Ling may affect the bargaining power of suppliers and buyers in the Skod market. As a group, it has revenues which exceed the Skod market total, so there may be possibilities for negotiating reductions in raw material costs and the profit margins of suppliers. If these savings are not passed on to the end consumer, then Ling's profitability will inevitably improve. If these savings are passed on, then Ling will begin to dominate a commodity market place.

A further element of suitability is whether the acquisition provides an opportunity to exploit the strategic capability of Ling. In one sense it does, as it provides an opportunity for it to exploit its technical capability in LED lighting, before the domestic industry can gear up its production levels. However, in another sense the strategy is not suitable because Ling does not have strategic capability in acquiring foreign companies. All of its growth has been achieved through setting up wholly owned distribution subsidiaries. Its only production factories are in Lindisztan.

Acquisition also has to meet the expectations of the stakeholders. In terms of the institutional stakeholders who hold 49% of Ling's shares, the acquisition promises the rapid growth which they are lobbying for. They have been critical of Ling's slow, cautious foreign growth and the maturity of the Lindisztan market means that there is little opportunity for growth there. The institutional shareholders have also been critical of the high levels of retained earnings and they wish to see a significant portion of it invested back into the company to fuel growth. The size of the retained earnings makes the acquisition financially feasible, although of course there is always the possibility that such funds could be better invested elsewhere.

The acquisition of Flick is also of personal significance to Lal himself. It provides him with an opportunity to show the country where he received his business education that he has succeeded. This tangible proof of his success and ambition is important to him. Acquisition is a speedy approach to growth, but it can raise issues of culture clash. This needs further investigation and will be one of the challenges which Ling faces, because it does not have any previous experience of this method of growth. It seems unlikely that the business culture of Skod and Lindisztan is exactly the same and so cultural issues can be expected. Perhaps this is contributing to Man Lal's unease about the acquisition policy.

The **acceptability** of the acquisition can also be considered in the light of Flick's financial performance in its market sector.

The profitability of Flick is currently below average for the industry sector. Gross profit margin in 2015 was 21·43% (industry average 30%), net profit margin 15·71% (industry average 24%) and ROCE 4·07% (industry average 5·74%). This may suggest to Ling's shareholders that there are short-term profits to be gained by reducing the cost of sales and overheads to a point where the company at least achieves the average performance of its sector.

In contrast, liquidity is higher than the industry averages. The current ratio is 3·33 (compared with 2·69 for the industry as a whole) and the acid test ratio is 1·83 (1·74 for the industry as a whole). It is possible that the high current ratio reflects a lack of investment in plant and equipment. At Flick, property, plant and equipment accounts for 63·33% of its assets, compared with an industry average of 71·09%. Inventory holding appears unnecessarily high and perhaps shows a lack of good inventory management practice. 15% of the total assets are held in inventory, compared with an industry average of 8·7%. Flick's liquidity is boosted by the amount of money it holds in cash or cash equivalents. This accounts for 11·87% of the asset base, more than double the industry equivalent.

Gearing is relatively low. The gearing ratio is 25·9% (compared with an industry average of 35·9%) and the interest cover ratio is 4·4 (compared to an industry average of 2·4). This points towards a cautious approach to investment and borrowing. It may again suggest that Flick has been reluctant to borrow money to invest in production machines and processes which, in the long term, contribute to more profitable products. It has preferred a lower risk strategy which leads, in turn, to the company making lower profits.

However, one area where Flick appears to excel is in its management of receivables. At an average of 104·3 days this is much lower than the industry norm. Its industry payables is broadly in line with the industry norm (192·5 days compared to 208·6 days).

Conclusion

The acquisition of Flick is, potentially, an excellent way of entering the Skod light bulb market. It appears to be a cautiously run company which has reported lower profitability, perhaps as a result of failing to invest in efficiency initiatives. The threat of import controls makes direct entry very risky and there is sufficient evidence to suggest that Ling's input will improve Flick's position in a very competitive market.

One reservation might be the lack of experience the company has in acquiring and managing foreign companies. Thus a comprehensive due diligence process to purchasing the company and a non-intervention approach to managing Flick when it is acquired is recommended, particularly while Ling gets to grip with the cultural differences which are bound to exist. Such an approach is also likely to partly appease any nationalist critics. Even in the short term, there appears to be improvements which can be made to Flick and profitability will improve by just bringing company performance into line with the national average. Although it is expected that Ling will supply most of the funding for expansion and equipping the factory to produce LED bulbs, liquidity and gearing data suggest that Flick itself has unlocked financing potential which could be used to help finance growth.

(d) There are many documented cases where acquisitions have been unsuccessful and so the caution of Ling's financial director is understandable. Strategic alliances appear to offer a less risky way of entering a market place.

A strategic partnership is where two or more organisations share resources and activities to pursue a strategy. The basis for an alliance between Ling and Flick would be co-specialisation, allowing each partner to focus on their core capabilities. Johnson, Scholes and Whittington suggest that 'alliances are used to enter new geographical markets where an organisation needs local knowledge and expertise in distribution, marketing and customer support'. This is exactly the situation Ling finds itself in. In such an alliance it could exploit a new market, retain all production in its own country and save itself the costs of acquisition and due diligence. In return, Flick would gain new energy-efficient products for its home market which would allow it to fulfil the requirements of impending legislation. Crucially, however, the profit of the alliance would have to be split, on some agreed basis, between the two companies.

There are different types of strategic partnership. In a *joint venture* a new organisation is created which is jointly owned by the parents. The parent companies remain independent trading companies. This is unlikely to be attractive in the Ling/Flick situation. It seems more likely that Flick would wish to sell the product as its own and not confuse the market place with an offering from a related company. A joint venture is probably more appropriate where the participating companies are entering into a different market place. For example, Ling and Flick combining their expertise to enter the energy management consultancy business. At the other end of the spectrum, a network of firms might collaborate without too much formality. For example, Flick could agree to brand and distribute Ling's products, paying a fraction of the sales price (or profit margin) back to Ling. This is in effect a licensing agreement, and this might eventually stretch to the company making the LED bulbs in Skod under licence, after testing the market first through branding and distributing them.

Different levels of formality of the alliance lead to different characteristics. For example, if speed to market is important, then an opportunistic alliance would be preferred to a joint venture. Indeed a joint venture might easily take longer to agree and legally establish than to complete an acquisition.

The form of the strategic alliance can be shaped to take into account the environmental factors which affect the industry and the different capabilities of the participants. It can also be made responsive to cultural differences. However, in the Ling/Flick situation, it is difficult to see how a strategic alliance will address the needs of the institutional stakeholders for growth and Lal's personal desire for acknowledged success and prestige. Furthermore, there may be concerns about the long-term viability of any such alliance. Trust is probably the most important ingredient of any alliance and it seems likely that Ling will be reluctant to licence a product which could be easily imitated by the licensee. Furthermore, just as Ling has limited expertise in acquisitions, it also has no experience of strategic alliances at all. Success requires expertise in setting up and monitoring clear goals, governance, financial arrangements and other organisational issues. There is no evidence in the scenario that Ling has this expertise.

2 (a) The Balogun and Hope Hailey model is used to explore the contextual features of change which need to be considered if that change is to be successful. Five of those contextual features were explored in this question.

Time – This looks at how quickly change is needed. There does not appear to be an immediate need for change as the business is doing well, but is looking at how to successfully compete in the future. Therefore there should be sufficient time to adequately plan the change, leading to a greater chance of success. Indeed, the actions leading towards the change are likely to be incremental, at least internally. However, the CEO has suggested that the entire switchover to the new strategy needs to take place in a single event. From an external perspective, this may be viewed as a 'Big Bang' change, which may lead to greater resistance from those external stakeholders affected by the change. However, if the marketing campaign is well-planned, then change may appear incremental, as customers will have time to get used to the changes which will be implemented.

Scope – This refers to the degree of change required. This may be considered a realignment of existing processes, or a transformational strategic change. Webfilms is planning to move from being a focused differentiator to a hybrid company operating with a broader customer base and a greater focus on cost efficiencies. This is a leap in strategy which needs to be very well planned in order for it to be successful. It is not impossible for a company to move around the strategy clock, but it may take time to gain acceptance from its customers. The continuing focus on quality, which may also be considered under preservation, should help with the success of the strategic change.

Scope also considers the type of business being carried out. This is being expanded to include services which have not previously been offered (e.g. broadband provision). The way in which business is to be carried out (boundary-less working) is also changing. These are areas unfamiliar to Webfilms and may influence the success of the change unless appropriate expertise is acquired.

Readiness – This examines how ready the workforce is for change. Webfilms has successfully undergone transformational change in the past and so its workforce may be well prepared for it to happen again. However, it appears there is resistance from a key player in this strategy. The creative director and his team are important to the success of the change and their resistance could jeopardise the strategy. The CEO will need to bring them on board for it to be successful.

Preservation – This looks at the organisational resources and characteristics which will be maintained throughout the change. The main business of the company will stay the same: offering programmes through the internet. This should ensure that the existing customer base remains, as long as it is still done successfully. However, the failure to preserve the advertisement-free approach may alienate existing customers.

Power – This looks at the power the change leader has to impose the change on the organisation. The CEO is the person driving the change and has the power to do so by virtue of her position in the organisation. She also has the experience, as she transformed the company from a postal-based to internet-based provider. However, it appears she plans to do this using force rather than consensus ('this is going to happen. It's up to you whether you want to be involved…'). This use of power may initially deter resistance, but it may have the opposite effect in the long term, demotivating the critically important creative development team.

There seems little doubt that the CEO is again suggesting transformational change as the company reinvents itself. Whether it is incremental or big bang depends on perspective. As mentioned before, internally it could be perceived as incremental and so the change would be classified as evolution. However, to external stakeholders it might appear as big bang, and hence represents revolutionary change.

(b) Boundary-less organisation structures increase flexibility of organisations in dynamic environments and require collaboration with external parties to work. The lack of traditional structures and use of external relationships is becoming common in organisation, particularly those in a hi-tech environment. Boundary-less organisations are frequently dispersed over geographical borders and so require good communications technology and integrated systems to succeed.

Three forms of boundary-less working are mentioned in the scenario, as options for change in Webfilms.

Hollow organisation structure – where non-core processes are outsourced to external providers. This does not seem to be far-reaching enough for Webfilms. It would assist with cost efficiencies but would probably prevent them from being able to implement the full new strategy as it lacks the resources to achieve this. However, if it considers some of the new services to be incremental and non-core, such as the online gaming service, then these could be outsourced to a company with expertise in this area. Similarly, advertising might be defined as non-core and sub-contracted to an organisation which has experience in this area. There may also be administrative services within the company, such as information technology, payroll, accounts, which could be outsourced.

Modular organisation structure – a hollow organisation which further outsources some elements of the production process. This would assist Webfilms in carrying out their new strategy. It could outsource some of the production processes for programmes, making use of external expertise to deliver those programmes with which it has little or no experience, such as documentaries and current affairs programmes. It could also outsource the translation of programmes into different languages. This would allow Webfilms' own creative staff to continue to provide programmes which they are familiar with and might ally some of the fears and concerns of the creative director.

Virtual organisation structure – an organisation with no formal geographical structure, but operates through a series of linked IT systems, partnerships and collaborative agreements. This appears to be most appropriate to Webfilms. It would incorporate the modular structure described above but further extend this to incorporate a range of agreements with external parties together with a more flexible approach to internal working. For example, agreements would be needed with providers of previously screened programmes, with advertisers and with local technical support services for broadband provision. Relationships may have to be developed with competitors and Webfilms may need to be willing to make compromises, for example, by offering competitors access to original Webfilms programmes and films. Internally, Webfilms could operate flexibly over geographical boundaries, allowing them to have local personnel in place to better understand the viewing preferences of the different geographical locations which it serves.

Overall, it seems that boundary-less working is necessary if the new strategy is to be successful. It will not only increase the flexibility of operations, but will also contribute towards cost efficiencies.

3 (a) Time series analysis uses a moving average to define a trend. In Figure 1, the moving average is upwards in a year-on-year basis, with each quarterly result being greater than the equivalent quarter in the previous year. However, that trend does fluctuate on a seasonal basis within each year, with Q1 and Q4 showing positive seasonal fluctuations and Q2 and Q3 showing negative seasonal fluctuations. Given the seasonal nature of the business, it would seem appropriate to use this as a method of forecasting sales.

Although there is no single agreed method of extrapolating the trend, it could be suggested that it appears to be growing at about $2m per quarter over the last few quarters. If this were to continue, estimates for 2016 Q4 and 2017 Q1 would be as follows:

2016 quarter 4: 134·0 (2015 quarter 4 figure) + 8 (growth over the year) + 14·60 (seasonal adjustment) = **$156·60m**

2017 quarter 1: 136·0 (2016 quarter 1 figure) + 8 (growth over the year) + 25·02 (seasonal adjustment) = **$169·02m**

The relatively low residuals would suggest that the method of forecasting is reasonably accurate and that residual factors have little effect.

Although this method seems appropriate when accounting for the seasonal nature in forecasting, it does not take into account *where* the sales are growing. It is mentioned that business growth is through both expansion of existing stores and through the introduction of new stores. It would be worthwhile understanding which is having the greater effect. The analysis also does not take into account external trends such as overall industry growth as the data used is completely internal to the company.

The least squares regression has more varying results. Because of the highly seasonal nature of the data, the correlation between time and revenue does not seem particularly useful. For example, if the formula were to be used to predict 2016 Q4 revenue, it would suggest $138·08m ($110·93m + ($1·81m*15)) which is much lower than time series would suggest, which takes seasonal factors into account. The 2017 Q1 revenue would be predicted to be $139·89m using this method, again much lower than that predicted using the time series.

The correlation coefficient 'r', with a value of 0·33, suggests that the two variables are weakly connected. The coefficient of determination (r2) suggests that 11% of the variation in sales (y) is due to the passage of time (x). This would indicate a weak non-linear relationship, as suggested by the seasonal variations.

Therefore, this approach would not be considered an appropriate method of forecasting.

The least squares regression considering number of stores and revenue is more closely correlated. With a correlation coefficient of 0·94, there is a strongly positive relationship. Indeed, the coefficient of determination suggests that 88% of the variation in sales (y) is due to the variation in store numbers (x). This would seem to add further insight into the information provided in the time series analysis, suggesting the increase in store numbers is the greater driver for growth.

Using this method, the analyst could forecast average quarterly sales for 2017 and 2018 as $143·5m (69·50 + 0·02*3,700) and $149·5m (69·5 + 0·02*4,000) respectively, given the increase in store numbers predicted. However, this approach makes no attempt to take into account seasonal variations. Additionally, this method is using a very small data set, which does not provide trustworthy results.

Overall, therefore, given the seasonality of the industry, it would appear that time series would be the most appropriate approach for forecasting future sales. However, it may be that a combination of methods is used to extrapolate the general trend so as to maintain relevance for future periods.

There also remains the issue that the data presented for all three figures is somewhat limited in that it allows only a summary forecast of revenue for the entire organisation, rather than incorporating segmentation or external data, for example. Additionally, only limited, historical data has been used to determine relationships.

These may be partially resolved by the use of big data.

(b) Big data is a generic term used to describe the exponential growth of data, provided from numerous sources, available to organisations. The data is not useful in itself, it is the analysis of such data which provides valuable insights to an organisation. The finance director is right to be interested in this, as it can lead to an in-depth insight into trends and the driving forces behind those trends.

The three Vs of big data, volume, velocity and variety, can be examined to determine their contribution towards strategic development.

Volume can enhance the understanding of customer requirements and behaviour. The more data available, the greater the reliability of the trends and relationships discovered. In the analysis provided, there was a limited volume of data, spanning less than three years and incorporating only two variables. The use of big data would allow multivariate analysis over a greater time period or a greater number of shorter time periods to understand purchasing patterns better. This could help RW to create better strategies to capitalise on discovered trends.

Velocity refers to the speed of use of real-time data. As the majority of business transactions are now carried out using technology, these transactions can be captured and processed in real time if sufficient processing capacity is available. This ensures that strategies can be continually updated, in order to deliver competitive advantage. For example, as a new product is trending on social media, RW may then ensure they stock this product and aggressively market it in order to capture greater market share. Similarly, when customers are shopping online, RW could analyse their transactions in real time and use current and historic customer information to make recommendations for further purchases.

Variety refers to the different sources from which data is provided. As sources take different forms and include those not in RW's control, this is a challenging aspect of big data. However, if managed correctly, the variety provides the most detailed understanding of the market place, segmentation and individual customers. This could include competitor and industry information, sourced through key words online, to hashtags on social media and discussion forums.

There are many potential benefits which could be obtained through the analysis of big data. RW could use the results to determine where to locate their new stores. By accessing customers' shopping habits from credit and debit card records, they could determine which competing stores are used, and in which locations. This could help in the strategic planning of store locations, especially as RW is intending to continue to grow store numbers, at least over the next two years. This could help maximise the additional revenue to be gained from new stores.

RW are clearly trying to identify trends and maximise the use of them. The use of big data will provide more reliable and robust trend analysis and could lead to the discovery of previously unsuspected trends, allowing RW to capitalise on these before its industry competitors have even recognised the trend.

Further revenue streams are also available through the selling of data. Given the industry RW is in, there will be a number of branded items on offer to customers. Manufacturers of these brands are keen to carry out their own analysis and will pay for information to help with this. RW could capitalise on this new revenue stream.

Overall therefore, it would seem that the finance director is right to consider the use of big data. Indeed, RW may well find itself at a competitive disadvantage if it fails to do so. However, as with all decisions, the cost-benefit implications would need to be considered before implementation.

4 (a) Currently, Maratec is using a traditional model of marketing, which is not fully supporting the needs of the company as it strives for growth. By adopting e-marketing, further growth would be made possible and the issues identified would be addressed.

Price – Maratec uses cost plus pricing, which may cause some lost sales, as the cost is unknown at the time of agreement with the customer. The use of the external procurement company and the procurement of small orders of specific materials is likely to increase the costs and therefore lead to higher prices. Whilst high prices are not necessarily a problem, the inability to set the price when negotiating with the customer is not ideal.

The use of e-marketing will require Maratec to be more specific with regards to pricing. Although it may display a 'contact us for price' instruction online, it would need to be able to provide a price within a reasonable time. Should it introduce e-procurement (see part b), then price links could be introduced to make this quicker.

E-marketing could be used to offer special discounts on large orders, or on pricing for a subsequent item of furniture, following a previous order.

Promotion – Maratec's current promotion model may work for a small company, but if the company wants to grow, then this is a crucial area for change. The current method of promotion is limited. The use of expensive brochures means that all potential customers see the same products, and the company only produces a new brochure very year. E-marketing allows individualisation, or personalised marketing. The website could record visitors' click patterns and use targeted promotion based on the patterns detected. For example, if a potential customer browses tables and chairs, then Maratec could send them an email focused on these products.

The reach of promotion is also limited, either to those who have an acquaintance with an owner of a Maratec piece of furniture, or those who attend certain exhibitions. Whilst Maratec has a focused differentiation strategy, this may be appropriate. However, Maratec is looking to increase its sales, including an expansion of segments, to reach corporate clients. Online promotion may be a good way to make initial contact with these potential customers.

Place – As Maratec produces bespoke furniture, it does not make sense to have many showrooms as each piece of furniture displayed only exhibits the style of Maratec and is not for sale. To open further stores would lead to high additional costs. However, by using e-marketing, the market reach is as wide as Maratec choose to make it; global clients could purchase products, on the condition that Maratec will support transactions from that country and will provide shipping to that destination.

Processes – Many of the processes, excluding the actual production of the furniture, could benefit from the use of e-marketing techniques. The clients' designs could be uploaded and progress shown when the client logs in to their own account. This would make the update process much smoother and overcome the difficulties of a client visiting the manufacturing plant. Maratec could post videos of the production process if required.

Details of the materials sourced and the expected date of completion could be stored and updated as appropriate. Corporate clients could have access to re-order screens, allowing them to place orders for duplicates of its previously produced products.

Physical evidence – This is critical to Maratec's success. As items are bespoke, there is no finished product to view before purchase. Therefore evidence of previous successes is important. Images of items may be placed on the website. This will help with visualisation for clients, as more images can be uploaded than in a traditional brochure. Maratec could also post evidence of the quality, in the form of quality standards awarded, and supplier quality statuses. Additionally, the word-of-mouth promotion may be extended through physical evidence, with customer reviews posted on the site.

If Maratec uses advanced manufacturing techniques such as computer aided design and manufacturing, the clients' designs could be transformed into 3-D images, which again would assist with visualisation and ensure that enquiries are converted into actual orders.

(b) Procurement involves the sourcing of suppliers and forming of agreements with them, enabling purchasing of the right quality materials, whilst ensuring that the time and price are right for the company. This is not currently carried out by Maratec, who chooses to use a specialist procurement company instead.

Principles of e-procurement

E-procurement makes use of electronic forms of communication to simplify the entire production process. It relies upon connections between suppliers' and purchasers' systems, enabling automated transactions.

The focus is on getting the entire procurement process right: materials are delivered in the right quantity and quality, at the right price, from the right seller and at the right time.

Most e-procurement systems require registration and login so that both supplier and buyer details are stored and both administrative (address, etc) and historical data are available.

E-procurement can be approached in a number of different ways. For example, in a B2B marketplace, suppliers and buyers trade through a third party site. The relationship, and contractual relationship, is with the third party, although buyers and suppliers may enter into regular trades. The third party sites usually focus on one industry, e.g. providing materials for the furniture trade. This would give Maratec access to many suppliers as needed for the growth of its business. This would be the closest to their current model, with the third party taking some of the procurement responsibility by providing appropriate suppliers in the marketplace.

An alternative approach suitable for Maratec could be buyer centric. Using this model, Maratec would have relationships with a number of individual suppliers. Systems would be integrated, and a procurement management system managed by Maratec allowing the selection of the best supplier for each requirement. This would also simplify management reporting, as the system would integrate with internal transactional systems, e.g. production control and accounting as well as internal reporting systems.

Benefits – There are many benefits of e-procurement, although not all would be applicable to Maratec. This would certainly pass the control of the procurement process to Maratec, who currently relies on a third party service. As Maratec uses specific materials for their products, it is important to have access to a wide choice of suppliers, as a specific piece may be difficult to find. Simultaneously, however, Maratec may build a relationship with a certain supplier, who may suggest certain raw materials as they become available.

There should be obvious cost reductions, as this would cut out the middle-man and enable Maratec to shop around for the best price, regardless of location. It should also speed up the process as there will be no need for communication with the procurement company, and Maratec could select suppliers who are able to deliver within a specified date range, or who are pre-approved on the system as they meet quality and reliability standards.

Risks – It is suggested that a procurement manager will only be recruited should the decision to use e-procurement go ahead. This may be risky as the e-procurement decision could be made without expert advice of a procurement manager. The model and method of implementation may be flawed and the system unusable for Maratec's purposes.

It is not known what agreement Maratec has with the procurement company currently being used. There may be a need to compensate the company for the cessation of the contract.

If implementation is successful, there are still risks. Maratec's strategy requires quality materials in order to succeed. There is a danger that quality may be compromised if purchases can be made from any source, anywhere in the world. There is also the danger that deliveries may not be made on time. These two risks alone could eradicate all the benefits of e-procurement.

E-procurement should reduce the administrative burden of purchasing, but cannot replace the strategic requirements such as sourcing and negotiating with appropriate suppliers, to help meet Maratec's strategic objectives.

Maratec will also need to consider data security. By making transactions online, it is possible that competitors may obtain access to their data, providing information about their strategy, products and customers.

1   **(a)**   Up to 1 mark for each relevant point up to a maximum of 7 marks.

   (b)   Up to 1 mark for each relevant point up to a maximum of 13 marks.

   (c)   Up to 1 mark for each relevant point up to a maximum of 18 marks.
            This will include marks for the accurate calculation of financial ratios and for correctly interpreting their implications.

   (d)   Up to 1 mark for each relevant point up to a maximum of 8 marks.

   Up to 4 professional marks for the structure, coherence, style and clarity of the answer.

2   **(a)**   Up to 1 mark for each relevant point up to a maximum of 3 marks for each contextual factor. Five contextual factors giving a maximum of 15 marks plus 1 mark in classifying the change as per the Balogun and Hope Hailey model. Total of 16 marks.

   (b)   Up to 1 mark for each relevant point up to a maximum of 3 marks for each configuration. Three configurations giving a maximum of 9 marks.

3   **(a)**   Up to 1 mark for each relevant point up to a maximum of 15 marks.

   This may include marks for the accurate calculation of:

   –   Extrapolated values for the time series analysis (up to 2 marks)
   –   Predicted values for regression 1 (Figure 2) (up to 2 marks)
   –   Predicted values for regression 2 (Figure 3) (up to 2 marks)
   –   Coefficient of determination (regression 1 and regression 2) (up to 2 marks)

   (b)   Up to 1 mark for each relevant point up to a maximum of 10 marks.

4   **(a)**   Up to 1 mark for each relevant point up to a maximum of 3 marks for each aspect of the marketing mix. Five aspects required giving a maximum of 15 marks.

   (b)   Up to 1 mark for each relevant point up to a maximum of 10 marks.

ABOUT BECKER PROFESSIONAL EDUCATION

Becker Professional Education provides a single solution for students and professionals looking to advance their careers and achieve success in:

- Accounting

- International Financial Reporting

- Project Management

- Continuing Professional Education

- Healthcare

For more information on how Becker Professional Education can support you in your career, visit www.becker.com/acca.

Becker Professional Education
is an ACCA approved content provider

Lightning Source UK Ltd.
Milton Keynes UK
UKOW07f0825150617

303311UK00020B/67/P